Man and Wife in America

Man and Wife in America
A HISTORY

HENDRIK HARTOG

HARVARD UNIVERSITY PRESS

Cambridge, Massachusetts

London, England

For Nancy

First Harvard University Press paperback edition, 2002

Library of Congress Cataloging-in-Publication Data

Hartog, Hendrik, 1948–
    Man and wife in America : A history / Hendrik Hartog.
        p. cm
    Includes bibliographical references and index.
    ISBN 0-674-00262-8 (cloth)
    ISBN 0-674-00811-1 (pbk.)
        1. Husband and wife—United States—History.   2. Separation (Law)—
    United States—History.   3. Marriage—United States—History.   I. Title.

    KF510.H37   2000
    346.7301'63'09—dc21   99-056466

Acknowledgments

To Nancy Hartog: friend, lover, soulmate, unsparing critic. Without you, a book on marriage would not have entered my mind.

To Elizabeth Battelle Clark, Vivien Hartog, Floris Hartog, and Marky Rath, in sadness and gratitude. Each taught me and helped make this book possible. Their absence is a constant and painful presence.

To Jacob, Liesbet, and Lucas Hartog: because the three of you were always present, even after you each left home. Jacob's disdain caused the death of many titles.

To Kathy Brown, Martha Fineman, Linda Gordon, Sally Gordon, Tom Green, Mike Grossberg, Peter Hoffer, Alan Hunter, Linda Kerber, Margo Melli, Martha Minow, Bill Nelson, John Reid, Dan Rodgers, Carol Sanger, Vicki Schultz, Molly Shanley, Diane Sommerville, Amy Dru Stanley, Chris Stansell, David Trubek, Barbara Yngvesson, and Viviana Zelizer: friends who talked with me and read chunks of indigestable manuscript at various early stages.

To Nancy Cott, John Demos, Linda Gordon, Sally Gordon, Mike Grossberg, Nancy Hartog, Carol Sanger, Molly Shanley, and Amy Dru Stanley, who read later drafts and offered questions, criticisms, and ideas that helped bring the project to closure.

To Jenny Pressman, Helen Glogovac, Jonathan Lipson, Leisa Meyer, Nancy Isenberg, Michael Millender, Claudia Charles, and especially Andrea Friedman and the late Marky Rath, who provided essential research assistance.

To Laura Nash and Laura Shiels, who helped me maintain whatever sanity I can lay claim to.

To Joyce Seltzer, a great editor. And to David Lobenstine, who helped cut many words.

Thank you all.

*   *   *

The work on this book began with research leave supported by the Smongeski Bequest of the University of Wisconsin Law School, the Graduate School of the University of Wisconsin (Madison), the John Simon Guggenheim Foundation, and the American Council of Learned Societies. Later, I received generous support from Princeton University.

American university law libraries remain a great and underutilized source for historical research. I have made heavy use of the University of Wisconsin Law Library and the New York University Law Library. I also found crucial material at the law libraries of UCLA, Yale, Harvard, and the University of North Carolina. Early on I sampled the amazingly rich holdings of the State Historical Society of Wisconsin and the New-York Historical Society. For the last six years I have relied on the immense resources of the Firestone Library of Princeton University. Librarians at all these institutions have been unfailingly helpful.

An early version of Chapter 2 was previously published as "Abigail Bailey's Coverture: Law in a Married Woman's Consciousness," in *Law in Everyday Life,* ed. Austin Sarat and Thomas Kearns (Ann Arbor: University of Michigan Press, 1993), 63–108. An early version of Chapter 3 was previously published as "Marital Exits and Marital Expectations in Nineteenth Century America," *Georgetown Law Journal,* 80, no. 1 (October 1991): 95–129. A portion of Chapter 7 was previously published as "John Barry's Custodial Rights: Of Power, Justice, and Coverture," in *Justice and Power in Sociolegal Studies,* ed. Bryant G. Garth and Austin Sarat (Evanston: Northwestern University Press, 1997), 166–193. A portion of Chapter 8 was previously published as "Lawyering, Husbands' Rights, and 'the Unwritten Law' in Nineteenth-Century America," *Journal of American History,* no. 1 (June 1997): 67–96.

Contents

Introduction

Throughout most of American history, marriage has meant "the legal union of man and woman, as husband and wife, for life." Today, we remain sure only of the first three words in the definition. Still, "union"—as in the uniting of two otherwise separate lives or the legal recognition of a common identity—endures as the mark of a legal marriage.[1]

But this is a book about American separations. And about women and men, who, as wives and husbands, made a law of marriage in legal struggles that percolated out of their separating or separated lives. It is through separations that we make sense of marriage in American law during the generations prior to our own. It is through separations, through close examination of struggles at the margins of marital life and marital identities, that we come to a historical understanding of core legal concepts: of wife, of husband, of unity.

I did not begin my study of nineteenth-century marriage fixated on separation. When I began I imagined that I was studying a world in which marital struggles took their meaning and significance from inescapable and lifelong coupledom. I imagined, as many others have and do, that the central difference between the present and the past lay in the contrast between the universal availability of easy divorce today and some coercive regime from which escape was practically impossible. The novelty of modern marriage seemed framed, determined, by the presence of exit.

But, like Nora's husband in Ibsen's *A Doll's House,* I had to learn that there were doors that could be opened and slammed, that leaving was a possibility, even where legal divorce was not. I had not yet noticed the significance of separation as the practice through which nineteenth-century marital rights came into being.

This book uses separations to explore the practical logic, the changing common sense, of legal marriage in nineteenth-century America.[2] What

1

did it mean to be married (man and wife) in a legal culture shaped by a deeply held and centuries-old faith that marriage was a permanent hierarchical relationship that made men into husbands and women into wives, in a legal culture that also offered unprecedented possibilities for escape from that permanent relationship? The chapters that follow try out a variety of answers to that question as they examine "telling" moments of tension and conflict in American marital legal history. I focus primarily on the improvisations of particular couples, their creative and sometimes playful responses to the changing legal scene they found before them. The goal is not to discover the universal in the particular. It is, rather, to watch marital selves—wives and husbands—at work: as they were coerced and molded in the law and as they molded and transformed themselves.[3]

This is, unapologetically, a work of legal history. Legal institutions and legal practices have been intrinsic to American life. Americans had law; they made law; they inherited law; they used law; they were subject to law. When wives or husbands were divorced, when wives tried to force absent husbands to provide support or to assert a right to sell their labor independent of husbands, when husbands worked to gain control over their wives' property, to wrest custody over children, to win compensation from wives' seducers, all looked to the law because courts were where one did such things. When they petitioned legislatures for changes in law or hired lawyers to challenge apparently fixed doctrinal understandings, they did so because they understood law as a crucial political resource. Obviously, they lost as often as they won. And it may be that few were ever satisfied with the law they got. But the question "Why go to law?" was rarely posed. And the central historical problem is to understand what happened when they went—and to understand the significance of what they did for an evolving marital regime.

The marital regime that is our focus was doubly legal: a body of rights and duties and relationships articulated and developed in the law, but also habits and dispositions revealed by law in the language mobilized by legal actors. Is that all there was? Was there nothing about nineteenth-century marriages more deeply private, less strategic, more intensely religious or intimate, hidden from law, yet definitive of marriage? Of course there was. But those "deeper" themes are not my subject. Still, in America law played a crucial role in the construction, the constitution, of nonlegal domains of marital meaning and marital experience.

Perhaps you didn't need law to fall in love. But you needed law to know that you possessed a "private" life and the capacity to pursue a happiness or misery that was distinctively your own. You needed law to know that your religious identity could remain inviolate. You needed law to know yourself as married "really," as committed beyond public conformity; you needed law to know that you possessed rights unasserted, legal opportunities forgone, virtue unqualified by strategic advantage.[4]

The legal history of marriage, often imagined as the evolution from "feudal" husband-headed households to "modern" companionate, relatively egalitarian, marriages, is a very old scholarly chestnut. Partially created by nineteenth-century woman's rights advocates and law reformers who saw themselves challenging a feudal atavism, the reform of marriage and the rise of no-fault divorce have been staple parts of the imagined modernization of western societies, including the United States.[5] Although debate remained on the questions when and how change had occurred, until recently no one much challenged the basic picture.

In the last few years, however, historical study of the law of marriage has been reinvigorated by the emergence of women's history and the still more recent appearance of feminist legal theory. In addition, we have lived through a striking transition in marital law and marital behavior. One aspect of that transition is the spread of no-fault divorce across the country in the years since 1970. But there is much else that has changed over the past quarter century, including the obliteration of legal language that once established and defined distinctive marital identities and the apparent triumph of an egalitarian and contractual conception of marriage. These changes, and their connections to the presence of female-headed child rearing, female impoverishment, the two-income household, changes in child custody practices, the rise of a men's rights movement, and the assertion of gay marriage rights (to take only a few notorious features of our modern "crisis of the family"), have all stimulated historical inquiry.

Nearly all recent scholarship on the legal history of American marriage has been shaped by explicit political and normative concerns. One side begins with a demonstration that traditional legal rules, identified with the term "coverture," were bad, like slavery. The narrative tells of a titanic struggle against coverture, one in which good (egalitarian law reform) is always pitted against bad (the patriarchal common law), although many apparent reforms merely reinscribed patriarchy. The other side glorifies the nineteenth-century ideology of permanent and highly structured marriage for the ethos of care, mutuality, continuity, and support that it produced. This side starts from the premise that too much has changed in recent years, too much lost in the rights-centered, individualistic, and selfish world ushered in by no-fault divorce.[6]

Most recent historical work, on either side, has imagined law, and in particular the opinions of nineteenth-century appellate judges, as covert political theory. The work of history is then to reveal the masked ideological assumptions and goals of the judges. This book challenges that methodological presumption. Judges and lawyers, like other participants in the legal system, had to improvise solutions to immediate and intractable conflicts, using the imperfect materials of an inherited and changing legal order. Judges were rarely the producers of a coherent system of normative values or beliefs. That wasn't their job. They were the managers of the legal process: of laws, customs, and inherited practices that incorporated incoherent and contradictory values and histories. Many judges, particularly trial judges, dealt with concrete lives, odd patterns of behavior, failed marriages. They improvised solutions to the situations before them from legal rules and from tacit assumptions they drew out of the larger culture. Occasionally, they might speak for a moment, a paragraph, in a prescriptive voice about the nature of marriage. But far more often they disciplined themselves according to their perceived institutional limits. They were necessarily concerned with consistency, with recognizing the force of precedent, applying it to situations that pressed at the boundary of inherited normative descriptions, choosing between competing, often equally applicable, precedents. But then again, consistency and precedent, while powerful constraints, were not the only concerns that tugged at the attention of judges. All this was a part of the work of deciding this case, at this time, with these particular litigants and lawyers before them.

Certainly, patriarchy and misogyny were present in the legal culture as well as in the words and worlds of judges. A nineteenth-century judge could always find reasons, if wanted, why the wife before him in court was not recognizable as a separate person from her husband, why her identity had been "covered over" by his. And many judges, like many other men, believed, passionately and adamantly, in a hierarchical, patriarchal order that they identified with the law of marriage and with coverture. Yet values never led inexorably toward particular legal results.

Most judges would have repeatedly confronted the contingency and the indeterminacy of the marital values expressed in the law. And judges, even intensely patriarchal judges, would have wanted a legitimate marital regime, one that distinguished good husbands from those who were dishonorable and abusive, from bad husbands.[7]

The story becomes still more complicated when we shift our attention to the uses that others—lawyers, jurymen, litigants, and the women and men who never appeared in court at all—made of the law. What they all thought about, as consumers and producers of law, is beyond the scope of any one book. Suffice to say they thought many different things. What we can learn about, and what does shape the framework of this book, are the improvisational performances of some who participated directly in the nineteenth-century marital legal order. And chapters of this book are structured around the voices and actions of particular individuals caught in the web of the law.

This book explores the distinctive legal culture within which Americans lived lives as married between the 1790s and the 1950s. Although it describes many changes within that regime and although it also tracks the emergence of understandings of marital identities that resemble our own, it does not try to explain how "we" got from there to here. Throughout, I have struggled to look at past marriages as shaped by understandings that are only distantly connected to present controversies. I have tried to convey my fascination with the marital ways, the rights and wrongs, the practices and habits, of those who came into my historical field of view. I have also worked to present sympathetically perspectives and points of view—such as those of many nineteenth-century husbands—that today seem unattractive. My point is not to deny the oppressions and repressions, the miseries, of either past or present. It is, rather, to insist as a historian that we come to understand ourselves better through imagined dialogue with those who came before us. And it is also to query the assumption that to know law (past or present) is to know the source of our present miseries and difficulties. We will understand our parents and grandparents better, and we will understand ourselves better in relation to them, if we explore their legal world as the terrain on which they lived their marital lives, paying less attention to the legal world they helped bring into being and more to the circumstances they confronted.

The Scene of a Marriage

Separation . . . is the living asunder of man and wife.
Giles Jacobs, The Law Dictionary *(1811)*

One day something pushed Lydia McGuire over the edge. Maybe it was Charles's refusal to pay the costs of a trip to visit her daughters. Or some winter morning when the furnace didn't work. Maybe it happened when she noticed that her neighbors had nicer furniture than she did. Or perhaps she woke up one morning and decided that she should not have to haul coal and ashes at her age. Maybe she just wanted an indoor flush toilet.

In any case, one day in the fall of 1951 she went to a lawyer and told him the story of her marriage. She and Charles McGuire had married in 1919. He was then in his late forties, a farmer with deep roots in northeastern Nebraska, the child of early white settlers. He was also a bachelor with "a reputation for more than ordinary frugality." She was in her early thirties, a widow with two daughters, who had inherited a one-third interest in an 80-acre lot from her first husband. Over the next thirty years, in her telling, Lydia had been "a dutiful and obedient wife," who recognized that her second husband was "the boss" and that "his word was law." Like other Nebraska farmwives, she worked constantly. And like many other farmwives, she also earned money separately, raising as many as 300 chickens to pay for household goods. Charles supported both her and her daughters, at least until they graduated from high school. She "cohabited" with Charles until 1950 or so, even though he was "a poor companion." Once every two weeks, he drove Lydia to the town of Wayne, the county seat, where she visited her mother. She had also made four trips over the previous ten years to visit her daughters (both of whom lived out of state), paying for the trips out of her chicken and egg sales.[1]

By the early 1950s, Charles was rich. He owned 398 acres of land, valued at about $84,000. He had nearly $13,000 in the bank and owned government bonds worth more than $104,000. Yet he and Lydia lived in a house without indoor plumbing. The kitchen was not "modern," lacking a kitchen sink, although there was electricity. The furnace had not worked well in years. He owned a 1929 Model A Ford coupe, equipped with an inadequate heater, and a 1927 Chevrolet pickup.

Charles would never tell Lydia anything about his finances. He doled out money to her in very small amounts, none at all in the last three or four years. He paid for all the groceries directly. She was permitted to make only local telephone calls. They belonged to no community organizations, and he had not maintained the Pleasant Valley Church, located on two acres of his farmland.[2]

The lawyer, we can presume, laid out some options for Lydia, and then asked her what she wanted him to do. One thing she did not want was a divorce. Nor did she want to separate from Charles, to move out and to live on her own. She wanted the law to make him do his duty as a husband, just as she had always done her duty as a wife. She wanted the law to compel her rich husband to make her life a little less bleak, to support her better. And so, dutifully, the lawyer filed an action in equity asking for "suitable maintenance and support," laying out the ways Charles had failed in his husbandly duties, his "extreme cruelty" in not providing Lydia with the necessities appropriate to her situation in life.

At first, her suit went well. The trial court held in Lydia's favor and ruled that she was legally entitled to use her husband's credit for the "necessaries" of her life. Charles McGuire was specifically ordered to pay for indoor plumbing for their house and to make a variety of other repairs and improvements. He was also ordered to buy a car with a working heater and to pay for a trip once a year for Lydia to visit each of her daughters.[3]

Charles resentfully complied with much of the trial court's order: buying a used car with a heater and making some improvements to the house. At the same time, he appealed the ruling to the Nebraska Supreme Court. The trial court, his lawyer argued, had based its decision on insufficient evidence. Furthermore, the ruling was contrary to law, and it violated Charles's "fundamental and constitutional rights."[4]

And the Nebraska Supreme Court agreed with Charles. There was no basis for the remedies the trial court had ordered for Lydia. The legal point was simple, according to Justice Frederick W. Messmore, writing for the majority: as long as Charles and Lydia were living together, a court, even a court sitting as a court of equity, had no business deciding what was or was not "suitable" support. Such decisions were the essence of the private domain of the family. "The living standards of a family" were "a matter of concern to the household, and not for the courts to determine." The court conceded that "the husband's attitude toward his wife, according to his wealth and circumstances," left "little to be said in his behalf." But, by definition, if the parties were living together, the husband was meeting his obligation to support his wife. "Public policy requires such a holding."[5]

Messmore's opinion appeared to reject both Lydia's and Charles's visions of their respective marital roles and identities (although in the process, it implicitly confirmed Charles in his conception of his rights). To Lydia, marriage created a reciprocal relationship between her obedience, her willingness to assume a subordinate role, and Charles's obligation to support her in a socially appropriate manner. If she did what was expected of her, he had to provide what most people would have thought minimally expected of a husband in his economic position—a flush toilet, decent furniture, a heated automobile, the ability to visit relatives, some sharing of family resources. As a wife, she had rights defined by his duties as a husband. To Charles, by contrast, his rights as a husband (rights that blended with his rights as a property owner) required a recognition that neither Lydia nor the court had any right to make demands on his use of wealth. Absent a demonstration of wrongdoing on his part, defined by the public laws of the state, he remained a free man, secure in his legal and constitutional rights, free to decide how what was his would be used.

But in Messmore's opinion, marriage was private, meaning that no roles or identities—whether phrased in terms of rights, duties, immunities, or expectations—could be imposed by law on a couple living in a state of matrimony. Who did what, who spent what, how much they spent, and on what—these were questions for the couple to decide "in private." Nothing in the court's opinion denied that Charles had a "public" duty to support Lydia, but the court refused to define the terms of the support obligation. These were matters "for the household," matters outside of the court's institutional competence.[6]

McGuire v. McGuire has a paradigmatic stature in American family law. Though it attracted little attention when decided and has rarely been cited as authority by other courts, it still lives an active life in most family law casebooks, used to introduce the concept of marital privacy and the legal significance of "the intact marriage." Yet no one really believes that *McGuire* is "right." To feminists and divorce law reformers since the 1960s, *McGuire* provides a useful "horror story" to illustrate the need for change in the marital regime. No modern casebook editor can resist pointing out the misleading character of the language of "household" in the case, making sure the student understands that the marital entity the case empowers is one in which the relevant decisions are entirely in the husband's control. In the standard modern rendition, Lydia becomes something close to an abused wife. And her lack of remedy reveals the continuing power of a patriarchal norm of coverture, of a wife locked within her husband's "household." "Well into this century," writes Ellen Wright Clayton, relying on *McGuire* as authority, "marriage legally extinguished the voice and identity of the wife. She could not enforce any claims against her spouse during the course of the ongoing marriage."[7]

It is tempting to treat *McGuire* as a container for present struggles over gender and inequality. But in fact the modern container is not *McGuire v. McGuire* as it was in 1953. That decision mobilized the language of marital privacy, not as a generalized value applicable to all wives and husbands, but as a way to describe this case as an exception to a general rule.[8] In Messmore's opinion, the relevant legal rule in Nebraska was simple: a separated wife was entitled to the support of her husband. That rule was defined by two late nineteenth-century cases, *Earle v. Earle* (1889) and *Cochran v. Cochran* (1894). In *Earle*, a husband had sent his wife away from his household and then refused to provide any support for her. The question that case raised was whether a Nebraska court could order maintenance or alimony for a wife who had not sought a complete divorce. The Nebraska Supreme Court decided that a court had such powers as a part of its inherent equitable jurisdiction, its capacity to ensure that there was "no wrong without some remedy." There was clearly a wrong; therefore, there must be a judicial remedy. A separated wife did not have to seek a divorce in order to obtain a support order against her husband. In *Cochran*, a husband left his wife in Wisconsin and went to Nebraska, where he owned land, ostensibly to see to some investments. Once in Nebraska, he divorced his wife without notifying her, on the false grounds that she had deserted him, and then he remarried (twice). Meanwhile, the Wisconsin wife continued to teach school and to await his return. According to the court, she never knew, during more than a decade of separation, that he had left permanently. But when she found her health impaired because of her teaching, she brought suit in Nebraska for support, and the court held in her favor.[9]

Over the next half century, many cases recognized that separated wives possessed an enforceable right to support payments from their husbands. And Messmore's opinion surveyed all those decided in Nebraska. He also noted a few situations in other jurisdictions where a wife had won, though still living in the same house as her husband. It was possible to be a separated wife, so long as there was strong evidence that wife and husband no longer shared a bedroom.[10] But there were no cases, in Nebraska or elsewhere, where a wife who insisted on her status and identity as a wife within her husband's household had successfully invoked the power of a court to make the husband give her things.

Thus, in *McGuire* everything turned on the absence of separation. Implicitly, the court defined the appropriate response for a justifiably unhappy or ill-treated wife—leave the marriage. Conversely, Lydia had accepted the terms of support by her willingness to stay with Charles. Or, to put it more provocatively, by her presence in the home, by her inseparability from her husband, she had participated implicitly in the decisions made by the household.

Modern readers of *McGuire v. McGuire* are not wrong to find a kind of false consciousness in the judge's evocation of an abstracted and ungendered "household" within a private sphere. Lydia didn't really participate; she lacked much of a voice in the household. No one articulated, or perhaps even imagined, the alternative of a companionate egalitarian marriage where decisionmaking power would be shared. No one, not even Lydia, recognized that she had played a crucial role in the creation of her husband's wealth. And the effect of the holding was to give her an unattractive choice: accept the "household" as is—that is, as a place where the husband's property rights ruled—or leave.

But there was institutional and moral logic to the holding in *McGuire v. McGuire*. It drew a boundary around the support rights of wives at a coherent point by refusing to intrude into an intact marriage.[11] Courts often recognized the need for remedies in a world where separated and ex-wives would otherwise find themselves without support and, often, without the means of earning an adequate living. But Lydia refused to place herself in the position of a separated or ex-wife. Indeed, Lydia's dedication to relief without separation gave her a somewhat morally compromised identity. We can imagine a judge thinking: What is marriage? What does it mean to be married? What it surely wasn't, what it didn't mean, was the simple quid pro quo Lydia had asked for—a quantum of obedience (or sex) for a quantum of support. To reduce marriage to nothing but instrumental calculation, to a balance sheet of rights and duties, would be to deny its moral and religious and cultural and political significance, its romance and its mystery. If Charles was everything Lydia said, why had she stayed? Only to inherit?[12]

A PLACE

To understand the decision in *McGuire,* we might begin by describing where and when the decision was made: the United States of America, as it was between the 1790s and the last forty years of the twentieth century. This was a huge country, defined, at least for the purposes of marriage, by its absence of central norms or directions. It was a place where many lost themselves or at least hid from marriages and from other commitments. Lydia and Charles McGuire were atypical litigants there: they spent their lives in one place, within one jurisdiction. And they spent their married lives living together.

The first thing to notice about the United States in this period of over 160 years was that the public officials, the authoritative legal voices, were all male. Judges, legislators, juries, treatise writers, all of them. By the early twentieth century, it was theoretically possible for a woman to become a lawyer, and by the 1920s there would be a sprinkling of women who were judges and a number of women who wrote texts (although not authoritative treatises) on family law.[13] As late as the 1950s, however, women were a miniscule fraction of the lawmakers. One of the many "unique" aspects of *McGuire v. McGuire* was that the lower court judge who had recognized Lydia's right to a remedy, the judge reversed by the Nebraska Supreme Court, was a woman.

Beginning in the 1840s, women's voices were increasingly and insistently present as voices of protest and critique. Women spoke on every side in the cultural wars over marriage. And a distinctive feature of this country, different from many other countries of the past, was the aggressive and active presence of women as marital litigants—suing for support, for custody over children, for confirmation of separate property rights, for divorce or for separation, for protection from creditors. But men made the law. It was still, they imagined, their country.

The United States of America was one nation; yet its distinguishing characteristic as a nation was the multiple jurisdictions that described its legal terrain. The constitutional authority of the central government grew in power and range of subject matter authority over the nearly two centuries between the Declaration of Independence and the end of World War II. Yet it remained at all times a constitutional regime whose legitimacy was defined by the recognition that its powers were limited, defined by the terms of the federal Constitution and the prior existence of states.

Many legal subjects were monopolies of the states. And one such subject was the law of marriage and divorce. Every state had a law of marriage. Every state had its legal peculiarities. Some states allowed judicially ordered separations—known at first as divorces *à mensa et thoro* (from bed and board). Others did not. Every state had its own changing list of what would constitute valid grounds for a divorce. Some allowed divorce after five years' desertion; others required a greater or a lesser period; some allowed no divorce for desertion at all. Every state had its own changing rules about what was marital property, about what managerial authority a wife could possess over marital resources, about what protections she had, if any, against a dissolute or impecunious husband. To know the law of marriage relevant to their marriage, spouses had to know the law of marriage in the state in which they lived.

Changes in the law of marriage occurred not through the instrumentality of a national legislature nor in response to the decisions of a national supreme court. They occurred according to the varying schedules of particular state political environments. In some states, notably New York and Massachusetts after the great Irish immigration of the 1840s, the Catholic Church played a distinctive, sometimes determinative, role in the politics of marriage and divorce reform. In other states, Protestant denominations held crucial power. Throughout most of the country, the enacted laws were imagined as deriving from an inherited English legal order, identified as "the common law tradition." In a few states, however, a European civil law tradition of community property, often borrowed from the French Civil Code, provided the imagined point of origin for the legal regime.

There were variations in the structures of courts in each of the American states. Prior to the middle of the nineteenth century, some jurisdictions maintained separate courts of equity, which became the only courts in that state where married women's separate property interests were recognized. These courts were understood as in continuity with the distinctive practices of the English Chancellors, and they provided equitable remedies unavailable at common law. Often, these were also the courts with responsibility over divorce and separation. In other states, equitable remedies were incorporated into the general common law court system. At first, most judges thought of doing equity as a separate and distinguishable task from common law decisionmaking, even when they worked within state court systems that had abolished or refused to establish separate equity courts. Over time, equity jurisdiction became a particular set of remedies within the larger common law system. After the beginning of the twentieth century, some states began to establish "family courts," with specialized responsibilities for divorce, custody, and other matters.

Often the lawmakers of one state—judges, legislators, and constitution drafters—imitated the laws or the practices of other states. Nebraska's marital support and separation laws appear to have been borrowed from Massachusetts and Ohio. There was a western migration of law reform: New York's married women's property acts of 1848 and 1849 were reproduced in Michigan, Wisconsin, and elsewhere. But legal change could as easily move in an easterly or a northerly direction. Texas's constitutional provision mandating marital property reform was debated, and sometimes adopted, in other states north and south. But when a law migrated from one state to another, it became subject to the interpretive energies of local lawyers, local judges, and local litigants, who soon transformed it into their law, not the law of a "foreign" jurisdiction. Judges would continue to check on the evolution of doctrine in other jurisdictions, but they were free to take the law in new or different directions—and frequently did so.[14]

State legislators and constitution drafters worked, with self-consciousness and ambition, to create legal regimes that were different from one another. Sometimes they did so for moral or theological reasons: to distinguish their jurisdiction from the evils and failures of other jurisdictions, because marriage was never merely a legal institution. Often they did what they did with more material goals in mind. The framers of the California Constitution of 1849 committed themselves to a community property system of marital property. They did so for many expressed reasons, including the desire to reduce the anxieties of the Spanish and Mexican settlers who had preceded them. A primary reason was that eastern states were governed by common law systems of marital property that gave the husband effective title to most forms of property that appeared in a marriage. By the late 1840s, the common law system was in widespread disrepute as an oppressive and "feudal" system. Community property, at least in 1849, appeared more egalitarian, more supportive of woman's rights. Thus, the framers reasoned, young white Anglo women, who were much in demand in Gold Rush California, would be drawn there by a liberal marital regime.[15] Throughout the nineteenth and twentieth centuries, one state after another became the divorce mill for the rest of the country—first Connecticut, then Indiana, then South Dakota, and finally and most famously, Nevada (I am skipping several). Each state made its reputation by liberalizing the grounds on which a divorce would be granted and, still more importantly, reducing dramatically the residency required to establish one's right to a divorce in the state. The process of divorcing would be simplified, becoming more of a bureaucratic process than an adversarial one. And along the way, residents of other states where the process remained more difficult would be moved to come. They could be counted on at least to spend money while undergoing the process, and perhaps to stay and establish roots.[16]

States competed with each other for settlers: for the unhappily married, for the inadequately divorced, for those who wanted to marry or remarry. Their marital regimes—the state rules that each state instituted and maintained, the courts and other institutions that enforced and interpreted those rules—became public packages of goods and services that competed against the public goods of other jurisdictions for the loyalty and the tax dollars of a mobile citizenry. In that sense, diversity within the federal system was simple product differentiation.[17]

And yet, although states often tried to insist on their autonomy as creators of marital regimes,[18] this federal system was less a free market of competing states and more a complex ecology where legal changes in one place would have uncertain but unmistakable effects on other places. Each state's laws were shaped in part by other states' laws. The existence of divorce havens (Indiana in the nineteenth century and Nevada in the early twentieth century) forced some states to liberalize their divorce laws and, on the other hand, allowed other states to keep their rules unbending. Practices elsewhere were often integrated into domestic state law. When, for example, the New York legislature abolished "common law marriage" in 1933 (common law marriage was the body of practices and understandings that allowed a long-standing public relationship between a man and a woman to "become" a marriage), the New York courts held that when cohabiting New Yorkers visited a state that still allowed common law marriage, the effect was to legalize their relationship, though the relationship had begun after 1933.[19]

In part, variety resulted from an almost playful spirit of legislating that Europeans and others found mysterious. In 1860 New York's legislature granted wives equal custodial rights over their children. A judge of the New York Supreme Court looked at this new law and declared that no rational legislature could have meant to divest fathers of their rights. The New York legislature obediently changed its mind.[20] Legislatures and courts tinkered constantly with the rules of marital property, the rules regarding child custody, and those regarding divorce. In some states, particularly in the Midwest and West, lawmakers appeared to treat the law of marriage not as an unchangeable inherited structure but, rather, as a testing ground for changing social theories. In the United States of America, government became, as Justice William Johnson of the U.S. Supreme Court said in 1821, "the science of experiment."[21]

There were connecting threads that helped produce an impression of unity across the multi-jurisdictional complexity of the American polity, made it possible for observers to imagine that there existed a singular American law of marriage.[22] Lawyers and judges across the nation shared an identity—constructed out of a common socialization, a historical sensibility, and participation in the growing national economy. Particularly after the imperial expansion of Harvard's case method of legal instruction in the late nineteenth century, all lawyers began careers with the same framework and methodology of analysis.[23]

New York, from 1820 through 1960 the most populous and most diverse state in the Union, played a crucial role—symbolically and practically—in the production of an American law of marriage. Because New York City was at the center of the print culture of the nation and because New York State exported many lawyers, New York law—both as texts and as practices—always spread widely. New York's complex court structure meant that New York as a state produced more case law and more opinions from more perspectives than elsewhere (particularly after the 1846 state constitution created intermediate appellate courts across the state). As commentators often noted, New York law was always cited as precedent because any lawyer could always find authority for his position somewhere in the New York cases.[24]

By the 1830s, professional treatise writers discovered a national law lurking in the shadows of the apparent multiplicity of state lawmaking. These men chose between better and worse rules, approving the doctrines in some states, rejecting others, publicizing some reforms, decrying others. The authors of these works understood themselves as participants in an international community of professionals at work refining and applying an objective and limited body of principles freed from specific political contexts. Their governing myth, one strengthened by legal education and other forms of lawyerly socialization, identified that body of rules with the common law tradition, with a continuing taught legal tradition dating back to an indeterminate time in medieval England. They worked to "find" a law of marriage that could be imagined as coherent.

Yet the results of the treatise writers' labors were paradoxical. On the one hand, treatise writers, in particular Joel Prentiss Bishop and James Schouler, gained enormous authority, and their statements of "the right rule" were adopted by many courts. Cases were decided with the phrase, "According to Bishop . . ." They became lawmakers of a sort, although they conceived of their work as "law-finding." The primary and emerging use of these treatises, however, was not as repositories of legal truth. Rather, lawyers bought these works as compendia, as repositories of all the possible positions that could be raised with regard to a particular legal problem. They bought them for the footnotes and the indexes, as short cuts to precedents and arguments they could use as well as those they would have to counter. And the treatise writers responded to the market demand with larger and larger editions that incorporated and distinguished every possible variation and alternative. Instead of countering complexity with coherence, in the end the treatises recreated complexity.[25]

For the better part of two centuries, the agencies of the federal government claimed little constitutional responsibility or interest over the law of marriage. During the framing of the Constitution in 1787, the topic never arose. That implicit denial of constitutional responsibility was reaffirmed, explicitly and consciously, during the debates over the Fourteenth Amendment after the Civil War.[26] From the middle of the nineteenth century until the constitutional revolution of the 1960s, there were repeated moments of passionate talk about the need for a national law of marriage and for uniformity, particularly in the face of the threat posed by Mormon polygamy in the Utah territory. And there were particular institutional responsibilities of the federal government, such as immigration law, that implicated marriage. Nonetheless, throughout the first 175 years of national government, marriage law was not the business of Washington.[27]

In this constitutional regime, there were no constitutional mandates requiring gender equality, even after the 1868 ratification of the Fourteenth Amendment. Neither the requirement of "equal protection" nor that of "due process" was understood to apply to the law of marriage. In the late 1950s, after *Brown v. Board of Education,* the U.S. Supreme Court could still view antimiscegenation laws as the private business of the states.[28] As late as the 1960s, the state of Wisconsin refused to grant in-state residency for tuition purposes to young women, born and raised in Wisconsin, who were married to soldiers fighting in Vietnam. Those women were wives, and wives had their domicile, their official residence, wherever their husbands were.[29] A constitutional challenge to the explicitly gendered law of marital support would have been unimaginable in 1953, at the time of *McGuire v. McGuire.*

All of which is not to say that the federal Constitution was not of significance in the constitution of marriage in America. Although each state was a sovereign lawmaking unit, there were external federal constraints on their freedom to act. Three explicit constraints came out of the text of the Constitution. Two relatively unimportant constraints were the contract clause, obliging each state to abide by its own contracted commitments, and the takings clause of the Fifth Amendment, forbidding takings of property without compensation. One could imagine that the application of either clause would have led to limits on the powers of states to change the terms of marriage or divorce, on the theory that when couples married, each spouse relied on an explicit marital regime and that valuable property rights vested as a result of the act of marriage. Neither clause, however, really made much difference in the practices of the states.[30]

On the other hand, the "full faith and credit clause" played a crucial and determinative role in the legal history of marriage. "Full Faith and Credit shall be given in each State to the public Acts, Records, and Judicial Proceedings of every other State." The clause articulated a founding premise of American federalism: that American citizens, though residents and citizens of states, should not be deprived of rights or identities that were validly theirs when they moved from one state to another. They always remained Americans.

Although full faith and credit was a clear constitutional mandate, nineteenth-century state courts interpreted the clause through the lens of state sovereignty and insisted on their right to act as if their state were a separate country. They talked in the language of conflicts of law, of "private international law," as if the laws of other states belonged to other nations, as if Nebraska were France or Argentina. The result was that open interjurisdictional conflict lurked at the edges of that innocent phrase, full faith and credit. Things became quickly complicated for the residents of federal America—people who married in one state, lived in others, owned property in still others, divorced in another, and remarried, sometimes repeatedly, in others. When litigation occurred, the "public Acts, Records, and Judicial Proceedings" of several states were often put on the record, and a judge had to decide which jurisdiction's laws were relevant to a particular question, whose laws were entitled to full faith and credit. If the judge decided that the laws of another state were determinative, entitled to full faith and credit, that meant he had to interpret the probably contested and uncertain laws of that other sovereign state. But as often, particularly in child custody conflicts and in divorce, a judge would rule that local law trumped the laws of all other jurisdictions, even when separated spouses had been fighting over the matter for many years and across many jurisdictions.[31]

Two kinds of critics observed this system and called it corrupt. One, whom we today would identify with woman's rights and feminism, saw through the jurisdictional multiplicity and found the continuity of male power and authority, the constitution of marriage as an oppressive structure. There were lots of states, but there were only men in control, all the way down, from the chief justice of the state supreme court to the members of trial juries. After the Civil War, these critics looked to the federal government and the federal courts as institutional locations where new, more universal, rights could be constructed, and they claimed that the federal Constitution embodied an ungendered and critical standard that delegitimated the received laws. Though they were long disappointed, most continued to hope for an ultimate victory.[32] The others, pious men and other conservatives (and more conservative women), looked at the federal system and saw only a field of action for manipulative and strategic men. To them, the weakness of the federal system threatened to destroy the constitution of Christian marriage. It tempted fallible men and women toward the sin of believing that they could undo what only God could undo. The only remedy, they believed, lay in a unitary national law of marriage, incorporating a national (anti-) divorce law.[33] Both shared a general revulsion of the diversity and complexity of the system, and both participated in the construction of a widely shared perception, one that resonates with us still: that marriage was in a state of constitutional crisis requiring drastic and immediate national action.

Disorder may have been the rule in law and in many personal lives. Nonetheless, this was the country in which Americans lived their marital lives—one with many jurisdictions with imperfect forms of policing and regulation, with a national post office and a developing communication structure, yet with inadequate and locally based forms of property and marriage recordation.

In those United States (the plural remained for many years the normal designation), many lived long and orderly lives, as the McGuires did, never leaving the county of their birth. But even those ensconced in an isolated cultural community would still have come across couples who moved—who had come into their marital world, who would leave their marital world, sometimes together, sometimes apart. They would have met men who appeared single, who would sometimes court and sometimes marry the single women in the community. And then the new couple would move. Or the man alone would move. Or, later, the new wife would return to her family of origin alone or with children. Sometimes the couple would get a divorce, but not usually. Usually, they just went on living apart. At one time or another the McGuires might have encountered apparently unmarried women, who might have appeared with or without children. A woman might call herself the Widow Jones. No one in the community questioned her widowed status or her prior marital status. Who could know? (Though sometimes, accidentally, a marital past would become known, and then litigation appeared on the horizon.)

Marital mobility marked American legal and constitutional life. States were the powerful legal institutions in the government of marriage. They were where marriages were constituted legally. Still, many Americans understood themselves as only loosely tied to a "home" jurisdiction. They moved unconstrained, across state boundaries, apart and together. Such movement was, in fact, a crucial aspect of the sense of living in freedom in America, in the "imagined community" of the United States.[34]

American mobility is the oldest and most durable cliché of post-Revolutionary American historiography. Families moving together across the great American wilderness. Families moving north to the cities to escape first slavery and then the Jim Crow South. Families coming to America and moving from community to community, looking for free, or at least cheap, fertile land, looking for work. On the move.

Yet the image of families moving together was often an illusion. People moved for many reasons, and not only to improve the well-being of their families. Frequently they moved to leave unhappy marriages or to find a jurisdiction to authorize a union that was not possible where they and their (prior) family were known. Though such conduct could always be construed as bad, as morally reprehensible, it was also understood as legal, as part of the range of legal improvisations that American federalism made available to American citizens. As the 1870 brief for one recent Wisconsinite put it, "The fact that in addition to seeking a home where he could invest money and do business to advantage, he also desired to locate where the divorce laws were liberal, made him none the less a resident of the state."[35]

Too many men went to the Gold Rush, leaving wife and children, and never returned. Sometimes men left for the West intending to return, but they or their wives changed in the interim. Sometimes they left, meaning to abandon. Meanwhile, wives went to cities, took jobs in domestic service or factory work or opened boarding houses. They were widows, they told people around them, and then they remarried. Andrew Jackson's beloved wife Rachel lived one of those narratives. She and her first husband parted; they went their separate ways, to different jurisdictions. Then she met Andrew Jackson and married him—except she was still married.[36] During much of the nineteenth century, the divorce laws of a few states forbade the party at fault in a divorce from remarrying during the lifetime of the faultless party. Did that stop people from remarrying? Of course not. But it did require them to go somewhere else, usually to another state, to do their marrying business.

Cochran v. Cochran, the 1894 case that established much of the relevant doctrine for the *McGuire* case, told a classic version of the American story of marital mobility. Warren Cochran married Letitia in 1866, six months after his first wife had died leaving five children. They lived in Oshkosh, Wisconsin, where they raised his five children, plus two more that they had together. He divided his time between "preaching, speculating, and farming." She taught school. In 1873 Warren and his five older children went to Nebraska where they "began housekeeping" on a farm. Letitia joined them in 1874, staying until 1876 when she returned to Wisconsin to attend her parents' golden wedding anniversary. She remained in Wisconsin thereafter. In 1878 Warren filed suit for divorce in Nebraska, alleging desertion, but he dropped the suit and moved back to Oshkosh, where he remained until 1883 when he took a trip to Nebraska. He returned briefly to Wisconsin. But in December Warren "moved" for the last time to Nebraska. Three months later, he advertised in the *Omaha Bee:*

> Wanted—To correspond with a Christian lady of culture and refinement between the ages of 25 and 50, without children, who could unite with a genial husband to make his nice home in Omaha one of prosperity and happiness. This is in good faith, and deemed a proper method of introduction. Address under assumed name if preferred. (Signed) Otis Myrtle, Omaha, Neb.

In May 1884 Warren brought suit against Letitia in Nebraska, alleging that she had "willfully abandoned him."[37] The only notice of the divorce was in the *Nebraska Watchman,* an Omaha paper of limited circulation. Though he obviously knew where she lived, she was never sent any notice. The decree awarded Letitia no alimony nor custody of the two younger children (who had in any case remained with her in Wisconsin). At the time of the divorce, Warren was the owner of several parcels of land in Nebraska. To cheat her out of her marital interest in those lands, Warren conveyed the parcels to his older sons, who held them for him. In September he married a third wife, from whom he was soon divorced, and by 1894 he was living with his fourth wife. Meanwhile, Letitia remained patiently in Oshkosh, until the day in 1894 when she really needed his support.

Did Letitia Cochran have the right to sue Warren for support in Nebraska in 1894? Except for two years between 1874 and 1876, she had never lived in Nebraska. She had, one might think, no standing to sue in a Nebraska court twenty years later. Yet the Nebraska courts allowed her suit and ordered Warren to convey property to her in lieu of support payments. Why? Because her domicile, at least for purposes of this suit, always remained wherever her "husband" was. Her actual place in the world was covered over by her husband's.

But was Warren Cochran still her husband? The court didn't bother to answer that question. The judges weren't going to waste institutional resources subjecting him to a bigamy prosecution, nor would they have been interested in endangering the moral standing of the two wives who had followed Letitia. But for purposes of Letitia's petition, the court held that she had, as a separated wife, a right to her husband's support.

Although the court turned the case into a sentimental story about a deserting husband who had tried to deprive his long-suffering wife of her share of marital assets, we don't know what really went on: whether they cared about each other, whether they stayed in contact with each other over the years of separation, what they had negotiated when he left in 1883. Indeed, it is altogether possible that the two of them together constructed this story for the court because it was one that courts heard easily and sympathetically. Perjury, collusion, fiction were all crucial parts of divorce practice. Letitia may have been as strategic as Warren about their separation. There were worse fates for a middle-aged woman without a husband than to have it be known that he was "temporarily" away in Nebraska, engaged in preaching and land speculation, away in a place far enough from Oshkosh that no one Letitia knew was likely to run into Warren. Only at her retirement from teaching (at a time when teachers lacked a retirement pension) would she have needed to change the terms of their arrangement. And, as for Warren, he was surely less than scrupulous in his marital habits. Yet we need to remember how important being married was in nineteenth-century America: important in terms of the labor of maintaining a household, important as a public matter of being recognized as a competent (male) adult, important as a defense against the emotional isolation that always threatened in mobile America.

Europeans and other non-Americans saw the American marital regimes, their freedoms, their possibilities for remaking identities, and they were drawn to come. This was one, usually unspoken, feature of the American ideal, of the freedom that America offered.[38] At the same time, for many Americans, especially for many poor and vulnerable women, marital life in the multi-jurisdictional landscape of the United States was filled with dangers. The search for work, for land, for economic survival, split couples apart as they moved across the United States. While men were away—looking for new land, at the Gold Rush, on a whaling expedition—houses burned down, inheritances were lost, children became ill and sometimes died, mortgages were foreclosed. Meanwhile, husbands changed their minds about returning to their marriages; they found new loves; they "remarried" in new jurisdictions; they never came back. Some wives looked for poor relief from towns that had no obligation to provide it, since inherited legal rules declared that a wife could only receive poor relief from her husband's "settlement," his legal residence. Other wives claimed rights as wives—to support, to marital assets, to child custody—against abandoned husbands and their estates. These wives too often found that they had no rights; they could only sue where they were "domiciled," and that turned out to be (at least under the inherited rules) wherever their husbands might be, not where they were.

LAW

Behind *McGuire* lay the assumption that marriage was a legally constituted private relationship between one man and one woman. It was not a marriage if it was not legally recognized. But if it was so recognized, then the marriage—the entity, the household, the couple—gained the privileges of private freedom, including some sense of security from the prying eyes of communities and the state.

Everything about the last paragraph can easily be reduced to absurdity. The boundary between the legally constituted and the non- or illegally constituted was porous and fuzzy. Who was legally married, who was not, was often uncertain, particularly across the vast reaches of an American continent. Even for those not married by any of the standard rules, even for those who could not marry because they were already married or because of some civil disability like slavery or infancy, the technical illegality still might not matter. Some of the time courts recognized the unmarried and even the unmarriageable as married. More important, some legal and political theorists had long recognized that marriage was not a private institution. At the very beginning of the eighteenth century, the English writer Mary Astell had already identified marriage as a political institution, signaled by the public power of husbands. When woman's rights advocates of the mid-nineteenth century analogized marriage to slavery, their point was that marriage, like slavery, rested on the mobilization of public power. Privacy was nothing more than the law's euphemism for the powerlessness of subordinates, their reduction to the level of property, "as so many *things* belonging to a master." Public power constituted the private sphere.[39]

And yet, despite contradictions and incoherence, the opening description retains its validity as a historical understanding. A marriage was both legally constituted and private. Law was not everything in a marriage. Love, lust, hatred, duty, friendship, respect, affection, abandonment, commitment, greed, and self-sacrifice, all the feelings and practices that made up a nineteenth-century marriage, were not primarily legal. But law was always there as well. Law was there when a marriage began; it was there when it ended. And in between: law was there when a husband and wife struggled or negotiated over the terms of power between them; law was there when a married couple constructed or reconstructed a relationship with a world of others—including children, parents, and third party creditors; law was there when husbands or wives thought about themselves as husbands or wives; law was also there when those same husbands or wives denied or repressed their identities as husbands and wives.

In an ordinary legal consciousness, say the legal consciousness of Charles McGuire, the law of marriage would have appeared in two guises. The first would have been as the constitutive structure for beginnings and endings. About those, within the ongoing marriage, little more need be said. To marry, you usually needed a legal form and a little law. When your spouse died, you needed a legal form and a little law. If you divorced, you needed a lot of law. For the rest, law usually appeared as public interventions into a private relationship. Like private property, marriage was a realm of private choice and freedom, except when the public good required regulation. Government needed strong public reasons to justify entering that private sphere—whether of property or of family. How strong—how well proven—that public interest had to be in order to justify intervention varied across the time and space of the United States of America. From an early time, from a time before the creation of the United States, local governments had intruded whenever a husband refused to support wife and children on the theory that he was thereby making his dependents into public charges. Likewise, a husband (and theoretically, a wife) who abused a spouse or children could be forced by the local sessions court to secure a bond guaranteeing his good behavior in the future. But, so long as the marital unit did not become a burden on public welfare and so long as moral failures within the family did not come to public consciousness, for so long the family would remain private, untouched (but not untouchable) by public power. Anything more was an abuse of public power. Or, as Charles McGuire's lawyer posed it, after the district court in Wayne County had ordered Charles to make improvements to his home and to give Lydia McGuire an allowance: "The Court erred in assuming authority to regulate the private life of the defendant . . . in assuming to establish by judicial fiat the standard of living in defendant's home . . . in finding and decreeing that it is the duty of the husband to provide luxuries and comforts for the plaintiff beyond those which he deems necessary and desirable for himself."[40]

For Charles and his lawyer, as for many other men and some women, the law might appear as a friendly visitor, occasionally as a facilitative resource, sometimes as an invading army. But it always remained distinct from the marriage itself, which was private, distinctively so, more so than other relationships.

For such Americans, the law was more than just the words and practices of state legislatures and state judicial and semijudicial institutions. The decisions of courts—rather, the decisions of any particular court in any particular state at any particular time—were never the last word on any subject. There should always be a way to know the law—the normatively and singularly right answer. The law, at least the law as it ought to be, filtered out local and multiple answers, found the "sound," the "tried and true," the "principled" truth.

Throughout nineteenth-century America, the statement "The law is . . ." made apparent sense in its singular form. When ordinary men and women thought or talked about "the law" in their daily lives, they drew on a vision of law as a text that derived many of its categories and forms of understanding from legal treatises and other "mandarin legal texts." They knew that there was some text called "the law of husband and wife," and they knew that it had an objective existence separable from the particular rules enforced in any particular jurisdiction.[41] They would have read in newspapers of widely publicized scandal cases of the day—for example, the 1850 divorce suit of Edwin Forrest, the great Shakespearean actor, or the 1874 action for criminal conversation brought against Henry Ward Beecher, the famous liberal minister, for the seduction of Theodore Tilton's wife—or the more local scandal cases that flourished in every American city, and they would have thought and talked about what it all meant for the "law of marriage." They would have read and responded to (and sometimes written) pieces in the flood of articles and polemics about the crisis in the law of marriage that began in the middle years of the nineteenth century. They would have engaged in arguments that began or ended with the statement "There ought to be a law," or with the premise that the law as a whole was hopelessly corrupt, in need of a thoroughgoing reformation.[42]

But when husbands and wives found themselves "in the law," or when they looked to it as a strategic field of action, or as a domain they worked to avoid, then the law became something different. In the law office, in the court, facing the social worker, dealing with the trustees of a separate estate, petitioning the Freedmen's Bureau, as a husband packed his bags to move quietly to Indiana or South Dakota or to join a whaling expedition, as a wife looked over at her sleeping husband and thought about the likelihood that he was going to leave or that she was, the law lost its literary and textual and metajurisdictional qualities. Suddenly, it became a force, perhaps not the force wanted, perhaps not enough of a force to do what justice demanded that it do. Still, a force. In its jurisdictional identity, as the mobilization of legitimate violence that is (sometimes) the state, it became "the law," concretized by the "It is so ordered!" that concludes a legal decree.

That law, the law defined by public power and coercion, sometimes carried within it the conventional moral philosophy of an era and its cultural commitments. It always involved the landscape of institutions that lawyers and their clients explored. The paradigmatic legal question was not the theoretical question, does a husband have a right to beat his wife when she disobeys his command? Rather, it was the concrete problem of a particular court, which had to decide whether it should punish him if he had beaten her under such circumstances. And how, if at all, would he be punished? Not, did a wife have the right to worship God in her own way? But rather, would she have the right to a court-ordered separation? Or would a court (in this jurisdiction, at this time) order a "judicial" separation if her husband kept her from going to church?

Lawyers ordinarily looked to doctrine as a body of materials useful as predictions without regard to moral or ideological content.[43] It was a repository of possibly persuasive arguments and images that might, or might not, get this court at this time to do what the lawyer believed needed doing. What would lead a court to declare Charles a guilty husband and Lydia an abused wife? What would justify breaching a husband's private sphere of authority? Under what circumstances would Lydia be justified in leaving Charles? What would it mean for her legal identity, her ability to act as a competent individual in the world, if she had left Charles?

Lawyers' predictions led husbands and wives to assume identities recognizable in the law, to make themselves into legal subjects. Lydia McGuire told the lower court that she had been "chaste, obedient and dutiful." Letitia Cochran described herself as someone who had always "performed and discharged her duties . . . as a dutiful, chaste, obedient, and faithful wife to the best of her ability." Predictions about how a court would react also led litigants to impose identities on their opponents. Lydia made sure the court saw Charles as a "poor companion," as "headstrong," and as selfish and greedy.[44] Some characterizations, like "obedient" or "headstrong," drew sustenance from the wider culture. Others could only be explained within the institutional context of local law. My father came to this country in 1940, sent by his family to figure out what was going on with his younger brother, then in New York, who had written my grandparents in the Netherlands that he was going to "sleep" with a prostitute in New Jersey, so that he could become "an adulterer" and thereby he and his wife could get a divorce in New York.[45] The "adultery" that my uncle was going to commit, while related to the moral category, had been shorn of its moral meaning, had become, at least in twentieth-century New York, a formal mechanism, a way of getting something done legally.

All those predictions and identities were never more than guesses, sometimes more successful than others. Becoming "an adulterer" assured you a divorce in New York. During the early 1950s, being slapped exactly twice entitled a wife to a divorce in Chicago.[46] But the legal significance of many characterizations was never quite determinate. Or, rather, apparent consequences would be belied by changing contexts and alternative doctrines. Lydia clearly proved that Charles was a tightfisted old coot who didn't support her in a way that was appropriate to her station in life. Doing so, however, didn't get her a legal remedy. Ninety years earlier, after losing one of the most widely publicized divorce trials of the nineteenth century, Edwin Forrest tried to reduce or eliminate his continuing obligation to pay Catherine, his ex-wife, the huge sum of $4,000 a year. Edwin had evidence that proved Catherine had led a life of "extravagance, intemperance, immorality, and vice" ever since they had separated and that she had repeatedly committed "adultery." The court denied his request, even though he had made a prima facie case that she was exactly the kind of separated wife who ought not to be entitled to the support of her husband. But, according to the New York courts, she was no longer a wife (and therefore not an adulteress). Her conduct since the marriage, her identity as an unmarried woman, was irrelevant, had no effect on an obligation that had been fixed at the time when they had legally been husband and wife.[47]

Knowing the law, as best one could, meant knowing what it meant to be a "wife" or a "husband." It also meant knowing that one had "private" rights, realms of private freedom, including the capacity to ignore many public or community expectations. According to the district court in *McGuire v. McGuire,* no one in the McGuires' neighborhood lived as they did, with such old furnishings, with so few "modern conveniences." In denying Lydia material comforts, Charles was not fulfilling his public responsibilities as a "husband." No matter. Charles did not need to do so as long as Lydia was not placed in need of public support.[48]

From an early point in the nineteenth century, some Americans drew out of the constitutional culture a vision of individual liberty that challenged the governing premises of the law of marriage. One would be hard-pressed to find any established institutional voice, prior to Justice William Brennan's in 1969, willing to declare publicly that marriage was legally nothing but "an association of two individuals." But some Americans long had acted on that intuition, and they were some of the men and women whose cases made the law of the era. They rooted their autonomy and their identity in a willingness to make marriages, to become wives and husbands, but they also insisted on their capacities to construct marriages and to leave them according to their changing desires. They assumed, and often found, that the American legal order, as a federal system, with many jurisdictions and with relatively easy forms of exit, would do little to challenge their practical understanding of their rights.[49]

A PRACTICE

Throughout his opinion in *McGuire,* Justice Messmore kept returning to separation as the necessary but absent "condition precedent." Lydia's allegation of "cruelty" was dismissed because "the fact that she did not separate" was "quite incompatible with the allegation." Without separation, the "family" remained inviolate. Without separation, there was no way to challenge the presumption that Charles was "legally supporting" Lydia, that "the purpose of the marriage relation" was "being carried out."[50]

But what was separation? And how would Messmore have understood its legal significance?

Today, we imagine separation as a transition between marriage and divorce. It comes into being in order to be resolved by divorce, although occasionally couples reunite instead of divorcing. Once married, one either remains married or one divorces.

This understanding of the law and of marriage is both empirically misleading and historically anachronistic if applied to Lydia's situation. For two centuries commentators have singled out America as the home of divorce, as the place where marital exits lived. America was always a comparative divorce haven.[51] And yet, until quite recently, few Americans would have regarded divorce as a remedy for their private marital situations. Marriages were meant to be permanent, for life. Divorce was understood as an occasional public remedy for a limited list of public wrongs, not a private right.

When unhappy nineteenth-century couples lacked the legal grounds or the financial means or the moral or religious support to seek a divorce, many separated. In doing so, they entered a complex legal netherworld, one framed by uncertainties of legal jurisdiction and authority as well as of moral identity and responsibility.

Judges and treatise writers inherited from eighteenth-century English law a stock set of pejorative phrases about separation. A standard doctrinal statement described separation as "that anomalous condition of a married pair which involves a cessation of domestic intercourse, while the impediments of marriage continue." A separated couple was something close to an oxymoron, a wife without a husband and a husband without a wife, a site of moral danger. "[E]ither from choice or necessity," separated couples had thrown aside "the strong safeguards of a home and mutual companionship." They had forfeited "their most solemn obligations to protect, love, and cherish through life." They were "united in form and divided in fact." "The spirit" of the marriage contract, "all that dignified and ennobled it," was gone; the letter remained. They were "cast loose upon the world without the right to love and be loved again." Even to think of "kindling fresh flames at the altar of domestic happiness" was criminal. No public policy could possibly "favor" such a way of being in the world.[52]

Throughout the long nineteenth century (which ended by my reckoning sometime after World War II), American judges and other law writers liked to chastise separated individuals: they had no right to live apart from their spouses, no right to renegotiate their contracted obligations to live together, to care for one another, to support and to be supported. The more important point, however, is that judges basically felt helpless before the crude reality of separation. The courts—at least in the United States—were fundamentally powerless to compel couples to live together, powerless to coerce an abandoning or deserting spouse to return, powerless to make men and women live as husbands and wives. By the 1840s, perhaps earlier, separating had become an exercise of unchallengeable private freedom.

A separation did not necessarily imply marital conflict. The possible reasons for separation were as multitudinous as our social and political history. One might begin with the search for work, for land, for gold, for economic security, for freedom, for escape from a stultifying social environment, religious conflict, warfare. Often couples who separated with the expectation that they would soon reunite, didn't. They fell out of love, found others to love, found that life was better alone or as part of a different community. The distance between them was just too great.

Other couples separated because they couldn't stand to live together, because they had to get out of the immediate intimate relationship, because of marital conflict. Few of those separations were legally justified, for the law only recognized a limited number of reasons for separating. The number grew during the long nineteenth century, yet remained small. Basically, one was "right" to separate when remaining required a spouse to "condone" the uncondonable: adultery, physical abuse to the point of danger, cruelty. Separation was also right when remaining placed one in immediate moral or physical danger. Beyond that, the explicit message of the law was to accept the imperfections of the other. Marriage meant "for richer, for poorer, for better, for worse."

Still, the legal standards cannot contain the reasons why American women and men separated from spouses. A husband's petty oppressions had crossed some line, from the bearable to the unbearable. A wife's attachment to her parents made her unloving. Her incessant religious proselytizing made home a living hell. Hidden sexual pasts were suddenly revealed. A mother-in-law's presence in the household challenged a wife's identity and implicit authority. Indebtedness or impoverishment could make anyone cranky, let alone the seductions of the tavern, outside religious communities, or a world of others who had "alienated the affections."

There came a point when separating became a felt necessity. Traditionally, at least among the upper-class Englishmen whose separations had constructed the inherited law, separating meant returning a wife to her parents' household. That was also a possible response in the United States, but distance and prior moves often made that an impossibility. In the usual case, separating meant that one (usually the husband) or both had to leave the community in which they had lived together. There were social costs to being separated and staying, even when one was not wrong to have separated. Separation was a mark of failure in a marrying society. Moreover, from the husband's perspective, if he and his wife remained in the same place, but separated, he would probably have to support two households. For both husband and wife, if they stayed in the same place, they would remain under the scrutiny of those who knew them as married, making new relationships and remarriage difficult, if not impossible. It made sense to leave and to recreate oneself elsewhere.

A possible recreation was for wife or husband to go to a neighboring or a distant state where divorce was possible. Going to that state and getting a divorce might, but also might not, gain the traveler a recognizable identity as unmarried in the state from which she or he had come. One was surely separated. One might be divorced. Sometimes one could be separated but married in one state and legally divorced in another. Or, as in the *Cochran* case, divorced, yet still responsible for the support of a woman who for some purposes remained one's wife. In a land of mobile Americans, multiple jurisdictions, and an inherited marital culture, divorce and separation were intertwined with each other.

Another possibility was just to leave, to disappear, to desert, to abandon, and then to remarry—and then hope that no one would appear where you now lived who knew or cared about your original marital status.

Enough people separated so that separation became the crucial practice through which the legal culture of marriage in America developed. Yet the relative numbers, the proportion of separated as compared to the divorced and the "intact" married, are and will probably remain unknown. There is no simple way to quantify how many men and women exercised their right to leave without a legal decree. Unlike divorces, which left a mark in the public records, separations mostly lived in a private and indeterminate world.[53]

From the perspective of law and lawyers, separation assumes a more public role yet also an ambiguous one. Appellate judges and the authors of legal treatises insisted on their hatred for separation because it called into question the salience and the coercive power of the inherited rules. They tried to minimize the subject. Nonetheless, separations percolated through their work, and almost every difficult issue in the law of marriage resulted from the lives and the legal problems of the separated. Many judges found it intolerable that couples had managed to renegotiate the purportedly non-negotiable terms of Christian marriage. Yet the paradigmatic cases of nineteenth-century marital conflict—cases involving struggles over support, obedience within marriage, sexual exclusivity, marital property, child custody—were about couples separated or in the process of separating, negotiating the terms of settlement. "Separation" cases provided the occasions for most of the standard family law language about the legal unity of husband and wife and the legal indissolubility of marriage. Rules framed by a commitment to marital unity and to the legal reality of a couple becoming "one flesh" by marriage emerged out of cases dealing with couples who were clearly separated and apart. Judges who pontificated on the permanence of marriage often did so with regard to parties who, though not divorced, were certainly not joined together. If *McGuire* is a guide, one would almost say that the law came to encourage separation, offered incentives to its use, that marital rights eventually depended on separation.

The narrative of woman's rights law reform in the nineteenth century—the story of the slow recognition of a wife's right to child custody, to separate property, to her earnings, to a separate legal identity, to the possession of her own person—was, for the most part, a story about the emergent rights of separated wives, most of whom would never again live with their husbands. Bringing separation to the fore allows us to see marital property reforms as institutionally realistic efforts to deal with the situation of separated wives, who remained otherwise in the law in a state of coverture, subject to their absent husbands and without the legal capacity to contract or act in the world. Legislators were not revolutionaries, but they were making significant changes in the law in response to the separations they saw all around them.

Separations took their shape within the constitutional landscape of the United States. The multiplicity of American states encouraged people to separate by offering the possibility of shucking off one marriage by moving to another state. Meanwhile, the full faith and credit requirements of the federal Constitution left uncertain the degree to which marital escapes would ever be complete. You could run, and you could hide, but if you were found, the law of your past might reclaim you.

The paradigmatic story was told in *Barber v. Barber,* decided by the U.S. Supreme Court in 1858. A New York wife abandoned by her husband went to the New York court of equity and received a judgment ordering her husband to pay her alimony of $360 per year. He moved to Wisconsin and divorced her there, alleging her "abandonment." She followed him and tried to enforce the New York alimony judgment in Wisconsin. When she failed in the Wisconsin courts, she went to federal court.[54] There she faced a problem of self-presentation. Who was she, a separated wife or a divorcée? Her ability to sue in federal court rested on diversity jurisdiction, on her right as a citizen of New York to sue a citizen of Wisconsin in federal court. But was she a citizen of New York, if, as she insisted, she remained her husband's wife? As a divorcée, she would have her separate identity, including a separate residence in New York. The effect of a divorce, however, would be to make her a single woman, and then she was not entitled to enforce the judgment, which rested on her right to support as a wrongfully abandoned separated wife. If, instead, she insisted on the continuity of her marriage, wasn't she, rather, domiciled in Wisconsin, where her so-called husband lived? And then she would not meet the diversity of citizenship requirement on which federal jurisdiction rested.

Justice James Wayne, writing for the Supreme Court majority, refused to let Mrs. Barber's dilemma stop him from granting her relief.[55] This

husband, like many other husbands, had obtained his Wisconsin divorce on fraudulent grounds, on the spurious claim that his wife had
abandoned him. Such a divorce did not release him from his liability on
the New York decree, which was founded on his misconduct in leaving
her. His misconduct not only released her from the obligation to reside
with him, but gave her immediately a separate identity and a separate
domicile as a separated wife. According to Wayne, abandonment meant
that a husband had tried to rid himself of his "conjugal obligations" to
support his wife. As a result, he lost his "marital control" over her, and
he gave up "that power and authority over her which alone makes his
domicil hers." Thus, his abandonment gave her instantly, by automatic
operation, a separate domicile wherever she wished to live. She could
sue him as her (separated) husband in federal court under the diversity
jurisdiction mandated by the U.S. Constitution.[56]

Wayne's opinion tells part of an important story: how American
judges changed elements of an inherited legal order to give wives, and
especially separated wives, legal capacity as individuals, how separated
American wives achieved recognized and usable legal identities. At the
same time, it is important to acknowledge how contested and uncertain
Wayne's constitutional vision was. We can assert, retrospectively, that
his was the winning side, yet Justice Daniel dissented, joined by Taney
and Campbell, and for the rest of the nineteenth century this dissent was
treated as nearly as authoritative as Wayne's majority opinion.[57]

Daniel's opinion took seriously two doctrines that Wayne had
brushed aside: the received orthodoxy that husband and wife were always and inherently one person at law and the constitutional assumption that marriage law was a matter of state law alone. (This was, of
course, 1858, and one can read strong echoes of *Dred Scot* and the slavery crisis on both sides.) A wife, wrote Daniel, only had rights "as a
wife," and those rights arose from the duties she performed as a wife. A
wife, as a wife, could not become a citizen of a state other than her husband's.[58] Furthermore, nothing in the federal Constitution granted federal officers, including judges, any right to enter "with a kind of inquisi-
torial authority . . . the habitations and even . . . the chambers and
nurseries of private families, and inquire into and pronounce upon the
morals and habits and affections or antipathies of the members of every
household." Only state officers and judges had that right. In this case,
those officers in Wisconsin had divorced the husband from his wife. If

Wisconsin declared him (and her) divorced, the federal courts had no business challenging the decision.[59]

Then Daniel turned the story around, focusing on the judicial separation. He found two fallacies in the notion that a judicially decreed separation made husband and wife into citizens of different states. First, nothing in such a decree made a wife a citizen at all, a legally recognizable person, while she remained a wife, "still bound by her conjugal obligations, the faithful observance of which, on her part, is the foundation of her claim to maintenance as wife." Second, her right to alimony depended on her continuing "personal merits and conduct" as a wife. But only the state that ordered the decree, in this case New York, could judge whether she had continued to meet the standard, not the federal government, which had no such power, no capacity to judge the moral behavior of "the several States and their people."[60]

Still, Mrs. Barber, the separated wife, won. She gained the right to enforce her judgment in federal court as a citizen of New York. The principle of the case, however, was a difficult one to generalize, and for the separated, no Civil War, no Reconstruction, resolved the issue. It continued, and festered, for the next century. Separated wives' domiciles became the stuff of continuing constitutional controversy. In America, the problem was everywhere the same, in state courts as well as in federal courts: what kind of legal unity was there when people were separated? Alternatively, did the federal courts (or the courts of other states) have any right to interpose their judgment about the substantive rights of separated parties, to interfere in the functioning of marital regimes that belonged to each of the states in the Union?

To be separated meant that one had taken on a partially new identity. One lived life in the awkward condition of a wife without a husband or a husband without a wife. There would be everyday legal consequences in terms of the capacities of both husband and wife to carry on a variety of legal transactions—buying, selling, borrowing, inheriting, remarrying, fornicating, and disciplining children, among others. Legally much would change when one became a separated wife or husband, but, at least in legal theory, one always remained a wife or a husband. A wife was still a "feme covert," except insofar as she had successfully escaped some of the consequences of coverture. A husband was still legally responsible for the support of his wife and children, except insofar as he had successfully renegotiated or abandoned that responsibility. Separa-

tions occurred within, although at the boundaries of, marriage and coverture.

In the law there were a variety of separations. To make a quick (and
incomplete) list, there were:

1. divorces à mensa et thoro (that is, judicially ordered separations,
   sometimes also called limited divorces from bed and board);
2. separations founded on equitable agreements (separate
   maintenance agreements) or enforceable contracts between
   husband and wife;
3. informal separations of a variety of sorts, including separations
   founded on legally unenforceable contracts, abandonments, desertions, and bigamies.

In addition there were two other categories that did not exist legally at
all, but that still had an important presence in the legal culture:

4. "temporary" separations, not founded on marital conflict;
5. divorces in one jurisdiction, unrecognized in another.

It is possible to arrange these separations along a continuum from
the legally recognized to the criminal. Or, alternatively, from the highly
formalized divorce à mensa et thoro (which in most American jurisdictions was identical to a full divorce in all its effects, except the right of
remarriage), through the informality of abandonment or desertion, to
the illegality of bigamy. Yet one should not work too hard to rationalize
or systematize the varieties of separations. Desertions were surely more
effective as "divorces" than were formalized judicial separations. Many
"permanent" separations would be entirely unacknowledged legally.
There might be marital significance in a husband's whaling expedition or
trip to the gold fields of California or in the wife's job as a domestic in a
wealthy household in the city—or there might not. Such "separations"
perhaps covered over more emotionally felt breaches in marital unity,
but such separations also reemphasize for us the private content of the
situation. Outsiders could never know what the couple meant by their
decision to live apart, and the couple may have liked it that way, enjoyed
keeping their private business private.

How did husbands regard the status of being separated? How did their
sense of themselves as husbands change as a result of a separation? One
answer, probably the common answer, was that they stopped thinking of

themselves as husbands or at least as the husbands of their separated wives. They moved on to new lives and new relationships in new places.

Some husbands, though, knew themselves as both married and separated. Formally, little had changed, since marital rights and duties survived a separation, but in practice separation changed everything. Indeed, the doctrinal material of nineteenth-century American law suggests one paradoxical conclusion: separation invented marital rights. Not just structurally, in the fact that it would ordinarily make little sense for a husband to be insisting, for example, on his rights to custody of his child within what we today would call an "intact" family, but experientially as well, as husbands discovered that as (now-separated) husbands they had rights they had better assert or risk losing. Only at the time of separation was it legally appropriate for a husband to assert his marital rights. The "private" relationship had become at least partially public, and he had to claim what was his. The control of the household had fractured, and power had to be exercised explicitly. Some husbands tried to use their custodial rights over their children as a way to compel wives to return to them. Others wrote letters to their separated wives detailing new rules and expectations.[61]

Wives, like husbands, often regarded separation as nothing less than the end of their marriages. Many of them became, so far as others knew, widows or single women. Yet when they found themselves in the "anomalous" situation of a "wife without a husband" when they were publicly separated, they seemed to have had contradictory reactions to their legal situation.

A wife could draw on important cultural and religious themes and understandings to justify a decision to separate. There were situations where separation was the morally right thing to do, where a wife had a moral obligation to separate herself from her erring husband. Temperance advocates told wives to separate from their drunkard husbands. Even conservative antidivorce polemics sometimes distinguished the evil of divorce from the legitimacy of separation. Although voices in the religious culture told wives to live with husbands' failings, to accept imperfections, to condone, still a woman had to look out for her own soul, for her own salvation. In the end, her relationship to God came first, ahead of her relationship with her husband. Eternity sometimes trumped "for life."

But who was she, once separated? In litigation, a separated wife might present herself as still dependent and incompetent, as still under her husband's control. She might describe the separation as coerced by her dishonest husband, that he had manipulated her weakness, her relative powerlessness. She might describe herself as wanting and needing to be supported within his household. Indeed, one of the oddities of studying lawsuits between separated wives and husbands is the discovery that wives—or their lawyers—so often claimed coverture as a right, against the contrasting claims of husbands that their wives had become competent and capable legal individuals who ought to be held responsible for their own debts.

And yet wives also insisted that separation had changed—had transformed—the identities of both husband and wife. One result could be autonomy and a sense of freedom. Many women rejected the inherited doctrinal premise that marital rights and duties were unchanged by separation and called upon courts and legislatures to recognize the changed situation. Marital property reform, earnings acts that allowed a wife to keep the money she earned outside the home, proposals for mothers' pensions and other forms of poor relief that did not threaten an unprotected woman with the loss of her children, all responded to the autonomy claimed by separated wives. In custody cases, wives rarely challenged the common law rule of husband's rights to the custody and control of his children; rather, they insisted that those rights were modified both by formal and informal separations. Separations, even separations without fault on the part of husbands, made mothers into the proper custodians of their children.[62]

Still, everyone knew that separation remained a part of marriage. In divorce, husband and wife became estranged and emancipated from each other. In separation, by contrast, they remained legally bound together. The rights of the separated remained marital rights, at least in the sense that they were possessed relationally within a zero-sum universe where what husband had, wife did not, and vice versa.[63] Courts rarely reduced marriage or separation to an explicit quid pro quo. More often, as in *McGuire,* they worked to leave the terms of a marital relationship within a private sphere. Still, separation often intensified the unequal but reciprocally constituted relationship between wife and husband. Separation challenged a husband's need to be recognized as a head of household, called into question his honor and identity by demonstrating his wife's independence. Her life apart from him could become a continuing provocation. Wives may have often felt emancipated by separation, yet they also lived with the knowledge that the legal regime left them vulnerable to the reimposition of a husband's authority. What autonomy wives gained was always partial and tentative.

McGuire v. McGuire belongs to the past but to a more complicated and interesting past than where family law casebooks have consigned it. The past to which it belongs is the past of the long nineteenth century of American marriage law. In that past, there still existed a legal and religious culture, a tradition, that appeared to make the terms of marriage compulsory and coercive. Lydia McGuire's claimed right to a legal remedy relied on that tradition, on an inherited vision of what it was to be married and of what a husband owed his wife. And if we believe the court papers, she had lived her life with Charles in accordance with its precepts, being a wife in relation to the being of Charles as a husband.

The categories and values the Nebraska Supreme Court mobilized as it rejected her claim—what was articulated and what was taken for granted as the court ruled that nothing about her performance as a proper wife was relevant legally—are immensely revealing. Nearly everything important about the law of marriage in the years through the middle of the twentieth century is somewhere in the court's opinion: about the nature of law, about the capacities of the institutions of the American states, about the significance of separation as the catalyst of legal rights. *McGuire v. McGuire* was, in that sense, both a telling and a typical case. It offers an introduction into the distinctively American law of marriage, into a law that used a legal vocabulary continuous with a long patriarchal tradition, but a law that also inflected and transformed that vocabulary in the American context, on the American continent, through multiple marital regimes.

2

Abigail Bailey's Divorce

It is indeed painful in the extreme to have occasion thus to deal with
one, who ought to be my nearest and dearest friend on earth.
Memoirs of Mrs. Abigail Bailey *(1815)*

One hundred sixty years before Lydia McGuire lost her case in court, an-other farm wife successfully divorced her husband. Like Lydia McGuire, Abigail Bailey initially rejected divorce as a remedy; unlike Lydia, she learned, after an extended and tortuous process, to understand herself as a wife entitled to a divorce.

Abigail Bailey's memoirs, published posthumously, tell a dramatic story. Born in 1746, she lived in New Hampshire and was married to a violent and hard man who, after twenty years of marriage and the birth of fourteen children, sexually abused one of their daughters. The bulk of her memoirs details her struggle to separate herself from that hus-band after she became aware of the incest. Eventually, she learned to think of him as her "enemy," and from that time on the modern reader can begin to see her as an individual in modern dress. But that transfor-mation of husband into stranger happened late and incompletely. Abi-gail's struggle, for what in the nineteenth century would be called "self-ownership," occurred entirely within a legal and religious culture that identified her with her husband.[1]

Throughout the memoirs, Abigail Bailey's unswerving focus is on her conversations with and monologues about her husband. The work rep-resents an intense reflection on her marital relations. Carefully recon-structing arguments, prayers, and invocations of religious authority, she monitors the changing discourse of her marriage.

Law played a prominent role in those conversations and monologues. Talk about rights and remedies—about what Abigail's husband had a right to do to her if she would not abide by his wishes, about what she could do to him if he would not abide by hers—was central to their marriage, particularly in its latter days. Their conversations reproduced power relations and legal notions of the self within marriage.[2] Yet the central normative structure in Abigail Bailey's life—a structure that radically constrained her options as she struggled with her husband—was never law. For her, human law was always secondary to God and his "wonderful" plan. Legal power was ultimately ineffectual against the power of prayer and submission to God's will.

Unless one appreciates the distinctive parallax of her evangelical Christianity,[3] there is no way to make historical sense of the pivotal problem in Abigail's narrative: that is, knowing when it would become right for her to act separately from and in opposition to her husband. From the time she first became aware of the incest, she theoretically possessed legal rights against her husband. She might have had a right to a full divorce. She certainly had a right to a separation from bed and board (a court-ordered limited divorce), including an equitable distribution of marital property. She had a right to have articles of the peace drawn up against her husband. She could always threaten him with indictment for a capital crime. Instead, she waited and prayed and suffered for the better part of four years before invoking formal legal processes.

Why? Was she so abused, like the "battered wife" of the modern legal imagination, that she had lost the will or the capacity to act, to leave? Was her delay a measure of her victimization? Perhaps.[4] Yet such a response, which so easily suggests itself to us, misses Abigail Bailey's own understanding of prayer as active and primary and of legal rights as secondary and derivative. She did not regard her prolonged delay as passivity or as resulting from victimization. For her, waiting was essential for her moral identity. She could not act until she knew and understood God's will. What to do about her husband was a question only to be answered at the end of a long spiritual journey.

THE SUBMISSIVE SELF

Abigail Bailey, like other eighteenth-century women, understood marriage as a move from the domain of her parents to that of her new husband, exchanging one dependence for another. "As, while I lived with my parents, I esteemed it my happiness to be in subjection to them; so now I thought it must be a still greater benefit to be under the aid of a judicious companion, who would rule his own house." Unlike later nineteenth-century young women, who often viewed the transition to marriage as one involving an exchange of a life of freedom for one of bondage and separation, Abigail did not describe her marriage as requiring the loss of a prior self.[5] Indeed, we might better think of her as finding herself through her hierarchical relationships. She was, at least as she described herself in her memoirs, fulfilling her destiny, being true to her nature.

Although she longed for a relationship with her husband founded on friendship, she soon learned that he would only intermittently offer that. She insisted, however, that she could be happy as his wife. God had, she believed, given her "a heart to resolve never to be obstinate, or disobedient," to her husband. Rather, she would "be always kind, obedient, and obliging in all things not contrary to the word of God." She thought, "if Mr. B. were sometimes unreasonable, I would be reasonable, and would rather suffer wrong than do wrong." She would be so because it was her nature so to be. When he treated her badly, as he did from the first, she hoped that it resulted "not from ill will" but "from the usual depravity of the human heart." She felt, during a good period in their marriage, "the tenderest affection for him as my head and husband. I ever rejoiced when he returned from abroad. Nor did I see him come in from his daily business without sensible delight. Much pleasure I took in waiting upon him, and in doing all in my power to make him happy."[6]

Abigail Bailey's willingness to subsume her identity into that of her husband, to live as a dependent within his household, might seem to reflect the normative vision of common law coverture. She knew that she was "under his legal control," and that "he could overrule all my plans as he pleased." As she told him in one of their many conversations after the discovery of the incest, "I well knew I had been placed under his lawful government and authority, and likewise under his care and protection. And most delightful would it have been to me, to have been able quietly and safely to remain there as long as I lived. Gladly would I have remained a kind[,] faithful, obedient wife to him, as I had ever been." Like other wives, her place within her husband's household, subject to his control and power, left her dependent on his honor and restraint.[7]

Despite the apparent prescriptions of law and theology, marital submission did not mean a loss of personal identity. Abigail Bailey may have been "covered" by her husband; the consequence of their marriage was not, however, that they became "one flesh" in anything other than the most formal legal sense. She knew herself as a distinct and separate child of God. Her identity and her ultimate interests always remained her own.

Her relationship with God was primary; her relationship with her husband never more than secondary. She implicitly but absolutely rejected the Pauline admonition that "He [the husband] [lives] for God; she for God in him." Indeed, passages in the text where she longs for emotional connection with Asa Bailey are immediately followed by admonitions against the sin of idolatry. "On a certain day," for example, something she had said infuriated him, leading him to abuse her verbally and then to leave the room. She grieved "to see him in so wicked a frame; and the more, as I had been (though without design) the cause of it. I mourned, and longed for his return, and for his friendship, as a hungry child longs for the breast." Nonetheless, no sooner did she write this than she "recollected, that in all my troubles, Christ was my hiding place." She had been wrong to look to her husband for a succor that only God could provide.[8]

When Abigail Bailey thought of herself as a wife, she did not think in terms of merger, of "one flesh," of an obliteration of a prior self. Instead, she thought of a self "covered" by her husband during marriage. Submission was not a denial of her self. On the contrary, it constituted the central test of her self and of the strength of her religious identity. For Abigail Bailey, marriage was both destiny and achievement. "[I]t had ever been my greatest care and pleasure (among my earthly comforts) to obey and please him." What she called "the habit of obedience" was a learned and practiced habit, crucial to her because in it she would find her salvation. She had hoped when she married "to find a companion of meek, peaceable temper; a lover of truth; discreet and pleasant. . . . But the allwise God, who has made all things for himself, has a right, and knows how to govern all things for his own glory." It was, she quickly learned, "the sovereign pleasure" of that same "allwise God" to try her "with afflictions in that relation from which I had hoped to receive the greatest of my earthly comforts."[9]

Thinking of submission as a test helps to suggest some of the complexity in the eighteenth-century idea of a feme covert. To some men, coverture perhaps suggested simple merger and unity. To Abigail Bailey, it suggested the task for a lifetime, a way of establishing credentials as a worthy Christian. Coverture was hard but necessary work for a distinctively female self that would realize salvation through submission.

To understand Abigail Bailey's legal identity, the reader must work through pages in which she reflects on God's goodness in testing her through the affliction of her husband. It was God's wondrous ways to make her life so miserable. When her friends and relatives told her that Asa was "a cunning, crafty man," who was likely to leave his family destitute if she did not take legal action against him, she replied that there was "a time to speak; and a time to keep silence, and that, at the present time, the latter was my duty." Like Job, Abigail found the difficulty of her situation came close to providing a measure of the strength and quality of her faith.[10]

And yet the test God had given her was more difficult even than bearing up under the burdens of an oppressive husband. She knew that there would come a time when she must "henceforth look out, and take care of" herself, when she must rid herself of her husband, when the habit of obedience would no longer be a virtue.[11] At some point the time for marital submission would have passed, to be replaced by a time for separation.

But when would that point occur? And what would mark the change? Her husband's oppression, as such, would never justify resistance and rebellion. Nor would his sinful conduct alone. All these were little else than the markers of God's wonderful (and inscrutable) plan. As she wrote, in describing her reaction to her first suspicions of her husband's incestuous behavior, "I saw that it was as much my duty to submit to God under one trial, as under another."

ABIGAIL'S STORY

Abigail's trials had begun with her wedding in 1767. Although she had not expected her husband to be a religious man, she had hoped when she wed that Asa Bailey "would wish for good regulations in his family, and would have its external order accord with the word of God." She soon found, however, that he was rash and frequently unreasonable, capable of hard and cruel treatment. Still, she worked at loving Asa and "confided in him, as my real friend."

Three years into their marriage Asa had an affair with a serving girl working in their house in Landaff, New Hampshire. The girl was eventually sent away, but Abigail felt as if her "earthly joys were fled." Yet she kept her troubles to herself and, in effect, "condoned" the affair by staying with her husband.

Abigail did, however, begin to "vent" her grief and "broken heart" by keeping a journal of her spiritual situation. In these writings she focused on man's depravity, on how those who should be friends often become the worst of enemies, on how it was wrong to put one's trust in mankind.

Three years later, in 1773, Asa sexually assaulted another serving girl, who would eventually go before the local grand jury to charge him. When Abigail confronted him with what had happened, Asa "fell into a passion" with her. He was overcome with anger and took to his bed. Abigail went out milking and while there tried in prayer to intercede on his behalf. She still believed he could be brought to repentance. She then returned to the house where she was met by her husband, who told her that he had thought about killing her. But suddenly he had had "a most frightful view of himself. All his sins stared him in the face. All his wickedness, from his childhood to that hour, was presented to his mind, and appeared inexpressibly dreadful. All the terrors of the law, he said, pressed upon his soul." He had cried out to God for mercy. And then, he said, he had experienced a sudden revelation of grace.

Abigail knew better than to believe that. But she continued to live in "peace and comfort" with her husband, "willing to forgive all that was past, if he might but behave well in future." Over the next fifteen years, they grew prosperous, and Asa became a leading citizen of the town, holding a variety of local offices.[12]

In 1788 Asa Bailey took a trip west, through New York and perhaps to Ohio. He was gone for several weeks, and while he was away, Abigail had several frightening dreams. When Asa returned, he proposed that they all should move west.

In December he began to behave strangely. He told Abigail again of his plan to move to Ohio, and he asked for her consent and the consent of the children. None of them were pleased with the idea, but all "wished to be obedient"; all agreed "to follow our head and guide, wherever he should think best, for our family had ever been in the habit of obedience." Asa proposed to take one son and one daughter to help him while he looked for a place for them all to live, a plan quickly altered to one where he would take only the one daughter. Abigail later realized that all this had been a ruse to get the daughter, Phoebe, alone with him.

Asa began spending extra time with Phoebe, while avoiding his wife and the other children. He told Phoebe stories and riddles and sang songs to her, pursuing "a course of conduct, which had the most direct tendency to corrupt young and tender minds." He tried "to make his daughter tell stories with him[,] . . . to make her free and social, and to erase from her mind all that fear and reserve, which he had ever taught his children to feel toward him." Phoebe found all this uncomfortable and disagreeable. She tried to stay out of his way, to avoid him. "But as his will had ever been the law of the family, she saw no way to deliver herself from her cruel father." She also did not dare talk to her mother, or to any other person, about her situation, for she knew that her father watched her constantly.

Soon, Asa's conduct changed again. Instead of "idle songs, fawning and flattery," he beat Phoebe for imaginary infractions and forbade her from doing anything with her mother or with any of the other children. He kept her confined in the house. His conduct became more and more violent. Sometimes he beat Phoebe with a "rod," sometimes with a "beach [sic] stick, large enough for the driving of a team"; sometimes he threatened to whip her to death if she tried to run from him again. Phoebe, who had always been "obedient to him in all lawful com-mands," was ashamed, would not look anyone in the face.

Meanwhile, Abigail slowly had to admit to herself what she saw hap-pening before her. She did not, at first, see any way to stop the evil. Even when convinced of what was going on, she did not believe that she could testify in court against her own husband. Her daughter would not confide in her, let alone testify against her father: "Fear, shame, youthful inexperience, and the terrible peculiarities of her case, all conspired to close her mouth against affording me, or any one, proper information."

To Abigail, the incest had an ambiguous meaning. To some extent, she thought of it in terms of the harm—the pain and cruelty—inflicted on Phoebe. To a much greater extent, however, she thought of it as a revela-tion that she was the wife of such an evil man, that she was part of his household and under his government. "It was not an enemy; then I could have borne it. Neither was it he that hated me in days past; for then I would have hid myself from him. But it was the man mine equal, my guide, my friend, my husband!"[13]

While the assault on her daughter continued, Abigail Bailey was also pregnant (for at least the fifteenth time), and in September 1789 she gave birth to twins, one of whom soon died. Once her health returned, she decided to "adopt a new mode of treatment with Mr. B." She told him what she thought of his wicked conduct. She had waited until God told her that the right moment had come. Now it had, and she would do what she could to stop Asa's "abominable wickedness and cruelties." For, if she didn't, she would be condoning his sins.

Asa's response was to assert his legal power over Abigail. "He wished to know whether I had considered how difficult it would be for me to do any such thing against him? as I was under his legal control; and he could overrule all my plans as he pleased." She answered that while she would gladly have remained his faithful and obedient wife, he knew he had violated the covenant of their marriage and "hence had forfeited all legal and just right and authority over me."

Asa quickly realized how bold and determined she was, and he became panic-stricken. He tried to flatter Abigail into abandoning any plans she might have to begin a legal process. He took an oath of innocence, which disgusted her. He then asked her forgiveness, which she said she might grant if she had real evidence of reformation, but, at the same time, she insisted that she could never more live with him "in the most endearing relation." He grew terrified at the thought of her seeking a separation. Abigail told him that he had brought it on himself by his actions and that she regarded it as her duty to save her family from further moral destruction.

Then she thought again of the difficulties of proving his guilt, since Phoebe had not yet agreed to testify. She gave Asa one last chance to reform.

A few weeks later Abigail learned that he had again assaulted their daughter. She confronted him, told him she would never believe him again. He offered to leave, to move "to some distant country," where she "should be troubled with him no more." They did not need, he said, a formal legal separation. He would simply go.

Meanwhile, Phoebe turned eighteen and moved out of the house. She remained for a time unwilling to speak against her father. Abigail, however, would eventually hear more about what he had done to Phoebe from another daughter, and then, soon thereafter, Phoebe agreed to talk to her.

Abigail fasted and prayed. Gradually, she came to the settled conviction that she should seek a separation. Should Asa also be turned over to criminal justice? Doing the latter looked to her to be "inexpressibly painful." She convinced herself that if he would do the right thing by her and their children, relative to their property, and if he would go far away, she should not have to prosecute him.

Abigail told Asa her resolution. "I informed him, I now could see no better way for him than this; that I had rather see him gone forever, than to see him brought to trial, and have the law executed upon him, to the torture of myself and family; as it would be, unless he prevented it by flight." She proposed that Asa sell a 100-acre farm and keep the proceeds of that sale for himself, leaving the rest of their holdings for her and the children. She then packed his belongings, including in his saddlebags some letters directed to his spiritual salvation. One of these described how his conduct had probably brought on an eternal separation between them. She closed the letter labeling herself as his "afflicted and forever deserted wife." And on September 8, 1790, he rode away.[14]

After Asa left, Abigail tried to keep the cause of his going a secret, but she soon learned that others in the community already knew of his conduct. She told the children that they could "no longer expect to derive the least advantage from being known as the children of Major Bailey."

Five weeks after his departure, Asa returned. He tried to convince Abigail to take him back, to convince her of his moral reformation. He had known no peace of mind while on the road. He was constantly tormented by the sight of other men with their wives and children. Abigail was hurt at seeing him so broken, felt compassion for his situation, began to weaken. He played on her fear of taking over full responsibility for their family.

In the end, though, Abigail did not believe in Asa's penitence. His situation must, she said to him, be distressing. "For a man of such a temper, such a disposition, who had ever felt so important, so wilful, and haughty, and so unwilling to acknowledge any wrong;—for him now to be upon his knees, upon his face, and begging of me to put my feet upon his neck . . . appeared like a strange turn of things!" She agreed with him that the family needed "a head, a kind friend, a comforter, a guide, to protect us from the thousand evils, to which we were exposed." Yet she still insisted on a separation and a property division. Without the latter, Abigail worried that Asa would retain the power "to injure and distress us."

He again prepared to leave, but before he did the local selectmen came one day to talk with him. Asa tried to avoid them, to escape the shame of talking to other men about his situation. They found him, however, and he confessed to them that his conduct had been bad, and he promised that he would leave his family well provided.

Asa left again.

When he returned several months later, he was no longer humble or penitent. His attention was focused on their property and on the property division. Although he said he would stay only for a few days, he stayed longer. He proposed one plan of division after another. Sometimes Asa told Abigail to forget the past. Sometimes he called her "stubborn and rebellious." He warned her that if she ever complained to the selectmen he would kill everybody. He suspected, moreover, that she prayed for his damnation. He was clearly frightened of her religious authority.

In fact, Abigail was still unwilling to begin a legal process against him. She was also pregnant again.

Finally, Asa agreed to a fifty-fifty split of the property. They would sell all the land and divide the proceeds. The property was put into the hands of Asa's brother, who, Abigail thought, was ordered to sell it. Asa left, taking two of their sons with him to work for him.

She heard nothing for eight months, until one day a lawyer named Ludlow appeared. Asa was living in Whitestown, New York. Ludlow was to purchase their property and exchange it for "wild land" in New York. Abigail refused to consent to the transaction. Ludlow told her that if she did not reconcile with Asa she was in danger of losing her interest in the family property. Abigail replied that he could "talk very fast, and make things seem smooth, and fair:—But his talk was in vain." After speaking with some of her neighbors, Ludlow left.[15]

In the winter of 1792, Asa came to Newbury, Vermont, across the Connecticut River from Landaff. He was unwilling to come to Landaff (perhaps for fear of legal process). Abigail crossed the river to meet with him to settle their affairs. They talked for several days and agreed to trade the Landaff farm for one in Bradford, Vermont, on the theory that it would be easier to sell.

Asa then told Abigail that a Captain Gould in Granville, New York, would give them $500 pounds for the Bradford farm, but they needed to reach him before spring in order to close the transaction. She must come along because her signature would be necessary, presumably in order to release her dower rights. She did not wish to go, since she would have to leave eight young children behind, but she saw no other way to conclude the business between them.

The trip to New York was a terrifying experience. As they went along, Abigail became more and more convinced that the trip was all a trick. Still, she remained passive and obedient. Asa continued to deny any bad motives, but then on the fifth day of their trip, he added "that if he had been so crafty as to lead me from home, as he had done, to answer his own worldly purposes, he could not be to blame for so doing." The next day, after they had crossed into New York, Asa admitted that he was not selling their property to any Captain Gould. His sole purpose was to get Abigail into that state, whose laws were "more suitable to govern such women as you," away from her relatives and friends, where he could bring her to more advantageous terms. "And now," if she would "drop all that was past, and concerning which" she had "made so much noise," and if she "would promise never to make any more rout about any of those things; and to be a kind and obedient wife to him, without any more ado; it was well!" If not, he threatened to carry her on to Ohio, or take her among the Dutch, or to Albany, where he might sell her on board a ship. She would never go home again, he assured her. Should she escape and reach home, he would empower his brother to keep all property out of her hands and to advertise in his name that she should not be trusted with the purchase of any necessaries on his credit. No one could harbor or trust her.

Later, when Abigail pleaded to be allowed to return to her children, Asa told her that she too was tarred by the same brush as he, and she should be ashamed to live with her kindred in their old community. What crime had she committed, she asked? "He replied that he understood my fault was, in being too favorable to him, after it was believed he had committed such abominable crimes." She replied that even if this description of how people felt were true, she would never run from them.

They traveled on, Abigail now thinking of herself as Asa's captive and of him as her enemy. They reached Whitestown where there was small-pox. Abigail decided that she had better have herself inoculated. They lived in a dirt hovel, where she became quite ill and weak.[16]

Asa had told Abigail that he was going to leave her in Whitestown, re-turn to New Hampshire, settle their property relations, and pack up the children and bring them to New York. She was convinced that he meant to disperse the children into other households, not to bring them to her. She began to plan her escape. She had never before ridden anywhere un-accompanied. Now she had to travel 270 miles alone.

Asa left Whitestown on May 9, 1792, about two months after they had first begun the journey from Landaff. A few days later, Abigail also left, even though she was still quite weak. Everything was new and hard for her. She had, for example, to stay in a tavern by herself. But every day she felt stronger. On May 30, she crossed the Hudson River. "Now God smiled" on her. "His providence smiled. And all his works and creatures seemed to smile." No longer was she a captive in the hands of "the man who vaunted over me, and seemed to rejoice in the imagination, that no power could take me out of his hands."

Abigail reached the Connecticut River only a few days behind her husband. She crossed over on a Saturday with her brothers (who lived in Vermont) and found her children well and still together, as well as her husband. Asa was, needless to say, shaken, tried to talk with Abigail alone. She turned to return across the river. He asked if she did not mean to stay with her children. She said she could not, so long as he was pres-ent. Although he tried to forbid her brothers from harboring her without his permission, they ignored him.

In Newbury, Abigail swore out a warrant against her husband before a justice of the peace. The justice issued a writ to have Asa Bailey arrested on Monday, but before he could be taken into custody, Asa told a confed-erate to put the children in a cart and to drive on as fast as he could. Abi-gail and her brothers went immediately to an attorney; the lawyer told her that he knew of no authority by which she could take the children back. "The law had given a man a right to move his children where he should think best, and the wife had no right by law to take them from him." But, he added, no law kept her from trying to frighten her husband's confederate. Abigail wrote a note to Asa's confederate, telling him that he might expect serious trouble if he did not return the children. One of her brothers rode after the cart, gave the man the note, told him that no one would harm him if he would comply immediately. The children were "released from captivity."

During the prolonged negotiations that followed, Asa sat in the local jail. Abigail and her brothers had decided that if he came to an honorable settlement, they would rather he simply left. They put off the court hearing while trying to get him to come to terms. Still, Asa procrastinated and resisted. He did not want a formal legal separation, insisted that it was "costly to settle in law," tried to get Abigail to agree to an informal separation. He still relied on her "tender feelings," believing that they would "set him at liberty."

Finally, Abigail and her brothers threatened to take Asa across the river to New Hampshire and have him indicted for incest, a capital crime. He broke down and quickly came to terms. They divided the property. He relinquished his rights over all the children, except for the three oldest sons, with whom he soon left.

Abigail petitioned for a divorce, which was quickly granted.[17]

THE USES OF LAW

Reduced to its barest legal essentials, Abigail Bailey's memoirs appear to tell a very modern story. Mr. and Mrs. Bailey married; he misbehaved; they divorced. As it is for many modern couples, periods of separation provided a necessary, but nearly inevitable, transition toward the divorce, which was the final (and relatively complete) conclusion of the marriage.

That rendition, however, is not the legal story of Abigail and Asa Bailey. It misunderstands the struggle over separation that lay at the heart of her narrative of their marriage. Abigail Bailey worked to separate herself from her husband, not to be divorced. That the story ends with her divorce is perhaps an accidental conclusion to the narrative.[18]

In Abigail Bailey's legal world, separation would have been understood as a more or less permanent condition—all that she needed or wanted. Nothing in her situation would, in the absence of her husband's extraordinary conduct in kidnapping her, have driven her toward divorce. A permanent separation was what she aspired to. Indeed, one suspects that divorce was never in her consciousness until the very end of her story.

Abigail had to demonstrate Asa's guilt if she was going to achieve a secure and legally enforceable separation. In that respect, the separation she needed was legally indistinguishable from a divorce, even though it would have left her still married in name. Such a separation usually required a judicial decision recognizing Abigail's right to live apart from Asa. That decision presumed proof that Asa had breached a fundamental marital obligation: adultery as the paradigm of marital guilt, abandonment as a distant second choice. From a formal legal standpoint it probably did not matter a great deal, then, whether Abigail "ended" her marriage with a formal separation or with a divorce. Either way, Asa would have been publicly identified as guilty, as a moral failure as a husband.

A wife's duty to obey and to live under her husband's continuing authority was conditioned on his good conduct as a ruler. In that sense, Asa's misconduct gave Abigail an immediate right to live apart from him. Indeed, she had a legal obligation to act immediately on that right. Otherwise, she would be condoning his conduct, as she had with his earlier infidelities, and she would have lost her right to leave. Conversely, in separating, in asserting her right to live apart from him, she was making public both his misconduct and her moral separation from his sinfulness.

What, however, was the significance of separation—formal or informal—for a Christian woman like Abigail Bailey? A marriage was more than a relationship for life. Although both Protestant theology and Anglo-American legal theory declared marriage a civil contract, there was another aspirational vision that competed with the formal contractual understanding. Marriage promised the permanent union of two souls through eternity. Did a separation that ratified a temporal breach in the unity of husband and wife also breach their eternal unity? Perhaps, but perhaps not. They were, after all, still married. Abigail Bailey predicted that Asa's conduct had brought on an "eternal separation" between them; she described herself as "forever deserted." These suggest the imagined consequences of separation. They also tell us something of the complexity of the relationship between marriage and separation for a serious religious individual. On the one hand, Abigail was not asserting that a separation by itself ended their eternal relationship; on the other hand, Asa's conduct probably had done so (presumably because he was going to Hell, while she had hopes of a better future). Because of their presumptively eternal relationship, moreover, Abigail had to separate from him or risk being implicated in his own sinful conduct, which would result in her own eternal damnation.[19]

And yet, in this world, Asa's misconduct did not necessarily free Abigail from the moral or legal bonds of matrimony. The indissolubility of marriage was a serious commitment for wives and husbands in early America. Marital unity meant that one's moral identity was intertwined with that of the other. One took the spouse as he or she was, for better and for worse. Conflict was an expected and accepted part of the relationship, not an opportunity for termination of the relationship. Sinfulness was inevitable.

The law did not require a wife's physical or moral suicide—to accept abuse or treatment that endangered her or her children or that put her in a position of public disgrace. Nonetheless, knowing when separation was proper and called for remained a tricky business. Figuring out how to achieve separation forced Abigail to assume a new identity, as a competent negotiator with her husband.

Out of Abigail Bailey's narrative we can reconstruct at least six negotiating sessions with Asa. The first two occurred in the approximately nine months between September 1789 and late spring 1790, when he was first confronted with her knowledge of his conduct. The third occurred when he returned from the first separation, the fourth when he returned after the second separation, the fifth when she crossed the Connecticut River to talk with him in Newbury, and the sixth occurred while he sat in jail after their separate returns from New York.

When, after the birth of her twins, Abigail first told Asa that she would do what she could to stop his abusive conduct, he tried, as we have seen, to assert his legal power over her—arguing that she was "under his legal control" and that he could overrule her plans "as he pleased." Her response was that because of his violation of the marriage covenant he had "forfeited all legal and just right and authority" over her. He had "done all" in his power "to bring about . . . a separation, and to ruin and destroy" their family. It was her "duty now to do all" in her power to prevent "further destruction." Thus, her actions were founded on "principle."[20]

He must have been convinced; from then on, Asa never challenged her legal right to separate. He intimidated her; he played to her fears of managing a family alone and losing her long-standing identity as a married woman; he tried to convince her of the high costs of seeking a formal separation; he worked to make her feel implicated in his conduct; he worried her about difficulties of proof; he threatened her with the loss of her children; he asserted his repentance. He knew, however, that she had a legal right to live outside of his control and authority in the wake of his immoral and illegal conduct.

Abigail gradually came to understand that she had not just a right but a duty to make a final separation. Early on she announced that she could no longer live with him "in the most endearing relation," that she no longer "*could,* or *ought* to do it!" But in the end she gave him one more chance. When, however, she received new evidence of incest, she came to the "settled conviction" that she "ought to seek a separation" from her "wicked husband." After talking to Phoebe, she told Asa of her resolution: "He asked me, what I intended to do? I replied, that one thing was settled: I would *never live with him any more!*"

She wanted him to leave immediately, without any public trial or proceedings. He should take a horse and enough property "to make him comfortable." (At this point, she had obviously not considered that an informal separation would leave her without any control over the property remaining.) She hoped he would repent and reform, and she wished him well, "and so much peace as was consistent with the holy and wise purposes of God." But under no circumstances was she willing to live with him again.

From this moment, in the late spring of 1790, until the end of the narrative two and one-half years later, when Asa had left and she was about to get a divorce, Abigail's settled conviction never wavered. She did not change. She did not, all of a sudden, come to a realization of her rights as a married woman, that she did not have to put up with his sexual abuse of her daughter or with the other actions of this violent man. She knew early on that she had those rights, although her husband often tried to threaten her with visions of his violence and his unilateral authority. She understood that it was "no small thing for a husband and wife to part, and their family of children to be broken up; that such a separation could not be rendered expedient or lawful, without great sin indeed: and that I would not be the cause of it, and of breaking up our family, for *all the world*." But that cost was one she knew she had to bear, given what he had done.[21]

Still, Abigail did not know or realize how resistant her husband would be. Asa's increasingly desperate and erratic responses to her settled conviction, his unsuccessful efforts to regain control over his wife, shaped the story of the end of their marriage. For too long, she assumed that he would eventually come to an appreciation of his own sinfulness, his own evil, and withdraw. She fantasized that the decision to separate would be a decision they could come to together, a shared understanding, based on what he would learn from her that he needed to do. In a sense, the decision to separate would be a decision to live (apart, not together) in a different marital relationship. She assumed—in common with much legal doctrine—that separation was intertwined with marriage, not an end to marriage. And that was her great mistake.

In their negotiations, Abigail and Asa made a variety of assumptions about separation law. Some of them conformed to doctrinal statements of that law; some did not. Although they constantly referred to law as an external force shaping their conduct, the legal shadow within which they bargained was in large part the product of their own interpretations, interpretations constructed out of mixed images of legal and religious and local authority.

Neither of them, for example, knew or cared much about the differing legal categories of separation. Both, by contrast, saw a sharp and important practical distinction between a "formal" and an "informal" separation, between one involving a public statement of grounds and legally enforceable remedies and one in which the two of them simply parted, perhaps with a property settlement. Asa continually pressed Abigail to accept an informal separation. When she first told him that she would no longer live with him, he replied that she "need not be at any trouble to obtain a legal separation. For he would depart to some distant country, where I should be troubled with him no more." At the very end of the story, while he sat in the jail, he again worked on her "tender feelings," to convince her to come to an informal agreement. He emphasized how costly a legal settlement would be, that their resources would be wasted "as dew before the sun," and that their "poor little innocent children" would suffer for their "folly." If only she would take their problems "out of the law," he would do "what was fully right."[22]

For Asa an informal separation would blur the line between a parting caused by his immoral conduct and the sorts of separations that occurred regularly—and more or less innocently—between couples when jobs or military service or lack of love drove them apart. The "meaning" of their particular separation could remain ambiguous and private. Such a separation would, moreover, leave him with the option of publicly regarding himself as a husband and also with the possibility of later reinserting himself back into the family.

Abigail had her own reasons for preferring an informal separation, for not invoking a process that would have brought Asa's domestic conduct into public view. She wished only "for an equitable adjustment of our affairs of interest; and then for Mr. B. to be gone." She worried that she lacked sufficient evidence to bring legal charges against him. More important, she felt that suing him—making him "a monument of civil justice"—would be "inexpressibly painful," and she wanted to spare herself "the dreadful scene of prosecuting my husband." Reading slightly between the lines, one senses her own feelings of being implicated in the failure of the marriage. She too would be shamed in a public process.

Abigail mistakenly assumed that the unexercised but continuing threat of public exposure would force Asa to make an adequate property settlement, so that she and their children would be supported. And that would be enough. She must have assumed that a property division between husband and wife would be legal and enforceable if the two agreed.

In fact (meaning in formal law), absent a transfer to trustees, such a division—even one voluntarily arrived at—was patently unlawful. Given the unity of husband and wife under coverture, a husband would only be giving property to himself, a transaction he could undo at will. Moreover, until the very end, Abigail apparently did not understand that a simple parting, even with a property division, would not necessarily change any of the terms of the marital relation. For too long she did not worry about the fact that she might still be formally under his legal control and power, even if they lived 270 miles apart.[23]

One senses that for Abigail Bailey the best resolution of their marital situation would have been one that left her unchanged in her social position as a married woman, even as she rid herself of the presence of her husband. She was a wife, and she wished to retain her identity as one, even as she demanded a separation. Thus, it makes sense that she, like her husband, at first hoped for an informal separation. What she learned from her trip to New York was how degraded her position as a married woman had become, how little social value that identity provided. As a result she finally became willing to sue out articles of the peace against her husband, to make him the subject of a public process, and to force him toward a formal separation.

Legal concepts and ideas played three different but overlapping roles in their negotiations: as organizing assumptions, as background threats, and as tactical tools. The distinction between formal and informal separations was an organizing assumption of their discussions. The usually unstated but always present possibility that Abigail would charge Asa publicly—either by suing for a formal separation, or by taking out articles of the peace against him, or by charging him with the crime of incest—exemplifies the use of law as a background threat, as does Asa's implicit threat that he would disperse all of their children if Abigail were anything but compliant in New York.

The tactical uses of law litter the narrative. Asa was clearly much more legally sophisticated than Abigail and unscrupulous. Thus, the trip to New York; thus also, his attempt in New York to convince her that she had waited too long to act, that she had implicitly condoned his conduct and had therefore lost her right to act alone. Asa's tactics were designed to make Abigail believe that he knew the law and that the law gave him full and continuing power over her: that New York's laws gave him the right to make her live anywhere he chose, even to sell her to a ship if that were his pleasure, that he could advertise her as a runaway if she escaped from him. When she confronted him after their separate returns from New York, he tried to reassert his control by trying to keep her brothers from "harboring" her. Sometimes, as in the latter example, these tactical uses of legal power failed. Often, these tactical invocations of legal rights were fraudulent. No husband had the right to sell his wife onto a ship. Asa, in particular, would not have had the right to advertise Abigail as a runaway and to refuse to pay for her necessaries if she escaped from his control. Given her relative ignorance, however, these threats could be used to terrify her, whether or not they were accurate.

By the end of the story, Abigail too had learned to use legal knowledge tactically. When Asa attempted to have their children driven away after his arrest, she had the autonomy and the character to ignore the attorney's statement of the legal rule that her husband had the right to move his children where he chose. Instead, she focused on the attorney's advice that no law would stop her from trying to scare Asa's confederate. When Asa continued obdurate even after his arrest, she used the explicit threat of criminal charges, of the shadow of the criminal law, to force him to terms.

Still, we are left with the question of what role, if any, the law played in helping Abigail break the habit of submission mandated both by coverture and by the religious norms of marital unity. We can tell her story in a way that makes law crucial. That is, Asa violated a series of legal expectations implicit in legal marriage: he committed adultery, he was violent and abusive, he committed incest. Abigail responded by declaring that she had both a legal right and a duty to separate from him, that his legal authority over her should be at an end. That statement led him, in terror at the shame and the loss of control over his domestic situation, to increasingly desperate acts, notably dragging her to New York. These acts brought her to the realization that she shared nothing with him, that he was merely her enemy. And thus she became free from him, willing to invoke legal processes against him, no longer just a feme covert.

Of course, their story was a distinctively "legal" one only if we choose to characterize it as such. We could, as easily and more convincingly, emphasize Asa's violation of moral and religious norms and Abigail's assertion of religious authority. Such a religious characterization would also be limited by its terms, just as the legal story is limited and partial, for, in part, hers was a story of legal change. Neither variation—legal or religious—is complete without the other. But an emphasis on religious motives would better capture Abigail's understanding of what went on in the last days of their marriage than one focused exclusively or largely on legal identities and legal tactics.

In Abigail Bailey's complex normative world, law and religion mixed freely. At times, they appeared to contradict each other; more often, they reinforced each other. Both provided a symbolic universe of justifications for domestic submission. Both also provided a vocabulary of aspirations, of restraints and constraints on the exercise of power, and of justifications for resisting arbitrary power, all of which served as tools in her narrative of separation.

WHAT DID NOT CHANGE

At the end of the story, Asa Bailey was a broken man, "beaten and de-feated." He gave Abigail half of "his" property, they divided their fur-nishings, and of their children Asa "relinquished" to Abigail all but their three oldest sons. He had wanted to take "several more of the young sons" and made plans to do so, but these young children had cried so plaintively at the thought of being separated from their mother that he had given in on this as well. Abigail noted that in this final concession, Asa's "self-interest here wrought in my favor. He knew not what to do with them."[24]

In the disposition of their children, Abigail assumed she was without legal power. Even after all that had happened in the family, even after what Asa had done to his daughter, nothing would change the legal fact of his patriarchal authority. Abigail might receive custody of the youn-gest children because Asa had alienated his custody rights over them, but if he wished to retain control over the three oldest boys until they reached their majority, nothing in his past conduct prevented that. He was and remained their father, the only relevant parent in terms of legal authority. Nothing in her legal world told Abigail that separation neces-sarily gave her any increased rights over her children. Nothing about his more or less public guilt as an incestuous and abusive parent countered Asa's parental authority.

Much of Abigail Bailey's narrative is taken up with reflections on her love and concern for her children. As she and Asa moved through New York, every child she saw reminded her of her lost and abandoned chil-dren. She used her fears for her children, her belief that they needed her, as justifications for her return from the desolate land Asa had dragged her to. Yet, in taking action to complete her separation from her hus-band, nothing changed in her legal relationship to her children. Until Asa voluntarily transferred custody of some children to her, Abigail re-mained, in Blackstone's famous (or infamous) phrase, "entitled to no power, but only to reverence and respect."[25] While Asa's actions taught Abigail that she had to act (and had the right to act) as an "uncovered" person, nothing in his actions gave her a sense that she possessed legal rights over her children.

Taking seriously her sense of legal powerlessness over her children may help us to understand a mystery lurking in Abigail's narrative: her relative insensitivity toward her daughter, Phoebe. Abigail insists on her "anguish" in witnessing her husband's abusive behavior. Her "soul" was "moved with pity for [Phoebe's] wretched case." Yet she sketches the abuse quickly and in relatively distant and abstract tones. And she constantly reminds the reader of her own powerlessness in the situation.[26]

We might expect more from Abigail. But in doing so, we would be committing an anachronism. Many today blame mothers for passivity in the face of their husbands' and lovers' abuse of their children. Mothers, we assume, are responsible for their children's well-being; they have moral and legal responsibility, a legal capacity as well as a legal duty, to act. But what should we expect of a mother in a world where parental rights are exclusive, a male monopoly? How should she have acted?

Within the terms of Abigail Bailey's narrative, Phoebe's incest was an opportunity as well as a disaster. Phoebe's plight gave her mother the legal and moral right to seek a separation. Phoebe was their daughter, but she was also the passive object of her father's adulterous lust. Because Phoebe had been nearly destroyed, in part as a result of her "habit of obedience," Abigail could imagine breaking up her marriage. Asa had destroyed domestic peace, had violated his responsibilities as the head of the household and a parent. He had also committed a form of adultery that she would not condone. Abigail was not responsible for the event because she was only a wife and mother, a victim herself.

In a sense, then, Asa's assault on Phoebe was simply a particularly aggravated form of adultery, different only in degree from his earlier adulteries. It was an act that gave Abigail the right to act to separate herself from him. Because of her legal powerlessness over her children, she could act without feeling complicit in her husband's conduct.

Thus, to some extent the marital change detailed in the narrative rested on what Abigail Bailey implicitly took to be an unchanging structure of parental power. Her capacity to resist and to reconstruct her life depended on her submission to a patriarchal order.

Abigail Bailey's memoirs end with her discovery of a less encumbered self, one capable of relatively greater agency and of separation. It may, however, be a mistake to tell her story in terms of its apparent conclusion. The point is not that she yearned for and achieved separation from her husband, that she changed, but that she found in her commonsense understanding of law and morality support for the claim that she had a right to a separation. From Abigail Bailey's own perspective, her story was less about change than about sustaining a moral identity in the face of moral danger. The right to separate existed not to permit its possessor to reconstruct a new life, but, rather, because without it she would be publicly (and legally and morally) joined with her husband in sin and moral disorder. In early America a wife risked assuming the moral colors of her husband. The right to separate offered an escape from that disaster, offered the possibility of continuity and protection from the cruelty and the chaos of a fallen life.

Abigail Bailey claimed rights in order to undo the corrupted power of her husband. Her claim offered no challenge to his ordinary legal authority over her; indeed, it rested on the same normative assumptions that underlay his conventional assertions of authority. He had changed, had abused his legal rights; thus, she had to claim her right to separate, else she would be complicit in his abuse. She would separate not in order to end her marriage, but so she could remain a good wife.

3

Early Exits

Americans, unlike the animals who set forth on the voyage in the ark, have not always journeyed in pairs.
Albert C. Jacobs and Julius Goebel, Jr., Cases and Other Materials on Domestic Relations *(1952)*

Behind Asa and Abigail's story, behind Asa's wavering between authority and abandonment, behind his fear of exposure, behind Abigail's uncertainty about her rights, behind their tortured negotiations, lay the legal mechanisms that late eighteenth- and early nineteenth-century American couples mobilized as they worked to leave or to end their marriages. Nothing such couples did, whether their final acts took the form of legal divorce, contractual agreement, abandonment, or desertion, were novelties. All replicated patterns found in England, colonial America, and elsewhere. Their practices—their private choices and the forms those private choices took—can be absorbed within a long history of the ways couples have always responded to marital unhappiness—fighting, running away, asking for public recognition of marital breakdown, remarrying with or without a divorce.[1]

Yet these American couples, like Asa and Abigail, acted on the terrain of American federalism, of states with expanded conceptions of lawmaking and a willingness to experiment. That terrain gave these couples new possibilities, new ways to frame their negotiations, and new ways to understand themselves as exiting wives and husbands.

Novelty and experimentation did not mean that the basic understanding had changed. In all the new American states, as in the rest of the Christian world, marriage still meant, at least in its inception, a commitment to stay together for life. Throughout the United States, the law was dedicated to discouraging separations and divorces and to punishing

63

those responsible. Courts and litigants shared a sense that marital breakup ought to be shaming, and many courts worked hard, at least sometimes successfully, to make sure that shame was experienced and publicly known. Remarriage might make one into a bigamist. Children born after the breakup might be bastards.

Still, the case law of marital exits in the years between 1790 and 1850 suggests that American courts understood themselves as possessing only three powers with regard to exit itself: the power to declare one spouse "guilty" of conduct that freed the other spouse from her or his commitment to stay in the relationship, the power to rule on the legality or illegality of a separation, and the power to prevent remarriage. Each framed the doctrinal expression of a distinct mode of exit: of divorce, of separate maintenance agreements, and of abandonment and informal separation. Together these powers produced a repertoire of legal forms that the law made available to wives and husbands who wished to end marriages. Powers intended to deny legitimacy to those who exited from marriages, to make exit appear a morally impossible act, created an array of legalized forms of exit, each with their own costs, advantages, and consequences. Legal policy became legal doctrine, became a structure of obstacles and choices, a decision tree, that could be negotiated with the help of a lawyer along the way to marital freedom. Couples became consumers of the law, choosing the best mechanism for their particular circumstances (within the bounds of cost and religious belief and culture and taste).

Like Abigail Bailey, husbands and wives looked at a field of legal possibilities. Unlike Abigail, they sometimes chose divorce first. Unlike Abigail, many of them never chose divorce at all when they left their marriages.

DIVORCE

Divorce existed everywhere but in South Carolina. How to get one? Answers varied across the United States, but as Abigail Bailey learned, the one sure way to do so, everywhere but in South Carolina, was to prove that your spouse had committed adultery.[2]

Here is how the lawyers for Eliza Jumel, Aaron Burr's second wife, succeeded in the mid-1830s, when Burr was almost eighty. Early on,

Burr had contested his wife's claim that he had committed adultery with Jane McManus, a young adventuress and publicist for the Anglo colony in Texas. In the end, however, he allowed the case to go forward "pro confesso," that is, uncontested. Whenever a divorce was uncontested, the chancellor, who controlled the equity courts where divorces were granted in New York, appointed a master to review and evaluate the accusations and evidence of the petitioner.[3] In the Burr case, the master recommended the divorce be granted, and his report included the following excerpts of testimony by Maria Johnson, a black servant in the Burr household:

Q: Where was you when you saw them the first time?

A: I came up stairs to fetch a pitcher of hot water to Coln Burr through the front room and . . . saw Jane McManus on the settee and Coln Burr had his hand under her clothes and . . . saw her nakedness.

Q: Were they sitting or lying?

A: They were sitting at the present time and Coln Burr had his trousers all down.

Q: Did they see you?

A: They could not help seeing me when I came in the room with the pitcher of water.

. . .

Q: Do you swear that Coln Burr at that time has sexual connexion with Miss McManus?

A: Yes sir—and I saw him several times before.

Q: How old was he then?

A: She does not know exactly—he was a very old man.

. . .

Q: Did you ever witness any thing between them at that house in Reed Street?

A: Yes, she sometimes had her frock unpinned & open all behind.

Q: Did you ever catch them together there?

A: Yes sir I did one Sunday and Coln Burr gave . . . [me] a new pair of shoes not to tell—but I did tell and will tell & always meant to tell because I was ready to go to church and he gave me orders to go to Bear Market and get oysters for Jane McManus' dinner. . . .

Q: When was it that she caught them together?
A: Before she went to get the oysters.
. . .
Q: What did you see?
A: She saw Jane McManus with her clothes all up & Coln Burr with
   his hands under them and his pantaloons down.
Q: What did Jane McManus say?
A: She said Oh la! Mary saw us.

In the face of such evidence, it is scarcely surprising that Burr did not
resist. The vice-chancellor accepted the master's report as drafted and ordered the Burrs divorced. (After the court ordered the divorce, Burr
came back to ask for a rehearing on the grounds that he was too old to
have committed adultery. This was denied by the vice-chancellor.)[4]

In the practical world of lawyering and legal strategy, the Burr divorce
could serve as a template of how to prove adultery. Don't rely on the un-
corroborated confession of the defendant. Find a witness to testify in detail about the defendant's acts. Servants were good witnesses, as they had
access to their masters' intimate lives (although they could be challenged as employees of the interested parties). So were prostitutes and
hotelkeepers (although the former were seen as corrupt and inherently
dishonest, and the latter were often challenged as confused about the
identities of the persons they thought they had seen). So were doctors,
particularly if they could testify to venereal diseases. All were subjected
to close examination by the master in chancery (or cross-examination, if
there were a real trial) as to their reasons for testifying and as to their
corruptibility.[5]

But easy cases like Aaron Burr's last (known) adultery or Asa Bailey's
incest played little part in the doctrinal law of divorce, which was mostly
constructed out of failed divorces. Even where one spouse had committed adultery, had been unfaithful, had committed immoral acts, adultery
alone was never enough. Divorce required guilt, and it required innocence, and it required a public decision and clear proof that one spouse,
and one spouse only, had fundamentally breached his or her obligations
as a spouse. Since adultery occurred in the shadows by people who almost always had a stake in not talking about what they had done, and
who did not leave or reveal evidence of their acts, and since adultery
often occurred in marriages where neither spouse was precisely "inno-

cent," nor necessarily "guilty," and since people lived complicated lives that might never fit into the stories that the law recognized as justifying divorce, many adulterers were not divorceable. Acts that apparently justified an order of divorce remained unproven or, if proven, demonstrated instead that a couple was not entitled to a divorce.

Consider the case of Jane Williamson Parisien, a case in which, as it happened, Aaron Burr served as defense counsel, and a case that became an important precedent in the American law of divorce. Daughter of a New York shipmaster, Jane had married Peter Williamson in 1780. Williamson was the British captain of a prison ship in the port of New York during the British occupation. When the occupation ended in 1783 with the end of the Revolutionary War, he left, ostensibly for a short voyage. He and Jane had two small children; she was pregnant with a third. He left her twenty guineas. All his other property went with him.[6]

According to Peter, he wrote his wife frequently after his departure but was shipwrecked and unable to return to New York. According to Jane, she heard nothing from him, and he went to Jamaica where he became a wealthy man. Jane, destitute and abandoned, struggled "with very great difficulties and distresses." Nevertheless, her conduct remained "irreproachable and above suspicion," and "by the most indefatigable industry and the most rigid economy" she maintained herself and their three children "in a reputable manner and suitable to there [sic] sphere in life."

After seven years "passed in sadness and disappointment," Jane was advised, by whom we do not know, that Peter Williamson's long absence had released her from her matrimonial obligations, left her free to make another marriage.[7] Still, she continued to hope that Peter might return to a sense of duty toward his wife and his children. After another year, however, she decided that he really had abandoned her and that, in any event, if he was alive, he had no reason ever to return to the United States. So she married again, to Philip Parisien, by whom she had six more children and with whom she spent the next twenty-three years.

In 1792, shortly after Jane had entered into her second "marriage," Peter Williamson returned to New York, where he and Jane saw each other. Evidently, he made no claims at that time that she was still his wife nor did he make any provision for their children, except for one gift of $70. He soon returned to Jamaica, and he would not return again to New York for twenty years.

But in 1812 he came back and, for unexplained reasons, began an action before Chancellor James Kent for divorce on the grounds of Jane's adultery with Philip Parisien. She, through her lawyer Aaron Burr, resisted and denied the charge. Her conduct had always been "chaste and discreet and free from reproach or suspicion." By contrast, Peter had led "a dissolute and licentious life." He had, she said, committed adultery with a number of black women, "of whom one was called Dinah or Diana, another called Margaret and another was called Mary or Maria." She also believed he was now keeping a woman as his mistress in New York. She had hoped he would leave her alone to live quietly with her present husband; but since he had acted "to vex and harass" her, she asked the court to force him to reveal his own adulterous relations and that, if the court decided that her marriage to Williamson still survived, that it grant her a divorce from him and award her alimony and make him pay her court costs.

Kent dismissed Peter Williamson's bill on the technical grounds that he had introduced no evidence to prove that he was a resident of the state of New York. Kent, however, took the dismissal as an opportunity to comment on the extraordinary circumstances of the case. Williamson's conduct had "a cruel aspect," and Kent was happy to be compelled to dismiss the bill. At the same time, in rejecting divorce he was not legalizing Jane's second marriage, which was undoubtedly null and void. "[N]o length of absence, and nothing short of death, or the judicial decree of some Court, confessedly competent to the case, can dissolve the marriage tie."[8]

A few months later, Peter Williamson again instituted divorce proceedings. We do not know what had happened between the legally reunited couple in the interim, but this time Jane did not contest the adultery charge, allowed it to be taken "pro confesso." Probably Jane and Peter had negotiated an agreement, perhaps with the help of friends. She, we might imagine, had come to the sensible conclusion that if she confessed to technical adultery, she could put her past behind her (where pasts always belong), could return to her second husband, and get on with what remained of her life.[9] His adultery was probably unprovable, certainly as compared to her public relationship with Philip Parisien. If proven, all that she would achieve would be a verdict of "recrimination," that is, that Peter was as guilty as she, and that therefore he had no right to seek a divorce. On the other hand, being divorced by reason of adultery would not be the worst thing that could happen, better by far than a reinstatement of her marriage to Peter Williamson. And so, once she had come to that decision, we and she might expect Jane's "first" marriage to have come to a swift legal conclusion.

Kent, however, refused to allow the divorce to be taken by consent, and he resolved to "consider this case precisely as if a serious controversy existed." The case, he began, should not be reduced to "the single dry question" of whether or not an act of adultery had occurred. Factually, of course, it had. But the statute that gave the court of equity jurisdiction to order divorces where adultery was proved left discretion in Kent to decide whether divorce was the appropriate remedy for the wrong. Condonation—the conditional forgiveness by the wronged spouse of the act of the other—and recrimination—the proven adultery of the accusing party—were two legal situations that justified rejecting a divorce petition, even where adultery was proved. Kent thought he saw a similar situation in the Williamson case, framed both by the husband's negligence and the wife's relative innocence.

Peter Williamson had come to New York in 1792 and found his wife newly remarried. Kent wondered why he had not "reclaimed" her then. Instead, he had gone back to Jamaica, implicitly "acquiescing" in her second marriage, "and suffering her offence to aggravate and become inveterate." She had had children and spent the "best part of her life" with her second "partner." "If ever lapse of time, or long acquiescence, formed a just bar to this kind of prosecution, this is one. Can it be fit, or decent, or useful, that, without any reason or apology for this delay, he should now be permitted to come into Court to expose and disgrace this woman? Most certainly not." And so Kent concluded the case by denying the divorce.[10]

Jane, Peter, and Philip disappear from the records thereafter. We might suspect that Jane returned to her home with Philip and continued to live with him as his wife. But how did the case affect the "respect and good will" that she had previously earned from her neighbors? Perhaps, like other Americans in similar situations, she and Philip moved to another state (or maybe just a new neighborhood), where they held themselves out as husband and wife. And what happened to Peter? If, as we might suspect, Peter began the divorce case because he wanted to marry someone else, did he "marry" her anyway? Did he return to Jamaica?

The legal effect of Kent's decision was that Jane and Peter were declared to be irrevocably and continuously married to each other in spite of her twenty-three-year "marriage" to another man, in spite of their shared desire to put their marriage well behind them. Their long separation changed nothing; her long bigamous second marriage changed nothing; their joint decision to divorce changed nothing. Indeed, their joint decision, their collusion, was itself a reason to deny the divorce. The unstated but inescapable conclusion of the chancellor's opinion was that bigamy was a less serious moral and legal problem than an unfair but technically correct charge of adultery. Better two marriages than one divorce, even if that divorce was desired by both the parties and would have resolved their tangled domestic situation.[11]

To make sense of Kent's decision in *Williamson v. Parisien,* we need to understand that in 1790, in 1815, even yet in 1840, divorce was not conceptually part of the law of marriage. To Chancellor Kent, as for his contemporary and successor judges, legislators, and treatise writers, divorce was a public process, available only for public reasons. Litigants may have seen things differently, wanted divorces for their own private reasons. But for judges of the early nineteenth century, divorce was a species of public law, a public remedy for a public wrong. If a husband and wife agreed to divorce because they, as private individuals, wanted a divorce, their agreement, all by itself, was reason enough to deny the divorce. "It would be aiming a deadly blow at public morals to decree a dissolution of the marriage contract merely because the parties requested it," declaimed Chancellor Reuben Walworth in 1828. "Divorces should never be allowed, except for the protection of the innocent party, and for the punishment of the guilty." A couple would be divorced (the passive tense is important here) because one or the other had so violated a public and legislatively defined norm that it became important for the moral identity of the innocent spouse to be freed from identity, or unity, with the other. The "innocent" party "prosecuted" a divorce. The guilty party had committed a "crime."[12]

Prior to the American Revolution, absolute divorces—divorces with right to remarry—had been available only in the New England colonies. Other colonial legislatures had followed English understandings of divorce as inconsistent with a well-run polity. After the Revolution, all but one of the new state legislatures passed statutes that created regularized divorce practices. By and large, these statutes articulated quite limited grounds for divorce. Even so, public and legal recognition that there were circumstances justifying absolute divorce constituted an important break with past English practice. The new American divorce jurisprudence that resulted from these statutes provided, moreover, the only significant change in marital legal rights to occur in post-Revolutionary America.[13]

Legislatures tried different divorce regimes. South Carolina stood alone in allowing no divorces. In New Hampshire, by contrast, the legislature in 1791 passed a statute granting both husbands and wives the right to seek complete divorces from the Superior Court of Judicature for incest, bigamy, adultery, abandonment for three years, or extreme cruelty.[14] Courts often added complex interpretive glosses to the legislatures' intended requirements. In an 1818 New Hampshire case, for example, the New Hampshire court denied a divorce sought by a woman whose husband had abandoned her for more than three years on the grounds that the husband was too poor to make any provision for her. To the judges, a divorce was only justified when it provided a support award to the divorced wife.[15] As late as 1850, to take a second example, New York's highest court declared that a wife who divorced her husband because of his adultery was still entitled to dower, to a share of her ex-husband's estate after his death. In an important sense, he remained married to her, even though they had been legally and fully divorced since 1825.[16]

By the first years of the nineteenth century, there existed a diverse jurisdictional landscape of divorce. All states, however, understood divorce as a public process allowed only for public reasons. Divorce laws did not modify or "impair" the marriage contract. If they had, they might have violated the federal Constitution's prohibition on laws impairing the obligations of contracts. But, properly understood, all that divorce laws did was, in the words of Chief Justice John Marshall, "to enable some tribunal . . . to liberate one of the parties, because it [the marriage contract]" had "been broken by the other." Legislators were simply providing a public remedy for a public need. Divorce laws were a part of the "police power," the residual power of legislators and other public actors to maintain a "well ordered society."[17]

Until the middle of the century, some state legislatures granted "legislative divorces" to petitioners for discretionary reasons unavailable under the general divorce jurisdiction granted to the judiciary. A few states followed inherited English parliamentary practice and made a legislative act the only way to get a divorce. Such divorces gradually disappeared as revised state constitutions of the middle years of the century included bans on special legislation (and sometimes specifically on legislative divorces), and as state legislatures gradually developed a modern understanding of their institutional roles.[18] Yet the presence of legislative divorces through the first half of the nineteenth century also underscores both the political character of divorce and the perception of divorce as extraordinary relief that public authorities would only make available under unusual circumstances.[19]

New York's lawmakers were often congratulated by nineteenth-century treatise writers for the "purity" and consistency of their divorce statutes, even as their laws also became notorious for their rigidity and inflexibility. They first passed a divorce statute in 1787, a statute in which adultery provided the only grounds for divorce, guilty defendants were forbidden to remarry during the rest of their lives, and courts of equity became the only courts with jurisdiction to grant divorces. In 1813 the legislature reconfirmed its understanding that only proof of adultery justified a full divorce. At that time, however, the legislature added that either a husband's proven adultery or his extreme cruelty would warrant a divorce à mensa et thoro (from bed and board) in favor of the wife. Such a limited divorce was, essentially, a judicially ordered separation as a result of which a wife gained the right to live apart from her husband and might gain, at the chancellor's discretion, the right to recover property brought by her to the marriage, to an alimony award, and, sometimes, to the custody of her children. At the same time, the legislature slightly weakened the "penal" provision, forbidding the guilty defendant from remarrying only during the lifetime of the "innocent" spouse. There were minor adjustments in New York divorce law after 1813, but basically New York's divorce law was unchanged for 150 years.[20]

When New York was congratulated for the "purity" of its laws, what was meant first of all was that New York's legal practice clearly identified divorce with "crime," and secondly that the state followed the word of Christ in identifying adultery as the only divorceable crime. It was never enough to assert one's own marital rights or marital virtue. To be divorced, one should have proved that one's spouse had committed a "criminal" act, a wrong on a scale sufficient to justify an order that the marriage had been fundamentally breached. Like the criminal law, divorce law subjected the guilty party to punishments (like loss of dower and support in the case of ex-wives, and loss of husbandly control, custody, and property in the case of ex-husbands). As important, the guilty spouse was labeled as a failure, had her or his marital identity taken away, and, at least in New York, lost the civil right to remarry, at least during the innocent spouse's lifetime. Because these were seen as serious punishments, as penal provisions, courts of equity had to act with care and restraint. The defendant (particularly a female defendant) was presumed innocent until proven guilty. He or she ought to be charged only with a divorceable offense that was clearly and statutorily defined and that was provable. He or she ought not to be subjected to open-ended charges, such as incompatibility or neglect. And evidence of the wrong, while never subjected to the "beyond a reasonable doubt" standard of criminal practice, ought to be compelling and overwhelming. Particular acts had to be proven unambiguously through a contested process.[21] Only a legislatively defined wrong justified divorce. But only a judicial determination of guilt provided a basis for breaking the bonds of matrimony.[22]

The defendant had, moreover, to reveal a guilty mind. As in the case of Jane Williamson Parisien, technical adultery alone was never enough, at least in New York. Insanity usually excused adultery, as it excused criminality generally. And the courts resisted the attempts of petitioners to escape from insane spouses.[23]

Although a "pure" divorce law identified the guilty party with criminality, the judicial divorce process was a peculiar mix of criminal practice and equity practice. A divorce freed one spouse from marriage to another, but the right to be divorced belonged only to an "innocent" spouse. Only a party with "clean hands" was entitled to the remedies of a court of equity. Thus, there existed the peculiar doctrine of "recrimination." If wife or husband sued for divorce by reason of adultery, one automatically successful defense was to prove the accusing spouse's own adultery. A successful defense, however, did not mean that the defendant then became entitled to a divorce. According to the received law, if both husband and wife were "guilty," then no divorce at all was possible. Where both parties were adulterers, legal policy declared they became thereby "suitable and proper companions for each other," locked in permanent matrimony.[24]

New York's lawmakers—both legislators and judges—worked hard to maintain a pure divorce law. From the first, however, they had to face the constitutional difficulty of dealing with the significance of extraterritorial divorces. What legal recognition did New York courts owe to "foreign" divorce decrees made in less "pure" jurisdictions, decrees based on norms that would not have been available in New York? If New York was required to grant full faith and credit to such decrees, then a wife or husband unable to obtain a divorce under New York law would only have to find a jurisdiction with a more satisfactory divorce law to nullify the policy of New York law. The impure would trump the pure.[25]

Foreign divorces were not the only threat that confronted those who worked to maintain the purity of state divorce policy. Equally challenging was the availability of ordinary legal processes for manipulation and strategic action. The policy might be clear and restrictive; only a wife or husband whose husband or wife had committed adultery was entitled to a full divorce. Yet so long as a husband or wife was willing to confess publicly to adultery, whether or not adultery had actually occurred, there was little a judge could do to avoid implementing a divorce law that did, in the end, allow couples to decide when and whether they would end their marriages. As Kent knew, sometimes the sin of adultery was committed (or feigned) for the very purpose of the divorce. Couples often colluded in constructing a case to meet the technical requirements of the law.[26]

New York's chancellors and vice-chancellors confronted collusion repeatedly as they tried to implement the state's divorce law. The procedure Kent developed for the court of equity hinged on whether the accused party denied the charge of adultery. If he, and it was more often he than she, did, then the factual issue of whether adultery had occurred was sent to a common law court to be presented to a jury as a "feigned issue." If, on the other hand, the accused did not deny the accusation, that is, took the charge "pro confesso," as Aaron Burr had, then the case was sent to a master in chancery, an appointed lawyer, who was to make a report to the court that tested the confession and set out the relevant evidence.[27]

The goal of the process was to prevent couples from achieving a voluntary, consensual legal end. But the danger of that corrupted conclusion did not disappear once a case was sent to a master for report, for, noted the judges, the masters (whose fees were paid for by the litigants) were predictably lax in their examination of the facts in the cases. The judges wanted a report that established clear and convincing evidence of adultery. They required masters to hear testimony from at least one independent witness, such as a servant, a doctor, or a prostitute. Yet, even when a witness was provided by the litigants and examined by the master in chancery, judges often rejected the masters' reports. In one case, for example, the vice-chancellor rejected a report of adultery founded on the testimony of a witness who was allegedly peering through a window when the "crime" occurred. According to the vice-chancellor, the witness could not have seen what he claimed to see because there was not enough light available. In another case, the witness was an illiterate prostitute who claimed to have slept with the respondent. Her deposition read like a fill-in-the-blanks form, however, and thus could not be regarded as probative. As far as the judges were concerned, the issue was not so much whether or not adultery had occurred. The goal of the proceeding was, crucially, to establish that there was "no collusion between the parties in laying a foundation for the suit."[28]

Still, collusive divorces may well have been inevitable in a jurisdiction like New York with clear and limited grounds for divorce. The chancellors and vice-chancellors were fighting a losing battle in their efforts to prevent collusion and strategic behavior, a failure they often acknowledged.[29] Let us imagine a couple no longer interested in living as a couple; perhaps each intended to remarry another. If the two came to an agreement that they would do whatever it took to obtain a divorce freeing each from the other, then the law became simply a landscape to be traversed by strategically minded litigants on the road to marital freedom. And such litigants could find skilled lawyers who would help them on their journey. Even the rules and practices designed to prevent collusion would become nothing more than directives or instructions that explained how to get away with a collusive divorce. If you needed a persuasive witness, then you would find or create a persuasive witness. If you were told that a deposition should not read like a fill-in-the-blanks form, then you would develop a form, or a set of formulaic questions, that did not read like a fill-in-the-blanks form. The art of lawyering is a wonderful thing for the instrumentally minded.

Nevertheless, judges struggled to separate marriage from divorce. As the historian and treatise writer James Schouler put it, writing in 1874 but reflecting an older understanding, divorce laws belonged to the public, not to the parties themselves. They were not intended to allow couples to escape identities assumed in marriage. Divorce punished the guilty for "criminal" conduct. Conversely, divorce allowed an "inno-cent" spouse to escape the moral contamination that might accompany continued cohabitation with a guilty spouse. In a world where marital unity meant something, it was important that divorce exist. At the same time, it was still more important that divorce not be understood as a form of voluntary exit available to all married couples. It was, wrote Schouler, because marriage was "*not* on the footing of ordinary con-tracts, that husband and wife" could not, "on principle, compromise, ar-bitrate, or modify their relationship at pleasure." Or end it.[30]

SEPARATE MAINTENANCE AGREEMENTS

At the end of the story, while Asa Bailey sat in jail, he and Abigail negoti-ated a final separation agreement. We don't know the precise terms of their agreement, but we can be sure that they included, on Asa's side, a conveyance to Abigail or more likely to trustees who would hold the property for Abigail's benefit. Also, he would surely have acknowledged that she was free to maintain her own domicile, to act in the world in most ways as if she were a single woman, a feme sole, buying, selling, and managing property. And he would have granted her the right to cus-todial control over the children who remained with her. She, on the other hand, would have declared that in exchange for the property and the right to act as a feme sole (and perhaps for the custody rights), she released him from any continuing obligation to provide for her support.

Was this final (or nearly final) agreement between them legal and en-forceable, assuming it took roughly this form? What if Asa had returned to New Hampshire and attempted to take one of the remaining children out of Abigail's custodial control? Or if he had reneged on a promise to convey property to Abigail? Conversely, what if Abigail had tried to make Asa liable for debts she had incurred with local merchants? Would a court have held the terms of their contract superior to the received expectations of marriage, superior to the core understanding that a hus-band had "paramount" rights to children and property but also had con-tinuing responsibility for his wife's debts and support? In Asa and Abi-gail's case, the answer is almost surely yes. Any sane court would have regarded their agreement, not as a "voluntary" contract between hus-band and wife, but as a compensatory and corrective act defined by Asa's misconduct, by his fundamental breach of the marriage contract.

But what if they had achieved a separation agreement earlier, before Abigail's forced march to New York? So far as the outside world would have known, such an agreement would have been nothing but a private, voluntary agreement between a wife and husband. She would have acquired some of his property; he would have been released from any further obligation to support her; he would have left; she would have stayed. That would have been it, at least as far as the outside world would have known. No court would have learned anything about Asa's behavior.

Would that "private" agreement have been legal or enforceable in court? The answer is uncertain at best. Throughout the years between 1790 and the middle of the nineteenth century, couples across America separated. And before or as they separated, they often renegotiated the terms of their relationship. When they did so, when they contracted about fundamental terms of the marriage—about support, obedience, domicile, custody, and property—their actions were of unpredictable and dubious legality.

Couples' negotiations occurred in the shadow of a complex and fuzzy doctrinal structure, framed by an important chapter in English judicial history. The English story is usually understood as having begun in 1783 when Lord Mansfield, Chief Justice of the Court of King's Bench, ruled on the separation of Lord and Lady Lanesborough. Like many other English and American separating couples, the Lanesboroughs had negotiated a "separate maintenance" agreement, settling property on Lady Lanesborough in trust "to her sole and separate use." By the agreement, she gained the right to live alone and assumed responsibility for her own debts. His lordship moved to his lands in Ireland while she remained in England. In England, she contracted debts, and, when the creditors sued her for payment, she asserted her coverture—her identity as a married woman—as a defense. As a wife, she could not be held liable for debts contracted to supply her with "necessaries," debts contracted with the implied consent of her husband.

According to settled law, the creditors should have been nonsuited, that is, should have been compelled to seek their remedy from Lord Lanesborough (or, rather, the executors of his estate, since he was dead by the time the case came to trial). The agreement between husband and wife was a nullity. A contract to vary one of the public terms of the marital relationship—a husband's support obligation—violated a fundamental notion of what it meant to be married. Parties, even very wealthy and aristocratic parties, should not be able to slough off the duties and responsibilities that accompanied marital rights.

Yet when Lord Mansfield decided the case in 1783, he noted the prevalence of these "separate maintenance agreements" that recreated the wife as a single woman, a feme sole. Mansfield understood that at common law a wife had "no civil Capacity or Power of acting without her Husband, under whose absolute Controul She [was] supposed to be." But, to Mansfield, separate maintenance agreements reflected a successful alteration in "the usages of society." Such agreements should be binding on wives because "the law must adapt itself to the various situations of mankind," including the new "fashion," unknown to "the old law," of husband and wife living apart and possessing separate property. A wife who negotiated with her husband for the right to act and receive credit as a feme sole should be liable as such.[31]

According to a familiar expectation of Anglo-American legal history, that might have been the end of the story. Like other areas of law transformed by contractualism—commercial relations, landlord-tenant relations, and labor law, for example—domestic relations law, at least in its attention to third party creditors, would have confirmed the contractual capacity of wives and recognized the validity of separation agreements. Mansfield's goal, here and in other cases, was to make it possible for husbands and wives to agree under delimited circumstances to change given terms of the marital relationship.[32] Status should have become contract. Marriage law should have become modern, under the guidance of a great judge concerned to shape law appropriate for a commercialized society.

Instead, Mansfield's successor as chief justice, Lord Kenyon, quickly overruled all Mansfield's decisions concerning married women's contractual capacity. In *Marshall v. Rutton* (1800), the language of which provided the clichés of marriage law in England and America for a century, Kenyon held that, at least as far as common law decisionmaking went, a contract between husband and wife that altered the terms of the marriage relationship would never be enforced. Such a pretended contract, Kenyon wrote, contravened the law's established domestic rules, rules "the public" meant "to preserve." Legal recognition of such an agreement produced "all the confusion and inconvenience which must necessarily result from so anomalous and mixed a character." Wives and husbands should not be authorized to change "the character and condition which by law results from the state of marriage, while it subsists."[33]

Words to live by, and words American courts repeated regularly throughout the first half of the nineteenth century. For example, when the Kentucky Supreme Court in 1836 ruled against a wife's attempt to enforce a separation agreement, the opinion described the principle as "of deeper consequence" than "mere adherence" to common law and to equitable precedent. It went directly to the public policy of maintaining the inviolability of marriage. "The well-being of society, as well as the policy of the law and the objects and duties of the marital contract require, that those who are united in marriage should live together." The court noted that the law provided "no coercive remedy" to enforce this duty. The law, however, had created powerful incentives to keep couples together, chief of which was the knowledge that courts would not enforce separation agreements between husband and wife.[34]

Courts contrasted the good of compulsory matrimony with the bad of voluntary separation. Consider the case of poor Mrs. Beach of Oneida County, New York, who in 1842 appealed the dismissal of her slander suit against Mrs. Ranney. According to Mrs. Beach's complaint, Mrs. Ranney had falsely called Mrs. Beach a thief and sexually incontinent. As a result, Mrs. Beach, who already lived apart from her husband, had suffered "pain of mind and body." Her husband had "abandoned" her, that is, he had apparently stopped recognizing her as his wife and no longer provided financial support. Her neighbors refused to assist her as they had done in the past. In particular, neighbors Smith and Raymond, who had once provided her with fuel, clothing, and provisions, no longer did so. She had been turned out of the local moral reform society, and children threw stones at her house and called her a strumpet.[35]

The case before the New York Supreme Court revolved around the "deed" of separation between Mr. and Mrs. Beach that "allowed" her to live apart from him. This agreement contained a covenant by the husband that his wife could sue, either under her own name or in the names of herself and her husband, to recover property or "for any damage or injury which she might sustain to her person, character, goods &c," and that he would do nothing "to hinder the progress of such suits, or in any way interfere therewith." Such a provision was routine in separation agreements and, from the wife's perspective, absolutely necessary if she were to have any security in her "separated" life. Because she remained a married woman even though she lived apart from her husband, a wife like Mrs. Beach needed the right to sue in her husband's name, since she usually would have had no standing to sue in court in her own name.[36]

When Mrs. Beach sued Mrs. Ranney, she sued in her husband's name as well as her own, relying on her separation agreement for her right to do so. As she and the courts soon discovered, however, Mr. Beach had gone to Mr. and Mrs. Ranney soon after she initiated suit and had waived any rights he might possess to sue them for slander. And so when the case came to trial, Mrs. Ranney defended on the grounds that Mr. Beach had "released" all rights under the cause of action. The result was that the lower court dismissed Mrs. Beach's suit.

The New York Supreme Court affirmed. Chief Justice Samuel Nelson, in his opinion for the court, began by reviewing the English authorities. Since Lord Kenyon's opinion in *Marshall v. Rutton,* it was, he said, the unquestioned rule that husband and wife cannot voluntarily "change their legal capacities and characters." As a result, all of the "numerous covenants" typically contained within separation agreements, covenants intended "to enforce a continuance of the separation," were void and not enforceable at law.[37] Nelson knew, and conceded reluctantly, that courts of equity sometimes enforced such provisions. But even equity would never enforce the particular covenant at issue in this case, a covenant by which a husband delegated to his wife his legal right to sue. The fact that the husband had promised not to do exactly what he had done was beside the point. His written promise, their contractual agreement, was all "waste paper," condemned "by the soundest principles of policy, morality and law."[38]

There were important alternative voices within American law. Chief among them was James Kent who, first as chief justice of the New York Supreme Court, then as Chancellor of New York, and finally as the author of the renowned *Commentaries on American Law* (1826–1830), consistently argued for a less formalistic and more realistic perspective on contracts between husbands and wives. To Kent, the goal was not to insist on a fictional marital unity. It was, rather, to look at the parties in terms of their actual relationship and their moral responsibilities. To Kent, as for a few other American judges, separation meant that there had been a real change in the relations between a married couple, a change that could not properly be ignored by a court.[39] Likewise, in Tapping Reeve's *Law of Baron and Femme* (1816), lawyers found a sustained defense of the capacities of wives to deal with their husbands and to make separate maintenance agreements. There could be no doubt, Reeve conceded, that separation agreements sometimes led to abuses "by proud vicious women." On the other hand, husbands were "not always perfect." They had "their caprices, vices and follies, as well as wives." Thus, the evil that resulted from recognition was more than matched by the great good produced. "Many an amiable, virtuous wife" had, "by this means, been secured against the tyranny and brutality of an unfeeling, dissipated, libertine husband, and delivered from poverty, distress and the most shameful abuse." Children became "ornaments of the age in which they lived," who would otherwise have been "lost to the world, or, what is more probable, have been a curse to it." The institution of the separate maintenance agreement was justified by its "powerful tendency to promote the comfort of the better half of the human race."[40]

In their very argumentativeness, however, Kent and Reeve suggest that they knew they were contending against a dominant tide. While Reeve kept insisting that separate maintenance agreements were enforceable, and so understood by all lawyers and judges, he also had to concede that "some late decisions" (like *Marshall v. Rutton*) had rendered this doctrine questionable. The editors of later editions of his work would challenge both his conclusions and his reading of the relevant doctrine.[41]

Some judges—particularly those sitting in courts of equity—shared Kent's and Reeve's legal understanding. They regarded it as settled law that some provisions of well-drafted agreements between husband and wife via trustees would be enforceable. These judges often wrote as if they hated those agreements but felt disabled by precedents that appeared to confirm their partial legitimacy. In 1834 Reuben Walworth, Kent's successor as chancellor, labeled a contract between husband and wife as "an assumption of a false character" and as "contrary to the real status *personnae*" of the parties. Still, in other cases he felt himself bound by established principles to enforce provisions of just such contracts.[42]

In part, the differences between judges derived from contending streams of precedents. Equity chancellors like Kent and Walworth identified their roles with a broader conception of institutional discretion and responsibility than did common law judges such as Samuel Nelson. The chancellors thought they had a responsibility to look behind formal legal status. They also thought of themselves as delegated protectors of the rights and interests of dependent women and children. The desire to protect would not necessarily lead them to enforce contracts between husband and wife. In *Rogers v. Rogers,* for example, where Walworth had labeled a contract between husband and wife as an assumption of a false character and therefore unenforceable, the marital right that Walworth regarded as non-negotiable, as beyond the private ordering of the couple, was the wife's retained right to seek a formal separation where her husband's fault justified it.[43] Chancellors often worried about the use of separation agreements as ways of freeing husbands from their duties to support their wives. But equity law also provided a rhetoric for enforcing contracts not enforceable at common law. Indeed, the jurisdiction of equity had always been framed by the unavailability or inadequacy of common law remedies.[44]

Still, the predominant legal position was that contracts between husband and wife, in particular contracts that varied significant terms of the marital relationship, were presumptively unenforceable and void. The precedents reflected "different sentiments and different decisions, by different men, at different times." Even when judges ruled in favor of the validity of such agreements, they did so with a long (and usually long-winded) preface that set the scene as one where such agreements were, necessarily, inconsistent with marriage as it ought to be understood.[45]

We are left with two related mysteries. One is how nineteenth-century American judges—practical men of the world—could continue to use the language of marital unity and marital transformation to describe marriages that had practically ceased to exist. Many of these cases involve couples who had been long separated. Indeed, typically, the plaintiff's or complainant's goal was to undo an agreement on which both spouses had relied, often for many years. Yet the judges by and large refused to recognize the reliance interest of the couples, refused to recognize their separated status, and insisted on treating an imaginary and long past marital unity as the foundation for judicial decisionmaking.

We can marshal stock explanations for this mystery. In deciding these appellate cases, the judges' concern was with the law and with public policy, not with the situation of the litigants before them. Recognizing and enforcing a contractual agreement would have given other potential litigants the "wrong" message, would have told couples that they could, at least sometimes, renegotiate the terms of the marital relationship.

That would have had baleful consequences for the society. Second, judicial rhetoric masked institutional anxieties, among them fears that the courts were relatively incompetent at the task of evaluating which contracts were and were not illegitimate, particularly in the face of the relative weakness and dependence of married women. A woman's "voluntary" decision to contract away her right to support often carried with it more than a whiff of coercion. Courts could avoid having to confront the difficult questions involved in deciding when dependent wives were really acting freely by holding to the "bright-line" proposition that marital terms were non-negotiable.

Still, the explanations leave unexplained the intensity of the rhetoric. At times, judicial language lapsed into near solipsism, as if marriage was what the judges said it was and nothing else, as if, by refusing to recognize the separation of interests implicit in contract, judges were recreating marital harmony and unity. Did they really believe in such a formalistic universe, in a marriage made from black-letter legal categories? Much else in the nineteenth-century law of marriage bespeaks a realistic appreciation of marital behavior and of the power relations between wife and husband, an unwillingness to invoke abstractions, as judges ruled on the unhappy lives of the couples standing before them. In these situations, however, the couple's willingness to act as if they were free to govern their own lives sometimes produced a furious judicial response.

The other mystery is why, in the face of frequent and intense judicial hostility to contractual separations, so many men and women continued to draft and to mobilize separation agreements? That many did so is clear. The number of cases appearing before state courts was large. And these cases must be, almost by definition, the tip of a relatively large iceberg of cases that ended in negotiated agreements or in unappealed and unpublished lower court decisions.

An odd feature of this mystery is the apparent changelessness of the terms of separation agreements. Courts struck down covenants identical in form and content with covenants struck down repeatedly years previously. For example, agreements to separate, that is, agreements for future separation (as contrasted with provisions dealing with the consequences of existing separations), were always held to be void by all the courts that dealt with them.[46] Yet couples continued to make agreements for future separations. It is almost as if they were oblivious to the enforceability of an agreement until, of course, one or the other of them ended up in court trying to enforce it. More oddly still, their lawyers continued to draft provisions identical to ones previously struck down.[47]

Why did couples rely on formal contracts as the foundation for their separations? One answer is that divorce was not a possibility for many people. Divorce was not a right, only a remedy for a wrong. Even when the wrong existed, divorce offered a very public, near criminal, sanction. For couples who wanted their marital troubles to remain private, that law was unattractive. As Asa said to Abigail while he sat in jail in Vermont after their separate returns from New York, "it was costly settling difficulties in the [public] law." Their "interest"—by which he meant both their property and their public standing—would waste, "as dew before the sun," and their children would suffer for their folly if she insisted on a divorce.[48]

Nonetheless, saying divorce was not a possibility may come close to an anachronism, in the implied assumption that if it had been possible, American couples would have acted on the possibility. Divorce existed almost everywhere, and by the 1850s divorce had become a cultural presence in public debates and in the scandal reporting of the penny press. For a very few couples the relatively liberal divorce laws of some states may have existed as a resource that could be turned to if need arose. But divorce as a public closure was not yet an alternative course for a marriage, not even an unavailable alternative. To explain contractual behavior by the relative unavailability of divorce would mean that those making separation contracts imagined a divorce they would have sought but for the rigors of the law. Yet that sense of an imagined but unavailable option is only rarely revealed in the language of separating couples. Marriage was for life; we need to understand separate maintenance contracts as drafted by couples who usually thought of themselves as still married. Indeed, as we saw with Asa and Abigail, the imagined alternative to a separate maintenance contract was not a more formal divorce but simple abandonment or desertion.

In nineteenth-century America, the sanctity of contract competed, perhaps on equal terms, with the sanctity of marriage. To contract was to identify oneself as a competent and responsible adult. One understood oneself as a person through the contracts one made (including, of course, the marriage contract). And, as many historical works have shown, the actual making and doing were more important than theoretical legal capacity.[49]

For a separating married woman, the act of contracting with her husband would have been experienced as transformative and regenerative, as a way to assert possession of an individual self capable of acting in and on the world. In making a contract, a wife claimed a formal equality that was at war with conventional and legally approved understandings of a wife's identity. More, the act of drawing up an individual contract would have given a wife a sense of herself as an individual with individual needs and wants and an individual history. Marital unity was torn apart, the identity of a wife replaced by the self of a contractually capable actor in the world. In place of the nearly unbounded relationship of husband and wife, in which a wife might experience herself as open to her husband, as unable to resist or control his power, a separation agreement posed a limited and mutually agreed-upon list of rights and duties. In that sense, to contract was itself a crucial form of separation, a near emancipation. A separation agreement was thus, regardless of its ultimate enforceability, an enormously important performance.[50]

At the same time, it is important to underscore the instrumental uses and significance of a separation agreement. Contractors could not be confident of the enforceability of their agreements to separate, but not acting carried great dangers for both wives and husbands. A wife in particular had to get her husband to agree to allow her to live alone. If she had any hope of surviving the separation, she needed a property settlement or, at minimum, the use of the property she had brought to the marriage. (Usually, she would need a trust device and trustees to give effect to either of these.) She needed her husband's clear agreement that she could use her own earnings. She needed him to promise not to advertise her as a runaway, so that merchants and others would trust her and grant her credit. She needed him to promise to allow her to keep custody of their children. Now, it may be that all or many of these promises were unenforceable in court. Yet in a society that placed great value on keeping one's word, contracting offered her hope that he would not trouble her. A husband too had good reasons to contract, had incentives to bargain with a separated or separating wife. An agreement might fix and limit his responsibilities. Otherwise, his absent wife would al-

ways remain his responsibility. He would still be legally obligated to provide for her support, to supply her with "necessaries," wherever she
lived, no matter with whom, no matter the circumstances of her life
away from him.

The point to remember is that all of the rights and duties of marriage
survived a separation in the absence of an effective contract. And, to
go farther, a husband's marriage rights often came into their full felt
flowering only at the time of separation. During a "working" marriage,
the social expectation—and often the reality—was of accommodation
and restraint in the exercise of power. There would be little talk of legal
rights or duties in many ongoing marriages. But once a separation had
occurred, once a wife was living outside of her husband's physical control, legal rights became a staple of marital discourse and conversation.
An angry and frustrated insistence on "my rights" and the absence of
"your pretended rights" was a standard refrain of correspondence from
husbands to their separated wives. The very forcefulness with which
marital rights would be articulated in the midst of marital conflict and
dissolution provided additional incentives to try to find a contractual
resolution. Suddenly it was clear what one should be bargaining over,
and why it was crucial to reach agreement, even in the midst of doctrinal
uncertainty.

Finally, many husbands and wives contracted not because they
wished to end a marriage, but because they found themselves married
but separated. As the literary entrepreneur Rufus Griswold put it, borrowing (perhaps unconsciously) phrases from Lord Kenyon's opinion in
Marshall v. Rutton: "For years I consented to live in the painful and
anomalous condition of a man who was suspected of being single, yet
without the right to marry, and of being married, without the existence
of a wife."[51] The point of a separation agreement was rarely to create a
private contractual form of divorce. Simple abandonment could have
produced that end. The point of a separation agreement was, rather, to
resolve conflict within a marriage by allowing the parties to live apart
from each other. Separation agreements modified the terms of the marriage, but the contracting parties remained, in legal theory and in their
own minds, married. Some of the time, indeed, their separate maintenance agreements expressed their continuing belief in the permanence
of marriage.

BIGAMY

Not everyone was as scrupulous as Rufus Griswold presented himself as being. And not every married person who did not divorce continued to think of herself or himself as married. Couples exited from unhappy marriages, often without judicial sanction. Then one or both spouses remarried, to become functional bigamists. Like Jane Williamson Parisien, they assumed—or hoped—that their former spouse would not return to embarrass them. Sometimes, as in Jane's case, the "former" spouse did return. Sometimes a former marriage became public, became a source of social stigma. The United States was an unimaginably large country, and many could disappear permanently from discarded pasts. Even so, husbands and wives, children, other relatives and neighbors, all had a way of turning up at the most inopportune times, leading to shame and to litigation.[52]

Bigamy or, rather, serial monogamy (without divorce or death) was a common social experience in early America. Much of the time, serial monogamists were poor and transient people, for whom the property rights that came with a recognized marriage would not have been much of a concern, people whose lives only rarely intersected with the law of marriage. Often, the first marriage was a relationship between very young people, who split at a point when they both were transient and without resources. Instead of looking to a legal resolution to marital unhappiness, a husband (or, less often, a wife) would move away, perhaps to another state, and remarry—as would the wife (or husband) who remained. Or both husband and wife would move elsewhere, away from each other, and remarry.[53]

Most of the time bigamous unions did not result in criminal prosecutions. Yet the traces of bigamies, or of the exits that preceded them, are everywhere in the appellate court records, particularly in cases involving contested inheritances, for poor people did not always remain poor people.

When bigamous second (and sometimes third) unions were challenged in court, judges were remarkably accepting and accommodating of the bigamous pair. Indeed, one discovers the same judges who struggled to maintain the rigid purity of divorce law, and who dismissed the legality of separate maintenance agreements, developing presumptions that protected bigamous marriages from challenge. Judges refused to convict someone of bigamy on the basis of confession or reputation. The actual recorded marriage license—the title to the first marriage—had to be placed in evidence.[54] By contrast, the general legality of an informal, possibly bigamous, "second" marriage could be established on the basis of notoriety—public appearances—and, in general, could only be challenged by a prior spouse.[55] And after 1830 in New York, a second marriage contracted in good faith, where the first husband or wife had been absent for five or more years, was merely voidable, not absolutely void. The aggrieved spouse's only remedy would be to file a bill in equity to annul the second voidable marriage. If the second husband and wife continued to live together after the annulment decree, then the "true" spouse had adultery grounds for a divorce. But, as Chancellor Walworth noted in 1836, the complainant's own adultery (as demonstrated by remarriage perhaps) would provide a "perfect answer" to the complaint.[56]

Courts implicitly analogized issues of serial matrimony to property disputes. Present possession—that is, the existence of an apparent marriage by a man and woman who held themselves out to the public as husband and wife—was, if not nine parts of the law, then at least very important presumptive evidence of a valid marriage. Theoretically, a husband, like Peter Williamson, harmed by the later marriage of his spouse, could attack the title of that later marriage. But, as with adverse possession in property law, so in these cases the "rightful title holder" could eventually lose the capacity to challenge the marriage if he sat on his rights, if he abandoned what was his, in the face of his wife's "open and notorious" adultery in living as the wife of another man.[57] And then the second, originally bigamous, marriage would become legal and enforceable by the very absence of anyone capable of challenging it.[58]

Consider the typical case of Abigail Rose, who in 1841 asked the Rensselaer County surrogate for her widow's portion of her "husband's" estate. Fifty years earlier, she had married Jonas Frink. They separated after a short while. Jonas soon married another woman and moved to Massachusetts. In 1830 he died in the poorhouse in Hoosick, New York. Meanwhile, Abigail worked as the housekeeper of J. Owens. Around the turn of the nineteenth century, she married S. Thurston, who left her the next day "and never claimed her as his wife." She then lived with Owens as his wife until his death in 1826. Two or three years later, she married Rose. She continued to live with Rose until his death in 1838.

According to the surrogate, Abigail's marriage to Rose was void when entered into. After all, Jonas Frink was still alive in 1829. But her continuing cohabitation with Rose as if she were legally married established an inference of an actual marriage after the death of Frink. Therefore, she should be awarded a wife's portion of Rose's estate. The chancellor agreed.[59]

Or, alternatively, consider the more dramatic story of Tillatha Catherine Bennett and Isaac Graham, both early Anglo settlers of California. Isaac had deserted a first wife in 1830 in Tennessee. In 1845 he married twenty-one-year-old Catherine, who lived with her mother and brothers on land near Santa Cruz. They married by signing a document prepared by Graham, presumably because there was no available Protestant minister. Her mother disapproved of the "marriage" and tried to get both the local justice of the peace and the U.S. consul in San Francisco to separate the two. The j.p. wrote to the consul of Graham's refusal to comply: "Graham said that they were well married and that he would lose a thousand lives before he would give her up." Besides, since "other Gentlemen . . . approved of his Marriage, . . . nobody could force a separation."[60]

In 1849 a son from Graham's first marriage arrived in California and learned, unexpectedly, that his father was still living. A few months later, while Graham was away with his son on business, Catherine took their two children and a disputed amount of gold and fled, helped by a handyman and her brother. In a letter published in a San Francisco newspaper, she justified her flight on the grounds of Isaac's cruelty, not his bigamy: "I was so tired of being beat and having bowie knives drawn over me . . . (for twice that old brute Graham drew his bowie knife across my throat till the blood ran down my breast, and I expected every day he would kill me)." In any case, her flight took her, dressed as a man, to Hawaii and then to Oregon, where she was discovered by her husband, who took from her the children and what was left of the gold.[61]

She then came back to Santa Cruz and brought suit against Graham for custody of the children. Suit followed countersuit between them. One judge granted Catherine custody rights, but when Isaac seized the children while she was away in San Francisco, another judge confirmed his right to their custody. She sued Isaac for personal damages and assault and for ruining her good name by inveigling her into a bigamous relationship. The point of this cause of action, one suspects, was to establish the illegitimacy of the children, as a result of which she, as mother, would have sole legal right to their custody.

When this last case came to trial, the central question was whether Graham had married her in good faith. He gave a variety of alternative explanations: that he believed his first family had been massacred by Indians on the way to Texas, that he believed that his first wife had remarried and had an illegitimate child, that Texas law allowed a marriage to be invalidated after seven years' absence. At the end of the trial, he was acquitted of assault but held liable to Catherine and ordered to pay $2,500 damages.

But then, on appeal, the California Supreme Court reversed, in a decision that incorporated common law marriage into California law. "Marriage is regarded as a civil contract, and no form is necessary for its solemnization," declared Justice Elcan Heydenfeldt. So long as both man and woman were competent to contract, "an open avowal of the intention and an assumption of the relative duties" that marriage imposed made their agreement "valid and binding." Where, as in this case, there was such a marriage, a father's children were "entitled to look for and demand from him, his care, maintenance and protection." Children became legitimate. And, as a correlative, a father gained "the unquestioned right to their custody, control and obedience." Meanwhile, the mother, as nothing but a wife, was left without any rights at all.[62]

To American judges bigamous marriages were less threatening to the institution of marriage than either voluntary divorces or contractual separations. Perhaps the tacit recognition of a second, more or less informal, marriage represented a recognition of the existence of human fallibility and change. Family law could not demand that husbands and wives lead perfect lives. The ideal of the abandoned wife, who remained at home like Penelope, sewing (or taking in laundry, or farming, or whatever), chaste and pure, waiting for her one, true, but long-absent husband, was an important cultural icon in nineteenth-century America. But, in the real world, wives knew they needed husbands to survive. Their need was, of course, exacerbated by a legal order that left a wife—a feme covert—ordinarily without the means of contracting or engaging in most legal or business affairs. So, like Jane Williamson and Abigail Rose, they often remarried. And when their cases came to court, judges recognized the felt necessities of their situations.

Husbands (and wives) who abandoned first spouses were understood as morally wrong to have done so. They would have to live with their sin through the rest of their lives. Yet, when they made new "marriages" that demonstrated their commitment to the conventional order of marriage, courts saw little reason to challenge the order they had reestablished in their lives. In typically American fashion, the judges were giving precedence to the present over the dead hand of past entanglements and obligations.[63]

Judges gave crucial weight to the "fact" that the new or newer couple was leading a life that substantively reflected a public understanding of being married: that husband and wife held themselves out publicly as married, that there was a present community that recognized them as married. As the California Supreme Court held in the Graham case, it was crucial to find that there was a real "assumption of the relative duties" that marriage imposed. Being married in a way that a court might recognize required evidence that one lived conventionally: as if man and woman had been united by marriage, as if their identities had been transformed, as if they had no right to vary the terms of their relationship, as if their relationship was necessarily one for life. If a couple lived as if those conditions were necessarily true, then the technical and legalistic reality that these conditions articulated roles that a man and woman were assuming voluntarily and privately (and without legal ceremony) gave way to the realer reality that the man and woman had publicly become husband and wife.

By contrast, those married couples who made contracts with one another to live apart and to change the received terms of their marriages or, worse yet, who colluded with each other to subvert legal processes in order to gain "legal" divorces from unhappy marriages challenged the public structure of marriage. Their lives defied orthodox expectations. Their willingness to alter legal rights and remedies through strategic use of legal forms, sometimes through perjury, undercut the law's legitimacy. Such couples put into question the capacity of public marriage to unite a couple within the bonds of matrimony, to transform them permanently into husband and wife. That subversion was much the greater danger.

The law of marriage created a public structure of rights and duties, theoretically not alterable by the wills, goals, or desires of husbands and wives. The legal act of marriage united a man and a woman into a public and permanent relationship, one that gave each prescribed and non-negotiable identities. Yet, out of the very concern of judges to protect the integrity of marriage, to protect its nature as a public institution, came a recognition of marriages "made" as knowing expressions of the private wills, goals, and desires of men and women publicly incapable of so acting. What that ironic result suggests is that for the judges the most important feature of marriage was the public assumption of a relationship of rights and duties, of men acting as husbands, of women acting as wives. The legal institution of marriage rested on the structured and intertwined identities of husbands and wives, not the other way around.

4

Being a Wife

Such are the chief effects of marriage, from which it is evident, says
Brown, that the law regards the fair sex with peculiar favor; but Smith
maintains that such politeness on the part of the law is like amiability
from a hyena.

The New York Legal Observer (1845)

What did it mean to be married in nineteenth-century America? It
meant that one had become a wife or a husband. By marriage, a host of
property rights, obligations, losses, gains, immunities, exemptions, remedies, and duties had come into one's life. By marriage, a wife became a
feme covert, and a husband possessed a dependent wife. Without marriage, none of this existed. Without marriage, sex was fornication; with
marriage, it became duty and right. That was the law. That was marriage.

Thus, one could not be both a slave and legally married. Slaves, at
least throughout most of the southern United States, lacked the legal
capacity for matrimony: a slave wife could not commit herself to her
slave husband, nor a husband to his wife. She would never live within
his household, for a slave could have no household. He had little capacity, no legal power, to protect her. Her person and her children belonged to the slave master. Their union was always subject to separation
by sale or gift. Slaves were never married because they always remained
unmarried.[1]

Single–married, that was the fundamental legal divide. And the sharp
boundary between marriage and nonmarriage was everywhere in the
law. It played a particularly important and continuing role in shaping the
meaning of coverture. Throughout the case law in nineteenth-century
America, judges worked to maintain the line between the two states of
being, between marriage and nonmarriage, to impose order on men and

93

women who often lived on the boundary between marriage and non-marriage, in separation, in a liminal state of marital being. That was, we might say, the basic ideological task of the law of marriage: to make sure that the married and the nonmarried were clearly divided from one another.

But you did not need to be a formal legal actor—a judge, a legislator, or a treatise writer—to participate in that work. On December 2, 1840, William Whetten wrote his employer, Harriet Douglas Cruger, to explain why he was quitting his job.[2] He had been her agent, her investment adviser, and consultant. His employer, rich and notoriously difficult, owned lands in upstate New York and in Scotland and had quite complicated business affairs. She was also hell to work for, and it may have been that he was looking for a graceful way to quit. His stated reason, however, was that, the night before, Henry Cruger, who had been separated from Harriet because she insisted on retaining sole control over all her property, had come home to their house in New York City. Harriet was no longer a separated woman. She was, again, a wife. And as such, William Whetten found it impossible to work for her any longer.

The change in Harriet's "domestic relations" had made William's position both "false" and "painful." While separated, Harriet had been able to deal with him in a straightforward manner. They could argue, they could disagree, they could work through the managerial problems of her estate: "I knew that you could singularly bear and forbear under candid rebuke and honest opposition." If she "in the heat of argument" said something rude to him, he had simply "to exercise the forbearance of a gentleman and await the atonement" that her "returning good sense and good feeling would infallibly award" him. (A reading of Harriet's correspondence suggests that he may have exaggerated her willingness ever to apologize. Yet at this point he had no reason to flatter her.) But "now," he continued, with the apparent reconciliation of the couple, "any harshness" used in her husband's presence seemed "unavoidably . . . to call for Mr. Cruger's intervention, either as sponsor or in expiation." Likewise, if during her separation William's "freedom of expression ever transgressed the limits of friendly license," he found it easy to apologize to her, "an unprotected Lady." Once she was again "under aegis" of her "natural protector," however, he could not help looking at Henry and "weighing, by scruples, as man does to man, the concession against the provocation." Relations had become too complicated, and so William resigned.

William Whetten's letter raises a number of themes. For him, a woman was either married or not, and whether she was or wasn't made all the difference in the world. He found it "painful" to deal with Harriet in her distinctive and ambiguous, her "unnatural," married state as a woman with her own property. On the other hand, so long as he understood her as separated, as practically unmarried, she could be treated as a competent contractual actor, as a woman of means and intelligence, as an employer. But her husband's return into her life made that impossible. She could no longer have a separate identity. She could only be understood as within her husband's domain, as united with him, and only Henry ought to represent her interests. The present situation turned the two men into competitors of a sort, fighting for the ear of imperious Harriet. And that situation made Whetten feel like an adulterer or an "enticer." To the extent that he continued to deal with her as a competent contractual actor, as his employer, he knew he was challenging her husband's competence and identity, calling into question Henry Cruger's honor. A criticism of Harriet became, by definition, a criticism of Henry.

If we take Whetten at his word, on December 1, 1840, Harriet became a wife, which changed everything. Before, she was one thing—a separate person. After, she was another—a feme covert, a wife whose public identity had been covered over by her husband. Yet Harriet Douglas Cruger was not a single woman on November 30. She was as married then as she would be two days later. During the days prior to December 1 when, according to Whetten, it had been easy to deal with Harriet, she was not a spinster, a widow, a divorcée, a feme sole. There had been no separation agreement authorizing her to live apart from Henry. The bright line that divided November 30 from December 1 rested not on the clear antinomic legal relationship of married/single, but on the much fuzzier opposition of unity/separation. Whetten imagined that everything turned on marriage; but what really mattered to him was not marriage as such, but Harriet's identity as a wife, united with spouse.

What did it mean to be married? According to the mid-nineteenth-century edition of *Webster's Dictionary,* marriage was "the act of uniting man and woman, as husband and wife, for life."[3] To nineteenth-century eyes, including William Whetten's, those words raised two overarching implications: marriage *transformed* men and women into husbands and wives, changed them fundamentally. Marriage *united* wife and husband, gave them a singular identity.

Now that's not all that marriage was. Some aspects of marriage—for example, the definitional certainty that marriage was only available to heterosexual couples—were so foundational as to be beneath the contemplation and the attention of a nineteenth-century dictionary. Others—like the possibilities for exit and abandonment, or the sexual rights of the husband (or the wife), or the intertwined relationships of property rights and support obligations, or the parental rights and duties of spouses, or the theoretical non-negotiability of the terms of the contract—were so convoluted and complex that no short definition could possibly have captured them. *Webster's* definition centered on the most legalistic aspects. In the midst of a culture that made marriage into the centerpiece of an affective and emotionally rich family life, that made romantic love the precondition of marriage and that usually imagined love as necessary for the survival of marriage, in a pluralistic religious nation in which many diverse practices and habits flourished, *Webster's* identified marriage as an "act" with significant and permanent legal consequences. Much of marriage would, then as now, never be captured by *Webster's*.

Still, "transformation" and "unity" are good starting points for an exploration of what it meant to be a wife or a husband in nineteenth-century America. All participants in legal or political discussions of marital rights and duties agreed on their centrality. No discussion of female subjectivity—of what it meant that a woman's legal identity was "covered over" by her husband when she married, of what it meant to be a wife—could avoid reflecting on those two words. And when, in the middle years of the century, woman's rights activists constructed a critique of coverture, they looked to "transformation" and to "unity" as repositories of everything that needed to be destroyed.

TRANSFORMATIONS

Mr. Barnes and Mr. Allen were neighbors. One day in March 1857, Allen went to Barnes's house and drove Barnes's wife and son to her father's home. Shortly thereafter, Barnes brought a lawsuit for damages against Allen. The complaint alleged that Allen had induced Barnes's wife to leave him, had "enticed" her away.

At trial, several witnesses testified that Allen believed that Mrs. Barnes was abused by her husband and that Allen had advised her to leave her husband's house. Allen was not permitted to introduce testimony as to Barnes's general reputation in the community. The trial judge charged the jury that an action for enticement compensated a husband for "an act of interference in the husband's affairs." If Allen had accidentally met Mrs. Barnes outside the home, her tale of abuse would have justified him in protecting her and carrying her to her father. That is, a good Samaritan could act without fear of liability. But Allen wasn't an innocent stranger; he had gone to her home by appointment. As a consequence, he had to prove that Mrs. Barnes was actually abused, and not just that she had complained of abuse. Otherwise, he was an enticer, someone who had violated a husband's private sphere. The jury found for the plaintiff Barnes and awarded him $800 in damages.

Three years later, the New York Supreme Court affirmed. *Barnes v. Allen* was one of a series of cases in which the New York courts attempted to work out the boundaries of the action for enticement, to distinguish and isolate the active promoter of "domestic discord" from those who, "from motives of kindness and humanity," sought to shelter a wife "from the oppression of her own lawful protector."[4] In the first of those cases, decided two generations earlier, James Kent had held that a father would never be held liable simply because his married daughter had returned to his house, even if he had encouraged her to do so. The doors of a father's house were always open to his daughter.[5] On the other hand, "strangers," that is, neighbors and friends, had to be much more careful. Their conduct was "perilous," subject to "misconstruction," and "never to be encouraged." The burden of proof lay with the enticer; he had to prove that he had good, lawful reasons to take the wife away, for a husband had a right "to the society and assistance of his wife." If a wife was wrong to have left her husband, anyone who "knowingly and intentionally" assisted her in violating her duty was implicated in her wrong. And a wife's allegations did not "extend immunity" to those who assisted her, unless the allegations were proven.[6]

Then in 1864 the New York Court of Appeals reversed the New York Supreme Court's decision in *Barnes*. In a dramatic and broad ruling, the high court held that husbands were without legal remedy against those who helped their wives leave them. Once upon a time, actually until that very moment, there had existed an action for "enticement." But, according to Judge Thomas Johnson, the action for enticement derived from an archaic understanding of a wife as "the chattel of the husband, over which he had complete and perfect dominion as property." The time for that understanding had passed, "happily for the interests of society." In spite of marriage and "for certain purposes, the merger or incorporation of her existence into that of the husband," a wife remained "in law an individual." She possessed "separate rights," which the law upheld and protected "even against the husband." Those rights included "the right to invoke and receive aid, shelter and protection from others, even strangers, against the oppression and cruelty of the husband."[7]

To us the holding hardly seems the stuff of revolution. Indeed, we might stop and wonder at the atavistic "merger or incorporation" of a wife's "existence into that of the husband." Yet the language of this opinion, language that affirmed the wife's partial autonomy as an individual, would have been difficult to imagine thirty years earlier. In 1864 it still had a radical quality.

Prior to the 1850s, notions as intuitive as the idea, today identified with the Fourteenth Amendment, of inherent rights to "equal protection of the laws," or that everyone has certain inalienable rights—including the right "to invoke and receive aid"—would have seemed nonsensical when applied to wives. Rights, remedies, autonomy, a sense of self, all the accoutrements of legal personhood were won and lost within the institution of marriage. The physical self that we have learned to identify as the home of our rights, the body that perhaps marries and works, that uses contraceptives, that lives through numbers of marriages and relationships, but is always itself, counted for little. The conceptual or fictional self, the wife, the self created by marriage, the self that, in important respects, could only exist in relation to a spouse, counted for nearly everything.

The point is not that a wife, prior to 1864, was remediless against her husband's abuse. The point is, rather, that her remedies would have been regarded necessarily as belonging to her as a wife, not as personal, individual rights preexisting her marriage. Her rights as a woman, as a human being, had been "merged" into the terms of the marriage contract.

What did merger mean? In property law, there long existed a notion of "merger," which defined the significance of a legal deed. "Merger" had nothing to do with "unity." Buyers and sellers were never "united." Rather, past identities as separate contracting individuals were replaced by the fixed legal identities of, for example, landlord and tenant. The past was extinguished, annihilated, "sunk or drowned" into the deed. The past was nothing but prologue.

A similar notion pervaded the inherited law of marriage. Once married, you had only the rights and remedies derived from an identity as a wife or a husband. Reasons entirely sufficient to justify breaking an engagement—for example, the fact that a woman was carrying another man's child, or that a man was impotent, or insanity on the part of either—were almost never sufficient to obtain an annulment. When you broke an engagement, you did so as an individual, as unmarried. Once married, though, you were theoretically stuck, bound by your new identity.[8] Even the birth of a mulatto child to a white woman after her marriage to a white man, even in the South, did not give her husband legal grounds for a divorce or an annulment. "[P]ersons who marry," wrote North Carolina's Chief Justice Thomas Ruffin in one such case, agreed "to take each other *as they are*," meaning that once married they took each other, inescapably, as husband and wife.[9]

Preexisting remedies or expectations sank or drowned in the marriage. Legal standards defining matrimonial incapacity became practically irrelevant. When Rufus Griswold, an editor and literary figure, went to bed with his bride in 1845, he was horrified to discover "that the person to whom I was thus united had been bound, in honor and law, not to receive any man's offer of marriage." No consummation was possible. In his narrative of the marriage, Griswold carefully described his bride as a "person" and insisted that marrying Miss Myers was like marrying someone of the same sex or of "doubtful" sex. Nonetheless, Griswold also knew that he was stuck in "the singular connection" into which he had been "betrayed." They never shared a bed again. Indeed, his bride returned immediately to "her" aunts. Yet marriage, not capacity for marriage, determined the relations between them from then on.[10]

In the "merger" of legal rights into the marriage, a wife lost control over property and her contractual capacity. If she had been, for example, the employee of her husband, say his housekeeper, the possessor of a contract for wages, once she became a wife she was no longer an employee and no longer entitled to wages for the work she did.[11] Meanwhile, a husband assumed responsibility for all of his wife's premarital debts and obligations. For Tapping Reeve in 1816, the existence of this husbandly duty offered a nice opportunity to bring out fundamental features—underpinnings—of the inherited law. By marriage, a wife lost her capacity to acquire property "by her industry." Her personal estate now belonged to her husband and was at his disposal. If, under those circumstances, the law still allowed her to be sued for her premarital debts, she could have been imprisoned for nonpayment of the judgments against her, and then she would have been entirely dependent on the good will of her husband, who was the only one with the means of "relieving" her "confinement," since he had all the property. But the law, according to Reeve, "would not trust to the caprice of husbands." In its wisdom the law provided not only that a husband should be sued along with the wife for her debts, but that he should be imprisoned with her for nonpayment. The law did not assume that the wife's liberty would be "a sufficient inducement" to a husband to satisfy his wife's premarital debts. It did assume "the obtaining of his own liberty would be a motive sufficient."

To Reeve, who carried this premise farther than almost any other law writer, no one should be held liable for obligations that the law had made them unable to fulfill. Since the law made wives, by the act of marriage, unable to satisfy their preexisting obligations, the law should put their burdens on their husbands, who could and should act. And Reeve thought this rule should be extended so far as to make husbands responsible for the support of wives' children from earlier marriages. "Why should he not be obliged, during coverture, to fulfill this duty of his wife, as well as other duties?" The fact that received legal doctrine universally rejected this extension he regarded as an "unnecessary exception" to the general principle.[12]

Reeve was distinctive in his insistence that the inherited law rested on a commitment to discipline and restrain husbands. On the other hand, he was entirely conventional in his assumption that marriage meant a woman had placed herself in necessary and inescapable relation to her husband, under his legal power.[13] What rights a wife had—over her body, her ideas, her property, her labor—existed as rights not possessed by her husband: as rights he lost, he gave, or he abused. Her place in the world, both metaphorically and spatially, was his place in the world; his home was her home wherever she actually lived. Citizenship—a public identity as a participant in public life—would, from this perspective, have been something close to a contradiction in terms for a married woman.[14]

For men, marriage constituted a less dramatic break in the life course.

Indeed, the marriage ceremony, with its "I now pronounce you man and wife," suggests the continuity in a husband's life. He remained a man whether married or not. Or, as Caleb Cushing put it in 1828, "His sex is to him a charter of freedom." It always remained "in his *power* to abandon his abode, if caprice or evil passions prompt him, without of necessity losing his claims to free admission in society, certainly without fatal prejudice to his means of subsistence and of enjoying life." Thirty-three years later, Elizabeth Packard, later to become a famous asylum reformer, met with her lawyer. Her husband Theophilus had abandoned her in the wake of her successful suit to be released from imprisonment in his house, and she asked what remedies she had, whether Theophilus did not have to share property with her. The lawyer told her that Theophilus was under no legal obligation to her at all. But, she exclaimed, "I had supposed that I was his partner, in law, as I am in society." "No indeed!" the lawyer replied, "there is your grand mistake. There is no such thing as a partnership relation in the marriage union. The man and wife become one, but that one is the man! for the rights of the married woman are all 'suspended during coverture,' while all the rights of the married man remain established and protected by law, just as they were before marriage."[15]

And yet a man's identity and his honor were deeply tied to his marital status. Being a householder, being someone who cared for and controlled a family, gave a man political significance. It was a foundation for republican political virtue. As the caretaker of a wife, children, and servants, a man became the sovereign of a domain, able to meet with other rulers and to participate with them in government.[16] Conversely, loss of a husbandly identity, loss of control over one's dependents, was a disaster, a source of overwhelming shame. A husband suing his wife's seducer for criminal conversation was described in 1807 as "driven almost to a state of madness and despair."[17] Asa Bailey's erratic behavior after Abigail began to insist that they separate becomes a bit more understandable, if we take seriously his own terror at losing his husbandly identity. As she noted, he was the first victim of his actions. "[H]ow distressing" his situation must be, that "a man of such a temper, such a disposition, who had ever felt so important, so wilful, and haughty, and so unwilling to acknowledge any wrong," should now be begging for forgiveness from his wife. He could no longer endure the sight of "men at home, with their wives and children." He hid in bed.[18]

Marriage was important to men. Still, it was the transformation of single woman into wife that defined marriage in antebellum America. Like others, Alexis de Tocqueville was struck by the contrast between the looseness of paternal discipline and the tightness of the bonds of marriage. What needed explaining was why American women (by which he meant free white women, the daughters of the lawyers who were his primary informants) were so willing to "sacrifice" the "enjoyment of freedom" without "struggle or complaint." His admiring description of the American wife imagined a free young girl confronting an inescapable structure of rules—rooted in law, custom, and religion. Yet she freely accepted "the yoke." She did not marry out of habit or without considering the consequences. When the time came to choose a husband, "her cold and austere powers of reasoning, . . . educated and strengthened by a free view of the world," led her to a considered and rational judgment. And then she accepted the legal consequences, the "bondage" of marriage, because she had chosen it. American women, Tocqueville smugly concluded, did not regard "conjugal authority as a blessed usurpation of their rights." Instead, they seemed "to take pride in the free relinquishment of their will."[19]

Meanwhile, to early woman's rights activists and others deeply shaped by various shades of anti-Calvinist Protestant theology, this transformation of the self was an insidious crime of the inherited law of marriage. Marriage produced a "new creature," "a monster . . . whom nature disowns," a wife, "a fictitious being, breathing a legal, not a moral atmosphere." The law, and the men who profited by it, had usurped God's authority. Only God could transform the self, in salvation. Only God had the right to be the "keeper" of a woman's conscience. No one, certainly no man, could assume responsibility for another's moral being. Yet in civil society, in the world created by marriage law and marital institutions, married women lost their "divine rights" of life and liberty and independent moral judgment, through the acts of men. And, like slaveholders, husbands were corrupted by the relationship produced by the act of marriage, by what they became in relation to their wives.[20]

Some orthodox voices imagined women's relinquishing of the will as conforming to a natural destiny. "[W]oman is what she is by a law of nature," intoned one member of the Indiana constitutional convention of 1850. The law of domestic relations, fantasized another delegate, had arisen naturally, "without the force of human legislation," as a simple and sincere expression of human natures.[21] Even a more moderate voice, like the legal writer Edward Mansfield, still regarded wifedom as firmly based on unchanging scriptural truth. In his 1845 legal handbook, published to be read by "intelligent women," he drew from both scripture and law the notion that a woman "was created to be 'meet,' that is, *fit* for man, her husband, and with the view of becoming his perpetual companion. To be separated from him, or, having become his wife, to live in an independent personality, is really to be exiled from the purposes of her being."[22]

Nearly as often, however, defenders of the existing rules justified marriage as an imposition of a public good on a recalcitrant nature. The identities of husband and wife were then viewed as produced by law.[23] An Indiana convention delegate, who had earlier described marriage as founded on a "primeval principle" and had spoken rapturously of the beauties of "one flesh," later described husband and wife as "the mutual hostages of each other." A nice friendly image, intended to suggest the social good produced by compelling husband and wife to live in "unity." The prominent New York lawyer Charles O'Conor described law as having "fixed" a wife's "domestic character."[24]

For these men, and for others (including at least some women), law was more than a ratifier of preexisting nature. Marital identities resulted, at least in part, from the legal and political transformation enforced in the legal contract of marriage, in the merger that was marriage. And that transformation produced marital unity and the law of coverture.

UNITY

In the October 1838 issue of the *American Jurist,* alongside arcane and sober discussions of "The Customs of the Germans as Described by Tacitus—A Source for the Common Law" and "The Requisites of Dower, and Who are Capable of it," readers found the anonymously written "State v. Henry Day," a poetic "jeu d'esprit," published to illustrate "the legal notion of the oneness of husband and wife."[25] The work described the recent prosecution of a "pale little man, with a twinkling eye," for having bruised, and wounded, and badly beat, his "Amazon" wife, "late Julia Sweet." He had long suffered under her curses and abuses. He was weak; she was strong. His lawyer repeated Day's excuses but quickly moved on to the serious business of legal argument. Whatever Day had done, he did as a husband, and since "man and wife" were "only one," he had done nothing at all, at least nothing that the law could recognize as a crime. Wife abuse was, definitionally, not assault because there was not another person assaulted. Henry Day had a right to whip himself.

The prosecutor dismissed the image of self-abuse. While it was true that man and wife were "only one," that truth was not intended to protect husbands from liability and responsibility. "Suppose in matrimonial strife," he asked, "[t]hat A should stab and slay his wife." That act was never suicide. In this case, the facts were unchallenged, and the law was clear. "And he his punishment must bear."

The judge agreed with the prosecutor. Turning to the defendant's counsel, he ruled that the defense was both right and wrong:

> If any ill the wife hath done,
> The man is fin'd—for they are one;
> If any crime the man doth do,
> Still he is fin'd for they are two.

Unity existed for the wife's protection and benefit, not for the husband's. And the jury should convict immediately.

Yet the judge must have known that his interpretation of the law would not convince all the jurors, that some would never regard wife beating as criminal, that their arguments within the jury room could go on forever, for he told the bailiff that the jurors should not get food or drink until they came to a verdict. Even so, twelve hours later, the jury had still not decided. Would they ever do so? We will never know, for meanwhile "the made-up pair were feasting and kissing." On that note "The State v. Henry Day" ends.[26]

The poem was a plausible fiction, coherent with the contemporary law. Versions of the defense argument were an accepted part of legal discourse as well as of a long trail of misogynist jokes.[27] Much in the law and the political culture taught a husband to think of his wife (and, to a lesser extent, his children) as an extension of himself, and husbands mobilized the image of marital unity as a justification for abuse. Wife beating was a practice of men who believed they owned their wives, who believed they had a right to do as they pleased with what was theirs, including beat them. Indeed, a heightened male consciousness of sexual power can be interpreted as an aspect of republican citizenship. Men who participated with other men in the making and maintaining of government, who ruled in public, also ruled in private. Indeed, their control over their private domain could become the foundation for their public rights.[28]

Both in England and in the United States, lawyers sometimes described a "rule of thumb," an imagined rule that divided legitimate from illegitimate husbandly violence. A beating where a husband used a stick or switch "about the size of one of his fingers (but not as large as a man's thumb)" should, they claimed, leave the husband immune from prosecution. In the United States, the argument usually did not work.[29] Nonetheless, many men escaped prosecution for their abuse of their wives. Unlike the court in Henry Day's case, American courts were often quick to excuse men who had been "provoked" to violence by their wives. Courts were part of a wider culture that distinguished the domestic violence of the poor (expected and ordinary) from violence in the homes of the genteel (inconsistent with a wife's legitimate expectations, abusive). Judges imagined small acts of violence as occurring in a husband's private sphere; not beyond all scrutiny, but located in a "place" where judges would worry about the limits of their institutional competence, about their right to interfere.[30]

Still, American courts of the early republic had largely discarded what Zephaniah Swift labeled in 1795 as "the savage doctrine of the common law." A husband was in theory punishable for "the unmanly act of chastising his wife."[31] When in 1821 a New York lawyer contended in defense of a client that under received English doctrine a husband "had a right to make use of moderate correction," to keep his wife "within the bounds of duty," Dr. John Graham, the lawyer for the complainant-wife, responded: "opposite counsel might, with as much propriety, have cited Pilgrim's Progress, and Bunyan's Holy War, as the authorities he had read; for it was not the law in this country, that a man had a right to beat a woman, and he hoped it never might be."[32] There were, Tapping Reeve acknowledged, "brutal" husbands who abused their wives. But no virtuous man claimed a right to "chastise" his wife, nor was "any such right recognized by our law."[33] Marital unity did not immunize husbands from punishment. In fact, marital unity dissolved under the scrutiny of a criminal court: "If any crime the man doth do, / Still he is fin'd for they are two."

Marital unity was everywhere in the legal rhetoric of the early republic. Marital unity explained why wives could not testify against, or in support of, their husbands. (It would contradict the privilege against self-incrimination as well as the maxim that no one could be a witness in his own cause.) It also explained their usual legal incapacity to sue as well as their inability to contract separately from their husbands. Because of marital unity, a wife's domicile remained that of her husband, even when she lived hundreds of miles away in a different state or country. Marital unity explained the impossibility of suffrage for women. (Can one imagine one being with two votes?) Marital unity explained why many marital obligations survived the separation of husband and wife. Marital unity also explained numbers of odd technical rules that were otherwise totally inexplicable: for example, the continuing prohibition on a widower marrying his dead wife's sister, which would be regarded as incest.

In American law (as well as in the broader culture), this deductive language was identified with the first volume of Blackstone's *Commentaries* (1766). His section on the legal relations of husband and wife began with the famous declaration, "By marriage, the husband and wife are one person in law." Unity was said to explain "all the legal rights, duties and disabilities" that followed.[34] Many law writers followed Blackstone's lead, indeed quoted him constantly. In James Kent's *Commentaries on American Law* (1826–1830), for example, "the legal effects of marriage" were deducible from the common law principle making husband and wife "one person."[35] Others used Blackstone's deductive imagery to tie the law to the religious sacrament of marriage, to the spiritual unity of "one flesh." According to James Wilson, writing in the 1790s, the most important consequence of marriage was that husband and wife became, "in law, only one person"; a wife's "legal existence" was "consolidated" into her husband. Almost all other legal consequences of marriage depended on this principle. "[S]ublime and refined," it deserved "to be viewed and examined on every side." It was "peculiar" to the common law, unlike the organizing principles of other societies. Yet it was "not uncongenial to the spirit of a declaration from a source higher than human—'They twain shall be one flesh.'"[36]

Marital unity pervaded early nineteenth-century legal rhetoric. Yet, as in "Henry Day," it was rarely determinative of legal results. Examined closely, canonical statements of marital unity quickly fractured. Legal doctrine could never hold husband and wife together as "one flesh." Legal authorities never imagined that an abusive husband was beating himself or that sexual intercourse was masturbation. Even Blackstone's famous declarative statement, "By marriage, the husband and wife are one person in law," was followed by a series of clauses that undercut the significance of unity. Each succeeding clause allowed for more separation, more recognition of a binary marriage. A wife's legal existence was "suspended" during marriage, "or at least" her legal existence was "incorporated and consolidated" into her husband's, "under whose wing, protection, and *cover,* she performs everything." Or, alternatively, she acted "under the protection and influence of her husband," as a result of which her condition during marriage was called her *"coverture."* At the end of the paragraph, Blackstone returned to the notion of a "union of person in husband and wife," but only because it explained "all the legal rights, duties and disabilities . . . that either of them" acquired. And then the rest of his discussion of the legal consequences of marriage dropped all pretense of unity. At all times, a wife was a being, a separate being, who performed, who was under the protection and influence of her husband, who acquired.[37]

Other writers went farther. For them, the law of marriage was never organized around the idea of marital unity; it was organized around the idea of "husband and wife" or "baron and femme," around the relational identities of separate beings with distinctive duties. Indeed, the most important American treatise dealing with marriage during the first half of the nineteenth century, Tapping Reeve's *Law of Baron and Femme,* entirely avoided the language of unity. For Reeve, all doctrine could be understood through the lens of two principles: the right of a husband, a legitimate but limited ruler, to the person (and the property) of his wife, and the right of the wife, a separate being in the power of a husband, to be free from unlawful coercion.[38]

Lawyers and judges used marital unity as a legal fiction, that is, as a set of imaginary "facts" created to achieve a legal result. It was a tool, not an explanation: existing only for particular purposes, to be discarded when no longer useful. Belief in the spiritual union of a couple did not require legal treatment of the couple as a unity. There existed a standard set of arguments to mobilize when a lawyer wanted to fracture unity, to challenge the fiction. Marital unity would then be described as "extremely artificial," as "unsatisfactory," as contradicted by real-life conditions, like separations.[39]

Courts and treatises often rejected the fiction. Indeed, the distinctive jurisdiction of courts of equity over marital property matters was usually premised on their capacity to recognize moral obligations that unity hid. Where equity demanded, where injustice would otherwise result, separate interests would be recognized immediately. Common law courts as well often broke wife apart from husband. Sometimes they allowed wives to testify against husbands, particularly where the couple had already separated. According to Kent, the rule excluding testimony was founded on a policy of preserving the peace of families. Where there no longer was peace or a family, then there no longer was a reason for the rule.[40] Or consider criminal responsibility. When wives were excused from criminal liability, as they often were, it was because they were under their husband's coercion, not because of marital unity. A wife, according to Zephaniah Swift, could not be guilty of stealing her husband's property because they were "one person." But if she committed crimes on her own against others, even if "by the bare command of her husband," she was theoretically punishable as if single because her duty to obey the law was "of a higher nature" than her duty to obey her husband.[41]

In the wider religiously-based culture, marital unity had emotional and moral weight. Marital unity implicated a wife in her husband's conduct; husbands, even more than wives, were understood to have assumed their spouses' external responsibilities, debts, and duties. Many didn't. This was, however, what was expected of men and women in a state of matrimony, and these cultural resonances provided the aspirational underpinning, the utopian subtext, of the inherited law.

But when lawyers and judges mobilized marital unity, it was usually as a synonym for marital privacy. "Unity" identified a private household, a bounded sphere, within which husband and wife would work out their collective life and their relationship. Husband and wife were understood to have left parents, friends, and others, to have come together, to have formed a private unity. Husbands, of course, lived in a public world as well, but even for them marriage carried an expectation that one found one's husbandly being—the meaning of life as a husband—within a private sphere.

This private sphere was private both in the sense that it was not, ordinarily, subject to public regulation and in the sense that it was private property. It "belonged" to the husband. And for a wife, being married meant being subject to a husband within his private domain.

Within a private sphere, within an ongoing marriage, a husband had much discretion. He might cede domestic authority, might defer to his wife, might reveal his dependency on her. Many husbands wrote and signed antenuptial contracts "yielding" to their wives the right to control and manage the property that the wives brought to their marriages. These contracts were usually enforced by courts of equity. A famous group of nineteenth-century husbands, including John Stuart Mill, Henry Blackwell, and Robert Dale Owen, promised their brides in documents labeled "marriage protests" never to use any of the rights or powers granted them by the law. Such documents had no legal significance, would never be enforceable by any court. Such men were contracting with themselves. More important, as in the case of private separation agreements, they were also "contracting" against a clear and explicit public policy that denied couples the right to modify the received terms of the marriage contract. Nonetheless, nothing in the law compelled a husband to exercise his vested rights. He could do as he pleased within his sphere.

A husband could also be abusive and cruel within his home, just as a wife could be disobedient or unruly. Yet neither spouse would necessarily have a remedy against the other, for marriage was a private sphere. There was, wrote Edward Mansfield, "a large class of cases of misconduct of husbands and wives towards each other, which no human law can reach, and for which it is in vain to expect any power of society to furnish a remedy." "Courts of justice," wrote one judge in 1831, did not "pretend to furnish cures for all the miseries of human life," as he denied a wife the separation she had asked for. Her husband's frequent drunkenness and verbal abuse were not enough. There had been, concluded the judge, only one instance of actual violence, and one event alone was not enough to authorize a court to interfere. Reliance had to be placed, wrote James Wilson, "on that legitimate honour," which is "the inseparable friend and companion of virtue."[42]

Still, there were occasions when such interference was justified. "Privacy" did not mean immunity from public scrutiny. Just as the police power would be invoked throughout nineteenth-century America as a constraint on private property rights where public needs demanded, so notions of moral order justified interventions into the private family. Privacy would be breached when a man indulged "in a base, unmanly temper, when he was in the habit of beating his wife, or, with brutish feelings, introduced lewd women with her into his household." Such interventions did not challenge "that public policy by which marriage is regarded as so sacred and inviolable in its nature." They merely reflected "a stronger policy over-ruling a weaker one." The law interposed its authority, as James Wilson put it, "whenever urgent emergencies" arose or whenever an "outrage" was "committed against the peace or safety of society, as well as against the refined rules of the conjugal union." The law, he conceded, had no power to "enforce its order for observing the latter." But it had all the power it needed to preserve or recreate the public peace.[43]

As a symbol of the proper place of a wife within her husband's household and of her dependency in relation to his rulership, marital unity had a crucial place in the political culture of early nineteenth-century America. It was a fiction that supported the principle of wifely dependency and thereby helped establish the terms of republican male citizenship. As a legal concept, however, marital unity was both protean and weak: unchallenged and ever present, yet of uncertain significance.

Its status would not remain unchallenged during the second third of the nineteenth century. "Marital unity" as a legal concept became the focus of continuing political debate. That debate occurred in many locations: in state legislatures, courts, sermons, newspaper columns, and magazine articles, as well as within families. It also occurred in constitutional conventions.

Between 1845 and 1860, nearly every state in the union, new and old, held a convention to draft a new constitution. These constitutions mark a sea change in American legal and constitutional history, in particular in the history of American legislation. They created—or ratified—a modern understanding of legislatures as institutions in the business of systematically appropriating and remaking whole areas of legal life once controlled by the judiciary. Legislative drafting, which had once been directed at giving particularized grants or local privileges, exemptions from continuing and general legal practices or expectations, would now turn to the production of statutes that challenged long-standing and apparently permanent bodies of Anglo-American jurisprudence, including private law areas like the law of husband and wife.[44]

The members of each convention—those who drafted and debated the new constitution—fought clause by clause through sentences that defined new "fundamental laws" for their state. In several conventions, a particularly intense struggle erupted over narrowly drawn provisions that directed legislatures to pass laws that allowed wives to keep the property they brought to the marriage, or acquired during the marriage, apart from their husbands' estates. It may seem odd that anyone imagined such provisions as belonging in state constitutions at all. Many of these provisions offered only slight expansions of state legislation that had been enacted without serious debate over the previous quarter century.[45] Yet delegates debated them as if the imagined legislation would produce a fundamental challenge to the liberties of free men and to the virtue of a republican society. In New York in 1846, in Wisconsin in 1846–1847, in California in 1849, and in Indiana in 1850, to take four examples, men declared that these were the most important, most fundamental measures considered within the draft constitutions. Sometimes they were passed; sometimes they lost. Always what the delegates argued over was not the details of marital property but the salience of "unity" as a metaphor for marriage.[46]

In 1850, for example, the Indiana constitutional convention debated whether to include a provision on the rights of married women among its list of fundamental rights:

Women hereafter married in this State, shall have the right to acquire and possess property to their sole use and disposal; and laws shall be passed securing to them, under equitable conditions, all property, real and personal, whether owned by them before marriage or acquired afterwards by purchase, gift, devise, descent, or in any other way, and also providing for the registration of the wife's separate property.[47]

Robert Dale Owen, a woman's rights advocate and the son of the famous English socialist Robert Owen, was the author of the measure. (In the convention, he represented Posey County, the county where his father thirty years earlier had established the utopian community of New Harmony.) His opening speech was strategically moderate. His proposal, unlike those considered elsewhere, would only apply prospectively to marriages contracted after the constitution was ratified. And all it would do would be to allow new couples to choose the legal regime under which their marriages would be governed. Still, as he and other proponents insisted, reform was a matter of simple fairness. Women, who were unrepresented in the convention, deserved to have their interests protected. They needed to be recognized as separate legal subjects.

The point was not to destroy the "natural" relations between a married couple. Indeed, Owen believed those natural relations included a natural dependency that would lead many wives to ask their husbands to manage their property. The point was to redress wrongs that existed under the present legal regime, and that aim required the end of marital unity. The argument that harmony depended on a wife's dependence within her husband's sphere presumed "in the husband kindness, indulgence, generosity." It presupposed a husbandly spirit that "virtually abrogates the law." There were such husbands, Owens recognized. But it was "not for such men" that laws were made. It was "the province of law to restrict, not the generous and the just, but the violent, the unjust, the encroaching." It was for the bad, not the good, that legislation was required.

Owen then retailed a staple reform story. We might call it the "bad unity" story, a tale of the dissipated husband who neglects to provide for his children, leaving it to his wife to do so.

> Say that he has been absent for weeks or months, squandering what money he has in dissipation; say that, in the mean time, his wife, faithful to her home duties, has contrived, by constant labor as a seamstress, perhaps, or a washerwoman, to supply his place; suppose that she has laid by in her trunk—the same trunk, perhaps, in which her mother had packed, with careful hand, on her daughter's marriage day, the little property she had to give her—suppose that the wife had laid by in that trunk a few dollars, hardly and bitterly earned, saved with difficulty as a scanty fund to purchase clothing for her children against the inclemency of winter; and suppose—alas! how often is the case a real one!—suppose, that the drunken husband comes home some evening, breaks open the trunk and carries off the money; is that larceny? has he stolen? By no means; he broke open his own trunk; he took—so the law declares—his own money.

Thus, the need for reform.[48]

To reformers like Owen, legally imposed unity meant oppression. The indeterminacy that we saw in "The State v. Henry Day" did not exist (or was unacknowledged). One reformer characterized conservatives as talking as if "[w]hen the husband eats, it satisfies the hunger of the wife—when he puts on his garments, of course, in virtue of this unity, it clothes the wife—or if he even deserts her and finds a shelter for his own head, hundreds of miles distant, that shelter protects the wife and her babes!" A nice fantasy. But, until that fantasy became reality, "[u]ntil the unity so much spoken of in this debate . . . shall do this for the wife, some property for her wants would seem to be needed."[49]

Both reformers and the guardians of orthodoxy often contrasted marital unity with conceptions of partnership. To opponents of reform, the heretical notion of partnership, the notion that individuals collectively pursued particular, jointly held, ends, was antithetical to the received, sacramental, common law idea of marriage. Marriage transcended the identities of those who entered into it, joined them together into a "state of matrimony." As Charles O'Conor declared in the New York constitutional convention of 1846: "If . . . man and wife [were] converted as it were into mere partners, . . . a most essential injury would result to the endearing relations of married life."[50]

Reformers of the 1840s and 1850s agreed that marriage was not, legally, a partnership. For them, on the other hand, that was precisely the problem, and a partnership was what marriage should become. In the just society they were bringing into being, "personal independence and equal human rights" would "never be forfeited, except for crime." Marriage ought to be "an equal and permanent partnership, and so recognized by law." One delegate to the California constitutional convention of 1849 rejected "all this talk about the poesy of the marriage contract." Those who preached "poesy" needed instead to convince him that there "should be this merging, this annihilation of the woman," that "the wife should have no rights, and that the law should give her no protection." Confident that they would fail to do so, he concluded: "Sir, the marriage contract is a civil contract—not a sacrament."[51] To reformers, in fact, marital unity was a cruel joke, a sanctimonious gloss on the reality of male arbitrary authority. "One flesh" might be all very well in theory, but were wife and husband "one in purse?" Of course not. "No, sir," declared a reform delegate to the Indiana constitutional convention: if one took "gentlemen in the common run," one would find that they kept "their purses in their pockets," that they distributed money "as their caprice" dictated. Meanwhile, their wives were always "asking and even begging for a solitary dollar" to purchase household necessities.[52]

On the other hand, mid-century defenders of legal orthodoxy labeled any reform, no matter how slight, as affecting the "oneness" essential to the marital ideal. They oscillated between visions of the slippery slope toward marital misery that recognition of a limited separate economic interest of the wife would surely impose and evocations of the bliss—the true and virtuous homes—that resulted from a rigid and rigorous adherence to the principle of marital unity. "If there was anything in our institutions that ought not to be troubled by the stern hand of the reformer," intoned O'Conor at the New York convention, "it was the sacred ordinance of marriage and the relations arising out of it . . . based upon the gospel precept—'they twain shall be one flesh.'" The old law had endured for centuries. It had "passed the ocean with our ancestors, and cheered their first rude cabins in the wilderness; it still continued in all its original vigor and purity, and with all its originally benign tendency and influences, unimpaired by time, undiminished in its capacity to bless by any change of climate or external circumstances." Political revolutions had left "the domestic fire-side . . . untouched.—Woman, as wife or as mother, had known no change of the law which fixed her domestic character and guided her devoted love." Still today (but perhaps not tomorrow), a wife knew "no debasing pecuniary interest apart from the prosperity of her husband. His wealth had been her wealth; his prosperity her pride, her only source of power or distinction." What could possibly justify change in this happy scene? "Must the busy and impatient besom of reform obtrude, without invitation, its unwelcome officiousness within the charmed and charming circle of domestic life, and there too change the laws and habits of our people?"[53]

In tension with these ideologically charged visions of marital unity were a variety of alternative conceptions. Romantic images of the ecstatic spiritual and sexual union of lovers joined in matrimony were a staple of nineteenth-century sentimental culture. That too entered into the constitutional discourse. Marital unity was often awkwardly juxtaposed with romantic imagery and with notions of individual and separate rights. And some speakers and writers searched for a middle ground between warring camps. Sometimes they used the image of "pants" or "breeches" as a way to capture a combined sense of unity and separateness. Each leg was separate and individual; yet both were needed to make *one* pair of pants.[54]

Edward Mansfield tried a different reconciliation. Though early woman's rights advocates regarded his book as sympathetic to their cause, he insisted that all the basic tenets of the law of husband and wife—including the notion of one flesh, the wife's obligation to obey, and the husband's possession of her person—were founded on holy scripture. He immediately continued, however, by noting that there was nothing unequal or unfair in this, "for, while they continue in the marriage state, whatever may be the husband's right to her, she has the same to him." Marital unity had always meant that the wife's custody belonged to the husband, resulting in a "striking difference" between the legal rights actually accorded a wife as opposed to a husband. But Mansfield thought marital unity could be reconceived to lead to legal recognition of the wife's custodial rights over the husband as well: "If the society and services of a wife" were, "as they ought to be, so valuable to the husband," were "not the society and services of the husband equally so to the wife?" If a husband had "a right to use gentle restraint upon the wife in case of *evil habits*," shouldn't she "have a right to demand of the law, that it should also restrain him from evil courses?" Mansfield's vision of marriage groped, hesitantly, toward a conception of equality between husband and wife while still trying to hold on to an orthodox notion of unity.[55]

Meanwhile, armies massed around him, on opposing sides.

COVERTURE

What did it mean to be a wife? The legal answer was easy, declared both critics and defenders of the inherited legal order. Coverture described it, and coverture was a simple notion. It named the condition of a married woman, who at common law was a "feme [sometimes, femme] covert," a woman covered over by her husband. In Blackstone's paradigmatic words, "the very being or legal existence of the wife" was suspended "during the marriage, or at least" was "incorporated or consolidated into that of the husband: under whose wing, protection, and *cover*" she performed everything.

In eight short paragraphs, Blackstone managed to inscribe most of the important features and consequences of coverture.[56] Coverture meant that a man could not grant anything to his wife or enter into any contract with her. Doing either would be to suppose her separate identity. On the other hand, a woman might be her husband's agent, for her representation of him suggested no such separation. Coverture meant that, in exchange for gaining full ownership of all of his wife's personal property and absolute control for life over her real estate, a husband was bound to support her, so long as she did not elope with another man. Coverture meant that a wife could not bring a legal action to recover for injuries done to her person or property without her husband's concurrence. All such actions, moreover, had to be brought in his name as well as her own.[57] Coverture meant that neither spouse would be allowed to give testimony either for or against the other in any trial because it was recognized that "it was impossible their testimony should be indifferent" and, even more, "because of the union of person."

There were, Blackstone conceded, English legal institutions that did recognize husband and wife as the possessors of distinct and separate legal identities. Notably, ecclesiastical courts and, sometimes, courts of equity. There also were legal moments, even in the common law courts, when a wife was recognized as a separate person but inferior and subject to her husband's coercive authority. For example, before a court would recognize her agreement to her husband's property transfers, the law required that she be separately examined by a judge to make sure that her act was a voluntary one. Likewise, she could not ordinarily give property she inherited by will to her husband, since the law assumed that she had done so as a consequence of his coercion. And she could not be convicted of some felonies if she acted in the company of or under the constraint of her husband, not because the law assumed her lack of identity but, rather, because it assumed her subordination and his power.

Coverture also meant that "by the old law" a husband had the right to correct his wife. Since he was legally responsible for her misbehavior, he ought to be able to use moderate "domestic chastisement," limited to what was necessary for the due government of his family, in the same way that he might correct his children or his apprentices. If he were irrationally violent, she could obtain a peace bond against him from the local county court, requiring him to provide guarantors who would insure that he kept the peace. By the latter half of the eighteenth century, Blackstone concluded, the power of moderate correction was exercised solely by husbands of "the lower rank of people," who, unlike members of the more enlightened and genteel English classes, still remained attached to the old common law.

That's it. And for many Americans, that's all that marriage was, "in the eye of the law." Blackstone's language was the common currency of legal and political descriptions of marriage, relied on by voices on all sides of the political spectrum. Treatise writers parroted Blackstone. Even those like James Kent, who regarded the law of equity as a significant limitation on the reach of common law principles, began their discussions with the certainty that the legal effects of marriage were "generally deducible from the principle of the common law," through which the wife's "legal existence and authority" were "in a degree lost or suspended, during the continuance of the matrimonial union." Courts, particularly equity courts, might act in ways that limited or contradicted the presumptive logic of coverture, but still they did so with reference to coverture. State legislatures, from the first days of Independence on, tinkered with small features of the law of marriage, and they created diverse divorce regimes that might allow a wife the right to recreate an independent—that is to say, unmarried—identity. Yet they too left marriage as a structure of vested rights. Coverture was understood as the general rule, as the first principle, as the distillation of an incontrovertible structure.[58]

Woman's rights activists and men concerned with law reform treated Blackstonian coverture as a true statement of a legal regime in need of change. In 1837 Sarah Grimké concluded that few things presented greater obstacles to the improvement and elevation of women "than the laws . . . enacted to destroy her independence and crush her individuality." These laws absorbed "the very being of a woman, like that of a slave," into that of "her master." The "old law" that granted a husband a right of moderate correction placed a wife in the hands of a man "subject like herself to the outbursts of passion, and therefore unworthy to be trusted with power." The law of coverture had "a debasing and mischievous effect" on women, lessening their estimation of themselves as "moral and responsible beings" and teaching them a "fatal lesson": to look to men for protection and indulgence. Similarly, when Lucy Stone and Henry Blackwell drafted their famous radical marriage "protest" to accompany their wedding in 1855, it began with a rejection of Blackstone. Legal marriage gave a husband "an injurious and unnatural superiority, investing him with legal powers which no honorable man would exercise, and which no man should possess." And they wrapped up their list of the "wrongs" of legal marriage by insisting on the corruption of the whole system by which a wife's legal existence was suspended, leaving her unable to choose her home, to make a will, to sue or be sued, or to inherit property.[59]

The mid-century defenders of legal orthodoxy often characterized the disabilities of coverture as elaborations on the Biblical truth that the married twain shall be one flesh. Yet those who based the legal construction of wifely dependence on "nature" or on God's handiwork faced some difficulties. Coverture could not, as a legal framework, be rooted easily in a naturalized dichotomy between male and female natures. If that were the case, why then were unmarried women not subject to the disabilities of coverture?

In fact, the fundamental contrast that framed the law of husband and wife in the treatises was not that between men and women but that between single women and married women.[60] An unmarried woman was not subject to the disabilities of coverture; single women possessed all of the rights married women lost. A single woman's legal status was, for the most part, indistinguishable from the legal status of many men. A single woman could contract, own, dispose, write wills, engage in most forms of business, testify, demand the obedience and the guardianship of her children. As reformers often reminded their audiences, it was better (if only from the rhetorical vantage point of formal legal status) to be the mother of bastards than to be a married mother.[61]

Blackstone himself had regarded coverture as a matter of "municipal law," a body of evolving man-made rules and policies to be contrasted with those that "God and Nature have established."[62] Most Americans disagreed. Many conservative nineteenth-century Americans understood coverture as the legal expression of God's will in mandating marriage. Woman's rights proponents, by contrast, insisted that coverture represented an area of legal life irrationally blocked off from the evolutionary processes that should characterize modern American life, a "feudal" or "barbaric" throwback. They often characterized coverture as an archaic structure that frustrated truly human relationships, a structure inconsistent with human nature.

What all these Americans shared was a particular historical (or antihistorical) consciousness. Coverture was complete, a frozen structure. Coverture was a finished product (although some hoped that it was soon to be truly finished). Statements in treatises were not distillations of evolving institutional practices. They were descriptions of a "true" or "false" or "received" or "unchanging" law.

When American lawyers and activists took Blackstone's lapidary paragraphs as a complete description of the received law of husband and wife, they reified what had been an evolving and changing—and limited—body of English law. Parts of that law extended back into a distant, partially mythical, medieval past. Parts, such as the law of separation and divorce, had been the subject of continuing political argument since the early Reformation. Parts that were sometimes characterized as of immemorial duration were in fact relatively recent phenomena. For example, the English legal doctrine that granted husbands complete custodial control over their children, regardless of their treatment or abuse of their wives, a doctrinal structure that reformers characterized as the embodiment of archaic and barbarous patriarchy, was actually a recent invention, an eighteenth-century novelty.[63]

English coverture itself, as it would have been understood by eighteenth- and early nineteenth-century English lawyers, was inseparable from England's complex jurisdictional map of courts. Coverture was a concept created by the English common law and by the royal courts that were responsible for the common law; it served to recognize husbands' title—ownership—to most forms of marital property. The royal courts, however, were not the only English courts and, even with regard to the law of marriage, the royal courts had limited reach. Coverture rules were intended to establish clear property rights for those men whose property holdings depended on centralized royal courts. The clarity of those rights would discourage contests between couples and, more important, between families joined in prolonged and complex marital negotiations. But the law of coverture had little to do with the intimate domestic relations between most wives and husbands of any class, not even the domestic relations of the upper-class families who were the intended objects of its concern. Coverture would not have been understood as destroying the independent personal identities of seventeenth- and eighteenth-century English wives, whose personal relations and conflicts with their husbands were ordinarily the business of ecclesiastical courts and county courts.[64]

Even with regard to property questions, common law coverture could be countered (and certainly complicated) through the recourse by wives to the competing jurisdiction of the chancellor in courts of equity. Whenever a wife's separate legal identity from her husband had to be established—either because of her separation from her husband or because of her (or her birth family's) particular desire or need to keep property "separate"—equity courts responded and played their accustomed role of modifying and supplementing the more rigid domain of the common law.[65]

In a world where title to property was the usual measure of public identity (and of the right to represent others), common law coverture was one crucial marker of a patriarchal and hierarchical society. More, coverture provided a distinctive English gloss on the Christian commitment to marriage as a merger of wife and husband, who become "one flesh." The civil law property regimes of western Europe offered different solutions to the universal problem of establishing title to household property while still remaining true to Christian marital unity. Only in Anglo-American common law jurisprudence was "one flesh" translated into an individualistic demand that there be only one owner of marital property, and that owner needed to be the husband.[66] English coverture thus was not merely an inevitable by-product of a monotonal Christian patriarchy. Like all things legal, it had its own relatively autonomous history, shaped by a changing complex of institutional forces, by its own legal logic. And it may be that English coverture had, compared with other marital property regimes, a distinctively repressive patriarchal cast.

Still, as Mary Beard once argued, common law coverture—at least in England at the time Blackstone published his *Commentaries*—was only a marital property regime (and not even the only marital property regime in England). Blackstone's language distilled the decisions of one important legal jurisdiction—the common law courts. It sketched one body of rules located in a society filled with multiple-rule bodies, many of which participated in the constitution of marriage. It was not, on its own, the compulsory imposition of a rigid religiously sanctioned patriarchy.[67]

But when Americans of the first half of the nineteenth century looked at this distillation, this text, they looked from the vantage point of a society with a radically altered jurisdictional map. For Americans, the law of marriage was not what it was in England: a complex and loosely related body of rules and institutions shaped by a variety of political, theological, and legal histories. It was, rather, a received structure that appeared to arrive whole and complete, as "the common law" of marriage. In nineteenth-century America, there was no ecclesiastical jurisdiction with coercive authority.[68] Local courts lacked the moral and political authority of a fixed and relatively unchanging local community. In post-Revolutionary America, local courts were expected to implement norms and rules enacted by state appellate courts and by state legislatures. And for the most part, they did so.[69] In republican America, moreover, many viewed equity courts with suspicion, as discretionary institutions that undercut the power and authority of majoritarian lawmakers. Equity jurisdiction was explicitly rejected in a number of state constitutions and merged into the common law courts. Where a separate equitable jurisdiction existed, as in New York, it offered at most a very limited alternative to common law jurisdiction, more a supplement than an alternative. Even Chancellor Kent, the most consistent and prominent defender of the discretionary authority of a court of equity, always framed his authority with regard to marriage and divorce in terms of legislative delegations.[70]

Nineteenth-century Americans imagined common law appellate courts and state legislatures as together filling up the lawmaking space of the society. Yet, prior to the 1840s, state legislatures played relatively little role in the regulation of marriage. Legislatures passed divorce laws and modified the rules of dower in order to prevent clogs on land sales. They left apparent legal authority over the law of husband and wife—including coverture—in the hands of the common law courts and courts of equity. Thus, state appellate courts became the primary articulators of the norms of marriage in America.[71] And when state supreme court justices, and the lawyers who argued before them, looked for authority about "the law," they often looked to Blackstone, whose statements of the law of England reinforced their sense of a unified and monopolistic common law.

So Blackstonian coverture described governing principles of the American law of husband and wife. We should not assume, as Mary Beard did, that those woman's rights activists who invested Blackstone's language with "truth" and who ignored the law produced by chancellors sitting in courts of equity were "wrong" to do so.[72] In law, there is no external position to establish the truth of what is law. If everyone makes the same "wrong" assumption about what the law is, then that assumption becomes right, becomes an accurate statement of what the law is. In nineteenth-century America, nearly everyone (that is, everyone except for a few equitably oriented and highly sophisticated lawyers, like James Kent and Tapping Reeve) agreed that Blackstone's *Commentaries* captured the central features of the received law of husband and wife. By definition, then, it did so, even if everyone thereby read Blackstone in a way that wrested the English law of coverture from its historical and jurisdictional contexts.

Of course, no sane man or woman, least of all judges or lawyers, believed in coverture's literal truth.[73] Coverture did not describe a wife's moral or social identity. No one believed that Blackstone's phrases described how husbands and wives ought to conduct themselves during their marriages. Much of the law of husband and wife, as practiced in courts and law offices, was concerned with avoiding or countering—through contracts and other means—the plain meaning of the Blackstonian text. Blackstone's eight paragraphs may have captured coverture's essence, but even long treatises could only sketch coverture's possible and changing implications.

But to play on the legal field of domestic relations required litigants—and their lawyers—to accept the starting premise of coverture: that by marriage a wife became a feme covert, a woman whose political and legal identity was covered over by her husband, who became responsible for her care. And this was true whether the legal terms of a marriage were argued in a court of equity or in a court of common law, or in the imaginations and fantasies of individual men and women.

WIVES AS THINGS

In August 1849, six years before she would marry Henry Blackwell, Lucy Stone, woman's rights activist and Oberlin graduate, wrote to her friend, classmate, and future sister-in-law Antoinette Brown Blackwell. She had been reading Edward Mansfield's *Legal Rights of Women,* and she urged her friend to do so as well.

What had Stone learned from her reading of the legal treatise? Not to marry.

> It seems to me that *no* man who *deserved* the *name* of *MAN,* when he knows what a *mere thing,* the law, makes a married woman, would ever insult a woman, by asking her to marry. It is horrid to live without the intimate companionship, and gentle loving influences which are the constant attendant of a true love marriage—It is a wretchedly unnatural way of living, but nothing is so bad as to be made a *thing,* as every married woman now is, in the eye of Law.[74]

The law made a wife into a "thing," a "nonentity," a "slave." Stone's letter played with a characteristic nineteenth-century ambiguity about the power of law to construct identity. In speeches, letters, and pamphlets, reformers declared that women became what the law said they were. If the law said that a wife was a feme covert—a being whose identity was covered over, obliterated, who became the property of another, who lost a self—then that is what a wife was.[75] At the same time, female reformers denied the moral power of law to construct them, resisted it, imagined themselves as moral beings with the capacity to create more Godly and human institutions. Reformers like Stone knew that the thingness of a wife was a legal metaphor, a fiction. Still, they often spoke as if the fiction was descriptive of social reality. And when they did so, they animated the law with demonic power.

The received law of nineteenth-century America provided powerful images of a wife reduced to the possession of her husband. A husband could recover damages from those who had alienated his wife's affections from him. He could sue his wife's seducer on a theory that the seducer had trespassed on his property. He possessed the theoretical right to "recapture" a wife from those who held her against his will. In such situations the desires of the wife were regarded as irrelevant. It was arguably of no legal interest what the wife had done or wanted: whether, for example, she had gone to her brother's house to escape from her husband, whether she had initiated the adulterous seduction. In the words of an eighteenth-century English treatise, the law always presumed "compulsion and force" when a wife left her husband because she was "not supposed to possess a power of consent." So long as the husband was not guilty of misconduct of a form that justified intervention by interested friends and relatives, he had a legal right to his possession, his wife, and a legal right to recover damages from those who acted to deprive him of what was his. It need hardly be added that a wife possessed no reciprocal or equivalent causes of action for harms done to her relationship with her husband.[76]

More important, every wife in nineteenth-century America would have experienced situations in which her husband's name and identity covered over her own. If "she" sued, it would probably be in his name. If she were sued, it would almost certainly be in his. If she traded or bought on credit in local stores, it would be understood that she was doing so as his agent, not on her own account. Her money—indeed, almost all her personal property—was his. Wherever she was really living, her "settlement," that is, her official place of residence, would remain wherever he lived. And in any number of situations, a wife would have to confront her dependency and her need to be "trusted" by her husband.

Sometimes not being "trusted" defined a moment of recognition. In early 1860, for example, the Presbyterian minister Theophilus Packard was desperate to silence his spiritualist, freethinking wife, Elizabeth. Eventually, he would commit her into the Illinois insane asylum, with immense consequences for both of them and for commitment laws across the nation. But in early 1860, he was still exploring alternatives, and she thought that he was still her "protector." Theophilus asked Elizabeth if she wished to make a three-month visit to her brother in Batavia, New York. In her later recollections, she first told him she should like it very well if it were not understood as "running from" her "post of duty." They agreed that she would take her baby and her daughter along (there were six children at the time). She then asked for $10 of her "patrimoney" to take for spending money. He refused her that. Her reconstructed dialogue went as follows:

> "Why not? I shall need as much as that, to be absent three months with two sick children. I may need to call a doctor to them; and besides, my brother is poor, and I am rich, comparatively, and I might need some extra food, such as a beefsteak, or something of the kind, and I should not like to ask him for it. And besides, I have your written promise that I may have my own money whenever I want it, and I do want ten dollars of it now; and I think it is no unreasonable amount to take with me."
>
> "I don't think it is best to let you have any. I shan't trust you with money."
>
> "Shan't trust me with money! Why not? Have I ever abused this trust? Do not I always give you an exact account of every cent I spend? And I will this time do so; and besides, if you cannot trust me, I will put it into brother's hands as soon as I get there, and not spend a cent but by his permission."
>
> "No, I shall not consent to that."
>
> . . .
>
> "Well, husband, if I can't be trusted with ten dollars of my own money under these circumstances, I should not think I was capable of being trusted with two sick children three months away from home, wholly dependent on a poor brother's charities. Indeed I had rather stay at home and not go at all, than go under such circumstances."
>
> "You shall not go at all!" replied he, in a most excited, angry tone of voice. "You shall go into an asylum."

Whether or not her memories were precisely accurate, she knew her readers would understand this dialogue as an expression of a husband's ordinary rights (and as an expression of a near-abusive—and foolish—insistence on those rights). Women readers would resonate to the problem she articulated: how to negotiate trust, how to sustain it, how to live with it, while still knowing oneself as a moral agent.[77]

Coverture was real; it had great symbolic weight in the construction of American womanhood. Yet it would be a mistake to allow Lucy Stone's comment to determine our understanding of the effects of coverture. Wives were never things in the law. Dependent, unequal, subordinate, surely. Often legally unable to act as competent legal subjects. At the same time, a wife always remained a person in the law, separable from her husband.

Conservative judges recognized the independent personhood of a wife even as they denied it in particular cases. Over and over courts would have to explain why it was that they were not able to take a wife's testimony, or to allow her to sue in her own name, or to have a separate domicile. In theory, to recognize a wife's capacity to represent herself was to imagine the end of the marriage. And much in the law and in the orientations of the judges moved them to reject that imagined ending. Yet so many cases involved couples who were in fact separated, who were suing each other, who presented judges with legal problems constructed out of their contending and opposing interests. In those cases lawyers worked to make real and plausible—possible—the imagined end of the marriage. Even where the possibility of a wife's reemergence as an uncovered female, as a feme sole, was not directly under discussion, or in situations where the suit involved a conflict between wife or husband and a third party, the submersion of wife within her husband's identity was never a tacit, unspoken assumption. In litigation, at least, it was never understood as an unchallengeable truth about human nature and human relations. It was always a conscious and artificial positive act of law, an imposition on a wife for particular legal reasons.[78]

An important use of coverture was, moreover, as a strategic tool of women seeking to avoid liability for their actions. As we have seen, it was women who affirmatively and individually asserted their coverture, their submersion within their husbands' legal spheres, in order to force their husbands to maintain them after separations.[79] Or consider *Ross v. Singleton,* decided by the Delaware chancellor in 1821. The story of the case had begun many years before, in 1785, when property that Sarah Singleton had inherited prior to her marriage was sold in execution of a judgment against her husband, Joseph Singleton. Apparently, she had never signed any document agreeing to the sale and releasing her rights in the property. This meant that she retained residual rights over the property, rights that would become vested and possessory on her husband's death. Then in 1791 Joseph left home and enlisted in troops under the command of General St. Clair, the governor of the Northwest Territory. St. Clair's army, composed of "men collected . . . from the stews and brothels of the cities," marched against the Indians of the Miami Confederacy and was massacred on November 4, 1791. Among those rumored to have died was Joseph Singleton.[80]

Soon thereafter Sarah asked John Ross if he wanted to buy her land. Ross first declined but, after receiving assurances that Joseph was dead, he agreed, contracting to pay fifty-six pounds down and the residue of ninety-seven pounds when Sarah provided good title to the whole. Sarah Singleton moved to Philadelphia, and in 1800, relying, one suspects, on rules that presumed death after seven years' absence, demanded full performance from John Ross. The sale was completed in April of that year.

But then in 1808 Joseph returned. He found his wife in Philadelphia, but she refused to cohabit with him. He wandered off to Kentucky, where he died in 1818.

On Joseph's death, Sarah brought an action in ejectment against John Ross for the land. She asserted her renewed ownership of the land that she had previously sold him (and that Joseph had previously allowed to be sold in execution of judgment). The common law court held in her favor, on the theory that her conveyance to Ross was void because she was a married woman at the time that she had made it (since Joseph was alive at that time). Ross then went to the equity court where he filed a bill asking that Sarah be compelled to pass title to him, and that he be quieted, that is, secured or protected, in his title, and for an injunction to stop further proceedings by her in ejectment. Under ordinary circumstances Ross was surely a likely candidate for equitable relief. Equity existed to ensure that bargainers did what they promised to do, to prevent unjust enrichment, to keep litigants from manipulating technical rules to achieve immoral results.[81]

But Chancellor Nicholas Ridgely refused to grant an injunction or to quiet John Ross's title. Ross had simply taken an imprudent risk. He had paid money to Sarah Singleton without direct knowledge of the death of Joseph Singleton, upon whose death the legality of his contract depended. The fact that Sarah had enjoyed the benefits of the contract, the fact that she had already been paid, was irrelevant. "A contract made by a married woman, without the consent of her husband, is void; and a court of chancery cannot give validity to a contract void in law." Indeed, a married woman could make no contracts during her coverture (during marriage) that would bind her after she became a single woman. Why not? Because once single, she had become a different person; there had occurred a new transformation of the self. She had crossed over the bright line between married and single. The covered past could not control the uncovered present. And so, at least for a while, Sarah Singleton was able legally to keep both the purchase price and the land she had been paid to convey.[82]

In a variety of ways coverture gave wives not an absence of identity but, rather, a particular recognized identity, one that sometimes gave them certain privileges. Coverture, moreover, was a limited concept. It existed solely during a husband's life. Good legal planning incorporated recognition of the likelihood of a wife's widowhood, at which point she would again become a recognized person in the law. Thus, legal doctrine insisted on a separate examination of a wife, whenever a husband dealt or traded in her property or in his property subject to dower. Thoughtful parents of marrying daughters insisted on separate use agreements and trusts not just because they didn't trust their soon-to-be sons-in-law (although they often didn't), but also because they knew that their daughters were likely, if they survived childbirth, to outlive their husbands.

The values expressed in the law of coverture were often balanced by courts against other values. The rule that one spouse could not testify for or against the other—framed by images of marital unity and the promotion of marital harmony—often was placed in tension with the "need" for the testimony or the factual absence of unity or harmony. In the much-cited case of *Ratcliff v. Wales*, for example, a man sued another for the seduction of his former wife, whom he had recently divorced for her adultery. His plan to call his ex-wife to the stand to prove the adultery was challenged by the defendant on the grounds that she was incompetent to speak about any fact taking place while she was plaintiff's wife. The husband appealed, and Greene C. Bronson, speaking for the New York Supreme Court and ordinarily a rigid defender of traditional coverture, held in the husband's favor. According to Bronson, it was indeed the case that a wife could not ordinarily testify against her husband, to promote the "perfect union" of their interests and to secure their mutual confidence in one another. In this case, however, the "fact which she was offered to prove, did not even come to her knowledge in consequence of the marriage relation." That is, her adultery, the "act" that ended the marriage and the relevant "fact" about which she was expected to testify, had nothing to do with her relation to her husband. Therefore, why reject her testimony?[83]

Two early nineteenth-century poor relief cases show coverture outweighed by other public policies. In early America, as in England, poor relief was defined by the law of settlement. Settlement was not residence. Free white Americans acquired a settlement by birth. But what happened when they moved, as most did at one time or another in their lives? Without a settlement in one's place of residence, one lacked any right to draw on community resources. Indeed, without a settlement one faced the likelihood of being "warned out," that is, ordered to leave. Most people did not leave a town immediately after having been warned out. Indeed, it is not clear that there was any real expectation that they would do so. The "warning" put strangers on notice that they could not rely on community resources, and it laid the foundation for a later process of removal. And when, to take a common case, an unmarried woman (or a deserted wife) whose settlement lay elsewhere became pregnant, the overseers of the poor would send the constable out to transport her back to the town where she had a settlement (thereby avoiding financial responsibility for a bastard child whose settlement, by birth, would have been in the town).[84]

By marriage, as a consequence of coverture and marital unity, a woman acquired a settlement in her husband's town, that is, the town in which he had a settlement. By marriage, moreover, her own settlement in the town of her birth would ordinarily be "covered over," suspended during coverture. When a husband was unable to support his wife, she would ordinarily become the responsibility of his town of settlement because that is where her settlement lay during his life.[85]

But what if the husband lacked a settlement in any town in the state? Maria Chadwick, originally from Otsego, New York, lived in Smithfield, New York, with her husband Elisha, whose settlement was in Connecticut. Elisha was a drunkard and did not provide for his wife and children, and in 1823 he had lost their house. When Maria turned to the charity of her neighbors, the town of Smithfield warned her out and ordered her removal to Otsego. The town of Otsego responded that her settlement there was suspended during coverture; she remained a member of her

wife had to be "uncovered," recreated as a feme sole, at least for particular purposes (such as control of her earnings or inheritance or child custody)? Had one or the other committed adultery, violated what the courts regarded as the fundamental marital vow of sexual fidelity, so that the relationship could be declared publicly to be at an end? To resolve such issues courts assumed that they had to give at least momentary recognition to the separate legal identity of the wife, including hearing her testimony against her husband.[90]

Courts recognized a wife's separate identity because many cases occurred at the margins—at the moments when the marriage might be dissolving, when the husband might be avoiding his responsibilities, when a wife might rightfully be asserting her moral obligation to separate from him. The law recognized some few circumstances in which it was appropriate for a wife to claim a separate identity. A woman would come before a court to argue that her personal situation fitted one or more of those circumstances. Even if the judge disagreed, in order to evaluate the claim he had to imagine her as a separate (and potentially separated) moral and legal being.[91]

Perhaps the point is an ironic one. Because a husband and wife would appear in court as separate and contending rights bearers only under circumstances when the continuation of their marriage was itself at issue, courts were precisely the arena where a wife's separate identity was most easily and commonly recognized. Legal doctrine created coverture. Legal processes provided public recognition of the separate legal identities of wives.

The apparent reality of the simple image of coverture, of wives as things, was easy to explode. Henry Blackwell did a particularly nice job of it in 1854, while successfully negotiating his marriage to Lucy Stone. Lucy had written him that marriage was impossible so long as the traditional rules existed. Henry responded that in imagining herself precluded from marriage because "the existing laws of Society do not square with exact justice," she was subjecting herself "to a more abject *slavery* than ever actually existed." Women, Henry continued, were not responsible for the law and should not feel morally compromised by it. The true degradation and disgrace rested "not with the victim but with the oppressors." Thus, the disgrace was more his than hers. "The Law by clothing me with unjust powers puts me in the position of the wrongdoer but it only puts you in that of the wrong sufferer." So he, not she, was in the situation "morally the most painful."

Would he marry, Lucy had asked him, if the laws placed men in the same position as they now placed women? He would, he answered, after making three sorts of preparations. First, he would satisfy himself that she would not try to lock him up, "or rather *attempt* so to do (for the *law* would soon get me out with a writ of habeas corpus, if you did)." Second, he would make her promise not to invoke any "unjust" laws that gave her control of more than half of his future earnings. Third, he would have a separate use agreement drafted to place all his personal property beyond her control. So long as the marriage were harmonious, he continued, "the laws *would not exist*" so far as they were concerned. The law was nothing much. It existed only where invoked. And even then, by taking appropriate action, a couple (or a worried potential spouse) could anticipate and alter its course.

He played out the fantasy of role reversal. What if, on the other hand, he had misjudged her and she, in her imagined role as abusive husband, tried to lock him up or mistreat him? A number of answers appeared: he would sue her for assault and battery. He would go into business in a friend's name ("a very easy & common matter"), and she would never get "one dollar" of his earnings. He would sue her for divorce "on the general grounds of gross cruelty & neglect," and if their home state did not grant such divorces, "at the worst I could easily move into one that did." He would "steal at least half" their children and put her to the trouble and expense of trying to get them back. If she succeeded in doing so, he would steal them again and give her "the same trouble over & over" until she compromised. He would always remain his own master "in spite of much unjust annoyance."

Henry thought Lucy's diatribe against marriage made two fundamental errors. Her first mistake was to assume that Blackstonian statements of the law described the practices of legal institutions. American women (and their children) were not subject to the exclusive custody of their husbands. "[H]owever true in old fashioned times—it is not *practically* so now at all & not even any longer true in theory." Any lawyer would tell her the same thing, "my life against a dime." A husband's only power lay in refusing to support his wife or in holding on to their children. As Lucy refused to be supported, the first threat had no "terror." More seriously, Lucy exaggerated the power of "external laws" over "internal power." A woman's moral identity remained her own, could not be involuntarily submerged in her husband. "Give me a *free man*—he can never be made a slave. Give me a free woman—she never can be made one either." Coverture was really nothing but "a few paltry enactments" that could quite easily be foiled. And the clincher for Henry as he pressed his suit: "[T]he *position of a wife* is based in Nature & is therefore *honorable*. All the perversions of Men cannot make the *married woman* other than a woman in a true relation to herself, to her husband & to her kind."[92]

Was Henry right? He was surely too quick in his dismissal of the constitutive power of coverture. In a culture that identified contractual capacity with humanity, the rules of coverture stood as a denial of female humanity. They were not everything, but they were something. Many women took from the general culture, including the law of coverture, a sense that they were not entitled to speak, both within their marriages and in the public sphere. They knew themselves as beings who had constantly to negotiate so that they would be "trusted" by their husbands. The Blackstonian image of a covering over was mobilized by authoritarian men like Asa Bailey, who looked to the phrases of the law for reinforcement and support. The limited legal and religious obligations of wives to submit before the legitimate authority of their husbands could easily be reinterpreted or misinterpreted as denial of identity, as submersion of the self. Still, Henry's response developed a sophisticated understanding of what law did to the moral identity of a woman, of its actual power as a shaping force.

Six years before Henry Blackwell's courtship of Lucy Stone, the theater critic Henry Hudson had written a conservative defense of Shakespeare's Desdemona. Desdemona was the pure embodiment of married womanhood, everything Lucy Stone wasn't. Or, more precisely, Desdemona was everything Lucy Stone worried that she would become with marriage. "Unfortunately for her reputation with the savans [sic] of the age," Hudson wrote, Desdemona was not "a champion of woman's rights." To Hudson, Desdemona was so good that her virtue could not really be described or encompassed by human language. But to give words to the indescribable, as he proceeded to do, the foundation of her goodness derived from her total and absolute obedience. She embodied what Hudson regarded as "the highest virtue of which woman, or rather, of which human nature is capable": that is, submission before legitimate authority. Othello's presence inspired her with "religious awe" as well as "awful respect," even "fear." "Meek, uncomplaining, submissive even unto death where she owes allegiance," her character was "not of the sort to take with a self-teaching, self-obeying generation." Her rights as a woman seemed quite worthless to her unless given and guaranteed by another. And all that made her better, purer, than Shakespeare's other heroines.[93]

There is a vast (political, religious, cultural) gulf that separates Henry Blackwell's picture of a good wifely identity from that sketched by Henry Hudson. We can imagine them as representatives of two radically opposed sides in the cultural wars of antebellum America. And yet neither would have regarded the being of a wife as the being of a thing. They both would have confirmed Mary Beard's insight that the meaning of marriage for women could never be captured by a list of the legal rights they possessed or lacked. To Hudson, Desdemona's acceptance of her husband's crazy cruelty, her loyalty to Othello, her submission, were signs of an extraordinary moral achievement: a stilling of a sinful self-will. Her virtue as a person was intimately connected to her commitment to her wifely duty and to her denial of any purported individual rights. A wife who regarded herself as having become a thing thereby would have been denying her own moral nature and destiny. Henry Blackwell, by contrast, refused to recognize any necessary connection between the legal structure of wifedom and moral identity. The law lacked power. It was nothing but an indeterminate, transitory, changeable, and manipulable arrangement of "rules." A woman who allowed those rules to define her was foolish and misled by outward signs of authority.

That neither Hudson nor Blackwell thought of coverture as a denial of moral identity does not mean that no one did so in antebellum America. Nor does the recognition of female identity within the strictures of the common law demonstrate that that recognition was the only meaning that could be drawn out of the law as it was understood. Laws exist to be misinterpreted and "misused," converted into new strategic resources, as early feminists like Lucy Stone surely did. It is impossible to prove the negative, impossible to prove that coverture did not make wives into things. Surely some women thought that way about themselves, some of the time, drawing on their understanding of the law. Many men often used the law to rationalize and legitimate their understanding of women's lesser humanity, of their diminished identity.

Yet even within common law doctrine there was no sustained denial of the separate and individual identity of a wife. The merger—the near-obliteration of the female self—implicit in the oneness of "one flesh" was always contradictory and inconclusive in the law, radically incomplete. If wives became their husbands' property legally, it was in a more complicated sense than the apparent analogies to trees and fields and pets and slaves that both feminist and misogynist literatures raised. Wives possessed the properties of wives. And husbands possessed them, at least some of the time, in some ways. But coverture did not turn women into things.

Rather, the twin achievements of the law of coverture were that it transformed women into wives and that it constructed and legitimated a structure of power within marriage, one that marital unity seemed to symbolize.

5

Acting Like a Husband

The only despotism on earth that I would advocate, is the despotism of the husband.

Charles Tyler Botts, California Constitutional Convention (1849)

The law created marriage as a husband's private sphere. Law gave him vested rights and limited duties within a domestic space that he owned. Being a husband meant that one possessed, one represented, one governed, one cared for. Or, to put it slightly differently, knowing oneself as a husband required knowing one's wife as a feme covert, as a dependent.

And yet the law also described the boundaries of that private sphere: when it would be penetrated by public power and when any sense of private autonomy should melt away, as a husband was remade as a dishonorable and unworthy man.

POSSESSION

The cases and the treatises of early nineteenth-century American law convey three overlapping images of a husband's rights. Two were publicly recognized and could be drawn out of the explicit language of the treatise writers. Coverture was understood as the representation of the legal self of the wife by that of her husband. It also constituted the terms of government within a family and between two individuals, terms that included both the husband's obligation to care for his wife and the wife's obligation to render obedience to him. Coverture as representation described a marriage in terms of its "foreign policy," when it, like other governments and corporate entities, would ordinarily be represented by a single voice. Coverture as government, by contrast, described the "do-

136

mestic policy" of a marriage, the narrative of how life was conducted within its borders.

Implicit in the idea of coverture was a third image: of a wife as the possession of her husband, as husband's property. Eighteenth- and nineteenth-century treatise writers found the image more than a little embarrassing. Defenders of orthodoxy preferred to talk about other things. Yet all had to acknowledge that a husband had the right to treat his wife as his, to defend his possession of her against others. A husband could recover damages from those who "enticed" her from him or who "alienated her affections." Theoretically, he had a right to sue out a writ of habeas corpus against anyone who kept his wife away from him, requiring the person to release the wife from improper restraint. The legal treatises also noted a husband's right to recapture and, in appropriate circumstances, to restrain and confine a wife. These were all rights possessed by a man, as a husband, against other men. They punished others for interfering with or taking that which belonged to him as a husband.[1]

The paradigm of a possessory right was the civil action for criminal conversation (commonly known as crim. con.), through which a husband recovered damages from his wife's seducer.[2] Criminal conversation was neither a criminal action nor about conversation. In form this was an action in trespass (*trespass vi et armis*), theoretically of a piece with a legal cause of action against someone who entered unlawfully onto one's land. The participation and desires of the wife were imagined as of no more relevance than the participation and desires of a tree in the theft of a man's lumber. Relying on what Tapping Reeve called "a rigid adherence to a maxim" that had "not the least foundation in common sense," the action proceeded "upon the ground that a wife was destitute of a will, and therefore could not have consented to commit adultery." The guilty defendant was, by definition, "a ruffian," who accomplished his purpose "by brutal violence," rather than "an unprincipled seducer, who, by art and intrigue," committed "the greatest of all injuries." And, though in legal practice "common sense" prevailed, and courts awarded damages in criminal conversation cases as if it were an action in case (trespass on the case), which allowed judges and juries to take into account the contributory negligence of the plaintiff and the conduct of the wife, still the wife often remained a shadowy presence in her own seduction.[3]

Three early New York City trials show how a husband's possessory rights played out in litigation. In the first, Jacob Blakney's wife Catherine was "dogged" by James Berrian until Berrian succeeded in seducing her, leading to the separation of Jacob and Catherine. Blakney's lawyer, Dr. John Graham, described the damages asked for as scant recovery for the "crime" committed: "his family ha[d] been broken up, his wife cast off a wandering vagrant upon the earth, and the husband left to bemoan in sorrow the loss of the love, esteem, and affection of the wife of his bosom, and to behold the wretched ruin of his affectionate and hopeful children." The defense conceded the act but insisted that the plaintiff was not the innocent Graham portrayed. Rather, he was an opportunist who had brought such suits before. The jury, however, held the defendant guilty as charged and awarded Blakney $1,500 damages.[4]

The second case involved a couple, the Parkers, who had not lived together for five years. Here again the sexual intercourse was never denied. One witness asked M'Dougall, the defendant, why Parker never noticed that his children were not his. M'Dougall answered that "Parker [was] such a damned fool he can't see"; further, that "Mrs. Parker wished her husband dead, for he could not please her." M'Dougall insisted that he was not the cause of the husband's loss. The Parkers had never lived together happily. Mr. Parker had beaten his wife more than once. He drank. She was always "an abandoned woman," promiscuous and sexually aggressive. There was even a suggestion of lesbianism: she was described as having "worked both ways" and as having been seen leaving a bedroom with a prostitute. If the wife were the seducer, according to M'Dougall's lawyer, then there could be no damages. A prostitute could not be seduced. More important, a man could "never have lost what he never had." Criminal conversation existed to compensate a husband for the loss of his sexual monopoly. Lacking that monopoly, there ought to be no recovery. But, again, the jury held for the plaintiff and awarded $250 damages.[5]

In the third trial a violin teacher sued his young pupil. William Sampson, the pupil's lawyer, laid his defense on four grounds: that the evidence did not sustain the charge, that the character of both the wife and the defendant was innocent, that the wife had a venereal disease that made her into "an object of disgust," not an object of seductive ardor ("Mr. Tyson is a young man, and we may therefore presume ardent in his desires, but you cannot believe that he wishes to indulge them where age and wrinkles combine with corrup[t] disease to disgust or *appal* his ardour"), and that the plaintiff and his wife were not happily married. The husband had lived in open adultery, and it was he, the husband, who had infected his wife. Furthermore, Sampson warned the jury, if the plaintiff recovered in this case, men like the plaintiff, men of the "middling and the lower classes," would "desert . . . their occupations in order to speculate in actions of crim. con." Sampson asked the jury to feel for the situation of the wife, to "remember" her "rights," to recognize "the injuries committed by a most abandoned and profligate villain, towards the partner of his bosom." He had never clothed her, yet he asked for $40,000 because his wife once had sat "upon a bed with the defendant." The judge, however, instructed the jury that the plaintiff's conduct was not a defense to a verdict, although that conduct might stand in mitigation of damages. The jury, obediently, declared the defendant guilty but only awarded the plaintiff $50 damages.[6]

Criminal conversation was an expression of the double standard. There existed no equivalent cause of action available to women whose husbands were seduced away from them. Yet, to speak in terms of the double standard is to risk immediate anachronism. The label "double standard" suggests a comparison of the legal rights of husbands and wives or those of men and women. But the right to sue for criminal conversation was not understood as a privilege given to men as a gender and denied to women. It certainly did not reward or protect male promiscuity. It was rather intended to remedy the wrongs that men did to each other, a part of a constellation of rights by which a husband defined his rights and his identity as a husband in relation to a world of men who were not married to his wife.[7]

The origins of the action for criminal conversation were rooted in a particular early modern understanding of male nature. Violent men (paradigmatically aristocrats), men inclined to duels and to murder if finding themselves cuckolded by their wives, would be disciplined by a legal remedy, would give up their weapons for the attractions of large money damages. The legal action formalized a husband's right to sexual monopoly over his wife, his ownership of her sexual fidelity, by granting him a remedy for its loss in a world without divorce. At the same time, the legal remedy directed a husband away from self-help, robbed him of traditional rights of honor, in a culture that assumed that men were naturally inclined to violence. Crim. con.'s emergence in eighteenth-century England was of a piece with the era's general commercialization and commodification of property relations, the reduction of all things, even honor, to a monetary equivalent, as much a diversion of the violent possessory impulse of men (away from violence and toward lucre) as it served as a legal expression of that impulse.[8]

Nineteenth-century American trials followed English precedents. Formally, two things only had to be proved: the existence of the marriage and the fact of unlawful intercourse between the seducer and the plaintiff's wife during the marriage. In other words, all the husband had to do was put his title into evidence (the marriage) and then show that the defendant had harmed what was his.[9]

In practice, the judges sometimes gave the evidentiary question of the wife's prior virtue a distinctively American cast. In *Torre v. Summers* (1820), for example, the defendant appealed a trial court's decision that rejected his attempt to call another man to testify as to his own sexual liaison with plaintiff's wife. The court ruled that the defendant had a right to such testimony if the witness were willing to take the stand. The court thought it was deviating in a republican manner from the traditional common law rule: "though we may not protect a seducer of women with all the feelings of men whose dearest rights are at stake, yet the meanest claim the equal distribution of rights."[10]

In criminal conversation, the plaintiff's general character was never at issue but his character as a husband might be. And yet courts construed "character as a husband" quite narrowly. Thus, in one case, testimony that a man was a low-class drunkard was not allowed, even in mitigation of damages. Evidence as to rank (which was admitted by the English courts) would have been "very uncongenial with our political institutions." After all, "The poor beetle that we tread upon, feels as great a pang as when a giant dies." In another case, the court refused an instruction to the jury to consider that the plaintiff and his wife had lived together unhappily and occasionally fought. A husband's bad temper did not lessen the seducer's guilt. The "occasional collisions" between a husband and wife inflicted "no wound on the husband's honour." A third court held that the plaintiff's own adultery could only be put into evidence in mitigation of damages. A husband's adultery did not bar his right to sue, although it did demonstrate that his "sense of moral propriety, and regard for chastity, could not be much offended by the loss of virtue in his wife." An adulterer sustained less damage than a more virtuous husband, but still he would have his remedy.[11]

In England, judges long debated whether a separated husband retained a right to sue his wife's lover. Throughout most of the eighteenth century, the view prevailed that a separated husband was still entitled to compensation for the violation of "inalienable" marital rights. This conclusion was reaffirmed in 1805, although juries increasingly regarded a prior separation as mitigating the size of damage awards.[12] In the United States, by contrast, the early (1798) Pennsylvania case of *Fry v. Drestler* established that separated husbands had no right to damages. Reeve took that holding and gave it an expansive spin: if a husband no longer had a concrete right to his wife's person, then, "of course," he suffered "no greater injury than any other member of the community" from her seduction. Others, including Kent, were more tempered, emphasizing that a wife, after a separation, still retained the character of a married woman, meaning that her seduction still constituted a "trespass" on the husband's possession. Well into the 1860s, the issue remained open. Separated husbands continued to prosecute cases against men who insisted that separation constituted a full defense. And sometimes the husbands won.[13]

Appellate courts refused to order new trials on the grounds that juries had awarded excessive damages. No award, indeed, was too large where guilt was proven. The loss to the husband was "very great." A guilty defendant was a villain, a "spider of society," a "reptile." To the argument made by one defendant's lawyer, that the defendant's innocent wife and children should not be punished by taking more than half his property and depriving them of support, Chief Justice Savage of the New York Supreme Court replied: "if the jury had not given the defendant's property to the plaintiff, it might have been dissipated in adulterous dissipation with the plaintiff's wife, and thereby doing the same injury to his [the defendant's] wife and children." Moreover, sympathy for his dependents should not diminish the defendant's punishment. "Remove from him the apprehension of suffering on behalf of his innocent family, and you remove from him the principal restraint upon his wicked propensities."[14]

Criminal conversation was understood as part of a punitive moral discourse that revolved around the problem of seduction. How to punish the adulterer? How to stop "the destroyer" of a husband's "peace and happiness"? By the middle years of the nineteenth century, a number of legal commentators had come to the conclusion that the wrong answer to these questions was by awarding private damages as compensation.

Crim. con. was a mistake. On the one hand, there was something decidedly unvirtuous about husbands who publicized their wives' disgrace in order to profit therefrom. Such men, often lower-class men, lacked honor. Indeed, much of the critical commentary carried the intimation that a real man would have killed, or at least thrashed, the seducer rather than taking him to court. "A grasping and conniving husband was seeking to profit from the degradation of another: the degraded wretches rise as the man of moral worth sinks."[15]

Adultery was too important to leave as a merely private wrong redressed with money damages. Crim. con. was too little, too late, an inadequate remedy for a serious social problem. In 1850 one anonymous commentator noted the "paramount importance" of laws that would provide "a wall of defence around the hallowed shrines of home." What was needed was "a flaming sword" to "guard the paradise of pure affections." Yet of all the commandments of the Mosaic Code, only the seventh, against adultery, had not been turned into a positive criminal statute in New York or in other states. As a result, "[h]appy homes" had "been invaded, and the altars on which were offered the pure incense of love" had "been cast down." The only remedy the laws provided to the men on whom these attacks were inflicted was crim. con.: "How preposterous to think that an injury, so deep . . . can be recompensed by the payment of silver and gold."[16]

Later on, in the late nineteenth century, legal commentators would debate whether possessory rights like those expressed in the action for criminal conversation ought to be granted to wives as well as husbands or whether they ought to be abolished entirely. In 1850, however, those questions were not posed in the law. As a sexual being a wife belonged to her husband, and anyone who interfered with the husband's exercise of his right committed a punishable wrong.[17]

REPRESENTATION

In the treatises on the law of husband and wife (or baron and femme) sexual possession was at most a furtive presence, allocated no more than a page or two. By contrast, images of merger and of the complex rules that described whether and when a husband substituted for or represented his wife dominated the treatise literature. Defenders of orthodoxy assumed the family was a private corporate entity that naturally spoke with one voice, the voice of the husband-father. In the case law and in the treatises, however, marriage constituted a complex collection of unstable rights and interests and duties and future expectancies. The separate interests, rights, and properties of husband and wife were supposed to become one. But what it meant "to become one" depended on the doctrinal and institutional context. Some things that had been the wife's became the absolute and permanent property of the husband (for example, nearly all forms of personal property); some remained formally titled in the wife, but the title was covered over or represented by the husband during coverture (for example, real estate); some became the property of the corporate entity, "husband and wife," managed and controlled by the husband (for example, causes of action for wrongs like slander against the wife). Some causes of action would be conducted in the husband's name alone, even if the interest were the wife's. Some causes of action would be conducted in both of their names. Some causes of action might be conducted in her name alone, represented by her husband. He was often, although not always, responsible for her actions if she committed a wrong subject to criminal penalty. He was usually, although not always, responsible for the torts she might commit that subjected her to actions for civil damages. By marriage, his real estate ordinarily became freighted with dower rights: that is, he would theoretically have to secure her agreement to any sale of his real property so that she could protect her dower rights—her survivorship rights in his property after his death. All of these doctrinal consequences had local variants. Dower rights, for example, varied widely from jurisdiction to jurisdiction.

The rules of representation and substitution constructed the technical substratum of the law of marriage. A husband's rights under coverture were structured by diverse and nearly incomprehensible pleading rules that determined whose name should be used in a particular cause of action. To all but the most sophisticated and learned lawyers, the structure must have seemed indeterminate, nearly incomprehensible, unshaped by any apparent logic. Furthermore, much of the law revolved around issues of creditor's rights and the rights of third party beneficiaries, seemingly unconnected to the discourses of marital struggle. Marital property law was often produced by husbands (and secondarily by wives) who were playing a strategic game with a universe of creditors and libelants and others outside of the marriage. Committed patriarchal husbands with financially dependent wives would, without a backward glance, assert the separate or separated interests of their wives if by doing so they could secure an advantage in this game. We can imagine that real marital unity was often demonstrated by the willingness of a wife to become a feme sole formally, to insist on her separate interest, so that particular pieces of family wealth could be placed away from the grasp or reach of a husband's creditors who had secured (or were about to secure) a judgment against "his" property and the property under his representative control. The rights and interests asserted in pursuit of a family's foreign policy—its dealings, commercial and otherwise, with an "outside world"—might have little to do with perceptions and understandings of individual rights within the family. Like many areas of private law, the law of baron and femme would often have been experienced as a domain of strategic calculation largely devoid of political values or principles.

And yet we need to be careful not to oppose identity and strategy. Many cases, like Sarah Singleton's described in the last chapter, show us wives "working" the system as wives and as separate (often, separated) individuals. Her short-lived achievement was to force the Delaware courts to declare her own acts void because those acts conflicted with her coverture.

More important, in family lives as in the lives of nation-states, foreign policy and domestic relations were inextricably intertwined. For any number of purposes, distinctively so in the case of real property transactions, husbands, though rulers, needed the support of their wives. The rules of representation may have been imagined as a strategic game played with nonfamily third parties. But crucial moments in that game were played out between husband and wife within the family.

Dower rights and their release offered the paradigmatic situation.[18] By marriage, a wife acquired a right to dower if she survived her husband. Surviving her husband meant that she became a dowager, the possessor of, to simplify a bit, a one-third life interest in any real estate held by her husband during his life.[19] Dower stood as the analytic correlate of a husband's right "by curtesy" in all of his wife's real estate, that is, his absolute managerial control of all the landed wealth she brought to the marriage.[20] But dower was not structurally parallel to curtesy. It was at most a one-third life interest in land, a limited estate, and it only became vested at a husband's death. Until then, it was a mere expectancy.

Curtesy, by contrast, represented or symbolized a husband's absolute managerial control over all of his wife's property from the time of the marriage ceremony until his death, whether or not he survived her.

In the real world, a world where men ordinarily (although not always) managed their wives' property, curtesy was just a fact of life, not of particular interest legally (although obviously of crucial concern to many separating women). Dower, on the other hand, was an important and problematic right that intervened into the everyday (male) ownership and use of land.

Dower was, notoriously, a clog on land titles and on the market in land because a wife acquired a dowable interest in any and all land held by her husband at any time during the marriage. That is to say, all land held by a husband at any time became part of the pot out of which her one-third life interest would be constructed. Unless she signed a release of her interest, land that he sold was still freighted with her dower rights. Dower had made sense in a world in which a family was rooted to its land, where the sale of land was understood as an occasional, perhaps extraordinary, event in the life course, a world in which there would be little mystery (or litigation) in determining what land was dowable when a husband died. But in an America where land sales had become routine as men and women moved across the continent (sometimes together), in an America where the basic economic lesson was to hold property lightly, dower became in the (male) legal imagination a problem, a constraint, an atavism, in need of law reform.

So what was an American husband, a player in a commercial land market, a man interested in selling land, to do? Worse yet, what was the purchaser of a husband's land to do, since the rules of the game held that he, or his own purchaser (since the land often stayed in commercial play), might be holding property subject to the dower interest of the previous owner's wife? Once the previous owner died, the new dowager could march in and take it from him, at least for the duration of her life.

One answer, a source of much case law in nineteenth-century America, was to ignore the wife. Husbands and purchasers traded in land without obtaining the release of wives. Then when the widow appeared and insisted on her vested rights, men (and their lawyers) worked to find and to develop exceptions in the doctrine, to remake or destroy dower in pursuit of a property law that from their perspective suited an active land market.[21]

For more scrupulous husbands, the traditional answer, a source of much litigation in England and in America, was to negotiate. English law offered an alternative property interest for a wife, a separate estate called a jointure, from which she could live in her old age in exchange for relinquishing her dower rights. Or, in exchange for a release of dower, a wife might gain an alternative piece of property to her own use in trust, or the return of personal possessions, or she might ask her husband to care for relatives, for example, her children from an earlier marriage. When couples separated, dower was an inevitable subject of negotiation since no sane man would have wanted to have to find and buy off a separated wife when next he wished to deal with his property.[22] For men, however, an alternative to negotiation (or, maybe better, negotiation by other means) was violence and intimidation. And the Anglo-American world was full of stories of men abusing their wives—beating, torturing, imprisoning them—until they would agree to release their dower interests.[23]

One legal solution to the problem of coercion and abuse, a solution substantively inadequate yet ideologically satisfying, was the odd institution of the "separate examination." Before a husband could sell anything, before a wife's release would be accepted, the wife would be interviewed out of his presence by a justice of the peace or other official. The official would ask if her actions were voluntary and whether she had been intimidated by her husband. And she would tell him that they were and that she had not been intimidated. One can't avoid feeling some skepticism about this institution. An intimidating husband was still an intimidating husband, even when he waited in the next room while she had her separate examination. A terrorized wife remained a terrorized wife.[24]

The separate examination is, however, interesting as one more legal recognition that wives existed within coverture, that they had an identity that the law could not ignore. Moreover, judges used this formal requirement as a protective tool. Apparently trivial errors in the form of an examination would void the transaction where judges suspected coercion.[25] Still, the real work of dower and its releases occurred in private: in bed, at the fireside, and in lawyer's offices, as deals were worked out between husbands and wives. The main lesson of legal doctrine was that such negotiations were valid and the results of those negotiations enforceable, at least by courts of equity. Husbands who wanted to deal with family property, to represent their families in the world of commerce and trade, had to come to terms, one way or another, with their wives.

Courts, particularly courts of equity, strained to balance the formal and singular representation rights of the husband against the substantive interests of wives to support and protection. The baseline expectation was that a husband embodied—stood for—his marriage. There were, however, many situations and family choices that countered that expectation—among others, the existence of a separate use agreement, the absence of a husband, or particular medical crises. Courts were flexible in their recognition that representation could not always be unitary. A husband's perceived misconduct sometimes mobilized an equitable rhetoric that effectively recognized the separate interests of the wife.

When a wife dealt with family resources, courts usually assumed she did so because her husband trusted her. Sometimes that assumption would be negated either by a husband's public advertisement that he did not trust her or by the terms of a separation agreement. But in the ordinary course of marital life, a wife who shopped, or who bought goods for the family farm or business, was presumptively entrusted with her husband's credit. She represented him as his agent. Third parties—creditors and others—who trusted a woman as a wife could rely on their legal right to go after the husband.[26]

And yet so many decisions dealt with situations at the boundary—or beyond the boundary—of ordinary marital life. A separated wife was still presumptively entitled to act as her husband's agent, still entitled to his credit. Many separated wives, however, had either contracted away their rights or lost them because of misconduct. Sometimes, particularly when a husband disappeared, a merchant preferred to recover directly from a separated wife. But could he do so?

In 1812 Joseph Emmerson abandoned his wife Sally, leaving their home in Vermont and moving to Canada. Over the next few years, Sally bought goods, dealing with merchants as a feme sole. In 1816 she married Elisha Reynolds. (No divorce is mentioned in the case report. And the court insisted on identifying her not as the wife of Elisha Reynolds, but as "Sally Reynolds, . . . called the wife of Elisha Reynolds.") A decade later, the merchants sued Sally and Elisha for payment of her old debt. Sally and Elisha made the predictable defense: at the time she had incurred the debt, she was still married to Emmerson. The Vermont Supreme Court agreed. Absence alone did not "deprive" a husband of his marital rights. As of 1816, there was nothing to suggest that Joseph Emmerson had not intended to return. (Indeed, the court continued, there was nothing "even now" to keep him from reasserting authority, except for the inconvenient fact that his wife had remarried.) Since Joseph Emmerson retained his rights, she retained her disabilities, and the merchants lost.[27]

Or consider the story of the Murray cow. Murray had moved to Ohio, probably to escape his debts, leaving his wife and family in Orange County, New York. Wife and family were packing up their things to move to her father's house when the constable arrived to take away their cow and other property in execution of a debt owed to a man named Woodward. Murray's wife told the constable that she would give up the cow if other property were released, and the constable agreed.

Murray, back from Ohio, then sued Woodward for the return of the cow, arguing that an 1815 debtor relief statute exempted the cow from execution for debts as a "householder's" necessity. Woodward answered that Murray was no longer a householder, or even a resident of the state, "as the family had abandoned their habitation, because they were no longer able to keep house." But the trial judge charged the jury that Murray was a householder (even if he was in Ohio) and that his wife had not had the legal authority to release his cow. The verdict that predictably resulted was in Murray's favor. That decision was affirmed by the New York Supreme Court, which held that a wife did not have a right to waive her husband's privilege, "by turning out an only cow," in order to protect other nonexempt property from execution. Such actions required special authorization by her husband.[28]

By the late 1830s, courts began to recognize the separate authority of a mother within a maternal domain over her children. But as yet few assumed that a wife had independent authority to act, as a wife or as a mother, absent very specific legal circumstances. When Mrs. Gardner's husband went insane in the late 1820s, for example, Chancellor Walworth removed her from the guardianship of her nephew and niece, a guardianship that she had previously shared with her husband. "If it is improper for him to have the management of the estate," wrote the Chancellor, "it is equally improper for his wife, who is subject to his control."[29]

The expectation that a husband would ordinarily represent his wife shaped conduct in many contexts throughout nineteenth-century Amer-

ica. Early in the century, active upper-class women involved in benevolent reform organizations began to incorporate their societies. The result was that state governments "created accountable and legally
autonomous entities composed of married and therefore legally dependent women." Corporate status circumvented married women's formal
legal disabilities, created a legal "person" who was, for all practical purposes, "not female." And yet even the drafters of these corporate
charters could not escape the dilemmas of representation. How to create
entities that were legally and financially autonomous to a degree that
their married members were not? The answer found in the charter of the
Boston Female Asylum (1816), which became a model for others, made
the husband of every married woman who belonged to the society accountable for the funds his wife received.[30] Likewise, in 1822, the new
Baptized Church of Christ Friend to Humanity at Turkey Hill, Illinois,
passed rules to govern its membership. These included rules forbidding membership to any person "whose practice appears friendly to perpetual Slavery." Were there cases where slaveowners might be admitted
to membership? No, except "in the case of women, whose husbands opposed . . . emancipation." Here, to lay out the obvious contradiction, we
see a church confirm that a wife might have a separate moral identity
from her husband as a committed opponent of slavery. Yet, at the same
time, the church could not escape the legal recognition that she was, if
her husband was, a slaveholder. Her "practice" was his practice. He represented her to the outside world, and it took extraordinary effort for
the church to look behind his apparent presence, "to pierce the veil" of
coverture, to find the antislavery wife represented by the slaveholding
husband.[31]

GOVERNANCE

Within the Anglo-American legal culture, love was the necessary prerequisite for marriage. No rational participant in the culture assumed that a
wife had an absolute duty of submission before her husband, regardless
of who he was or how he behaved. As a 1792 English text put it, "the
husband first promises to love his wife, before she promises to obey
him." His love became the condition of her obedience, and she needed
obey only if he were loving.[32]

Yet, to pose the implicit marriage contract in that way (love for obedience), is to recognize that obedience was also a salient and crucial part of marriage.[33] The corollary of wife's obedience was husband's authority. A husband had authority over his wife and their children. He was—legally, conceptually, definitionally, morally—in charge. And, for the most part, his general authority over the family derived from his status as a husband.

In 1857, for example, Julius Maguinay sued Joseph Saudek for the seduction of Maguinay's stepdaughter. A natural father possessed such a right to a legal recovery, based on the "loss of services" resulting from her seduction. A stepfather who reared his wife's child was theoretically in exactly the same position.[34] Saudek's lawyer defended by challenging Maguinay's right to maintain the action. The trial judge instructed the jury that while a husband had a presumptive right to be head of his family, the defense had a right to try to prove that this stepfather was not holding that position, "that he in fact exercised no authority, government, or control over it [the family]; that he was a mere *cypher,* and that instead of being served by the members of the family he became their servant." The Tennessee Supreme Court held that the trial judge's instructions had been wholly erroneous. "By the common law the husband is the sole and absolute head of the family: and of this character and relation, with its attendant rights and obligations he cannot be divested." The mother's authority had been suspended by her remarriage, and neither she nor her children could do any act to prejudice or limit her husband's rights. From "motives of expediency," as well as a desire to avoid "utter confusion and derangement in all domestic relations," no inquiry into the actual structure of decisionmaking within a family would be permitted. A husband was "conclusively presumed" to possess the status of head of family.[35]

"As a general rule," intoned the treatises, a husband had "an entire right to the person of his wife," and he might use "gentle means to constrain her liberty."[36] Rollin Hurd's 1858 treatise on the writ of habeas corpus and the right of personal liberty included a chapter that rehearsed the received clichés that justified a husband's authority over an errant wife: the law favored "industry, economy and a well regulated household." It required "the husband to maintain the wife and to repair whatever injuries she may inflict upon others." It held "domestic habits to be befitting the wife and mother," and it abhorred "a dishonored bed." Thus, Hurd continued, the law armed the husband with power to regulate his household: "If his wife inclines to extravagant living he may protect his estate and prevent her from squandering it. If she foresakes her duties to her family and gads about to scandalize her neighbors or reform the race, he may bring her home and keep her there. If she burns with 'free love' he may protect his honor and exclude her from all associations by which it is endangered."[37]

And yet the moment Hurd shifted his attention to the actual remedies the law provided authoritarian husbands, his discussion became confused and uncertain. The husband's right of chastisement and correction was never an unquestioned right. Yet, he insisted, a husband retained the right to confine and restrain his wife. But such restraint could not be intended as punishment, only as a preventative remedy, always limited by the "natural rights" of a wife, of which coverture had not deprived her. Except for one English case, widely criticized on both sides of the Atlantic, no case Hurd cited really confirmed the availability of the remedy of confinement. Indeed, several of the authorities he surveyed suggested that any attempt to lock up a wife would justify her in escaping, would entitle her to a writ of habeas corpus, would offer her grounds for a divorce. A husband had, Hurd still insisted (a bit desperately), authority to confine his wife to his dwelling when it was justified. In doing so, however, he could not lock her up, deprive her of light and air and exercise, nor of the society of himself or her family, nor could he exclude her from intercourse with neighbors. What he retained was the bare power to "make her live with himself at home as his wife."[38]

Most law writers wrote in similar tones. The law seemed to offer few real means for men to secure the obedience of their wives. And that was as it should be. Men did not need legal means—external intervention—to establish their legitimate authority over their dependents, and a husband endangered his standing, "both as a gentleman and a Christian, by an indiscreet attempt to enforce what he believed to be his marital and paternal rights."[39] When "recourse" was "had even to moderate chastisement . . . an everlasting farewell may be bid to all prospects of pleasure and felicity."[40] Or as Hurd dryly noted, "The precise value of a wife requiring such surveillance, the law furnishes no rules for estimating."[41]

The internal dialogue of the law—the discourse produced by judges and treatise writers—took blanket statements of patriarchal authority and interrogated them, exploring qualification and limitations in the black-letter rules. Edward Mansfield's 1845 work was typical. He began with the familiar statement, "As a general rule, the husband has an entire right to the person of his wife, and may use gentle means to constrain her liberty." He ended with a more elaborate set of qualifications, which overwhelmed the initial assertion: a wife retained "her personal responsibility for moral action" and her "rights of conscience." Her husband had no right to coerce her. She had remedies, "as much as any other citizen, against his illegal acts." She had a right to personal liberty. And if he used force, she had a right to charge him criminally.[42]

In the writings of reformers and woman's rights activists, however, such qualifications on husbands' powers of governance disappeared. Marriage was, definitionally but unnaturally, a structure of oppression. Coverture existed to destroy a woman's independence and to "crush her individuality." Through the law, man had "exercised the most unlimited and brutal power over woman, in the peculiar character of husband,—a word in most countries synonymous with tyrant." Central demands of the early woman's rights conventions, notably those at Seneca Falls in 1848, revolved around the legal consequences of marriage. "[M]arital bondage" was the operative phrase, and much of the rhetoric played nervously with an analogy between the legal power of the husband and that of the slave master.[43]

At the same time, a standard nineteenth-century story, found in fiction as well as in autobiographies and memoirs and trial transcripts, detailed a wife's discovery of her capacity for disobedience and resistance, of a less coverture-encumbered self. Implicit, never explicit, in that story was the complementary realization that the law offered a less monotonal picture of power than had been predicted. Abigail Bailey told one early version of that story. Elizabeth Packard detailed an elaborate, Civil War-era, variation. In Jane Swisshelm's version, her husband was not so much an evil and/or corrupt tyrant, as an ignorant and conventional man. When her mother was dying sometime in the early 1840s, she was called back to Pennsylvania from Louisville, where her husband had taken her. He tried to keep her from going, since, according to Jane, she had just started a business there that he was dependent on. He quoted scripture to her (Ephesians, verse 22) about wives submitting to their husbands. She worked through the passage and rejected it. He then told her that he had a legal right to detain her and that he would exercise that right. She "assured him the attempt would be as dangerous as useless," for she was going to Pittsburgh. And so she did.[44]

When she left, her husband had no way to stop her legally. Yet, although she had disobeyed him, she had not yet "separated" from him or from her disabilities as a feme covert. When, sometime later, her mother died, her mother's will left everything to trustees to hold separately for Jane and her sister. Her husband felt himself wronged, excluded, distrusted. Still, he had one remedy. As the "owner" of Jane's "person and services," he had a right to repayment by the estate for Jane's wages for the time spent nursing her mother (which she had done against his will), and he filed his claim against the executors. Of this act, Jane wrote:

> I do not know why I should have been so utterly overwhelmed by this proposal to execute a law passed by Christian legislators for the government of Christian people. . . . Why should the discovery of its existence curdle my blood, stop my heart-beats, and send a rush of burning shame from forehead to finger-tip? Why should I have blushed that my husband was a law-abiding citizen of the freest country in the world? Why blame him for acting in harmony with the canons of every Christian church—aye, of that one of which I was a member, and proud of its history as a bulwark of civil liberty? Was it any fault of his that "all that she (the wife) can acquire by her labor-service or act during coverture, belongs to her husband?" Certainly not. Yet that law made me shrink . . .

And soon thereafter she separated from her husband.[45]

One crucial nineteenth-century story of rebellion against a husband's authority was played out on the field of religious belief. A wife's obligation to take on the beliefs and the religious identity of her husband was an ordinary aspect of coverture, indistinguishable from her obligation to live where he wished or her obligation to take his settlement as her own.[46] The boundary between a wife who had to be disciplined because she "burned with free love" and one who merely insisted on her independent access to religious truth could be faint. According to Chancellor Walworth, writing in a notorious but authoritative 1832 separation case, if a wife's only reason for leaving her husband was that he had refused to allow her to attend a particular church, then she had no good reason for separating: "Although it was an act of great unkindness and of unreasonable oppression on the part of the husband . . . , I have no hesitation in saying that she mistook her duty in not submitting to the oppressor, if she could not win his consent by kindness and condescension."[47]

The figure of the devout wife unable to worship as she chose because of a loutish or drunken or unredeemed husband became a staple of nineteenth-century reform rhetoric. No other act by a husband seemed as inconsistent with the love and respect that ought to provide the foundation for a proper marriage. No other act, sanctioned by law, so clearly opposed the corrupted power of the received orthodoxy against the demands of morality. A man could be a drunk yet deserve the care and sympathy and fidelity of his wife. A man who used his legal power to keep his wife from worshipping according to her lights, on the other hand, had earned her disobedience.[48]

For Jane Swisshelm, the story of religious conflict preceded the breakdown of her marriage. When she was first courted by her husband, she was a strict and genteel Presbyterian, he a lower-class Methodist. She worried that he would make her convert, but he promised that he would never interfere with her "rights of conscience." He promised her that he would take or send her to her services "when possible," but sometimes she should expect to go with him to his services. As soon as they were married, however, he broke his word. He would not take her to her old church, leaving her to walk the seven miles by herself. "In this change, he but followed that impulse which led the men of England, centuries ago, to enact, that 'marriage annuls all previous contracts between the parties.'" His family wanted her to preach as a converted Methodist, since she was cultivated and well educated and spoke well. She, on the other hand, had been raised to believe the Pauline admonition that women should be silent in church. When she raised that precept, her husband responded: "Wives, obey your husbands [and preach]." But she stood her ironic ground and refused and continued to attend her own church.[49]

The law may not have provided husbands with a direct remedy for their wives' disobedience. Little in the law, however, challenged the continuing cultural expectation that a good wife was an obedient wife. Once in court, marital conflicts—about property ownership, about child custody, about all the technical issues that separations raised—almost always turned on the question of obedience. Litigants understood that the law required wives to be obedient or, at least, required wives to present themselves as if they had been so. Thus, wives seeking relief from courts uniformly began their pleas with the claim that they had been "always obedient." Obedience was the quality that entitled them to the care and support of their husbands or, more relevantly, to the intervention of the court. Conversely, the responses of their husbands recharacterized their wives as "always disobedient." Because of their wives' disobedience, they argued, courts had no right to intervene or to impose conditions on husbands' conduct.[50]

In legal texts of the 1840s one can begin to read sketches of alternative rhetorics. In a few custody cases, mothers argued that their failures as wives—their disobedience—did not disable them as mothers.[51] Much of the rhetoric of mid-century law reform developed images of marital partnerships, of marriages that joined two equal (or nearly equal) rights bearers together. But these were radical challenges to a prevailing and very long-standing cultural understanding of marriage as a structure of governance. The law may have been a weak enforcer of that understanding, but it was part of the same culture. In the law, as in the culture generally, wives revealed their virtue by their submission before their husbands' lawful authority. And husbands governed their families.

HUSBAND'S DUTIES

At the end of Shakespeare's *Taming of the Shrew*, after Petruchio has made a good wife of Katherine, the former shrew lectures her flighty sister on why a wife ought to obey her husband:

> Thy husband is thy lord, thy life, thy keeper,
> Thy head, thy sovereign; one that cares for thee,
> And for thy maintenance commits his body
> To painful labour both by sea and land,
> To watch the night in storms, the day in cold,
> Whilst thou liest warm at home, secure and safe
> And craves no other tribute at thy hands
> But love, fair looks and true obedience
> Too little payment for so great a debt.
> Such duty as the subject owes the prince
> Even such a woman oweth to her husband;
> And when she is froward, peevish, sullen, sour,
> And not obedient to his honest will,
> What is she but a foul contending rebel,
> And graceless traitor to her loving lord? (Act V, sc. ii)

This speech is often read as proof of Kate's submission, her defeat.[52] What is significant for our purposes are its evocations of central themes of early modern political theory, themes of continuing significance in the nineteenth-century law of marriage. At the heart of Kate's language lay a conception of the reciprocity that ought to exist between rulers and ruled. Wives owed fealty and obedience to their princes, so long as those princes behaved as princes. A wife gave her obedience "to his honest will," not to his willfullness. A wife ought not rebel against a loving lord. But nothing in the discourse required a wife to submit to cruelty or to tyranny.

A wife had a right to be supported by her husband. We need to stop and be very clear what that right meant. It did not mean that a wife had a right not to work or a right to be taken care of, as we might use the latter phrase today. The right to support grew out of coverture, out of a wife's distinctive legal identity. It also grew out of her labor within the household. A wife labored for her husband. If she worked for wages, her wages belonged to him. If she worked at home, the products of her labor belonged to him. He had a right to compel her to work. He was, however, obligated to provide for her, to use his resources to house, feed, and clothe her in a manner consistent with their place in the social order, in a manner suitable to their condition in life. He "kept house" for her (not the other way around), and within his house, he supported her.

The content of the duty to support was defined by the husband's material circumstances. Nothing about the duty suggested a minimum wage or a minimum level of support. To the contrary, courts took it as a given that the legally supportable needs of a rich woman would be very different from those that a poor woman could lay claim to.[53]

Within the law of marriage, the rhetoric of "duty to support" was pervasive, playing a particularly important role in actions for judicial separations and divorces and for enforcement of (or for voiding) separate maintenance agreements.[54] The duty explained a husband's privileges. "[A]s he cannot be heard, on the one hand, to allege, as an excuse for his failure to discharge the duties of husband or father, his own unfitness, or want of adaptation, to the character or relation he occupies, so neither on the other hand, can he be deprived of the rights, privileges and authority properly belonging to him as head of the family."[55]

Within the case law and the treatises, explicit discussion of the duty focused on two doctrinal subjects: the law of necessaries and the equitable theory of a "wife's equity" in an inheritance. The first of these, the law of necessaries, was, in form, framed by the right of a merchant to recover from a husband for goods purchased by a wife acting as her husband's apparent agent. In practice, necessaries cases always arose in situations where a husband had refused to trust his wife, almost always in situations where husband and wife were separated from one another, and the "merchants" bringing such cases often were parents or relatives or friends of the wife who sued to recover for the room and board of the wife. Such plaintiffs were probably surrogates for the separated wife.

Where husband and wife lived together, courts never substituted their judgment as to the needs of the wife for that of her husband. *McGuire v. McGuire* would have been good law at any time during the nineteenth century (or before). A court would not require a husband to account for what were and what were not necessaries for a woman sharing his station in life if she were living within his household.[56]

For separated couples, the basic rule was that a husband had a duty to provide those goods—clothes, food, housing—that would make it possible for his wife to continue to live at the level of society to which she was accustomed by marriage. The simple black-letter rule stated that he would be bound by her contracts for necessaries whenever he refused to provide them, whatever her conduct, however wanton or disobedient she might have been.[57]

Necessaries cases typically arose in two somewhat different situations, each of which evoked a distinctive theory of a husband's obligation. In the first, the wife had left her husband, and she was presumptively wrong to have done so. Did a husband still have an obligation to support her? No, according to the orthodox understanding of the law, assuming that he had "advertised" that she had abandoned him and that he did not wish merchants to "trust" her with any goods or wares.

The source of that understanding was the seventeenth-century English case of *Manby v. Scot*.[58] This was, according to Sir Robert Hyde, whose opinion in the court of Exchequer Chamber carried the day, the "meanest" case ever decided by that court, but one that "toucheth every Man in point of his Power and Dominion over his Wife" and that concerned "the Woman in point of her Substance and Livelihood." Hyde's opinion constituted a compilation of images of marital subordination. One flesh, a rigid and literal conception of coverture, the "fact" that "the Husband" was "Head of the Wife," as "the King" was "Head of the Commonwealth," all played a part, as did an assumption of institutional incompetence, that a court was presumptively the wrong place for such a wife to find relief for her needs. Hyde emphasized two arguments. A judgment for the merchant would be "inconvenient." If a wife's contract, made against the will of her husband, were to bind him, it would be in her power, in spite of the "Law of God and of the Land," to rule him and to undo him. Then the wife could be her own "Carver," able to judge for herself "the Fitness of her Apparel, of the Time when it" was "necessary for her to have new Cloaths, and as often as she" pleased, "without asking the Advice or Allowance of her Husband." Once wives possessed such powers, would they still "depend on the Kindness and Favours of their Husbands, or be observant towards them as they ought to be?" Second, judgment for the merchant would be wrong morally and politically, would ignore a wife's treason. Some might think that even when a wife left her husband, she still remained his wife, "and she ought not to Starve." But Hyde disagreed: "If a Woman be of so haughty a Stomach, that she will chuse to Starve, rather than Submit and be reconciled to her Husband; she may take her own Choice: The Law is in no Default, which doth not provide for such a Wife." If she were to die from starvation, it would have been her own fault. "Her evil demeanour brought it upon her, and her Death ought to be imputed to her own Wickedness."[59]

In *Manby* the wife had tried to return to her husband's household but had been turned away. To Hyde and the majority on the English court, her attempted reconciliation was irrelevant. Her abandonment was the definitive event. She had lost her place within her husband's household. American law writers disagreed, although they recognized the *Manby* rule as established doctrine (usually rendered as "Those who trust a wife, who has separated from her husband, do it at their peril"). And they highlighted a number of early nineteenth-century cases that modified and interpreted *Manby*.[60]

In 1801, for example, Ellen M'Gahey had left her husband, leaving him with a six-month-old child. Why had she deserted? The case record is sparse, but it seems that her father had moved away, and she wanted to visit him, but her husband had refused permission. So she had gone anyway, and when her husband asked her to take the child along, she told him she would not do so. Soon thereafter he placed an advertisement in the local newspapers: "Whereas my wife, Ellen M'Gahey, has left my bed and board, without any provocation, this is to forewarn all persons crediting her on my account, as I am determined to pay no debts of her contracting." Evidently, Ellen quickly changed her mind and over the next fourteen years tried repeatedly to reconcile. But M'Gahey always refused, saying, "that she had played him a trick; that she had left him with one young child, and if he took her back again she might stay till they had more, and then leave him with four or five." In 1813 she applied to the local overseers for poor relief. An overseer called on M'Gahey to try again to convince him to reconcile or, failing that, to secure her support. Again, however, M'Gahey refused to have anything to do with her.

Soon thereafter, Ellen's father, with whom she was living, brought an action against her husband for her room and board. At trial, M'Gahey proved that she had left him without his consent "and contrary to his entreaties." None of her attempts to reconcile with him were put into evidence. The jury held for him, and, when the case was appealed to the New York Supreme Court, the court affirmed the jury verdict. According to Justice Platt, to give her father a remedy "would encourage disobedience and infidelity in the wife." A husband was only bound to support his wife "in his family." So long as he had committed no act of "cruelty," and so long as he was "willing to provide her a house, and all necessaries there," he was "not bound to furnish them elsewhere."

Along the way to that decision, Platt had noted that the case would have been a much more difficult one if Mrs. M'Gahey had tried to reconcile with her husband and been refused. The reader will not be surprised to learn, therefore, that, shortly after the conclusion of the first appeal, her father tried again to recover her board and lodging. In the second trial, much was made of her "unblemished reputation" and of the many efforts she had made to reconcile with her husband. The jury ruled in favor of the plaintiff, and the New York Supreme Court confirmed, holding that where there was a proven offer to return on the part of the wife, as there was in this case, the husband would become liable for her necessaries.[61]

Decisions to enforce necessaries often had much to do with the desire of public officials to compel husbands to support impoverished wives. Much of family law, then as now, was shaped by the deep desires of public officials—including judges—to pass the costs of welfare on to private individuals, whether "deadbeat dads" or "heartless husbands."[62] Even if we grant that material cause as the explanation for decisions like *M'Gahey*, it is important to hold on to the salience of the label of heartless husband. To nineteenth-century judges and treatise writers, a wife was wrong to leave her husband of her own volition. But a husband was also wrong not to forgive her and "receive" her again, when she repented her wrong and tried to return to him. A good husband, one entitled to the rights of a husband, was a forgiving husband, a good ruler, not a mean-spirited man who insisted on his formal rights.

Adultery was the formal boundary of such legally coerced forgiveness. According to the orthodox understanding, no husband could be compelled to take his wife back, or to provide necessaries for her support, if she were an adulteress. Yet, even here, one senses some disquiet. Tapping Reeve regarded that principle, at least in its starkest form, as "liable to strong objections." Reeve who, according to Catherine Beecher, was noted for "his chivalrous devotion to woman both in and out of the domestic circle," thought that holding a husband chargeable for the purchases of his adulterous wife made perfect sense unless the merchant-plaintiff "had notice, or unless it [the adultery] had become a matter of notoriety."[63]

The second model situation for a necessaries case was one that followed the wrongful separation of husband from wife. When the husband was innocent, or at least not known to be at fault, courts were quite deferential to his discretionary judgment as to the needs of his wife.[64] But where he had abandoned her, or where he had abused her or misbehaved so that she was compelled to leave him, his discretionary authority was at an end. And courts felt free to substitute their judgment about the needs of a wronged wife. It was as if an institutional switch had been flipped. Judges no longer assumed a husband's right to organize his private sphere as he chose. How he fulfilled his duties became matters of public concern and scrutiny.

Thus, a husband whose wife had left him because of his adultery with a servant girl had no capacity to forbid her from purchasing goods as his agent. Indeed, his actions had effectively granted her "a credit with the whole community." Nor, according to the New York Superior Court, could he require her to reside in his house where he had promised to support her. "She had a right to live apart from her husband, and to be supported by him."[65]

When a husband was "at fault," he could avoid continuing responsibility for a wife's purchases only by agreeing to an adequate separate maintenance for her, by creating a fund that would allow her to act effectively outside of his control. Once the fund was in place, a court might free him from responsibility for her necessaries. But a mere "naked promise" to make a separate maintenance agreement was not enough.

And the substantive terms of any agreement between separated husband and still dependent wife were subject to judicial scrutiny. After all, too quick a discharge from responsibility might leave the wife "to subsist on charity."[66]

According to James Kent and other early nineteenth-century chancellors, the wrongfully separated wife was entitled not just to her necessaries, but to the continuing protection of a court of equity. And in the important 1830 Maryland case of *Helms v. Franciscus,* Maryland's Chancellor Theoderick Bland built on Kent's work to rule that Anna Gebetha Margaretta Wandelohr (Newhaus) Helms had a right to keep her long-separated husband from her recent inheritance.

According to Lewis Helms, he had married Anna in 1819, thinking she was a respectable widow keeping a store in Chambersburg, Pennsylvania. To his horror, he had discovered that she had an illegitimate child. After he confronted her, she and her friends "locked him in a room" and "by great threats of personal violence" tried to force him to release all his marital rights in her property and to leave the area. At first he refused. But then Anna got hold of family papers containing compromising information. She defamed and slandered him. He was sued on a debt and imprisoned. He tried to make peace, but she rejected his overtures. She made plans to have him again imprisoned. He, coerced and defeated, finally agreed to a separation agreement by which he relinquished his claims over her property. According to Lewis, he had signed knowing that the agreement was illegal and void. He had, he concluded, always treated her kindly, and he was still willing to do so if she wished to live with him. But, whether she lived with him or not, he was, as her husband, entitled to her inheritance.[67]

Bland's opinion quickly disposed of Lewis Helms's pretensions. The cause of this "angry separation" resulted from Anna's examination of his papers that revealed "his really vicious, sordid character." He was a fortune hunter who had married her only for her expectation of an inheritance. Their separation agreement was not coerced. It was, rather, the fruit of their "settled dislike" for each other. Helms had never supported Anna before or after the separation. Indeed, he had always remained "in the very lowest condition of insolvency," and he had never "made one single manly effort to rise above that condition." By contrast, Anna Helms sustained "a good character," was "industrious," and had run a boardinghouse. Her efforts to earn a living counted in her favor.[68]

Bland then set out the relevant law. He began by insisting on the non-negotiability of the marriage contract. In marrying, Lewis and Anna had imposed duties on themselves, duties intended as much for public welfare as for "private happiness," duties that they were "never permitted to cast off at their pleasure." But then Bland shifted. Although the common law left a wife "absolutely submerged and covered over" by her husband, deprived of all means of saving herself from "the most abject penury," thankfully there existed the principles of equity as a counterbalance. As a result, "the stern and ungallant" common law rules had been compelled to yield to "a better feeling" and to "wholesome modifications." Before a court of equity, a wife could be protected against an abusive, intemperate, or impecunious husband. Because of equity, a wife was not entirely "destitute" of contractual capacity and, "in particular situations," husband and wife might "treat together effectually, if they treat[ed] upon fair and reasonable terms." As they had in this case.[69]

Was their agreement enforceable at equity? Anna, of course, wanted the inheritance settled on her, under the terms of the agreement. But insofar as the agreement pretended to "dissolve" the marriage, it was clearly void. And Chancellor Bland worried about a direct recognition of her separate rights. Theoretically, a court of equity could have settled the whole inheritance on her. The Chancellor, however, would do so only if he were convinced that her husband's actions in marrying her were entirely "sordid" and "corrupt." In this case, all Bland had were suspicions. At the same time, Bland could not "assume or admit the position" that a married woman was "entitled to the whole of her separate property to her separate use, in direct opposition to the clearest principles of the marriage contract."[70]

What to do? Bland turned to the concept of a "wife's equity," a concept that New York's Chancellor Kent had elaborated on in a series of decisions. To Kent, a "wife's equity" was a fund to be drawn out of the property that a wife brought to the marriage, out of the resources that a husband gained control of through the magic of coverture. The fund was intended to provide reasonable support for her and her children. Such a fund did not exist in common law theory. Title and control of all personal property belonged entirely to the husband at common law. Such a fund was created out of the distrust of chancellors asked to help husbands secure their control. It existed as a counter to the common law rules, as a way to reconcile a husband's moral duty to support with the apparent absolute title of coverture. A husband could only get the inheritance to which he was legally entitled if he first did what equity demanded he do, which was to make "an adequate provision" for his wife.[71]

Petitioners like Lewis Helms needed courts of equity to gain possession of their wives' inheritances. Before the chancellors would act, though, the husbands had to show that they had made an "adequate" provision to their wives. In setting this condition, chancellors were not challenging husbands' private authority. They would use "no active means" to make a husband provide his "wife's equity"; they only proposed "to him who asks equity, that he should do equity." And one way a husband might "do equity" for his wife was by giving her the right to hold property to her separate use. The agreement between Lewis and Anna, rather than a contract between husband and wife changing the terms of their given relationship, became instead a constructive gift to the wife by the husband of his interest in his wife's estate. It became valid and enforceable because it came "in aide of the equity" that would give a wife "a provision out of her own fortune" when she was not properly supported by her husband.[72]

To Bland, following Kent's lead, courts of equity ensured the security of dependent wives. Equity law complemented and complicated common law coverture, incorporating into the orthodox legal discourse substantive moral standards of care and support. Amasa Parker and Charles Baldwin, who edited the third edition (1862) of Reeve's treatise on the law of baron and femme, characterized the general ascendancy of Kent's views as "a striking instance of the healthful influence of a court of chancery in guarding the rights of the helpless and unprotected."[73] We should remain skeptical. In the first place, Kent's conception of "wife's equity" was considerably weakened by later judicial decisions. In 1837, for example, Kent's successor Reuben Walworth denied that he had any capacity to compel a husband's creditors to make a suitable provision for a wife in the absence of clear evidence that they had conspired with him. Instead, Walworth deferred to the common law rule that a husband took an immediate vested interest in his wife's real estate and held an absolute right to all her personal property.[74] Second, chancery's capacity to guard and to intervene depended on a husband coming to equity. Sophisticated husbands with improper designs on their wives' resources learned to avoid the scrutiny of equity whenever possible. Finally, it is important to remember the restricted range of "the helpless and unprotected" that appeared before courts of equity. While it is not true that everyone who appeared before a chancellor was, by definition, wealthy, it is true that only women who gained resources during their marriages had a claim on the attention of courts of equity.[75]

Still, the language of a wife's equity demonstrates the complexity of a husband's legal identity under the traditional rules. For most purposes, a husband acted as a husband within a private sphere, without need to explain or justify his conduct by public standards. How he fulfilled his duties to those who depended on him was left to his own judgment. But once he had provoked judicial suspicion by abusing his wife's vulnerability, by exhibiting "conjugal unkindness," by insisting on excessive enforcement of his marital rights, everything changed. Suddenly, his rights as a husband no longer served as a kind of immunity. He became vulnerable to the discretionary judgments of public officials, including judges. All his capacities as a husband, his rights to possess, to represent, and to govern his wife, all might be limited and even destroyed.

And out of such remedies came the theoretical security that allowed wives to risk giving husbands the "love, fair looks and true obedience" that Shakespeare's Kate, at least, thought they were entitled to.

HUSBAND'S NEEDS

To nineteenth-century critics, remedies like the law of necessaries or the notion of a wife's equity to her inheritance were famously inadequate. A husband's capacity for abuse and misconduct remained fundamentally unsanctioned. Indeed, critics often wrote as if the law itself was the source of a husband's intemperance, violence, and fraud.

Some advocated a reformed and reconstructed law of marriage. Others imagined that resort to extralegal sanctions was required to bring a bad husband to an awareness of his duties. Jane McManus, whom we have met as the young lover of the aged Aaron Burr, worked as a publicist for the Anglo community in the Republic of Texas. In her description of the virtues of that new republic, she emphasized the availability there of the "stern primary law of self-preservation" as a singular protection for defenseless wives, a better law than the law.

There was a man in northeastern Texas who had the "amiable" habit of biting and pinching his wife, "just for his own independent amusement," when he was drunk, which was regularly. His wife, helpless and sickly, endured him because he had brought her and their children from Pennsylvania, and she knew no one in Texas. In Pennsylvania, the law had permitted the man "to squander his wife's little inheritance of three thousand dollars, against her will and entreaties, and leave her and her babes without a shelter." But now, in Texas, her new community resolved to protect her, even if she could not protect herself. "In full assemblage," it decided to impose one hundred lashes on the husband by "impromptu common law." Twenty volunteer sheriffs carried out the sentence, "while his wife in vain implored for him the mercy he had never extended to her." The results were salutary. "Lynch law effectually frightened him into better behavior—for the brutal coward who can raise his hand against a woman is exactly of the mould to yield to fear and brute force." And the wife became "a prosperous woman" in a "secure home."[76]

Jane McManus's moral was a familiar one. The law—the received law—would never make abusive men into responsible husbands. Only an organized moral community could coerce better conduct from bad men. The duties and rights inscribed in orthodox legal discourse were faint security for the wife of a malicious or abusive man. She was, literally, powerless.

For those committed to the traditional order, that powerlessness, that legal incapacity, was no argument for change. It was, indeed, what marriage ought to produce. The law of husbands' duties, along with the other aspects of the law of baron and feme, was not written for the benefit of wives, even for suffering wives. The various restraints on husbands' powers that judges and treatise writers found in the legal discourse were never understood as rights possessed by wives. Although some wives were able to use the language of restraint to gain relief from abuse, and occasionally to secure property to their separate use, that language did not exist for them.

The law of coverture rationalized and justified a structure of power. It existed for husbands as a ruling class, expressed a particular male vision of responsibility and duty and power. And, along the way, it confirmed good husbands in their identities as good husbands, among other things by identifying and sanctioning bad husbands.

The structure of reciprocity—of duty for obedience, rights for support—that appeared to organize the received law of coverture was less a distribution of rights between husbands and wives and more a way

of conceptualizing the terms of being a husband. Men became husbands through their commitment, their allegiance, to that picture of
who they were.[77]

The role of the law of coverture in constructing a husbandly identity
bears some resemblance to the role slave law played in stilling the moral
conscience of the American slaveholder. Just as slaveholders needed
slave law, so husbands needed coverture. Just as slaveholders derived
moral legitimacy from a slave legal code that represented them as virtuous by distinguishing them from their (more) abusive brethren, so conservative men emphasized the constraints and sanctions that defined the
boundaries of a husband's power and discretion. Just as slaveholders had
to contend with a liberal legal culture that challenged the rightfulness of
who they were, so conventional nineteenth-century American husbands
had to face growing conflict (not least of all within their own hearts and
minds) over the justness of rights they had been socialized to believe
were constitutive of identity.

"Would you make Prince Alberts of us all?" asked Charles Tyler Botts
of the reformers who promised to change the face of marriage by introducing marital property reform.[78] The question resonates with images of
female sovereignty and male incompetence, images of role reversal and
of a world turned upside down. The prospect of being a Prince Albert, a
man ruled by his wife, was a terrifying one for many Americans. Men
needed coverture. And when reformers talked of an end to coverture, of
an emancipation of wives, they hit men, literally, where they lived.

6

Coercion and Harriet Douglas Cruger

We know no way of preventing wives from presenting their husbands
either with their possessions or their earnings, if they feel so disposed,
and we have no doubt wives will continue to do so as long as wives are
women and husbands men.
    The New York Times, *February 10, 1860*

Coercion was all over the early nineteenth-century law of marriage. But
to understand the role of coercion in the law of marriage, we need to distinguish two different ways of using the word. One, today identified
with legal realism and critical legal theory (and with the later writings of
Michel Foucault), takes coercion as part of a systemic description of social institutions, as constitutive of power relations. Thus, one speaks of
the labor market or of marriage as a coercive institution.[1] The other
makes coercion into a synonym for abuse or mistreatment or duress. An
individual, within an institutional practice like marriage, makes a decision she would not have made but for coercion. Her will was "overborne." She had desires, wishes recognizably her own. Nonetheless, they
were taken away from her. She was coerced.[2] Both notions were important to eighteenth- and early nineteenth-century legal writers, but they
would only have identified the latter usage with the word "coercion."

Still, a tacit understanding of marriage as about structured inequality
pervaded the law of husband and wife. There was, of course, resistance,
but to the extent that wives and husbands bargained and worked together toward cooperative ends—for example, wealth, children, survival, happiness—they did so in the context of an unequal and coercive
institution, one in which women were systematically deprived of rights
that men gained.

Law was both marginal and constitutive within that tacit understanding. It was marginal in that power—at least marital or sexual power—was understood as prelegal, leaving the law in the position of a marginal actor, an occasional regulator, mopping up the mess that the social world or testosterone had left behind. It was constitutive in that the rights and duties of marriage, marriage as a practice, existed within a legal order. Husbands were ontologically more powerful than wives. Marriage was a husband's private sphere. A husband's will ruled. But a line also had to be drawn between the systemic coercion or inequality of everyday marriage and physical abuse and cruelty, between legitimate and illegitimate domination, between everyday domination and the coercion that the law should recognize.

The law of coverture articulated that line. And coverture helped make the structured inequality that was marriage morally acceptable. To the extent that one took unequal power as a preexisting fact, recognizing wives as separate legal beings—identifying them with separate legal rights and separated legal identities and contractual freedom—would never have been anything but a sham. Worse, such recognition would have invited men to violence and abuse, to coercion (in the second sense). Men would still get their way, but they would have done so through force and intimidation. A wife legally recognized as a separate legal actor, yet still weak relative to her husband, would either have given in immediately when her interests appeared to conflict with her husband's, or she would have been subjected to his violence, his cruelty, perhaps to murder. The law could not make her powerful, her husband's equal. So the law, in its Hobbesian wisdom, declared that men were entirely responsible for their wives. Then the law regulated husbands, sometimes even punished them, when they failed in their duties, their responsibilities to care for their dependents. What the law would control, it first legalized.

All of a wife's apparently independent legal acts could, presumptively, be understood as coerced by her husband. The law could never recognize her as free of his influence and power. In almost any possible situation, an investigation into the freedom of her will, whether her will had been overborne, what her true and free choice would have been, how she should have decided in the absence of coercion, was an impossible one, a task that no judge or decisionmaker could safely undertake. To decide whether coercion (in the second sense) existed, a court had to imagine or hypothesize a choice or decision *but for* her husband, in the absence of her husband's presence and influence. Yet in a legal culture that took seriously the transformation of woman into wife, that imaginative act, that counterfactual, was both difficult and morally dangerous, so long as husband and wife remained united. So, instead, the law declared her to be a feme covert and focused all its attention on the husband alone, holding him responsible for what otherwise would have been recognized as her civil or criminal acts.

Thus, if one takes the danger of coercion as a starting point for legal analysis, coverture, far from posing a moral dilemma for legal theorists, appeared to resolve some of the anxiety and disquiet the legal consequences of marriage raised for a morally sensitive male soul. It even makes a kind of sense out of the infamous last two sentences of Blackstone's chapter on the law of husband and wife, where he claimed that coverture's disabilities were intended for a wife's benefit and where he asserted that a wife became "a favourite" of the law.[3] Coverture meant that the law could limit the strategic behavior of husbands. Coverture denied a husband the capacity to use his wife's separate identity and separate estate to achieve his own ends. Meanwhile, the wife could become "a favourite," protected from responsibility.

And yet the "logic" of coverture could never explain the institutional settings and practices that grew up around it. Why did courts of equity recognize and legitimate separate estates for unseparated wives? Why did they create a separate equitable identity for some women, who would, we might imagine, then have become still more vulnerable to their husbands? Many eighteenth- and early nineteenth-century judges and chancellors asked these questions, as they decided cases dealing with the enforcement of separate use agreements and trusts. For at least some judges, the answer was clear. Separate estates existed because of the structural reality of marital coercion. Separate estates limited the structural power of husbands. For all that these judges venerated coverture's moral logic, they always knew that coverture alone offered little in the way of real protection for a wife. With a separate estate, a wife gained a more separate self, a self not fully incorporated into the marriage, a self that an equity court could recognize as having choices and wishes, a self that could be revealed to have been coerced when a husband compelled particular outcomes. And though that made the law less deductively coherent, more complex, it also made it more just.

THE FEME SOLE (SUB MODO)

In 1805 Mary Alexander, the wealthy widow of William Alexander, agreed to marry John D. Jaques, a doctor and a younger and poorer man. Prior to the wedding she did what many wealthy widows in early America did: she set up a trust to which she conveyed all of the property she held as a single woman. The trust empowered her to "take the profits thereof, free from the control of her husband, and at her absolute disposal." If she had not created such a separate use trust, her husband would have acquired by marriage absolute ownership of all her personal property and absolute control for the rest of her life of all her real estate. The premarital agreement and the resulting trust negated that legal result; all the wealth she possessed as a widow was transferred before the marriage to a trustee, who was to manage the property for her benefit, unavailable to the husband. Thus when they married, John Jaques gained control over all the property she held at the time of her marriage, which was exactly nothing.

Over the next eight years, Mary informally gave many of her assets to her husband to manage and use. Many of those he converted into property that ended up under his own name, although he claimed variously that he used the property to pay family costs, that his actions followed an informal agreement between the two of them, and that the property converted to his name was compensation for costs and burdens he had undergone. Mary died in 1813, leaving her estate to be divided into thirds: one-third to her husband, one-third to the children of a friend, and one-third to the Methodist Episcopal Church of New York.

The church brought suit against the husband, seeking an equitable accounting of funds that Mary had turned over to her husband but that properly belonged to her estate. Chancellor Kent followed usual equity practice and referred the case to a master, who heard testimony and wrote a report detailing specifically what property had been misappropriated and what the husband owed to the estate. Kent then wrote a long opinion that confirmed most of the master's report. His decision was appealed to the New York Court for the Correction of Errors (known as the Court of Errors), where it was reversed.[4]

Jaques v. Methodist Episcopal Church doesn't sound like a case of high institutional drama. The story of the Jaques-Alexander marriage, at least as far as we can tell from the case reports, reveals no real nastiness or abuse by John Jaques. While there was a bit of testimony suggesting that Mary had grown unhappy with her husband's actions in managing her property, that she worried about what he had done, there was no evidence that he had threatened or harmed or "coerced" her directly.[5] More, the issue that divided the Court of Errors from Chancellor Kent's court was one of mind-numbing technicality: whether the legal presumption should be that a wife was free to dispose of her property to whomever she pleased, including her husband, in the absence of explicit constraints in the trust document (the position of the Court of Errors) or whether the legal presumption should be that her freedom to dispose of property was limited to the terms explicit in the trust document, in other words, a legal presumption that she lacked capacity, absent explicit language to the contrary in the trust document (Kent's position). Hardly the stuff of a legal landmark.

Yet a legal landmark it was. And the reasons why were all rooted in the passion of Kent's opinion. In *Jaques,* Kent, who famously described his decisionmaking process as starting with the facts in the cause, then seeing "where justice lay," and only then sitting "down to search the authorities," which happily "most always" contained "principles suited" to his "views of the case," found a case in which the authorities were almost all against him.[6] But, rather than reconsider, or find a way to avoid the authorities, Kent labeled the judicial attitudes he found in his "march" through the precedents corrupt, mean-spirited, and misogynist. He worked to impose a particular picture of marriage on the law and to establish a boundary on the continuity between English and American equitable practices. The judges of the Court of Errors rejected his analysis, or, more probably, given Kent's status as the most distinguished legal figure in the state and in the nation, they discovered that they rejected his analysis and so were compelled to find reasons for their rejection. Along the way they rebuilt the law of separate estates, even as they appeared to be reclaiming an older understanding.

One has to start, though, with James Kent's outrage. Kent regarded John Jaques as a scoundrel who trafficked in his wife's property while pretending to be her agent. John Jaques had been a party to the premarital contract, the settlement. Indeed, the settlement was a necessary precondition to the marriage. He had agreed not to meddle with the trust, and he had agreed that Mary's property would remain entirely outside of his control. The estate "should be to her only use, benefit, and disposal."

To excuse him would have the effect of legitimating a husband's subversion of a trust agreement. And the result would expose wives like Mary Jaques "to the acts, machinations, and undue influence, which the general dominion and power" of husbands "must greatly facilitate."[7]

Kent characterized such trusts as offering a wife "a certain support in every event" and, more important, protected her against her husband's "misfortunes, or unkindness, or vices." Making a wife into a buyer and seller and giver of property was not the intent; the fundamental goal was, rather, to give her security against her husband. Wives and husbands contracted in the shadow of coverture, in order to make agreements against the automatic consequences of marriage.[8] Women like Mary Jaques put their property into trusts to protect themselves, through the intercession of trustees, from their own weakness. A wife (actually, a wife-to-be) immunized herself against "one whose influence" was "the greater in proportion to their mutual love and attachment."[9] Her property became inalienable, except in the mode provided (sub modo).

Kent's interpretation of the meaning of a separate use agreement determined his holding: the trust was valid, and the trust did not give Mary Jaques the direct right to alienate or give away the property in the trust (certainly not to her husband). Mary had conveyed trust property to her husband in violation of the terms of the trust, and her husband had taken control of that property in violation of his own express agreement to act in accordance with the trust. As a result, John Jaques became, with regard to her property under his control, a constructive trustee, bound as a fiduciary to manage that property for the benefit of Mary and her estate, and bound, in particular, to return it when requested by her executors. Case closed. Victory for the church.

The only difficulty was that nearly all of the English precedents disagreed with Kent's interpretation of a separate use agreement. Instead, they all assumed that a wife was not restricted in her capacity to convey to her husband, absent an express restriction in the document itself. According to Kent, the English courts had leaned "too much against the wife," had "too freely indulged" the presumption of a wife's consent, because they all believed it "against common right" that a wife should have separate property from her husband and that, therefore, all ambiguities would be resolved "against her." The judges and chancellors had carried the wife's power as a feme sole much too far. They continuously affirmed acts of the wife without the concurrence of the trustee, forgetting that the trustee "was created for her protection" and constituted "the only sufficient shield against the undue, secret, and powerful influence of the husband."[10]

Having made "the march" through the cases, Kent's conclusion was ordained: forget precedent. The English decisions were "so floating and contradictory" that they left him free to adopt "true principles." To Kent, generally regarded as the leading conservative judge in early nineteenth-century America, a man famous as an antidemocratic Federalist loser and as an Anglophile, the English precedents were both dishonest and unjust.[11] In denying that coercion was involved, in granting a wife a formal equality with her husband, they succeeded in their real goal: to destroy her individual and autonomous enjoyment of her property. Kent, sounding a bit like a late twentieth-century radical feminist, characterized marriage as a relationship of such overwhelming structural domination that granting a woman a formally independent right to use her own property, without the interposition of trustees, was nothing but a sham independence, one that merely subjected her to the greater power of her husband. A court committed to doing equity should not construct the wife in an empty and formalistic manner as a feme sole with regard to her separate property but "only" as a feme sole sub modo. She should have no power but what was specifically granted in the trust device.

Kent, however, was reversed by the New York Court for the Correction of Errors, which held, to reduce two long opinions to four syllogistic propositions:

1. that separate use agreements were inconsistent with the nature of marriage, as properly understood;
2. that separate use agreements were, however, an equitable mechanism available to wives, affirmed by long-standing precedent;
3. that when a wife held a separate estate she did so with all of the rights of a single woman, as a feme sole (not sub modo), without any need to involve a trustee in her transactions, the trustee being a mere formality. She became a free property owner like other property owners, with every right to give property to whomever she chose;

4. and who better to give her property to than her own dear and loving husband.

Along the way, Chief Justice Ambrose Spencer and Justice Jonas Platt
managed to introduce phrases that became obligatory quotations in
cases and other legal texts for the rest of the century. Their paeans to the
"pure" common law dotted and confirmed the arguments of opponents
of marital property reform. Platt in particular confessed his love and
veneration of "the primeval notion of that mystical and hallowed union
of husband and wife." Marriage, "in that old fashioned sense," was for
him "the purest source of domestic joys and the firm foundation of social order." He and Spencer both "bowed" to the established presence
of separate use agreements, but they lamented "the complicated and
artificial anomalies in the relations of domestic life" that had "grown"
out of their use. Such agreements constituted "an adulteration" of the
"holy union." A wife with a separate estate, "armed with distrust of her
husband, and shutting out his affections and confidence, by refusing to
give her own in mutual exchange," was "an object of compassion and
disgust." For such a woman marriage had degenerated into "mere form,"
sometimes "little more than legalized prostitution." Her marriage had
"no higher object than sexual intercourse, and the sanction of legitimacy
for . . . offspring."[12]

Kent's opinion had presumed a husband to be his wife's "worst enemy." If that were the case, a fact that both Spencer and Platt denied,
then the only appropriate answer was "marry not at all!" The "ancient
rule" that Kent had rejected was still the best rule for a simple society,
one like the America of 1820. Spencer and Platt were not naive; both
recognized that their decision immunized coercive acts that would remain protected behind marital privacy. It was, however, "better" that
trust "should sometimes be abused, that than it should not exist in that
relation."[13]

The equitable recognition of a wife's separate property was "a *fungous
excrescence*," which the judges knew they could not "lop off." At the
same time, they could "prevent its growth," paradoxically, by recognizing the wife as a fully competent separate property holder. And so the
judges articulated a stock interpretation of Mary Alexander's intent in
creating the trust. About to marry John Jaques, she had meant to keep
control over her real estate. She did not mean to make herself the de-

pendent of a trustee or "to guard against herself." She remained a liberal property holder. Thus, there was nothing her executors or the Methodist Episcopal Church had to complain about when, as the owner of separate property, she chose to give much of it to her husband.[14]

As so often happens in the law, the end of the case was not the end of the story. The case itself lingered on.[15] Meanwhile, Kent himself was unreconciled to his reversal. He felt that the Court of Errors had undone his best work. "After such devastation, what courage ought I to have to study and write elaborate opinions? There are but two sides to every case, and I am so unfortunate as always to take the wrong side." And he had evidently spoken to Justice Platt "in a way to mortify and offend him."[16] More important, he reargued the question, in muted form, in his *Commentaries*. There he wrote that the Court of Errors had even gone beyond the English decisions in its "rendering" of the wife as a feme sole, withdrawing "those checks . . . intended to preserve her more entirely from that secret and insensible, but powerful marital influence, which might be exerted unduly, and yet in a manner to baffle all inquiry and detection."[17]

For the next half century, some law writers continued to praise Kent's opinion as describing the better rule.[18] Yet in this case there was a winner, and it was not James Kent. The language of the Court of Errors' opinions provided obligatory citations for a variety of voices in husband-wife legal debates. Opponents of marital property reform mobilized the opinions constantly, finding in them a "salutary and solemn" warning of the dangers of reform and a "pure-minded" expression of truth.[19] Proponents, on the other hand, used the image of wives "naturally" turning over their property to their husbands as a way to counter accusations that they were advocating marital disunion.[20]

The analytic framework set out by the Court of Errors swept the doctrinal field. Whenever questions arose about the power of a wife to dispose of her separate estate, the answer was clear: she was a feme sole, a property owner with the same freedom possessed by other property owners. She did not need the concurrence or the involvement of a trustee to do what she wished with what was hers. Her acts were presumptively her own. Coercion, as such, had to be proved affirmatively, could not be presumed as inherent in the relationship of husband and wife. And a citation to *Jaques* settled the point.[21] By the late 1840s, in fact, just as state legislatures were passing married women's property acts that allowed a wife without a separate use agreement to keep her separate property as a separate legal (not merely equitable) estate, the New York courts ruled that whenever a wife possessed any form of separate property, not simply property created through a trust, she was to be regarded as a feme sole. This "principle," drawn from *Jaques*, could not "be controverted."[22]

SCENES FROM THE MARRIAGE OF HARRIET AND HENRY

About the time that the New York Court of Errors was reconstructing Mary Jaques as a woman independent and autonomous enough to be free to give her wealth to her husband, Harriet Douglas was making her own plans for her inheritance.

Harriet Douglas was rich. She was also strong-willed about some things. Although she had great difficulty making many decisions, including whom, when, and whether to marry (she was well into her forties before she did so), she had no trouble stating her terms for marriage. In order to become her husband, a man had to agree that she would retain full control over all of the money she had inherited. This she demanded "in obedience to, and conformity with the opinions and precepts of her parents." Furthermore, he had to change his name to Douglas. He had to give up his profession so that he could devote his full attention to her and her family's properties. He had to be willing to live where she wished them to live. Implicitly, she required that her husband become her wife.[23]

Initially, Henry Cruger balked. In 1823, when he, a young lawyer from South Carolina, first courted the not-so-young New York heiress, he expressed his "great aversion" to marital settlements and separate use agreements. He asserted that "the husband ought always to possess an absolute control over the wife's property." Harriet refused him, at least in part because he held these opinions.[24] Three years later he tried again. He did not, he claimed, know the extent of her wealth. For that reason, if for no other, he was unwilling to give up his "present independence" for a dependence on her property, "be it much or be it little." She refused him again.[25]

Soon thereafter, Harriet was off to Europe, where she spent the next six years pursuing literary figures as a kind of nineteenth-century groupie and weighing the proposals of a variety of suitors, including persistent Henry who came to visit her in London in the fall of 1829.[26] By then, he had obviously decided that marriage to Harriet was worth a reluctant partial compromise of his principles. In October 1829, he wrote a letter that described his qualities as a potential mate. He was, he wrote, unquestionably devoted to her, the best evidence for which was his new "implicit submission" to her terms, "however derogatory to proper pride . . . and self-respect." Yet he worried that in proving himself "as a lover," he had made himself "less worthy" as a husband. And he wished that she had not exacted from him "such humiliating, though unequivocal proof" of his devotion.[27]

In November, after more discussions, he placed a small note in her hand. It began: "I live for your happiness." It continued: "The property to be conveyed to Trustees. The income for the joint use of the parties, and of the survivor. The principal for their children; the eldest son to bear the surname of Douglas." Harriet rejected his proposal, as he had not gone far enough and she remained determined "not to submit her property . . . to the control of any husband whom she might marry."[28]

On Christmas Day, Henry pressed his suit again in a long letter. Again he tried to convince her that her conditions were unreasonable. He disapproved not simply because those conditions were "entirely out of the pale of customary arrangement," but, more important, because they would "frustrate the paramount, if not exclusive purpose . . . they both have in view, mutual happiness." On the change of name, he wondered how to do it? If through a petition to the legislature, he would be publicly humiliated. And what if he later wished to run for public office? As for Harriet's property, leaving her in exclusive control of her property implied "a distrust of the integrity of the person to whom" she was about to confide her "person and happiness." The world at large would learn from that distrust and therefore "lose . . . confidence in him also, and treat him with a disrespect" from which she herself would suffer. She was, he stated confidently, ignorant of the law.[29]

By spring 1830, Henry had come round, thanks, as Harriet later put it, to her "steady purpose and resolution." She would have her property "free from any control" by Henry, "so that she . . . should be vested, notwithstanding . . . coverture, with the fullest powers of control and disposition . . . that the laws of the . . . State would permit in a marriage settlement." He would not change his name to Douglas, but he "cheerfully" agreed that she would be known as Mrs. Douglas Cruger. He decided to add D. as a middle initial to his name, ostensibly in order to distinguish himself from his New York uncle, Henry N. Cruger, who was already a prominent lawyer in the city (he had been Mary Alexander Jaques's trustee). Evidently, Henry did not consider it a hardship to give up his profession and to retire to what he imagined would be a life of leisure.[30]

And so they wed three years later. Harriet, foolishly as it turned out, agreed to Henry's request that the marriage settlement agreement be signed after, not before, the marriage ceremony. He had told her that his request for this particular arrangement was rooted in appearances, not greed. If the settlement were made before marriage, it would be published on the record and embarrass him. If after marriage, it would be a more private transaction. But the result of this arrangement was that her later actions with regard to her inherited estate came under a cloud.

When they wed, Henry became absolutely entitled to all of Harriet's personal estate (said to be about $100,000), and he gained lifetime control over all of her real estate (worth at least $60,000). In fulfillment of his promise to her, he immediately transferred all of that property to trustees (of which she was one of three, the other two being her incompetent brothers), who would hold the property "exempt from his debts, contracts, or control, to be disposed of on her separate orders, or by her deeds or will, so that she may enjoy and dispose of the same."

What happened next was unclear and the stuff of litigation. According to him, Harriet, "surprised and gratified" by his actions, told him in front of her brothers that he would have the use of the entire income of her estate for life. This gift was soon reduced to a written order to the trustees to pay Henry the income. And in reliance on that "absolutely and irrevocably" made order, he gave up his "laborious and engrossing occupation" of the law.[31] According to Harriet, on the other hand, she was gratified, but not surprised, by his compliance with her conditions. She had always intended to exercise her rights and powers with regard to him in a "liberal" manner. In particular, she intended to give him by will the enjoyment of her property after her death. But that intention was merely an emotion "of her own mind," never communicated to Henry. She never turned over to him the income or any part of the income for life, never gave him more than a bare agency. She certainly never gave him an irrevocable right to the income.[32]

Whatever she had given him at the wedding it was not, from Henry's perspective, "absolute" and "irrevocable" enough to satisfy him that he had acquired a proper husbandly identity. He found it "irksome" that he was not trusted. And for the next eight years, he made the conversation of their marriage revolve around her property and his need to control it.

For six months during 1834, Henry was in England and Scotland, seeing after her family estates. At sea in May, he wrote Harriet a long letter in the form of a journal. Much of the letter detailed his doubts about the competence and good will of her beloved brother George. If conflict between Henry and George became open, which side would she choose? Was she, he wrote, "ready to fulfil the scriptural precept, and without reluctance" stand by her husband? He was not certain, and he worried (with reason). The letter then described her marriage settlement as a "thorn" in his side. Her friends, like everyone else, could not comprehend "how a Lady," who had confided "her person, her reputation and her happiness" to him, could "have any scruples as to her property." Implicitly, she had not yet recognized him for the man of honor that he was.[33]

In July Harriet responded in equally high-flown language. Her marriage settlement, she wrote, was exactly as she had always resolved it should be: "a security of the abstract rights my parents had left me: which I think I have no [more] right to alienate, or you to wish me to do, than taking the eyes out of my head, and give them to you literally, because I had committed my person to you." She did not mean the settlement as an indication of want of confidence in or suspicion of him. And she asked him what was the thorn in his side: whether it was her "supposed suspicion" or the settlement.

Harriet found many of his comments upsetting: it made "the waves roll" in her breast against Henry rather than against George. Still, she missed him terribly, and she wanted nothing more than to be in "a regular Chariot, as light and fashionable as it can be made, in which you and I can shut ourselves up from the world, while we look at it." In a later letter, she told him that his letters made her, in spite of herself, almost want to "*love, honor and obey.*"[34]

At the end of September 1834, Henry wrote her another long letter. It described his desire for a "settled" form of life and for a form of "independence." According to him, one way to gain that independence, if she would not bestow it on him directly, was for him to return to legal practice despite the dreariness it would impose on their life:

To breakfast at eight, and be at my desk at nine punctually—and as the clock struck three, start for home, the dinner being served while on my way. Returning at four, my stay in the afternoon would be until dark always, and frequently until ten at night. I should decline all invitations, make no visits, and resort to no place of public amusement: but be indeed what I professed to be, a man of business. The great competition in New-York, my newness there, and indeed my marriage itself, would all impose this assiduity, and self-denial upon me. It is not a life of pleasure, or perhaps of happiness, and has little to invite but stern principles.

But, of course, he had an alternative: let him have control of her wealth. "Take away this poignard of ice from between us—it is brittle, but it is cold. It portends that you and I are not one, and curdles the confidence that should flow to and fro. I desire no interests separate from yours, for I love you, and we are married."[35]

After he returned to the United States, Harriet made up a new "order of appointment," one that (according to her) merely relieved Henry from the need to keep detailed accounts and that responded to his endless complaints. He put aside his plans to reenter the business world and devoted himself to Douglas family affairs and to the building of a country estate. Meanwhile, the two of them continued to disagree about her family. He grew close to James Monroe (nephew and adopted son of the former president), the husband of her sister Betsy, and he came to feel that the Monroes were ill-treated by the rest of the family. Harriet remained close to her brothers, even after they tried to exclude both of the sisters from a Scotch inheritance.

During the summer of 1836, relations grew strained. Harriet disapproved of some loans Henry had made to his own brothers, and she and her sister jointly decided that they would not pay him for his legal services in representing them. According to her, he was often moody and sullen, revealing his discontent "in various very offensive ways." He refused to take wine at the table, "saying he did not own it." He refused to go out riding with her, "saying that he did not own any carriage." All the time, he kept up his "murmurings about his dependent condition."[36]

Harriet had a new "agency" agreement drawn up, naming Henry agent of her estate with some serious exceptions: decisions as to the sale of real estate were reserved to her, as was the question whether she would proceed in a lawsuit against her brother George. Henry was expected to apply any income he saved the estate to the debt he and his brothers owed. One of her trustees would examine his books each year to certify that they were living within their means.[37]

Henry understood Harriet to be questioning his honesty, and he moved out, into a boardinghouse. He would not return, he announced, until she stated her objections or withdrew them. Once the accounts were settled, she should decide whether to live on her means or on his. He was happy, he said, to go back into legal practice and to support her as best he could. But if she wanted them to live on her estate, it must be by making him "independent." She should have nothing more to do with business or accounts. He should not have to account for his decisions. "Every Lady but herself, is rejoiced to have a husband competent and willing to advise, direct and manage for her."

Uniformly friends and relatives took Henry's side and advised Harriet to relinquish control of her income, to set love above lucre. James Monroe wrote her that she had a duty "to relieve" her husband "from a state of dependence." As a "man of honor," Henry would never "live in harmony with himself" if she didn't. His present condition was "an unnatural state," a "degradation." Monroe's wife, Betsy, took a similar line. Harriet had to let Henry "be independent." Harriet should not "let it be said that the love of *accumulation*" was the "motive" for her actions, "holding out against the opinions of all."[38]

William Bard, her uncle by marriage, and William Whetten, her investment adviser, were asked to mediate. The two proposed that Harriet's income be divided into halves, one under Harriet's absolute control, one under Henry's for the duration of his life.[39] Henry was satisfied with this; he regarded the proposal as a reasonable compromise, consistent with the relationship of husband and wife. Harriet, however, refused to comply. Henry could manage the whole thing but on her terms. She remained true to what all should have understood as the "fixed principles" of her life. Henry would have to return to her, leave his boardinghouse, and "trust" to her "confidence and affection." She would never give him an irrevocable right to any portion of her income.[40] And after a sleepless night, during which he "communed" with his "inmost soul," Henry accepted her terms. He resolved to return and to "confide in the affection, honor and generosity" of his wife. "God grant, for her own sake, that she may justify that confidence."[41]

By 1838, they were living apart much of the time. He stayed at their country place. She lived in the city. When Henry asked her to join him for the summer, Harriet refused. She was, she wrote, "boiling over and at the same time frozen" toward him because of his extravagances. She was, she reminded him, the "grand-daughter of a man, who gave his earnings a dollar at a time to his Wife." Unconsciously, one assumes, she had equated him with her grandmother, while putting herself in her grandfather's shoes. "[T]here is," she concluded, "but one way for you to act and act right—co-operate with me in everything, pay your debts and watch over the happiness of your Wife."[42]

The endgame of their marriage began in fall 1839. As Henry later told it, he had stayed in the country while Harriet went to visit one of her brothers, who lived on Long Island. When he tried to pay for various expenses incurred over the summer, his check bounced. The trustees of Harriet's estate, under Harriet's directions, had shifted the income away from his account. Once again he "was made to feel . . . at the mercy" of her "capricious monied tyranny." Something had to be done, and quickly, to put their financial relations on a fixed footing, no longer leaving him at the mercy of her changing desires. Meanwhile, he made plans to return to legal practice and perhaps to move back to the South.[43]

James Monroe interceded. Under pressure from all sides, Harriet let Monroe know that she would sign an agreement giving Henry irrevocable rights, but that she would never live with Henry again if he accepted that agreement. Monroe told her that he would not convey any such condition "from a Wife to her Husband, or from a Husband to a Wife, as it would be regarded as an admission . . . that man and wife could properly separate for matters growing out of money."[44] She backed down. On October 26, she wrote to Monroe: "I hereby give to my Husband . . . the Power to draw the whole of my present Income, as it accrues, during his life." This "order" was not conditioned on separation. Henry rewrote the order in more formal language. He also included an authorization to her trustees to pay her one-half of the income. He did this to give effect to the arbiters' recommendation of 1836. The result would be, again, that each would have final control over one-half of the income in her estate.[45]

Meanwhile, Harriet had evidently changed her mind and decided, again, that she would not live with Henry if he accepted any version of an "irrevocable" order. She had been rushed or coerced into the earlier agreement. She did not wish, she wrote, to separate "from the only one who can make me enjoy this life," but she could not change her principles, although she had, she added, changed her name. (This letter, however, she signed "Harriet Douglas.")[46]

Henry denied that there had been any coercion. He dismissed her concession about her name. "[H]alf way measures won't do in matters matrimonial." She had, instead, to "go the whole life," if she meant to be happy and to make her husband so as well. If she intended to separate, she should say so. He himself acknowledged no reason for one. Indeed, he disapproved of separation as "contrary to both Religion and morality." Still, he would acquiesce, since he knew that if he didn't, if he returned to her on her terms, everyone would "misconstrue" his motives. He owed it to himself "to shun the injurious imputation."[47]

They remained informally separated for much of the next year, Harriet residing with her brother on Long Island. Henry canceled the irrevocable order and tried to renew his professional identity as a lawyer, to reclaim "that honorable independence he had always enjoyed before marriage." Both of them pretended that they were trying to resolve the issues that separated them. He made a show of inviting her to join him in his new and modest circumstances. But she refused, even though, as he put it, "she well knew it was in her power, at any time, to accomplish what ought to have been the parmount [sic] object of her existence."[48] Henry's tone in his letters had grown icy and precise, and the reader senses an increasing strategic calculation. Litigation was somewhere on his horizon. She, by contrast, seems to have been both adamant and deeply depressed.

Various friends and relatives again tried to mediate. As before, the weight of the advice was against Harriet. William Bard wrote Harriet a long reflection on the unhappy situation. She should be the one to give in because, in "such perilous controversies as controversies between man and wife," the one who wished "a quiet conscience" had to be very sure that she was in the right and that she had done all she could for peace. "Henry's present situation of absolute want of the means of respectable living" was not one "worthy" of her. She needed to act to "[p]ut it out of the power of others to say" that she had "kept him on the rack till" she had "forced an unwilling confession." She should avoid the appearance of "triumphing" in her power. She should not insist that Henry apologize, for Henry's situation had "in it humiliation enough." He was "dependent." She could "yield something with dignity." He had no dignity to give up.[49]

Obviously, Bard had hit the right notes. Harriet gave in, writing Bard that she would put at his disposal the whole of her income, leaving it to him to decide what portion of the income should be given to Henry. Bard decided to settle an annuity of $3,000 on Henry.[50]

Harriet had agreed to the yearly payments thinking that it would ensure that they would stay separated, as a form of separation agreement.
But one evening in late fall of 1840 Henry arrived at Henderson where
she was living, and "not seeing how she could do otherwise, she acqui-
esced in his remaining."[51] Until June 1841 they lived in "external harmony," but throughout that time Henry continued to complain about
the inadequacy of the annuity, continued "importuning and harassing"
her. In particular, he made, she said, a great show of the burdensome life
of a lawyer. She was "perfectly aware" that this conduct was not induced
by his professional obligations. Rather, "it was only a part of the system
of vexation," dedicated to overcome her "patience and powers of resistance" and to force her to settle the whole income of her estate on him.

During the summer of 1841, they separated for the last time. Or,
rather, she left him. Harriet regarded this as prudent defensive action.
Henry treated it as disobedience, leaving him in the position of wronged
husband, still entitled to all his rights. He played at the game of outraged
husband: writing letters to her brothers telling them that he would permit her to stay with them under limited circumstances, writing her that
it would not do for her to continue to live by herself in her house, a married woman alone, writing letters to the minister of Grace Church to
complain that she was still allowed to sit in her pew and take communion in spite of her sinful disobedience.[52]

In November 1841, Harriet gave Henry a new deed, entitling him irrevocably to one-half of her income for the rest of his life. But when Henry
applied to the trustees and agents of Harriet's estate for an accounting of
the estate, so that he would know what he was entitled to, he was
refused.

His next stop was to Vice-Chancellor William McCoun to gain equitable enforcement of his finally established rights.

Henry Cruger's first petition to the vice-chancellor asked for an accounting of the estate and that his letters and other documents be returned to
him. It proposed three alternative remedies for their marital situation.
The first asked for "the full benefit" of all Harriet's "promises" made over
the past years. That is, he should gain absolute control of one-half of the
income of her estate, and managerial control over the other half, in his
capacity as "head of the family." She could still retain "ulterior control"
over the latter half, "from abundant caution . . . and to provide for ex-

treme cases." This remedy was premised on the fanciful assumption that
they would be living together. If, on the other hand, the court found that
"the wife" had abandoned her duty and deserted her husband without
cause, "the means of wrong-doing should be withheld from her," meaning that she should lose her "ulterior control." Or, as a third alternative,
the court could simply give effect to the original agreement that he
claimed had been made at the time of the marriage. That is: "the principal to the heirs, the income [irrevocably] to the husband."[53]

That petition was soon amended. The amendment claimed that the
postnuptial settlement was entirely void, a legal nullity under New
York's Revised Statutes. Because she had not made a premarital conveyance of her property, Harriet had become just another feme covert and
Henry the baron of her estate.[54]

Harriet's response insisted that the postnuptial agreement was legally
valid or, at the least, enforceable by a court of equity. At the time of their
marriage the most Henry had was a revocable interest in her property, an
interest that repeatedly had been revoked by the time of Henry's petition
to the vice-chancellor. The real issue was the validity of the 1841 order
that appeared to give Henry an irrevocable right to one-half or more of
the income of the estate. That order was the product of an intense and
extended pattern of illegitimate and illegal coercion. Henry, in combination with James Monroe and Betsy Monroe and others, had coerced her
into making exactly the kind of settlement that everything in her up-
bringing and nature had taught her not to make. It was not the product
of her free will. Thus, Henry was entitled to nothing.

The two judges who dealt with the case of *Cruger v. Douglas* (sometimes labeled *Cruger v. Cruger*) over the next eight years agreed with
Harriet that the issue of "coercion" was central. They took the
postnuptial settlement as a valid conveyance, giving her control over her
property during marriage. But they disagreed with her that she had been
coerced by Henry and his minions when she made the irrevocable order
in 1841. Both found it difficult to imagine how talking with friends, ordinarily a protection against a husband's coercion, could have become
coercion. According to Vice-Chancellor McCoun, writing in 1844, her
friends and family had pressed her to make the irrevocable assignment
out of their mistaken belief that the result would be marital reconciliation. They were wrong; instead, the assignment reinforced her estrange-
ment from her husband and led, as well, to a break between Harriet and

her sister. Yet, wrote McCoun, such unfortunate and unintended consequences did not make the deed invalid. The fact that an agreement did not lead to happiness or peace did not mean that it could be disregarded or regarded as void because coerced. In any case, the document had been drafted while her husband and her "importunate friends" were away. It was the product of an independent will.[55]

In 1848 Justice Selah Strong of the new New York Supreme Court (created by the 1846 state constitution) described the situation somewhat differently but came essentially to the same conclusion. He regarded Henry's behavior as honorable and appropriate. He was right to have insisted on the dishonor of his economic dependence; he was right to have mobilized the "persuasion of her friends." Thus, there was no reason to regard Harriet's eventual agreement as coerced. She had simply changed her mind, been persuaded by others. Her acts remained those of a free and independent property holder, a feme sole. And, as one might expect, the opinions of the Court of Errors in *Jaques* were described as determining the relevant law.[56]

A DOCTRINAL CODA

Henry had won his half of Harriet's separate estate. The editor of the *New York Legal Observer* congratulated him, a fellow member of the New York Bar, for having "passed through this fiery ordeal unscathed, vindicated, and triumphant."[57] Henry retired to Saugerties on Long Island, where, in George Templeton Strong's words, he lived for another twenty years "on 'alimony' extorted by process of law from a wife he hated and whom he had married for her money."[58]

Harriet, as a symbol of her new emancipation, had her marriage bed cut in two, transforming it into two "slightly peculiar" sofas. She too lived for twenty more years, dividing her time between her country house at Henderson in the Mohawk Valley and a house in New York City, where she maintained a salon that Strong sometimes attended.[59]

"She was mad and he was bad, and the legal muddle they brought about between them was very deep and formidable." So wrote Strong on Henry's death in 1867. But Strong was wrong, at least about the complexity of the legal muddle. The case produced an extraordinary amount of paper; doctrinally, however, it was neither difficult nor particularly significant. The Court of Errors decision in *Jaques* remained the crucial authority on the power of the wife to deal with her separate estate. And *Jaques* meant that both courts of law and of equity regarded Harriet Douglas as she, by and large, wished to be regarded: as a competent actor and manager of her property. And that meant that she would be no more likely to succeed in claiming coercion than any other property owner who had lost property because of a stupid decision.

One might imagine that coercion had disappeared from the law of marital property. Or, at least, that it had become as difficult to demonstrate in marriage as it was in other areas of nineteenth-century legal life (labor law, for example). Inequality of power within marriage would not be presumed, and the decisions of a wife in possession of a separate estate would only rarely rise to judicial scrutiny.

And yet, in the wake of the passage across America of married women's property acts, acts that secured to wives full legal title to separate property, the language of coercion suddenly reappeared. Coercion was one of the categories judges mobilized as they worked to make sense of the new statutes, as they reconstructed the law of marriage in light of what would eventually be understood as a fundamental transformation of the inherited law and an undoing of central aspects of coverture.

The claim is limited. I am not convinced Harriet Douglas Cruger would ever have convinced a court that she was coerced. (On the other hand, the Methodist Episcopal Church might well have won, had Mary Jaques held her separate estate under the new rules.) "Coercion" never regained its status as a moral justification within the modernizing law of husband and wife. But "coercion" defined one doctrinal stream in the flood of cases that interpreted the new statutes, and its critical presence made for a telling contradiction within the liberal individualism of late nineteenth-century America, one that shaped the marital property law that wives and husbands faced as they worked out destinies as property holders.

In New York and elsewhere, the story began with the 1858 decision of the New York Court of Appeals in *Yale v. Dederer,* the most important of the early decisions interpreting New York's 1848 and 1849 married women's property acts.[60] Mrs. Dederer's husband wanted to buy thirty-eight cows from Yale. Yale, who knew that Mr. Dederer was insolvent, only agreed to sell the cows when Mrs. Dederer agreed to sign the promissory note as well. Yale went to court to have the debt charged against her separate estate. There the Dederers resisted, arguing that Mrs. Dederer's act had been void. She had no right to pledge her property; Yale could only recover against Mr. Dederer.

When the case first reached the New York Court of Appeals (after 1846 the highest court of review in New York), Judge George Comstock began his opinion by setting out a "well settled" doctrine he drew from the Court of Errors in *Jaques:* "that a married woman could deal with her separate estate as though she were a *feme sole.*" This doctrine extended, according to the judge, only so far as her own self-interested dealings with her own separate estate, not so far as to permit her to use her property as security for her husband's activities. The "well known" disability of coverture that stopped her from contracting debts prevented Mrs. Dederer from using her estate as security. Did the new married women's property acts of 1848 and 1849 change that? No, for she remained a feme covert. Statutes intended, to quote from their preamble, "for the more effectual protection of the rights of married women" should not be interpreted to remove a "far higher protection to married women than the wisest scheme of legislation can be." Any other rule would "go far" to undo "those checks . . . intended to preserve a wife from marital influences, which may be and often are unduly exerted, and yet baffle all detection." Judge Ira Harris, who wrote a concurring opinion, went even so far as to quote without attribution from Kent's rejected opinion in *Jaques,* describing the reason for a wife's separate property as being "to protect her weakness against the husband's power, and provide a maintenance against his dissipation."[61]

What of the capacity of a wife to give her separate property directly to her husband? In New York that question was faced in two distinctive factual contexts. The first involved a wife whose husband farmed on her separately owned land. Did the income from the farm belong to him or to her? In 1859 Justice Noah Davis of the New York Supreme Court was sure the answer was him. The Court of Errors in *Jaques* had established that when a wife's actions were "free and not the result of flattery, force or improper treatment," she might give her husband her property. The new marital property regime had not, Davis thought, changed the husband's marital rights, except with regard to the wife's separate property. He remained entitled "to the society and services" of his wife. And he remained "entitled to the results of his own skill and labor." If he had been a tenant under a lease, he would have had the right to keep the results of his labor. Any other rule inverted the relation of husband and wife, reducing him "to the condition of a servant of the latter" and "dwindling him to a *mere serf on her lands.*"[62]

Seven years later, the New York Court of Appeals reversed. The "authorities" drawn from "the old reports," meaning *Jaques,* had become "unsafe" as statements of ruling law. The married women's property acts of 1848 and 1849 had transformed the legal field and the inherited law; they constituted "a clear innovation" on and reduction of a husband's marital rights. In light of the statutes, there remained no principle on which to claim that the husband acquired any legal title in the produce of "her" farm. To the contrary, the court doubted whether the wife could convey such legal title to him, since the new statutes had not changed the husband's basic incapacity to enter into a valid contract with his wife. If that meant that a husband were reduced to the condition of a serf, that was a matter to take up with the legislature, not the courts.[63]

Could a wife, in contemplation of death, make a gift of her property to her husband? The early decisions interpreting the new New York law bounced around the question. In 1860 one state supreme court justice decided that the terms of the 1848 and 1849 laws proceeded on the assumption that a wife was "entirely competent" to do with her separate property as she wished, including giving it to her husband. The statutes had come into being in order to remove "the mischief" of "the husband's power over his wife's estate," including his power "to dissipate and squander it," under the common law rules. And the goal was to give a wife the same freedom over what was hers "as any other individual." She had, under *Jaques,* "always" enjoyed the equitable right to bestow her separate estate on her husband. The goal of the new law was not to curtail that right, certainly not to make a "complete and radical change" in that existing law.[64] Other judges rejected that interpretation. A wife's attempted conveyance to her husband, even one "in good faith and voluntarily," was wholly void, wrote Justice Charles Mason in *White v. Wager,* also in 1860. The intent of the new laws was to offer greater protection to the property of married women in the face of structured marital coercion. It was not to remove all of a wife's disabilities, certainly not to remove her incapacity to convey to her husband.

Mason rooted his decision in a picture of marital politics shaped by inequality, one very like Kent's. By marriage a husband had always acquired "an almost unlimited control" over a wife. That control justified

the traditional presumption that her criminal acts were committed under her husband's "coercion." In that context, what would be the effect
of the new statutes? It was in the "very nature" of the relationship that
a wife would remain "confiding" in her husband and "solicitous" to
meet his "desires, wishes and expectations." Husbands, on the other
hand, schooled in a common law tradition, assumed that it was "right
and proper" that their wives conveyed their property over to them and
could become resentful. Many husbands believed that the new laws had
wrongly deprived them of important property rights. They would, as a
result, seek to regain "control" through their wives' "consent." Most of
the time, if wives were permitted to convey to their husbands, the husbands would still get what they wanted. But where they didn't, where
wives stood out and refused and resisted coercion, where wives were
willing to incur the "displeasure" of their lords, husbands would subject
them "to very disagreeable importunities," to abuse, and the matter
would "end in bickerings destructive to the peace and happiness of
families."[65]

And in 1862 the New York Court of Appeals affirmed Justice Mason's
holding in *White* (in an opinion that still appeared in casebooks into
the 1950s). Judge Hiram Denio's opinion began with marital unity, described as "one of those stubborn mandates of the common law" requiring "absolute obedience from the courts." Then he moved on to a short
description of the traditional disabilities of coverture. No equivalent disabilities attached to the condition of a married man, who remained
"free" to receive title to property and to dispose of it as if unmarried,
putting aside the one exception: his incapacity to be his wife's grantee or
to make a grant directly to her. No one ever supposed that legislation
was needed to increase a husband's rights. "On the contrary, the complaint was that his rights were too great, and ought to be diminished,"
because a wife was "the victim" of an "oppressive legal system." And
that complaint was the foundation of the new laws of 1848 and 1849.
Those laws were designed to protect the property of a wife against her
husband, to grant her new rights by taking them from her husband. That
being the case, the drafters of the law would not have wanted to remove
the husband's incapacity to be his wife's grantee. Furthermore, the reali-
ties of marriage meant that "the greatest peril to which the separate estate of the wife" was "exposed" was "her disposition to acquiesce" to her
husband, her susceptibility to coercion. The law may have given her

powers to act "as if unmarried," but the law should not be interpreted in ignorance of the dependent relationship within which she lived.[66]

By the 1870s, the New York legislature had made it clear that a wife was theoretically free to use her property as she chose, including giving it to her husband. Yet in 1878 the Court of Appeals set aside Caroline De La Montagnie's 1851 transfer to her husband John of a very valuable long-term lease she had inherited from her first husband. The transfer had occurred at a time when his investment in a California steamship enterprise (using her funds) was deep in debt. John had told Caroline that she might be personally liable to the creditors of the steamship (she wasn't), but that if she transferred her title to him, it would be more secure than in her hands, and it might delay the creditors. In 1860, at roughly the same time that John separated from her and moved to California, Caroline asked him to give the interest back to her, and he promised to do so. But he never did.

The trial court had held that her gift to him had been founded on her "love and affection," and that was enough to justify the conveyance. But both appellate courts that reviewed the case disagreed. The judges did not challenge the possibility that a transfer for love and affection would be valid. Nor did they hold, as they might well have, that the husband had intentionally defrauded the wife. Instead, both courts held that Caroline had been induced to make the transfer by "untrue statements" and under a "misapprehension" about her potential liability, and that she was entitled to a restoration of her title. The Court of Appeals went on to develop a presumption about all conveyances from wives to husbands. The burden was on the husband to show that it was meant as a gift and that the whole transaction was "fair and proper." The husband's burden would not be met by a demonstration that the wife "consented." Wife and husband did not, the court ruled, "stand on equal terms." She remained entitled to relief.[67]

And in 1889 Justice Stephen Field, writing for the U.S. Supreme Court, restated the presumption. Whenever a husband acquired possession of his wife's separate property, with or without her consent, he would be understood as holding it in trust for her benefit, in the absence of direct evidence of her intention to make him a gift. Field acknowledged that there remained some jurisdictions where the presumption went in the opposite direction (as it had in *Jaques*): presuming the validity of a gift from wife to husband in the absence of evidence to the contrary. But his holding was, he believed, more in accordance with "the spirit and purpose" of the married women's property acts.[68]

Through the first half of the twentieth century, Field's presumption was recognized as ruling law.[69] Wives, though "absolute" owners with regard to their separate property, were still wives, living in a relationship where a husband's influence was inescapable. Courts refused to impose formal equality or liberty on an institutional context inconsistent with such abstractions. Wives were free and capable property owners but not within marriage.

Thus, "coercion" did not disappear. No late nineteenth-century or twentieth-century treatise writer or appellate judge could have imagined describing the reason for law as being the prevention of coercion within marriage. None of them defended coverture in the ways that eighteenth-century writers had. They were, like others in the society, in the thrall of a vision of marriage in which all acts within the institution were founded on "love and affection," in which power had no legitimacy. And they could no longer articulate a systemic justification of inequality within marriage. Yet their concurrent recognition of both the danger of coercion within the relationship and of the legitimate role of courts as restraining a husband's misuse of his power meant that "coercion" retained a place on the terrain of American marriage law.

7

John Barry and
American Fatherhood

The Law of Parent and Child is a very characteristic branch of the Law of Marriage.

George A. Hickox, *Legal Disabilities of Married Women in Connecticut* (1870)

What did it mean to be a free man? For freedmen, after the Civil War, one sure answer was marriage. The marriage covenant was "the foundation" of their rights.

What was foundational about marriage? The answer was, above all else, custody over dependents. Wife and children belonged in the household of a husband. Slave marriages, if recognized, would have threatened the central need of slaveowners in a capitalist economy: to keep capital mobile. Slavery had required slaveholders to retain the power to sell, to alienate slaves, including children and wives, whenever opportunity presented itself or the market demanded. Slavery had meant that wife and children, as well as husband, were all subject to the custodial powers of masters. Conversely then, free legal marriage meant the act of consolidating loved ones under one roof, protecting them and keeping them, creating a private sphere within which they would be cared for. For ex-slaves, husbandly custody over wife and children demarcated emancipation as well as marriage.[1]

The male ex-slaves' aspiration was the ordinary expectation of free husbands throughout nineteenth-century America. Descriptions of marriage emphasized control, care, responsibility—custody—over dependents, children as well as wife. A husband was the head of a household, and his children, until grown up, were expected to live within "the empire of the father."[2]

From the very beginning of the nineteenth century, however, American courts had sometimes refused to deliver children to married fathers who had gone to court to have children released from "illegal restraint" (that is, from the custody of anyone else, including separated mothers). And occasionally courts took a child from a father and gave the child to a separated or divorcing wife. Fatherhood was understood as a form of rulership, incorporating elements of possession, representation, and governance. Yet a ruler's powers were always limited, and his private sphere of authority would be penetrated when necessary. Bad fathers, like other bad rulers, lost their rights when they victimized those they should have cared for.[3]

It didn't happen often, at least at first. The patriarchal assumption that a husband/father possessed his children, that he had the right to keep them and to raise them according to his designs, and to keep others, including mothers, from them, retained a hold over the early American legal culture and the legal imagination. Fathers and their lawyers could take comfort from a body of English cases, all decided in the late eighteenth and early nineteenth centuries, that constructed father's rights in absolute terms, in terms that made the father's prior conduct toward his dependents almost irrelevant and that left both law courts and equity courts without power to shift custody to mothers, even to innocent and victimized mothers.[4]

Still, husbands occasionally lost custodial rights over their children. In 1816, for example, Chancellor Kent responded to a petition from a wife who had separated in 1808, after her intemperate and violent husband had tried to coerce her into giving up her separate property. Her petition alleged that her husband had reappeared and revoked their separation agreement and committed adultery, and she asked the court to protect her from him, that she be "vested" with the custody of their children, and that the marriage be dissolved. Kent denied the first and the third requests. There was not, he believed, any immediate danger to her personal safety, and his court was not the appropriate institution to provide protection. She had also not proven her husband's adultery, so she had no right to a full divorce. But he did issue an order giving her custody and control of the children. And he ordered the husband not to visit his children, except under the direction of one of the masters of the court.[5]

Kent took the right to determine custody as implicit in his discretionary power as chancellor, and as inherent in his legislatively delegated authority to determine the consequences of divorce and separation. For him, custody jurisdiction was unproblematic, to be decided quickly and without elaborate justifications, depending on the guilt of the husband. In his later *Commentaries on American Law,* the only mention of child custody began by asserting a father's right to use the writ of habeas corpus to gain custody over his children when "improperly detained from him," but then emphasized the responsibility of both courts of law and equity to investigate the circumstances and to act according to "sound discretion." Courts should not take a child from "the possession of a third person" (and a "third person" could include a wife, grandparents, other relatives, even a kindly stranger) and "deliver" the child back to a father against the child's will. A court even had a legitimate right to limit a father's right "to the possession and education of his child." Everything depended on the circumstances of the case.[6]

In Kent's language, as well as in the fugitive phrases of other legal commentators (for all of the early nineteenth-century law writers did no more than glance at questions of child custody), judicial power to decide questions of child custody could only be understood as a problem in the determination of a married father's right. Fathers had the right to the custody of their children, although they could lose that right. No one else possessed that right, certainly not married mothers, who were barely mentioned in any of the contemporary treatises. Indeed, the generic and seemingly ungendered word "parent," in Kent's treatise as in other early nineteenth-century works, incorporated mother only if father were dead or if there were no legal father at all, as in the case of bastards.

In 1839 Joseph Story defended an American conception of equity jurisdiction over child custody sharply at odds with inherited English notions. Chancellors had a responsibility to protect children whenever a father was "guilty of gross ill-treatment or cruelty towards his infant children," or was "in constant habits of drunkenness and blasphemy, or low and gross debauchery," or if he professed "atheistical or irreligious principles," or if "his domestic associations" tended "to the corruption and contamination of his children." That responsibility was, Story admitted, one "of extreme delicacy, and of no inconsiderable embarrassment and responsibility." But it remained a jurisdiction "indispensable to the sound morals, the good order, and the just protection of a civilized society." Was that jurisdiction in opposition to an ordinary father's right to the care and custody of his children? Story was at pains to deny the inference. The jurisdiction established "not a denial of father's right, but rather a way to confront" a bad father when he abused that right. Children were given to the custody of their fathers because fathers were usually best suited to provide for their protection, care, and education. So long as those needs were met, fathers' rights remained secure. Custody remained a right identified with good husbands and fathers.[7]

AN UNHAPPY MARRIAGE

John A. Barry was a widower with four daughters when he married Eliza Ann Mercein in the spring of 1835. She was the daughter of a prominent New Yorker, Thomas Mercein, a former labor leader, by then the head of the Equitable Insurance Company. Barry was a businessman from Nova Scotia. She was not young, at least twenty-five or twenty-six, perhaps older, but strongly attached to her parents' home in New York. He was forty-three.

Their marriage represented the conclusion of protracted negotiations. The two had entered into an engagement in November 1834, including an informal antenuptial agreement that Barry would move his family to New York within one year after their marriage. The meaning of that promise would later be much litigated and debated. He assumed that after spending time in New York, he was free to go where he pleased, and that he had a right to expect his wife to follow. Legally, he was right, but he should not have assumed her acquiescence. In a number of anguished letters Eliza had told him of the conflicts she felt between her attachment to her father's home and her desire to be with Barry. She could not, she wrote in January 1835, imagine a lasting separation from "home," yet she wanted to "unite" her destiny with Barry.[8]

There were conflicts from the beginning of their marriage. Barry had supposed, according to one judge, that "all was to be authority with him"; Eliza had assumed that "all was to be accommodation to her." Instead, they both were "led to the irresistible conclusion" that there was "no perfection short of Heaven."[9]

They moved back to New York in May 1836, after one year in Liverpool, Nova Scotia. Thomas Mercein provided capital to help Barry open a store selling lamps, glass, and china on Broadway, which went bankrupt within a year during the Panic of 1837, and in the spring of 1838 Barry returned to Liverpool, where he had been a prominent merchant and a member of the provincial assembly. When he left, he took the four children from his first marriage, while Eliza remained in New York with two infants. He visited New York a few weeks later to arrange Eliza's move to Nova Scotia and, evidently, to try to gain financial assistance from his father-in-law. She refused to help him talk to her father and announced that she would not leave New York.

A few days later, on June 7, 1838, they both signed a "separation agreement," one Barry later claimed he had drafted knowing that it was "illegal." The agreement declared that neither party then wished for a final separation. In the event of a final separation he relinquished his parental rights over their year-old daughter, Mary, while retaining sole custodial rights over their two-year-old son. He then returned to Nova Scotia, still hoping that Eliza would follow.

Later in the year, Barry came again to New York and picked up his son from the Mercein residence. In a long pamphlet he wrote in 1839 to defend his actions, Barry explained that he took the child in order to convince his wife to follow. To those who challenged the propriety of using the child as bait, he responded: "[T]he child was mine. I had a right to take it, and no one had any right to complain."[10] Evidently his wife and father-in-law agreed, for they gave the older child up without a struggle.

But when, a few months later, Barry demanded the return of Mary, Eliza Barry and Thomas Mercein resisted. And in the summer of 1839 Barry brought the first of a series of habeas corpus writs in the New York courts for the return of wife and infant child to his custody. These writs were uniformly directed at Thomas Mercein, who, Barry alleged, was unlawfully detaining his dependents and interfering with his rights. Early on, Chancellor Reuben Walworth ruled against Barry. Although the New York Supreme Court twice upheld Barry's rights, its decisions were overruled by the New York Court for the Correction of Errors. In all, Barry sued out at least seven writs, all of which eventually failed.[11]

In 1847 the last failure was ratified by the U.S. Supreme Court. According to Chief Justice Roger Taney, the Court lacked authority to review the district court's decision to leave Mary's custody with Eliza. The Judiciary Act of 1789 granted appellate jurisdiction only where "rights of property" were involved, "where the matter in dispute" had "a known and certain value, which can be proved and calculated, in the ordinary mode of a business transaction." Yet in this instance the matter in dispute was "evidently utterly incapable of being reduced to any pecuniary standard of value," as it rose "superior to money considerations." Custody could never be reduced to a property right.[12]

John Barry's custody case (usually known as the *Mercein* case) has come down to us as the leading child custody case of the nineteenth century, as authority for the proposition that children were not property. For nearly a century it was a constant citation in custody cases across America. It is still occasionally cited for the notion of *parens patriae,* the idea that public authorities, judges in particular, have the right, independent of parental interests or desires, to make decisions in the best interest of a child.[13]

At the heart of the case was John Barry's obsession with his rights. Although he was not a lawyer, he immersed himself in the minutiae of the old law of baron and femme and habeas corpus law and, after 1839, argued his own cases and wrote his own briefs. He felt slandered when Chancellor Walworth rejected his writ, and he published a long pamphlet to defend his character and legal rights. His passionate involvement reflected the challenge posed by judicial attacks on "his" rights as the custodial parent. He should have been recognized as being a responsible adult, meaning a man who kept and cared for dependents under his legal control. Yet the courts denied him the recognition he deserved. Wives, all men agreed, moved with and obeyed their husbands; yet his wife did neither, although there was no basis for a legal separation. Fathers were the natural guardians and custodians of their children; yet his youngest child was kept from him. If those events were legal, what sort of a father and husband was he?

Like John Barry, all the judges who tried to resolve the case knew that a custody case—meaning an attempt by a father to enforce a habeas corpus writ for the return of his child—concerned the identity of the father as a rights bearer within an ongoing marriage.[14] The question of which parent was entitled to custody was intertwined with Mrs. Barry's claimed right to live apart from her husband. In fact, all but one of those judges saw the case as raising precisely the issues that obsessed Barry. They understood that questions about a court's authority to determine a child's custody arose within a context shaped by the settled priority of a married father's legal rights (rights drawn from the law of coverture).[15]

JUDICIAL VERSIONS

The case began, over and over again, with the return of a writ of habeas corpus ad subjiciendum.[16] The writ was always directed to Thomas Mercein, initially commanding him to bring before the court both Eliza Barry and her infant daughter, later only the daughter. Each time, Mercein responded that he was not holding Eliza Barry against her will, that she was free to come and go as she pleased, that there was, therefore, no unlawful imprisonment, no constraint on her personal liberty. If a writ of habeas corpus were to be directed against anyone, it should, according to Mercein, be made to Mrs. Barry herself since the child was within her custody.

To this defense, John Barry answered that talk of Eliza's freedom to come and go as she pleased, talk of her legal right to stay at her father's, talk of the child in her custody, were all legal nonsequiturs.[17] The rules of marriage meant that only Barry's will, his freedom, and his rights ought to be relevant to the question of the legal responsibility of his father-in-law for keeping his wife away from him. Questions of her freedom and of her legal rights—more properly, questions of her status—depended, as Esek Cowen of the New York Supreme Court wrote in 1842, "upon a rule too elementary to require the adduction of authority; and too obvious to have been denied in the whole course of this particular controversy." That is, upon the foundational assumption that "the very being or legal existence of the woman" was "suspended" during marriage, "incorporated and consolidated into that of the husband." Because of coverture, Eliza Barry's father, who kept wife and child away from husband, was nothing but a wrongdoer.[18]

And yet here, as elsewhere, the received law of marriage was more complicated than it seemed, and one could not derive a legal result by invoking Blackstone's definition. In 1816, more than twenty years before the Barry litigation had begun, the New York Supreme Court had already held that a father did no legal wrong in taking in his married daughter.[19] John Barry might possess a theoretical right to Eliza Barry's custody, but it was an empty right, not one a court would enforce. Courts, according to Chancellor Walworth, never compelled "a wife to return to the bed and board of her husband and to the performance of her conjugal duties" when she "voluntarily" separated, "either with or without justifiable cause." Eliza Barry was at "perfect liberty . . . to return to her husband, or to seek the protection of any other relative or friend who may think proper to assume the legal responsibility of affording her a shelter," in opposition to Barry's marital rights. Courts could not make her return; she was left "only responsible to her own conscience and to her God, for such a violation of her conjugal duties."[20]

Barry learned his legal lesson. After his writ for the release of Eliza from her father's custody was rejected by Chancellor Walworth in 1839, later writs only claimed the court's assistance in regaining the custody of his daughter. Yet Thomas Mercein remained the appropriate person to be sued for the return of Barry's child, not Eliza Barry. The question was not, according to Greene Bronson, the chief justice of the New York Supreme Court, whether the child was actually suffering under imprisonment, but whether there was "that kind of restraint" that defeated "the right of the [infant's] father." Mercein had made it impossible for his son-in-law to see his child, except on terms "which a proper self respect made inadmissible." Such a denial defeated "the right of the father to the custody of his child" and laid "a proper foundation for asking redress by habeas corpus." Cowen was characteristically blunt in explaining why the father-in-law, not the wife, ought to be sued. It was, he declared, "impossible to avoid seeing that" Mercein was, "in fact, the principal offender." Without his support it was "morally certain that the relator [John Barry] would have been put to encounter no serious difficulty in reclaiming the custody of his child without a law suit." Without her father's protection, economic necessity would have driven Eliza Barry back into her husband's household, and with her would have come their daughter.[21]

Formally, the case pitted father against grandfather. Substantively, however, Eliza Barry's legal right to live apart from her husband was always the central issue for courts deciding Mary's custody. According to Chancellor Walworth, "if [John Barry's] misconduct toward the partner of his bed and his bosom" had "furnished her with good cause for seeking again the protection of the paternal roof," no law, "either human or divine," required him "to remove this infant from her arms, or from the same friendly shelter." The judges of the New York Supreme Court posed the problem more narrowly and more legalistically: only a finding that Eliza had effectively established a right to a legal separation could possibly justify her claimed right to the custody of her child. Either way, a contest over custody became a contest over the legal right of a wife to separate from her husband. And that depended entirely on his conduct.

Custody over dependents remained a central attribute of a good husbandly identity. A father could lose his rights; yet, according to the prevailing understanding, a father should not be required to subject his rights to the vagaries of judicial sentiments about appropriate child care, about the "best interests of the child," about who was the better parent. Bronson, reflecting the orthodox view, assumed that the goal of the court was to provide for the welfare of the child but "knew" that the law had already settled that the father was preferred by that standard, absent proof of such "grossly immoral conduct" as would disqualify him from "the proper discharge of parental duties."[22] Thus, absent limited circumstances that justified divesting him and transferring what was his to others, the child was Barry's to raise and to control. And all he should have to do to win was to show his authority or capacity to bring the writ, that is, his parenthood, in combination with evidence that the child was wrongfully being kept away from him. The relative or comparative parental capacity of another, Eliza Barry for example, was beside the point, entirely irrelevant. The respondent, the person (Thomas Mercein) holding the child, could challenge the father's right to bring the writ, typically by demonstrating his abuse or neglect or mistreatment of those he was bound to care for. But a father should not be subjected to a comparative judgment about who was the better parent.

And yet Chancellor Reuben Walworth's opinion began (shockingly, from John Barry's perspective) by insisting on his equitable obligation to conduct a "summary inquiry" into the "relative merits or demerits" of the conduct of each separated spouse. According to Walworth, a writ of habeas corpus was not the proper instrument to test the "legal right" of a father to guardianship (that is to say, the property right, the title, in the child). All the court could do under the writ was decide whether the child was being held under unlawful restraint. In making that determination, the court ought to exercise its discretion and its moral judgment.

Walworth's version of their marital history began with John Barry's agreement that the couple would return within one year after the wedding to live in New York City "for the future." Walworth understood that this was not a legally enforceable agreement since it would have changed a fundamental term of the marital contract, that is, the husband's right to decide where the marital home should be. Yet it was evident that neither Eliza nor her parents would have gone through with the marriage absent his agreement, and Walworth regarded it as imposing a moral obligation on John Barry. More important, it demonstrated Eliza's extraordinarily strong and "uncontrollable" attachment to her parental home, something John Barry should have understood when he married her.[23]

Walworth proceeded to give a sentimental account of the marriage of John and Eliza, one designed to show how both were "at fault" in the failure of their marriage. At first, Eliza had loved her husband, "as few have ever loved before." Her letters to and about him revealed "the strong and convincing language of nature and of truth—the natural language of a heart which must have been perfectly satisfied." John too loved his wife intensely, although the chancellor thought that he detected from the beginning some harshness toward his wife, a hasty temper, explained, in part, by his financial difficulties. Such a temperament would not necessarily make him an unkind husband, although it would "naturally" require "more prudence and circumspection on the part of the wife."[24]

Three events dominated Walworth's narration, all of them events about which Eliza had testified. Each of them revealed what the chancellor termed John Barry's "unworthy desire to enforce implicit obedience to an unreasonable command, with the view of triumphing over her." The first occurred while they were still living in Liverpool. Eliza had accidentally swallowed a peach pit. John thought her life was in danger, and he consulted a doctor, who prescribed cream of tartar and sulfur mixed with honey. She refused to take the medicine, as she hated sulfur. John regarded her refusal as "a mere whim." The feelings of both became "too much excited," and John made it a matter of "principle" that she should give in. When she still refused, he declared, indiscreetly, that he would leave their bedroom until she complied. And that night he slept on the sofa in another room ("to the manifest danger of his own health," for, as she reported, "it was bitter cold weather"). The next afternoon, when she agreed to take the medicine, "he immediately took her in his arms and kissed her, said she was a good girl, and carried her to her room." Eliza, on the other hand, was unreconciled to her apparent submission and declared (in front of a servant) that their happiness was now at an end.

According to the chancellor, the second and third "difficulties" were ones in which John Barry was more "clearly" in the wrong. Shortly after the birth of their first child, while Eliza was still bedridden, her mother, who was acting as nurse, was called back to her own home. John had promised to take her mother's place, but, apparently angered that Eliza had spent $2 for a cot without his permission, he left her alone with her infant. A few months later the two argued after their black servant Dolly gave notice. John, who thought her "the best servant that ever lived," blamed Eliza. After their quarrel, he went away and stayed at his offices for ten days until she came and "sued for peace." To the chancellor, John's conduct was "overbearing and cruel."

None of these events were in themselves sufficient to "sever the strong cord of affection" that bound Eliza to John. Yet they had led her to the unwarranted suspicion that he was unfaithful and no longer loved her. And she fell into what we (looking behind the chancellor's ornate language) can only assume was a period of emotional depression. By the spring of 1838, when John left New York for Nova Scotia to look for work, she had resolved never to leave New York City.[25]

According to Chancellor Walworth, if John Barry "had always treated his wife with kindness," he would have declared it her duty "to have followed him [to] any part of the world where he had a reasonable prospect of bettering his condition." But, given John's prior conduct, Walworth did not believe John retained the right to insist on her cooperation. Grounds did not exist to justify a "final" or formal separation. In particular, the separation agreement between John and Eliza was void because it was a contract for a future separation rather than an agreement determining the consequences of a present separation.[26] Yet enough had occurred to justify her "both legally and morally" to refuse "for the present to place herself under his entire control, in a land of strangers."[27]

John Barry's various acts of unkindness and authoritarianism played a part in this decision, as perhaps did some judicial parochialism. Walworth felt some reluctance to support a foreigner, a Nova Scotian, a subject of the British crown, in his efforts to force an unwilling New York wife to leave her birthplace. But the chancellor's judgment rested, above all else, on his disapproval of John Barry's adamant insistence on his rights. Barry had never learned the forbearance that the sentimental judge regarded as the crucial lesson for success in marriage. Instead, he endangered "his former high standing, both as a gentleman and a Christian, by an indiscreet attempt to enforce what he believed to be his marital and paternal rights."[28]

The chancellor ruled that Eliza Barry was "equitably" justified in her refusal to accompany John to Nova Scotia, and thus she was not living in an illegal and immoral state of separation. She was not, as a result, someone who should be kept from custody of a child. As a judge, he had discretion to deny the writ of habeas corpus. A mother, "all other things being equal," was "the most proper person" to entrust with care of "an infant of . . . tender age," and there were no good reasons to deprive this mother of that responsibility. Indeed, forcing the child back into her father's custody, out of a mother's care, would not be a proper exercise of discretion, would instead "violate the law of nature." The child was not improperly restrained.[29]

The New York Supreme Court, which reviewed the chancellor's decision in 1840, thought the chancellor had misconceived the nature of legal or equitable discretion.[30] And in sustaining a new writ of habeas corpus, the justices unanimously rejected his narrative and his analysis of the case. The issue was not open, according to Chief Justice Greene Bronson; the law was settled. In controversies between husband and wife, the husband had the better title to the custody of minor children. The law regarded him "as the head of the family," it obliged him "to provide for its wants," and it committed "the children to his charge, in preference to the claims of the mother or any other person." Any sympathy the justices might "feel for this lady," or "however strongly" they might have wished that Barry "had relinquished his claim to one of the two children," was beside the point. They had "no choice but to administer the law" as they found it.[31]

Eliza had not established her legal right to a separation and therefore had not succeeded in challenging Barry's custodial rights. The child still belonged within Barry's private sphere. The narrative of the marriage revealed a number of incidents of anger and unkindness on Barry's part. Yet nothing had occurred by the summer of 1838 legally sufficient to authorize a judicial decree of separation. And even if Mrs. Barry had been able to charge her husband with those "grossly immoral acts" that might have authorized a judicial decree in her favor, it did not necessarily follow that she would be entitled to the child. But she had "no such heavy accusations to bring against her husband." Her case relied "on a highly wrought picture" of trivial conflicts, but such conflicts did not "form a proper subject for judicial inquiry." They were merely part of "the many little things which go to make up the happiness or misery of married life."[32]

Late in 1840, by a vote of 19–3, the New York Court for the Correction of Errors reversed the decision of the New York Supreme Court.[33] John Barry had lost again. And during 1841, his efforts to obtain a new writ of habeas corpus from Judge Thomas Oakley of the New York Superior Court failed as well. According to Oakley, Mercein's refusal to permit Barry to enter his house, to allow "visitation," did not change the situation. The custodial rights of Mary Barry had been settled. Still, Barry refused to accept defeat. "Surely no court in a Christian Country can intend to countenance such a definition of the law! It is too *monstrous* to think of, and I cannot submit to it, without making another attempt to vindicate my rights."[34] So Barry again sued out a writ of habeas corpus for the return of his child, this time going directly to the New York Supreme Court. And in 1842, the New York Supreme Court voted in his favor, this time on a two-to-one vote of the justices.[35] The child ought to be delivered to John Barry. But again, the New York Court of Errors reversed.[36]

In 1842 Justice Cowen used the issue of the purported separation agreement as an opportunity to vent his general disgust with the liberal trends he saw around him. To Cowen, coverture meant that a man could not grant anything to his wife, "for the grant would be to suppose her separate existence; and to covenant with her would be only to covenant with himself." Cowen knew that many separation agreements had been enforced by courts of equity in both England and in the United States, but he inveighed against extension of the trend as inconsistent with sound public morals. "Husbands and wives with feelings and appetites already too violent for the restraints of duty or of shame" were "thrown into the highway of temptation." More important still, children were not alienable goods, to be negotiated over by wife and husband. A father was obligated, because of the "character and condition which by law results from the state of marriage," to provide and to care for them, and he should not be able to evade his responsibility by contracting away their custody. Private agreements should not be used to avoid public duties.[37]

Cowen's opinion directly challenged Chancellor Walworth's 1839 efforts "to oppose the supposed necessities of nurture to the demands of law." In 1839 and 1840, when the child was just weaned, perhaps a temporary denial of the relator's rights had been justified. But in 1842, with Mary now five years of age, "Why should this child be longer withheld?" Barry had a right to train his child "to serve him affectionately in the business of his household," and he had a right to see her "properly educated." Indeed, such training was "essential to the child's welfare." Conversely, the claim that a daughter should be left under the control of a mother who voluntarily separated herself from her husband would, "if allowed, work an entire subversion" of a moral marital order. For one thing, legal recognition of the mother's claim would teach the child an immoral lesson about the capacity of dependents (like wife and daughters) to escape from their rightful obligations to their superiors. For another, such recognition would reward the mother for her misconduct in refusing to return to her husband. In any event, Walworth's judgment that Eliza would be a better custodian than John was wrong. Whatever may have been his situation earlier, in 1842 John Barry commanded "a comfortable home with adequate means for supporting the child." He was "at the head of an interesting family," made up of "daughters, . . . bred under his care in the best manner." That he was "qualified, and eminently so, for the moral and mental instruction of this child" was "clear."[38]

JOHN BARRY'S VERSION

Barry himself found every element of Walworth's 1839 opinion outrageous and personally offensive. Only danger to the child—a charge not made—or immoral character—a charge refuted—would justify denying his right to custody of his daughter. He was not one of those "foul characters" contemplated by the law. He was, rather, a kindly, admittedly imperfect, husband, who had tried "to conciliate, and to bring to something like reasonable terms, in a peaceful and private manner, one of the most unreasonable—and inexorable, because one of the most romantic of women."[39]

Walworth's judgment had been twisted by Eliza Barry's "female artfulness," which overwhelmed his "moral courage." Walworth had seen her as "a very angel," as "all love, affection, and forgiveness." But she wasn't. More important, her claim to custody invaded "a province not hers," and it showed "her want of good, sound, discriminating common sense." In declaring that Eliza was the proper person to be entrusted with custody of their daughter, Walworth was denying "unpalatable scriptural truth" and violating "natural" laws. Walworth had done more than even Fanny Wright (the notorious sex radical) might imagine could be done to "break down the bulwarks, and loosen all the foundations of social and domestic life, and consequently of all civil society." In deciding that Eliza's separation from John was neither immoral nor illegal, Walworth had produced a legal situation "calculated to bring into the most sovereign contempt, all the doctrines . . . so elaborately advanced and asserted for the sanctity and indissolubility of the marriage relation." And he had imposed on Barry a "thralldom," a form of bondage, and inflicted "a suffering and an anguish which only the Almighty himself possesses the prerogative to impose."[40]

Walworth wrote as if the antenuptial "agreement" that the couple would move to and live in New York City had some sort of legal effect. Barry, following standard doctrine, insisted that such an agreement was clearly unenforceable because it changed a fundamental term of marriage. Furthermore, even if it were theoretically enforceable, it had been complied with when John and Eliza moved back to New York City one year after their marriage. He was under no legal or moral obligation to remain in New York in perpetuity. Indeed, no just legal order would ever compel such a reading. He had a right to move where he chose in pursuit of his livelihood, and he had a right to expect his wife to accompany him.

Walworth had also given inordinate weight to small and inconsequential conflicts, conflicts that Barry himself had forgotten. Such conflicts occurred within the private sphere of marriage. "For sound reasons of public policy," they should never become legal grounds for separation. These conflicts were, according to Eliza's own testimony, quickly resolved. If so, how could such petty stories become the foundation for her right to live apart? In none had John revealed or expressed the violence or the corruption that provided the legal foundation for a wife's separation.[41]

Walworth had claimed that he was not settling a question of guardianship or of legal right, that he had only decided whether the child was being held under such restraint as to justify the intervention of the court. Yet in ordinary legal practice the writ of habeas corpus was the means by which a father's legal rights were tested. If the writ were refused it must be because of proven misconduct on the father's part as a husband. And when Walworth held that Barry was not entitled to enforce the writ, he labeled (and libeled) Barry as an unfit husband and father, as a bad man, dishonored, lacking in virtue. Otherwise the writ would have been enforced. Worse yet, Walworth had entrusted the child to a mother who, as the chancellor himself acknowledged, did not have grounds for a legal separation, a wife who had left her husband because of what Walworth labeled a monomania about staying close to her father's family.

Much in Barry's polemic imagined himself as victimized by the dangerous powers of women. Behind John Barry's misogyny, however, was the question of his rights as husband and as father. If he did have rights in his child, and even Walworth seemed to concede the point, then how could the chancellor deny their enforcement? There was no foundation for the kind of equitable discretion, for the moralistic judgment, that Walworth claimed as rightfully his to make. It was "the province and the duty of the Court, to determine what the laws are, . . . not what it is desirable that they should be."[42]

Barry particularly resented Walworth's notion that his very insistence on his husbandly rights justified Eliza's separation. That insistence was not at all inconsistent with a course of conduct toward Eliza Barry marked by "liberality and generosity." He never intended to violate her rights nor to deal with her on any basis other than that of fairness and kindness. In the prosecution of his rights, however, he would not be intimidated or sidetracked by the chancellor's "bugbear." He would never allow "one solitary right to be wrested" from him. "Matrimonial and parental rights and claims" were "not to be measured in their importance by money;—nor placed in the scale with wealth." And he, John Barry, was not the sort of man who would "yield his child." "No!" He would never "submit," until he had learned that such was "the law of this land; yes, to use no uncommon phrase, of this 'land of law.'" But he knew it was not: there were too many millions of other men, similarly situated, who also needed to be protected by the same laws.[43]

MODERN VERSIONS

John Barry lost. And, what is more, the law of child custody soon assumed that the decision "who gets the child" was theoretically independent from conclusions as to a husband's fault. Judges drew on a liberal critique of parental power rooted in eighteenth-century educational theory, as well as on a vague but potent analogy between wrongful power within the institution of the family and the institution of slavery. Particularly after the Civil War, it became important to say that children were "not property" as a way to emphasize that they were not enslaved to their fathers.[44]

We can see important elements of this "modern" point of view in one published opinion in the *Mercein* proceedings, Senator Alonzo Paige's 1840 opinion as a member of the Court of Errors. The "great principle" that Paige found running through American and English cases was that judicial attention ought principally to be directed to "the benefit and welfare of the infant." Like the chancellor, he believed the mother was "the most proper person to be entrusted with the custody of a child of this tender age." He also shared the chancellor's sense that a good father would not press his claims to custody if inconsistent with the child's best interests.[45] Yet he rooted those judgments in a broader statement of judicial authority and in a different political vision of the nature of parental rights.

The evolutionary story Paige told began with the state of nature. There, a father had no rights superior to those of a mother. All he had was power over others in his family. With the coming of civil society, that power, the power of the "chief of a family," was transferred to the government of a nation, which then delegated to parents "such portion of the sovereign power . . . subject to such restrictions and limitations" as was thought "proper to prescribe." From then on no parental power existed independent of the state. And when civil authority deprived a father of parental authority, the decision did not "come in conflict with or subvert any of the principles of the natural law." A child was, first of all, a citizen of the country of its birth, "entitled to the protection of that government." Thus, in custody decisions the "welfare, comfort and interests" of the child were determinative.[46]

Contemporaries read the collective opinions as leaving the law of child custody in a deeply confused state. In 1841 Judge Oakley gratefully invoked res judicata to deny a new writ of habeas corpus brought by John Barry. If he were to decide the substantive issues, he wrote, he would have a difficult time of it because "[t]he legal principles . . . have not been rendered more certain . . . by the elaborate but apparently conflicting opinions" of the high court judges.[47] In his 1845 treatise, Edward Mansfield characterized the traditional rule of a father's right as barbaric and described *People v. Mercein* as unsettling and overturning that rule. Yet his statement of the holding of the case was narrow: "where the mother *was not morally guilty,* and a separation took place between the parents," courts would give the custody of *daughters* to the mother.[48]

Throughout the rest of the nineteenth century (indeed, well into the twentieth century), litigants and judges constantly claimed the various opinions in *Mercein* for every side and position. The case was authority for the state's interest in child care. It was also authority for parental autonomy and authority. It was relied on by women asserting the propriety and legality of a court determination in their favor. It was also cited by courts and lawyers that wished to reaffirm a father's right.[49] In his 1868 *Treatise on the Constitutional Limitations,* Thomas Cooley concluded a short discussion of the use of the writ of habeas corpus in domestic relations by noting that, on the one hand, the father's right was "generally recognized as best." That right, however, was not absolute and had to "yield to what appears to be for the interest of the child." Courts had great discretionary authority, and "the tendency of modern decisions" was to expand that authority. "Barry's case" was then cited as primary authority since it exhausted "all the law on the subject."[50]

Specialized treatises agreed on *Mercein's* significance, although they too struggled to reduce it to a particular holding. To Rollin Hurd, it embodied the novel "spirit of the American cases," although he also recognized that it was more "remarkable for great research and ability displayed in the discussion of the questions involved," and for the "exceeding pertinacity with which it was pursued" by John Barry, than for the legal issues it settled.[51] Other treatise writers used it to establish sharply conflicting points. In the seventh edition of Story's equity treatise, *Mercein* stood for the proposition that as "between husband and wife, the custody of the children generally belongs to the husband; and the latter cannot, by an agreement with his wife, . . . alienate to her the right to the custody and care of the children."[52] Some writers saw it as limiting a father's authority; others saw it as establishing a mother's right, particularly if the child were of "tender years." It stood as confirmation of the inability of the courts to compel a wife to reside with her husband. It also established that a custody determination (through habeas corpus) would be conclusive (res judicata) while the circumstances of the parties remained unchanged, a bar to subsequent writs of habeas corpus by the noncustodial parent.

Still, over the rest of the nineteenth century, the predominant meaning derived from *Mercein* was the expected one: that the authority of courts and other public officials to determine the best interests of the child stood superior to any parental rights, distinctively those of fathers. In 1847, for example, Judge Oakley of the New York Superior Court heard another custody case between a separated husband and wife, and again he reexamined the opinions of the higher court judges in *Mercein*. His conclusion: "The general doctrine" that a father had "an absolute right to the custody of his child, if personally unobjectionable," was not "sustained by the law of this state." Instead, courts exercised a "sound discretion" in pursuit solely of the child's best interests.[53] Or, as courts across America often put it, the best interests of the child became the "polestar" of child custody law.[54]

In part, this reading of the Barry precedent became increasingly persuasive as more mothers succeeded in divorce actions against their former husbands. Once a divorce had been decreed, once a wife was released "from all marital obligations or obedience to him," a husband was no longer her "superior." She had been uncovered, had regained an identity as an independent legal person. Courts found themselves compelled to judge between two competent individuals, and to resolve the dilemma they turned from questions of parental rights to "the harmonized interests of the community and of the child," to the "best interests" test, and to the "tender years" presumption in favor of mothers. When a man was no longer a husband, it was hard to grant him a right that was understood as part of a husbandly identity.[55]

Yet the ascendancy of the "best interests" test, and of the increasingly widespread practice of granting custody to separated or divorced mothers, did not mean the end of a father's right. Instead, precedents diverged into two contending streams, both of which drew sustenance from the Barry case. A structure of understandings that had once been hegemonic—tacit and presumptively true—was on its way to becoming ideological—contested, challenged, and recognizably partial. There were precedents on every side, and who won depended, not on the law, but on who judged.

A steady stream of appellate decisions relied on the opinions of Bronson and Cowen. In these cases, too, the best interests of the child were said to be the sole concern. But the question how to secure the child's best interests was understood as answered definitively by the inherited law of marriage and coverture, which established where a child's best interests lay. Judicial discretion to interfere with a father's right to custody of his children depended on a demonstration of his wrongdoing as a husband. Absent such proof, the authority of a head of a household remained secure within his private sphere, to the exclusion of judicial discretion. And courts had no business entering into an abstract and indeterminate discussion of who might be better as a parent or where the child's best interests lay. Their only business was to recognize and to give legal effect to a father's right.[56]

Nearly all of these cases involved struggles for custody between a husband and a wife who had "voluntarily" separated herself from her husband and who was not, as a result, entitled to a legal divorce. None of them followed from successful divorces or legally enforceable separations. The polestar here was the wife's reasons for separating herself from her marriage. If she had the right to leave because of her husband's misbehavior or cruelty, then things became complicated, although judges cautioned that even then there was no necessary obligation to award her custody. But once her separation was recognized as unjustified, as unlawful and illegal, as voluntary, then the rest was easy. The father would get the child. Her reasons for leaving were irrelevant because they were merely her reasons as a separate individual, not as an abused wife. Indeed, her selfishness in leaving established that she was not a proper custodian and allowed stern judges to counter the sentimental presumptions of a culture that sanctified motherhood.[57]

By the 1860s, a few legislatures began to pass statutes that explicitly granted married mothers guardianship and custody rights.[58] New York's 1860 version was part of a dramatic, potentially revolutionary statute that gave a married woman the right to keep and control her earnings and other property and established a procedure to allow her to act with regard to her separate estate without need for the concurrence or participation of her husband. According to Elizabeth Cady Stanton, who addressed the New York legislature the day before the statute was enacted, women needed only to be left alone, freed from the spurious protections of coverture. "In mercy, let us take care of ourselves, our property, our children, and our homes." The apparent intent of the statute was to create a new legal identity for a wife, one less dependent on her husband, one that included specific recognition as a parent, possessing power as well as love and respect. Every married woman was "constituted and declared . . . the joint guardian of her children, with her husband, with equal power, rights and duties with regard to them."[59]

The first and only judicial test of the custody provision of this new law occurred in 1861. Clark Brooks had applied for a writ of habeas corpus for the return of his son from the custody of his separated wife Lydia. Lydia, according to Clark's petition, had left him "without any just cause or provocation, and remained away without his consent and against his wishes." His writ should be granted because he was "of good moral character and habits, and in all respects suitable and competent to take care of" wife and child, and he had never "abused or ill treated" his wife. But the lower court judge held that the new law meant that a married mother retained custody of her child unless she was not of good moral character and habits. The father's moral character was irrelevant because the mother was presumptively entitled to custody under the new law.

That holding was, however, quickly reversed in an opinion drafted by Justice William Allen of the New York Supreme Court's Appellate Division. Allen did not hide his disgust with the new law. Some incremental modifications to the old husband-centered regime had already occurred. But anything further constituted a radical and incoherent interference into established rights and duties. Legal reformers had not, "as yet," taken from the husband the duties and rights that were part of being the legally responsible head of the family. Coverture had survived the legislative onslaught. A husband was still obligated to support his wife, to pay her debts, to "govern his house properly." He was bound to support his children, in return for which he was given the right to their labor. In that context, what could it mean to make a wife the joint guardian of children with power equal to her husband? Taken literally, as written, the new custody law implied a transformation in the whole inherited structure of legal marriage. A law that authorized a wife, "in the absence of any fault in the husband," to claim sole custody of the children, "preferring her to the husband," would have to impose upon her duties and responsibilities corresponding to those that had traditionally fallen on husbands, and the necessary power to discharge them. Was that what the legislature intended? If so, wrote Allen, if the legislature meant to effect such a revolutionary change, it had to say so in "very plain and explicit" terms, for "nothing should be taken in favor of social anarchy and domestic anarchy, by implication." If passage of the law meant that a wife could now leave her husband's bed and board, repudiate her vows and duties, and still keep custody of children, then "very great and sad changes [had] been made by a very short statute."

But, wrote Allen, one did not need to read the law as changing anything at all. One could simply interpret it as meaningless, as Allen proceeded to do. Since the law did not set aside a father's right, it conferred no new rights upon a mother, except for the right to enjoy parenthood jointly with the father. It gave her a form of custody that had to be exercised with her husband, "not away from him or exclusive of him." If a separated wife could gain custody against her husband's wishes, as the lower court had held, the effect would have been to give her exclusive control, not shared control. The statute would then have destroyed a father's common law marital rights, "at the option of the wife." But again, since nothing in the statute explicitly conferred rights on a wife separated from her husband, the law could only have effect when the parents lived together. When they moved apart, the husband regained his common law rights, including the right to custody over his children.[60]

And one year later the New York legislature amended the 1860 law, among other changes repealing the custody provision.[61]

In 1882 the New York Court of Common Pleas (a lower court) overruled the old rule that separation agreements granting custody to wives did not bind or stop husbands from recovering custody when they wished to do so. In 1916 the New York Supreme Court agreed. The "world" had "moved" since 1842, wrote Justice Clarence Shearn. New York State had finally "emerged from the Dark Ages, during which married women had the status of slaves and chattels." No "enlightened" court still held to a conception of the "being" of a wife "suspended" during marriage. A wife was free to contract "with the freedom of a feme sole," free to contract even with her husband (except that she could not release him from his obligation to support her). And her contract with her husband for custody would be enforced. A father no longer had a paramount right.[62]

Nonetheless, in decisions before and after, throughout the second half of the nineteenth century, well into the twentieth century, in New York State and elsewhere, some judges continued to rely on the opinions of Bronson and Cowen that affirmed a father's right as paramount. A notorious 1905 New York decision held, much as the old New York Supreme Court had, that a boy awarded to the mother two years earlier when the boy was three was no longer of so "tender" an age as to need maternal care, and so a father's right should trump a mother's claim.[63] Or, as the Illinois Supreme Court put it in 1921, a father (although a drunkard) had a right to custody against the world, so long as there was no demonstration that he had forfeited that right.[64] Even decisions that denied the principle of a father's paramount right often still incorporated the framework from which it derived. One judge explained that a mother should retain custody not because her rights were superior or equal, but because the wife had been "allowed" by her husband to live apart from him and to keep her children with her. The father's paramount right was demonstrated by the mother's custody.[65]

Courts committed to a father's paramount right often distinguished custody cases between divorced parents from ones between separated parents. And yet, even in the case of divorce, even where the husband was adjudged to have been the party at fault, even after a father had lost custody, still the shadow of his "paramount" right remained. Consider the case of Nancy and Alexander Burritt. In the early 1840s, while she was on a trip with her baby daughter to visit relatives in New York, he left their Illinois home with their sons and his lover and moved to Ohio.[66] She divorced him in Illinois in 1843 where she was awarded both custody of the baby and $50 alimony per year for six years. Fifteen years later, she went back to court in New York to "recover" $3,900 plus interest for the support of the child, alleging that Dr. Burritt had "abandoned . . . and neglected" his daughter.

The good doctor responded that he had done as ordered by the divorce decree, paying alimony and giving up custody in the daughter, and that he had not abandoned his daughter but owed nothing for her support, since he had been deprived both of the opportunity to care for her and of the services that she would have owed him. And the New York Supreme Court agreed. A father's liability for the support of his child derived from his position as head of the household, as well as his right to the child's "society and services." Where a divorced wife assumed her former husband's rights, she also assumed his former responsibilities. Any other decision, wrote the court, would be doubly oppressive: depriving him entirely of his child and then requiring his "compliance" with his ex-wife's demands.

There are two plausible readings of the holding. One imagines custody as the prerequisite to support (a position that resonates with the claims some fathers' rights groups make today), that a husband deprived of his parental rights no longer had parental duties. In other words, custody was not to be understood in the modern mode as a discretionary choice between two potential custodial parents, both of whom remained responsible as parents; rather, custody was a taking away of paternal rights, an intervention into a husband's private sphere, a deprivation. And once deprived of rights, duties disappeared as well. Alternatively, one can read the opinion as characterizing the Burritts' situation as one where the father had met his obligation to support by allowing his ex-wife to assume it. The father was free to "exercise" his obligation in a manner that suited his "convenience" or "comfort," and the mother could "intervene" only when there was a demonstration of "substantial omission" on his part. The fifteen years of no support was not such a demonstration.[67]

A close reading of *Mercein,* combined with a survey of the cases that relied on it, reveals how difficult it has been to separate child custody determinations from a husband's legal rights. Such rights were not simply atavisms from a rejected past. The presumptive right of a man to custody over dependents defined what it was to be a free man and a husband. And that presumptive right had a complementary impact on the legal consciousness of separating wives as well. Eliza Barry never challenged her husband's continuing custody claims over their young son. She conceded his right, whether because of the terms of their separation agreement or because she assumed that a boy beyond infancy "belonged" with his father. Nor was her defense of her custody over their daughter framed, at least at first, in terms of her natural right or even her daughter's needs. Rather, she or her lawyers devised her case as if the point was to give effect to John Barry's express alienation through the separation agreement of his right over his infant daughter. Her defense, her challenge to his custody claim, might be read as a concession of his legal right.

Those judges who worked to develop the notion of parens patriae—the notion of the state's responsibility for the best interests of the child—saw that notion as of a piece with conceptions of the police power. Parens patriae justified the regulation and modification of private (property or husbandly) rights, but it, like the police power, would not have made sense to most judges without the prior existence of private rights. Parens patriae epitomized the public values of a legitimate public sphere, of the state's growing responsibility to assure "the best interests of the child." As such, it would often (depending on the judge's sensibility and the precedents he found available to him) take precedence over traditional parental (husband's) rights. It was not, however, understood as an abrogation of those rights.

Unless we understand the continuing emotional power of the structure of husbandly parental rights, we will never fully appreciate the courage and ingenuity of the women—and their lawyers—who worked to undo coverture and the father's right. To many early feminists, the image of marriage implicit in the continuing reality of a father's legal powers made marriage law into an exact parallel of slave law and made any defense of the traditional law equivalent to a defense of the morally corrupt slaveholders' constitution. They believed that change would require a fundamental social and constitutional reconstruction.[68] Women like Eliza Barry pursued, of necessity, a different strategy. Their goal had to be to persuade male judges and other public decisionmakers both that there were socially and legally accepted reasons for denying husbands' particular vested claims and, as well, that the exercise of judicial discretion in such situations was part of the judges' institutional role. They had to make a father's right appear less vested—less certain of enforcement—than it had been (in the process reconstructing judges as benevolent patriarchs), in order to create the legal conditions for the undoing of that right.

And along the way, women like Eliza Barry made men like John Barry realize that a structure of rights and entitlements on which they had long relied, a structure they had assumed provided a foundation for a just society, could no longer be taken as given. Even when courts reaffirmed paternal rights, they did so in a context where those rights had to be asserted noisily, aggressively, in a context where rights were contested, partial, and indeterminate.

8

The Right to Kill

> By the contemplation of law the wife is always in the husband's
> presence, always under his wing; and any movement against her
> person is a movement against his right and may be resisted as such.
> *Edwin Stanton,* Trial of Daniel E. Sickles *(1859)*

By the 1850s, many aspects of family law appeared uncertain and contested. Law reform had altered the balance of legal power within marriage, and mid-nineteenth-century husbands had lost some security of
possession over their domestic domains.

Still, if a man found his wife in the arms of another man, and he killed
the other man on the spot, he would never be charged with murder. His
exemption was part of a complex of self-defense rights, at one with his
right to shoot a burglar or a malicious trespasser, to repel, violently if
necessary, someone who had invaded his property (although, like other
property holders, the man might be convicted of manslaughter). His exemption was part of the privileged identity of a husband. Other men in
protective or patriarchal roles—fathers, brothers, sons, fiancés—possessed no articulated exemption from prosecution for murder if they
killed seducers found in the arms of their dependents. Nor were wives
entitled to kill their husbands' lovers. All of them—wives as well as fathers, brothers, sons, and fiancés—often escaped conviction and punishment when juries refused to convict. But only a husband had a developed legal right.

And he had that right only if he had found his wife and her lover together in a seriously and unquestionably compromising position. And
only if he had acted immediately. Time was of the essence. The privilege
demanded an act "in the heat of passion." Otherwise, if he dawdled, if he
planned, he became a premeditating murderer. He became someone who

should have looked to his remedies at law for the harm the seducer had done him but who, instead, had taken the law into his own hands, subverting the peace of the community. His situation was no longer distinguishable from that faced by other men, all of whom faced provocations, all of whom were expected to resist the impulse to violence, all of whom were expected to look to the law rather than to self-help and to arms.

This was the unwritten law. That is, there was a particular practice called "the unwritten law" within the general domain of the criminal law (a practice that survived into the 1970s as a written unwritten law in the statute books of a few American states).[1] The unwritten law existed, if we take what American criminal courts did as our guides. Moreover, American lawyers and judges talked and wrote about it as if it were a recognized part of the law. And yet its status as law—as a part of the doctrinal structures of marriage and crime—was always uncertain and contested. Blackstone and Hale had denied that killing a wife's lover ever constituted justifiable homicide. Tapping Reeve had written that a man was never justified in killing his wife's seducer. The principle, according to Reeve, was that a husband, as the wife's representative, could do anything that the wife could do. Thus, he could kill her rapist, since she could have done so as a matter of self-defense. But, since the wife had no right to kill her seducer, so he did not. Other writers on husbands' rights and privileges ignored the unwritten law entirely.[2]

Still, it existed in spite of the treatise writers' denial. But only as an exemption for acts committed by husbands in the heat of passion, and never when there was "sufficient cooling time for passion to subside and reason to interpose." Then the act became "deliberate revenge"—murder—and the unwritten law, whatever its status in legal doctrine, ought to have been irrelevant.[3]

TRIALS

In 1859, in 1867, and again in 1869–1870, Americans were transfixed by the trials of men who had murdered their wives' lovers. Often identified in hyphenated form by the last names of both killer and victim (although who was really the victim became the subject of much legal argument)—Sickles-Key, Cole-Hiscock, McFarland-Richardson—each of these trials became major media events. In addition to unceasing and sensationalizing newspaper coverage and editorial commentary, complete transcripts were published, sometimes in multiple and competitive editions.[4] Pamphlets separately reproduced the opening and closing arguments to the juries of the defense attorneys.[5] The lawyers who argued the cases became celebrities, particularly the overlapping group of men who acted as defense attorneys.

These trials tell us much about changing understandings of gender, of contending visions of marriage, of the role of the mass media in American life, of the interactions between law and the mass media, of the ways Americans thought about honor and law and violence. They reproduced and developed a national debate about the legal and religious nature of marriage and the relative rights and duties of husbands and wives. Moreover, these trials reveal a profound sense of male disquietude because of lost or changing rights and traditions, and the cases themselves were used by defense lawyers and by parts of the media to create a new legal understanding designed to restore male honor and property rights in women.

The crucial facts were never at issue. In each case the injured husband had shot the adulterer in a public place in front of witnesses. Each defendant relied on the unwritten law, although none of them could claim that he had found his wife in the arms of her lover and done the deed immediately, as the received law appeared to require. And each defendant was eventually acquitted of all charges.[6]

Sickles involved a congressman from New York City, Daniel Sickles, a Tammany henchman, whose much younger wife, Teresa Bagioli Sickles, was engaged in an active affair with Philip Barton Key, the district attorney for Washington, D.C., and the son of the composer of "The Star Spangled Banner." When Sickles discovered the place of assignation, he made his wife write out a confession—"There was a bed in the second story. I did what is usual for a wicked woman to do"—concluding with the statement that she had written the confession "without any inducement held out by Mr. Sickles of forgiveness or reward, and without any menace from him." Then, the next morning, when Key walked by Sickles's house and gave the secret signal for Teresa, Sickles came out and shot him dead.[7]

In *Cole,* George Cole was a doctor and druggist who had become a major general of volunteers during the Civil War. When he returned to upstate New York, a wounded hero, he found his wife distracted and unwilling to sleep with him. Later he discovered that his old friend and lawyer, L. Harris Hiscock, had forced himself on her (at least that is the way her confession was phrased). Cole consulted with various men about what to do, including his wife's brother. Then he took a train trip to Syracuse, where Hiscock was serving as a member of the state constitutional convention. Cole walked into the convention hall and shot and killed Hiscock.[8]

The published McFarland-Richardson trial transcripts told a much more complicated and contested story, one that remains unclear in a variety of respects. Daniel McFarland was a well-educated Irish immigrant. He married Abby Sage, a young New England woman, in the late 1850s. They spent the next decade wandering around America, as Daniel fruitlessly tried to make his fortune.[9] Meanwhile, Abby Sage gained a small reputation as an actress and as a public reader. She also began to publish some children's stories. Both of them moved among the culturally and politically radical literary figures and journalists who circled around Horace Greeley's *New York Tribune*. She became the intimate of several politically active women, including Lucy Calhoun, a pioneering woman journalist. These women supported Abby's career ambitions and encouraged her to leave her marriage. At the same time, she also grew close (how close we will never know) to Albert Richardson, a nationally famous journalist and author.[10]

In early 1867 she left McFarland, later claiming that she had done so because he was an abusive alcoholic.[11] She moved first to the home of the publisher of the *Tribune* and then to an apartment in the same boardinghouse where Richardson lived. One month later, McFarland shot and slightly wounded Richardson, after intercepting a passionate letter Richardson had written to Abby. ("I never seek my pillow without wanting to fold you in my arms for a good-night kiss and blessing, and the few months before you can openly be mine will be long enough at best. No grass shall grow under my feet.")[12] Daniel began a habeas corpus action—a child custody suit—to recover his children. That suit ended with a negotiated agreement that each parent would have one child. He also initiated a suit for alienation of affections against Richardson, which may have led to a monetary settlement (and perhaps an offer of a consulate from some of Richardson's powerful political friends). Then, in late 1868, Abby moved to Indiana to establish residency so that she could get a divorce there. In October 1869 she received the divorce and returned to New York.

In November, after Albert Richardson had published a notice stating his intention to marry Abby Sage, and after rumors had circulated that Abby and Albert were living together in New Jersey as husband and wife, Daniel McFarland went to the offices of the *New York Tribune,* where he again shot Richardson, this time mortally. Richardson lingered for nearly two months, and during that time, two prominent clergyman, one of them Henry Ward Beecher, presided at a notorious bedside marriage of Albert to Abby.

Distinctive facts create distinctive stories. Yet these three trials were understood as a sequence. The lawyers in each succeeding case mobilized the previous trial as precedent and authority, recycling arguments and images from one to the next.

Commentators of all political persuasions understood them as a sequence in a different sense. *Sickles* through *Cole* to *McFarland* represented the complete breakdown of the traditional boundaries of the unwritten law. According to George Templeton Strong, *Sickles* already stood for the corrupt principle that "the seducing of a wife or near kinswoman (or even the erroneous belief in such seduction) justifies homicide."[13] Still Sickles, the defendant, could be viewed as having acted in a way that had traditionally entitled husbands to acquittal. He shot in immediate response to Key's signal. He had not waited and planned. Cole's lawyers, in contrast, faced the problem of proving his right to an acquittal in the face of the facts that the affair had occurred in the past and that their client had traveled a long distance to find and kill the seducer. The prosecutors sought to distinguish Cole's premeditated act from that of Sickles, but Cole's lawyers insisted on the likeness of the two cases. They emphasized their client's frenzy, his loss of control, his absence of agency in the face of dishonor and shame, all of which provided the continuity between commission, discovery, and killing that would substitute for an immediate act.[14] In McFarland-Richardson, the defendant's wife had left him more than two years before; she had been divorced from him; and the man he killed was publicly her fiancé, not her seducer. And in this case there was no clear evidence of seduction, no confession. Whatever had occurred had apparently resulted from Abby's independent decision to leave Daniel. Thus, his lawyers had to recreate the defense in a way that minimized the significance of traditional understandings of the unwritten law. They did so by focusing less on the discovery of adultery itself (although they emphasized the letters Richardson sent and

McFarland discovered as precipitating events) and more on the disintegration of McFarland's family life and marriage as caused by the misdeeds of Richardson and his henchmen, including the circle of men and women around the *New York Tribune*, "free lovers," who worked to destroy McFarland's marriage.[15] They had driven McFarland crazy, and thus Richardson's death was their fault.

Defense attorneys constructed persuasive narratives that justified their clients' acquittal by imagining an embattled husbandly identity, an identity confronted by evil men—seducers—whose only goal was the destruction of domestic peace. In the narratives, a wife's actual seducer was primary. But the lawyers' arguments implicitly connected that evil man to a larger world of law reformers and woman's rights activists, groups who had violated the sanctity of the "marriage bed," and who were busily remaking the holy institution of marriage. The nature of the threat was posed in broad and general terms, to be experienced sympathetically by the jurors. And the response that the attorneys demanded was a collective one where male egos would join together in solidarity.

Who were the lawyers who constructed these legal narratives? Two members from the three defense teams had particular prominence. James Brady represented both Sickles and Cole but died suddenly just before the trial of Daniel McFarland. John Graham represented Sickles and McFarland, and his closing address in the latter trial became one of the most famous speeches in nineteenth-century legal culture. The two shared a common ethnic and political viewpoint. Both were Irish-American, Catholic, and Democratic, although Brady did become a strong Unionist during the Civil War.[16] All the defense lawyers were legal professionals, not husbands' rights ideologues. One was Edwin Stanton, who became Abraham Lincoln's secretary of war. Another was Amasa Parker, co-editor of the 1862 edition of Tapping Reeve's treatise. A third was Charles S. Spencer, who would later deliver a eulogy for the abolitionist Charles Sumner. Brady was the author of a much reproduced speech in support of woman's rights. Graham represented wives in prominent, indeed notorious, divorce trials.[17]

As always with lawyers, we cannot know what they really believed. Nor can we know what juries actually took from the defense case, what persuaded them to acquit. And yet that inevitable mystery should not obscure the coherence and the power of the narratives that the lawyers constructed. These were skillful and successful courtroom advocates, with great insight and understanding of what would convince a body of male jurors to acquit. Their success was not preordained, and their professional eminence (however grudgingly conceded by more elite members of the bar) was not accidental.[18]

They were gifted improvisers on the culture, drawing on images and perspectives available to all men: emphasizing some things, minimizing others, reframing a common stock of knowledge and belief. Their rhetorical strategies reveal tacit assumptions about male authority and legal authority and about how men on juries understood (or learned to understand) the world around them.[19]

They succeeded because traditional notions of marital authority had become contested and uncertain in mid-nineteenth-century America, because wives were understood as having gained public rights that necessarily meant losses of rights for husbands. The lawyers pictured a corrupted present and advocated a return to the bedrock of the past. Brady and Graham in particular were masters of the "either-or" technique. Either acquit, thereby recreating Biblical truth, or accept a new world of independent wives and libertines. The refrain was that jurors needed to acquit so that they—jurors, like other husbands—could rest secure that their own families would remain true to the eternal verities.[20]

Eternal primordial truth required acquittal. Yet, to gain an acquittal, defense lawyers had to assume the role of law reformers, had to insist on the need for legal change. On the one hand, the lawyers were teaching the juries how to think about change and about events that were frightening and novel, and what they, as jurors, could do about those changes. On the other hand, the lawyers had to convince judges of the need to modify and reform "archaic" evidentiary rules. The lawyers worked to create new legal practices that would legitimize male honor and private vengeance. Those emergent practices improvised on, yet also stood in opposition to, inherited legal traditions.

ARGUMENTS AND STORIES

In each trial, opening and closing defense speeches made the same claims: that the lover deserved to die, that the husband was defending the home against an intruder, that he was doing what any natural husband would do, that his madness, if that is what it was, was one that any true man, including any member of the jury, would naturally experience were he confronted with the situation, that it was the job of the jury to defend the threatened and embattled traditional institution of marriage. Defense lawyers infused their arguments with a sense of crisis and of looming chaos, laying on the jury the duty to recreate moral order through acquittal.

Out of particular facts, the lawyers wove schematic images of the central characters. McFarland and Cole were both portrayed as mild-mannered, "domesticated" men, only seeking peace and a quiet home life. They were ordinary men, no different than those sitting in the jury box. While Abby loved to party, Daniel, according to his lawyers, wanted nothing more than a quiet evening by the fire educating his children. Cole was a wounded hero, only seeking to reclaim the love he had left when he went off to war, confused (not angered) by his wife's coldness. Trusting and open, he continued his friendship with Hiscock.

By the time of the trial, they were both "broken" men. In attorney William J. Hadley's opening argument for Cole, the jury was told that its deliberations were

to decide for him the solemn and momentous questions, whether he shall be restored (not to home, for home, alas, he has none); not to wife (for wife though living, is dead to him as though the cold grave enclosed her once loved form), but whether he shall be restored to liberty, and to the companionship and affection of his loved children, and be permitted to endure the remainder of his wretched and heart-broken existence, until a merciful God shall relieve him from further suffering by calling his crushed and wounded spirit home.

Both McFarland and Cole were portrayed as long-suffering, genteel, and gentle. But both had been driven to distraction.[21]

Sickles was harder to portray in this way, since he had a compromised reputation in Washington and had almost certainly engaged in several affairs during his marriage. As a result, his lawyers spent little time characterizing him, keeping the attention on Key, the seducer. Like the others, though, he was understood (undoubtedly correctly) as obsessed with his honor.

The seducers were portrayed monotonally. They were libidinous scoundrels, who deserved to die for having "polluted" the wife's "being." According to the anonymous editor of one of the two published editions of the McFarland trial, "The traitor who invades a man's sanctuary—

who steals into his Holy of Holies—thus to pollute it, expects nothing short of death if he is detected, and it would be a great pity to disappoint him." If husbands were seen as passionate and obsessed and innocent, their nemeses became strategic and calculating. Snakelike images abounded.[22] Hiscock became something close to a rapist. Defense attorneys made sure the jury understood that these were men who knew exactly what they were doing, that they understood the risks they ran in seducing weak women, in destroying husbands' peace of mind. Hiscock, they emphasized, was a lawyer and a legislator; Key was the district attorney in Washington, D.C.; Richardson was a sophisticated and accomplished man of the world. According to the lawyers all the libertines knew a fact we shall return to: that adultery was not a crime in the statute book and that, as a result, a husband would be forced to resort to the law of nature, would have to take the law into his own hands, were he to discover that his wife had fallen into the arms of a seducer.

In the rhetoric of the unwritten law, wives were barely relevant. The struggle was one between men. Just as you did not need to characterize the qualities of a farm in order to know that it had been trespassed on or flooded, so defense attorneys worked to minimize the presence and individuality of the wives. Their nature was to be protected by their husbands. "The person or body of the wife is the property of the husband, and the wife cannot consent away her own purity."[23] Their seduction dishonored their husbands, robbed their husbands. For the rest there was little to say about them or, rather, little that defense lawyers wanted to say about them. (Prosecutors, of course, emphasized the wives' agency and participation, their consent.) In the misogynist frame that the defense lawyers constructed, the wives were inherently weak and vulnerable to the wiles of seducers. Yet even that could not be emphasized too strongly because then the husbands became failures in what the lawyers identified as a husband's most important role: the production and maintenance of an impermeable private sphere within which wives would necessarily remain. To the extent wives had wills, hopes, wants, and identities, jurors would have had to recognize them as individuals and as capable of consent, as participants in adultery, and as qualifying and undercutting the idea of "seduction."

Both Mrs. Sickles and Mrs. Cole publicly conformed to the non-roles that defense attorneys assigned them. Neither played any part in the public trial. They were effectively ciphers. But Abby McFarland Richardson was another story. Because she had left Daniel, had separated from him, was building a career, struggled to gain custody of her children, went to Indiana to get a divorce, had taken on all of the characteristics of a modern woman, she could not be reduced easily to stolen property. Throughout the trial, Daniel McFarland's lawyers worked to label her as greedy, ambitious, vain, and as a failure in her wifely responsibilities. But all that language was ultimately mobilized to recreate her as the diabolical and passive product of the strategems of a "free love conspiracy": Richardson, in combination with Lucy Calhoun and others, had flattered her, fed her vanity, drawn her away from her husband's protection, made her a believer in her autonomy. "In an evil hour," she had fallen "into the sotiety [sic] of these fourierites, agrarians, Mormons, spiritualists, free-lovers, amidst whom every Jack has some other person to gill." Lucy Calhoun, "a plotter, conspirator, adventurer and procuress," had "instill[ed] into her breast the seeds of a discontent that she [Calhoun] hoped would ripen into an alienation from her husband, and dissatisfaction with her lot in life." They had made her into their weapon.[24]

McFarland's defense lawyers also worked to interpret the child custody suit that McFarland had brought in 1867 in a way that turned it into a struggle between men. McFarland's goal in bringing the suit had been to "make" Abby "virtuous," confronting her with the consequences of her separation. It was less a fight with his wife and more a way to fight "temptations that Richardson had thrown about his wife." They conceded to her "human nature," by which they meant motherlove. She was, Graham asserted, "vibrating between her affection" for her lover "and the desire to keep disgrace away from [her children]." And McFarland might have succeeded in bringing her back to virtue, but for Albert Richardson's interference. Without Richardson's support, she would have gone back to her husband "sooner than sacrifice her natural affection for her children." Conversely, Richardson had financed her defense against McFarland's habeas corpus case because he too knew that whoever had control of the children would control her.[25]

In each trial, the story the attorneys wanted to tell was simple and inherently attractive to a jury of men: of an ordinary honorable man who had acted in self-defense, who had done what everyone, including the seducers, knew husbands had a right to do. The problem they faced was that their story violated the law. Husbands had no right to act in that way. The law was against them. No existing version of "the unwritten law" excused their clients' acts.

In 1859, in *Sickles,* this problem was faced as a problem of evidence. How to make the fact of adultery the centerpiece of the trial? The defense tried to introduce Teresa Sickles's confession, arguing that Daniel had the right to waive the rules against spousal testimony. But, at least at first, the prosecution succeeded in keeping the document from being read to the jury. Teresa's confession could not be received into evidence, for neither husband nor wife could testify in support or in opposition to the interests of the other on the theory that either perjury or marital conflict was the inevitable result. Here, in the case of Teresa's confession, the problem was even more serious, since it was produced in the presence of, and perhaps under the control of, Daniel. According to the prosecutor, the attempt by the defense to introduce it revealed a cynical belief "that the age of progress had modified the law."[26]

The defense then shifted its strategy. Evidence of the affair between Key and Teresa Sickles would be introduced to demonstrate Sickles's state of mind at the time of the killing. The prosecution resisted, claiming correctly that the defense was simply trying to reintroduce the confession as a justification for Sickles's act.

In setting out its version of the relevant law, the prosecution laid great weight on the precedent of *State v. John,* an 1848 North Carolina case that upheld the conviction of a man who had killed the man he believed to be his wife's lover when he found the two of them alone in the "lover's" home. Using this case was a major strategic blunder for the prosecution. The defense pounced on the case, which involved the prosecution of a slave husband. "If Philip Barton Key had owned a married woman as a slave, he might place a halter around her neck and lead her to the shambles; but could he do so with a free woman? The Prosecution in their thirst for blood had forgotten the institution of slavery." To deprive Sickles, a free white husband, of the opportunity to introduce exculpatory evidence was to reduce him to the level of a slave husband. Indeed, *State v. John* was meaningless as a precedent, since John, as a slave, was no husband at all because legal marriage was not a recognized possibility for slaves under North Carolina law. Slave men by definition had no marital honor to vindicate.[27]

The defense won, more one suspects because of the failure of the prosecution than because of the quality of the defense argument, and the judge would admit any evidence defense counsel chose to introduce, in theory to demonstrate Sickles's state of mind and possible insanity. More important, the defense team had established a connection between Sickles's act and the liberties of a free (white) American man as a husband. Where a defendant's act "was committed under the influence of the marriage relation," where everything turned on the wife's conduct, defense lawyers would be permitted to demonstrate the acts of adultery and seduction that produced a husbandly reaction. This was, all sides conceded, a change in the law. The old law would not have regarded the behavior of seducer or wife as relevant evidence for the consideration of the jury. However, that old doctrine was, according to the defense, just that: old and out of date, made at a time when the law did not trust the democratic judgment of the jury. "The jury system is now developed and is perfect." So a new evidentiary regime would have to be established. Defense attorneys still had to contend with the competing interpretations of prosecutors and judges' instructions as to relevance. But from then on, in *Cole* and in *McFarland* as well as in *Sickles*, defense attorneys had no difficulty introducing evidence about adultery for the jury's consideration.

Much had been gained. Still, the law of murder remained as a barrier. The acts that constituted seduction might be before the jury, but seduction was still no excuse under the law. How to make seduction an excuse or justification for the defendant's act?

One answer was the insanity defense, a controversial exception within the law. It is possible to draw out of the language of the defense attorneys an intermittent but continuing effort, using the fuzzy and undeveloped terms of nineteenth-century psychiatry, to characterize their clients as made insane, or driven mad, by the seductions of their wives. Indeed, the Sickles case is regarded as one of the first occasions when the claim of temporary insanity was raised.[28]

And yet in all three cases the insanity defense was posed hesitantly, in a manner that suggested the lawyers' own ambivalence. Indeed, the defense attorneys in *Sickles* for the most part avoided speaking at all in terms of the insanity defense, and denied that they were seeking an acquittal on the grounds of insanity.

The claim of excuse by reason of insanity was posed peculiarly. Men and women of the nineteenth century thought, as we do, of the criminally insane as exceptional and distinctive, which is why they were excused from punishment for acts that everyone else was expected to avoid. But in these trials, with the partial exception of *Cole,* the defense worked to show that the defendants' actions were generated by feelings—by a frenzy—to which all good men alike were subject, feelings that were, indeed, the product and the markers of their goodness and their normality. As the prosecution in *Sickles* posed it, the defense was not claiming that Sickles was mad; only that he ought to have been mad. Or, as Graham put it, reflecting back on *Sickles* in his closing argument in *McFarland:* "We went to the jury upon the common sense of the matter. We knew that no man could be anything else than frenzied under a provocation like that."[29]

Their clients' insanity was less a medical or psychological defect and more a legitimate and appropriate attribute of male identity. "Where the cause of insanity" was "alleged to be an interference with man's marital relations, or his paternal rights in taking away his wife or child," the jury had "the right to judge the probability of the existence of such an affection, from their own and the known feelings of others as husbands and fathers." Graham and the other lawyers often came close to labeling their clients' insanity as logically entailed or compelled by the situation. (Indeed, the prosecution parodied Graham as arguing that insanity was a rational response.) At several points, Graham described the actions of Richardson and the "free lovers" as "maddening," a nice ambiguous word. And in each case, an expanded unwritten law became, in the defense attorneys' rendition, a reflection of a realistic understanding of the limits of husbandly rationality and restraint. The "tumult" or "transport of passions" created by knowledge of a wife's adultery justified the taking of a human life.[30]

A second way to make their story fit the law was advised explicitly by Amasa Parker in the Cole case and implicitly by all the other defense lawyers: do what juries have always done in such cases—ignore the (judge's) law. Follow "in the wake of the unbroken line of precedents" produced by every jury in the past 200 years that had dealt with such cases, for no man had ever been punished here or in England for slaying his wife's seducer.[31] The defense lawyers pressed the jury to ignore what they knew the judge was going to say in his final instructions on "the law" of the case. Apparently unworried about any risk that they would be held in contempt of court, the lawyers worked to empower the jury as a community of husbands and men. "I respectfully and earnestly ask you gentlemen of the jury," went a typical refrain, "you citizens, husbands, fathers, brothers, sons—with patience and attention to hear me, with a deep and solemn persuasion of your own position, of the sacredness and affection of your own homes, and of your tremendous responsibility, for your action in this case, to the defendant, to the community, to the Divine Creator who holds us all in the hollow of his hand, and by whom, let us pray and believe that you will be guided to the end aright."[32]

John Graham, in particular, constantly insisted that the jury had the ultimate power to decide questions of law as well as fact, that no technical doctrine or judge's instruction should stand in the way of the jury doing what he described as its moral duty. The result, if the jury did as he told them to do, would be a realization and acknowledgment of the "Divine edict" that jealousy "is the rage of a man, and that he will not, cannot, must not spare in the day of his vengeance."[33]

In each case judges instructed the jury to stick to the established law, to resist such arguments. Judges agreed with the prosecuting attorneys that adultery as such was not at issue, except insofar as perceptions of adultery might have driven the defendant insane. As Judge Henry Hogeboom put it in instructing the *Cole* jury, "neither manhood nor honor" was a relevant concern. Recorder John Hackett, the judge in *McFarland* (who was attacked by liberal and woman's rights commentators as biased toward the defense), used his jury instructions to attempt to inoculate the jury against the tide of language mobilized by the defense. They were "not to administer sympathy, but to execute justice; to carry into effect the laws of the land, to enforce its solemn mandates, and not to nullify or relax its positive commands by misplaced sympathy or morbid clemency." It was not their job to vindicate the sanctity of the marriage relation. In interpreting the law, "the inflexible rule of jurors should be that a man who takes the correction of wrongs into his own hands with pistol or knife, and is not in a state of insanity when he did the correction, is not to be acquitted."[34]

When all of the juries acquitted, in spite of judicial instructions for restraint and deference to the law, contemporaries thought they knew what had happened. Juries bought defense arguments. To woman's rights activists, the success of the defense demonstrated the corruption of male-only juries. Others concluded that the verdicts revealed the need for reform of the law of adultery. If "the murderer's counsel can successfully justify the act to the jury on the ground of a defect of law and justice," wrote one critic, "it is time that something were done to remedy such a palpable evil, and to end this line of ghastly precedents."[35]

The arguments made by the defendants' lawyers had mobilized the rhetoric of law reform usually identified with liberal (woman's rights) law reformers. In effect, sometimes explicitly, defense lawyers challenged the law as given. The jury, not the law, was the best representative of "enlightened moral sentiment."[36] And the jury, in acquitting, would be establishing new, better law. By rejecting existing law, the jury would establish a new legal right for husbands, one that was appropriate for a modern, democratic society.

The foundation for that right would be the Bible. John Graham made a particular specialty of the Biblical invocation. Reflecting in 1869 on his participation in *Sickles,* he pontificated that he had had "the honor—and it was an honor which I am glad belonged to me—of introducing into a court of justice the precepts of the Bible."[37] In 1870, in his closing in *McFarland,* he spent at least half a day quoting every possible Biblical passage justifying revenge and private vengeance and patriarchal authority. He ended that part of his closing by summarizing what he called "the law of the Bible": "That man was made for God, and woman for man; and that the woman was the weaker vessel, is meant to be under the protection of the stronger vessel, man. The forfeiture of that supremacy is as much an infraction of the husband's right as though it was the infliction of violence upon her or him." (According to one of the published transcripts, a "distinct hiss from some of the strong minded ladies present" was heard in the court at that moment.)[38]

The lawyers needed to "introduce" the jury to the Bible because of what they construed as a gap in secular law: adultery was not a crime in many common law jurisdictions, including New York.[39] What was the significance of a publicly unpunished "crime" of adultery? It was, in the first place, a stroke of good fortune for the lawyers and their clients, since it allowed them to claim a need for private self-help. Hadley, in his opening address for Cole, argued that the absence of an adequate remedy meant that a husband was thrown back on to "the law of nature." Hiscock, the seducer, must have known "that the fabric of society was built upon that instinct of the human heart which ever impels the wronged husband to vindicate the sanctity of the marriage bed." John Graham agreed. The absence meant that "society" recognized the right of "every man" to defend himself against an adulterer, "and that right" was "perfect under Divine law." Society, he continued, threw the wronged husband on to "the law" of his "heart." When he followed his heart, he reflected "the will of Heaven," and when he killed the adulterer, he fulfilled "the judgment of Heaven." Society "left the adulterer where the law of God" had left him: "to be the victim of that judgment . . . executed . . . by Heaven through man as its instrument."[40]

Other lawyers used somewhat less violent and crudely religious language than Graham. But all framed the issue the same way: in neither criminalizing adultery nor empowering husbands to commit private vengeance, the existing law stood as an atavistic reflection of an older and less moral English legal culture, one that had not properly fixed the value of the marriage bed. For Amasa Parker, who made one of the closing arguments for Cole, happily "the laws adapt themselves to our condition." The law was "made as we go on in the progress of civilization." And, though the lawyers never made the point explicitly, one could imagine that this particular evolutionary adaptation, like so many others elsewhere in nineteenth-century legal culture, involved a grant of private freedom in which the individual husband was freed from the dead hand of common law restraints.[41]

The worst feature of the old common law regime, according to all the lawyers, was its substitution of money damages for the loss caused by the seducer. Prosecutors constantly reminded the juries that the law retained a variety of remedies for injured husbands, including separation rights and actions for alienation of affection and criminal conversation. But what sort of remedies were these, responded defense lawyers? As Hadley put it, with heavy sarcasm:

> [T]he laws of society have . . . provided a sufficient, a perfectly adequate remedy . . . a safe, certain, and unfailing cure, . . . for all the rankling and agonizing wounds of degradation and dishonor. When the affections of your wife have been stolen and her person polluted, when your home has been broken up, your prospects in life destroyed, your hopes of happiness blasted, just go to a lawyer's office. . . . Tell him the story of your wife's disgrace . . . ; tell him what was the moneyed value of your wife when she gave you the treasure of her affections and committed to your trust the protection of her virgin innocence. He will advise you to make merchandise of her in a court of justice . . . ; He will advise you to coin your tears and groans into dollars and cents.

The law substituted money damages for lost honor, an impossible substitution and "an intentional insult" to the jury's "understandings." After
all, "The wounds of what husband could be staunched by dirty money
from the pockets of him who had defiled his wife?"[42]

In Edwin Stanton's closing speech for Daniel Sickles, modernity itself
required a change in the archaic structure of the unwritten law. At common law, in the constrained world of earlier centuries, a jury might well
have concluded that a wife's consent to commit adultery qualified the
adulterer's guilt and denied a husband the right to take vengeance. If
adultery continued, it was, implicitly, because of a husband's negligence
or even connivance, his lack of attention to his husbandly duty to keep
his wife safe. A wife's freedom was itself a commentary on her husband's
lack of honor. But in mid-nineteenth-century American society, even
more so in Washington, D.C., there was "a freedom from restraint and
supervision that exists nowhere else." Men necessarily devoted "a large
share of time to the cares of life, and to the duties of providing for the
family." Meanwhile, women were left "without protection." Families
moved constantly, and men lost the capacity to pick out those with
whom they and their family members might associate. The very "equality of our social condition" and the "frankness of intercourse" characteristic of American life required "a rigorous personal responsibility to the
death," if there was to be any hope for a secure "marriage bed." Thus, in
America, in a world where wives could not be easily controlled, a wife's
consent should not shield the adulterer from her husband's violence.[43]

The lawyers brandished a deeply sentimentalized notion of honor,
one that drew on the tropes of nineteenth-century domesticity. The defendants' love had led to vengeance because they, like others in the society, knew that there was no cash equivalent for love. The husbands were
the victims of romantic and obsessive love (their own romantic and obsessive love, not that of the seducers). Love for their wives—their need
to be united with their wives—had driven them forward toward murder,
not simply the insult given by another man.

Still, it was the relations between men that made the lawyers' stories
work. Indeed, in the finale to Brady's closing in *Cole*, George Cole's act
was transformed into a Christian gift to all men. One imagines Brady
lowering his voice, forcing the jurymen to strain to hear him. "If you
convict him, if he does ascend the scaffold," Cole will have one consola-

tion. Just as he fought to preserve "the honor of this native land" during the Civil War, so he fought to preserve his family, and to keep for his children "an honorable position and an honorable name." In so doing, he also "strengthened the security of the homes" of his "fellow-citizens." He would have led a "soldier's life," and he would have died a soldier's death. And as he was led to the scaffold, he would know that he had done the right and honorable thing. "And so," Brady concluded (to applause), "if he dies, he will die for you [the men of the jury], and for all of us."[44]

Brady's closing evoked an image of male solidarity and sacrifice, of heroism and community, along the way forgetting the killing of one man by another. In *McFarland* as well, the lawyers worked to make the jury imagine Daniel McFarland as a kind of hero. The enemy he faced, however, was very different than the simple libertine embodied by L. Harris Hiscock. In McFarland-Richardson, the libertine became first a free love conspirator and then, implicitly, a member of an extended world of law reformers and busybodies who threatened the homes of all good men. The right that McFarland's lawyers worked to establish was necessarily a right that stood in opposition to a body of law reforms and legal changes that threatened to remake the nature of legal marriage. The right that would free McFarland was a right that countered the emerging (or threatening) rights—to separate, to divorce, to keep custody of their children, to earn an income, to live an independent life—of wives.

Defense lawyers' exploration of his 1867 custody suit became an occasion to demonstrate McFarland's obsessive and total love of his children, his virtue as a good nineteenth-century father. They called one witness after another to report on McFarland's obsessed state of mind during the custody suit, his fears that Richardson would steal his children away.[45]

The focus on child custody was determined by the particularities of the McFarland-Richardson story. One suspects, though, that Graham and his associates had more in mind than demonstrating McFarland's increasingly distracted manner. The jury was surely aware that mothers, even separating mothers, were regularly receiving custody in cases throughout nineteenth-century America. And when Graham focused on custody rights, he was not simply exploring aspects of McFarland's life; he was also identifying McFarland's case with a central arena of struggle in nineteenth-century American family law. Daniel McFarland's attempt to use custody of his children to regain his wife (an effort that several witnesses characterized as foolish and crazy) became, in Graham's rendition, a noble albeit losing struggle for rights possessed by all husbands.

At the end of his closing, Graham described the nightmare scenario that McFarland had faced and that, by implication, loomed on the horizon for other men. This was not, he emphasized, an ordinary case of a wife separating from her husband. "In ordinary cases," where a wife eloped, she left her children with her husband, and she left him free to get a divorce as the injured party. An abandoned husband retained two crucial marital rights: "his paternal right and his right to get a divorce from her because of her degradation and infamy." That was "the usual course." In this case, however, Abby had "put herself in a position where" she could "declare herself independent of him." That was accomplished (the passive voice is important here) by putting her on the stage. "She was an abortion there. She had no talent as an actress." But that wasn't the point. The goal (of Richardson, of the "free love conspiracy," of unnamed others) was to give her financial independence in order to destroy marital unity. The goal was to make it possible for such a woman to leave her husband when she wished, to assert an independent identity, not simply the identity of a wife in a state of coverture.

She had left without conceding her guilt. She had no justification for a separation. Yet, she insisted, mouthing the words of others, on her right to leave. Then she struggled against her husband's efforts to establish his custodial rights, so that "this man's child" might "become the staff of Richardson's declining years and a lackey for a stepfather?" Richardson had "taken" the prisoner's wife, made her "free," supplied the money needed to take her husband's child out of the state, all in order "to make her cohabitation with him more certain." This was, all in all, "a villainy" unparalleled "in the annals of infamy or vice."[46]

Then Graham shifted his ground. The gentlemen of the jury were to determine the "highest interests of society." They needed to meet their responsibilities "like husbands, fathers, men." This was a case about a "home in ruins, how distressing the desolation." They ought to remember what home was supposed to mean:

> Home is home though ever so lonely. The best home for us is that which receives us with the warmest heart and welcomes us with the most cordial hand. . . . Within the walls of the family mansion, how

happy, how joyous those words. At their mention does not the memory revert voluntarily to the abode of our earlier days, where, gathered around the family fireside, in which a correspondence of love and affection—father, mother, brothers, and sisters constituted a little community in themselves[.] . . . Who, if we could, would not be a child again?

But then back to the burdens of judgment: "You are to reflect in your action the value you place upon your own hearths and the affections with which you regard your own firesides."[47]

WHAT'S A HUSBAND TO DO? ONE ANSWER

The unwritten law, in its changing incarnations, was one of a number of contested and unstable rights that framed struggles within and about marriage in nineteenth-century America. The trials where the right was articulated were among the disruptive moments that shook and ultimately remade the inherited law of marriage. In the three trials that we have explored, but with distinctive intensity in *McFarland,* lawyers manipulated a sense of desperation and uncertainty about the legal climate. The world was changing and, in the lawyers' rendition, husbands were losing control of their private domain, justifying murder.

As New York's last chancellor, Reuben Walworth was a participant in those changes. In *Mercein,* in particular, he had articulated a vision of the Christian husband in sharp contrast to the vision that the lawyers in these murder trials had developed. For him, a good husband did not need to insist on his rights, and gained his stature as a good husband by his restraint and by his willingness to withdraw when challenged or provoked.

His own eldest son did not leave home with those lessons well learned. Mansfield Walworth was a moderately successful novelist but a failure as a husband. His wife, Ellen Hardin Walworth, was his stepsister, the daughter of the chancellor's second wife, and they had grown up together in Saratoga Springs. They married in 1852. Between 1853 and 1871, Mansfield and Ellen Hardin had eight children, five of whom survived infancy. But already, by the summer of 1861, Ellen Hardin Walworth had moved alone to Kentucky with her children.[48]

Between 1861 and 1867, she kept a country inn three miles from Louisville, by means of which she supported her family. The retired chancellor visited her there often, but her husband Mansfield came only once. In 1867 she moved to Washington, where she obtained a government job and where she enrolled her eldest son Frank in Georgetown University. She remained in Washington for eighteen months. Then she returned to Saratoga Springs where she opened a boardinghouse. During this period, Mansfield lived with her some of the time, but he was never the family's primary support.

Then Reuben Walworth died. She and Mansfield "discussed the question of a future residence" without coming to any agreement. He was evidently furious that the old chancellor had left him only a beneficiary of a trust while he had given his stepdaughter a direct inheritance. Though they lived together in New York City between November 1870 and January 1871, she soon moved back to Saratoga Springs. In April 1871, she received a judicial separation. The "cause" of the final separation was his violence. He had beaten her, and she had screamed, and then their son Frank had come in and stopped him. The decree allowed Mansfield to visit his children under supervision, but he never came to visit.[49]

Mansfield Walworth, however, did begin to send his wife abusive letters. In them, he obsessed about the wrong his father had done him, about his fear that his children were alienated from him and would convert to Catholicism (his brother, Clarence Walworth, who also lived in Saratoga Springs, was a leading American Catholic), and about the many ways Ellen Hardin had robbed and humiliated him. His state of mind was, at best, unhinged. In several of these letters, he threatened to kill his wife and children.[50] On May 30, 1873, in his last letter to Ellen Hardin, he told her to prepare herself for "the inevitable." He was coming to call on his children.

[M]y heart is starving for their caresses. . . . I will see them—peaceably if I can, or with tragedy if I must. . . . Popish cruelty must bend to the demand of a father's breast, or the Walworth name goes out in blood. Keep Frank Walworth [his eldest son] out of my way. You have taught him to hate me. . . . Beware that you do not in any way arouse the frenzy which you have known to exist since you left me. . . . I am a broken-hearted desperado. I admit it. Save this letter for lawyers and courts if you please. God is my lawyer; not the remorseless, brutal god that you . . . worship, but that God who has planted love in my heart for my little girls, and that says to the tiger bereft of its young, "Kill!"[51]

Ellen Hardin Walworth never read this last letter; nor had she read many of the earlier ones. Her son, Frank, had taken it upon himself to be her protector, and he hid the letters from her.

After reading the last letter, Frank, who was nineteen, went to New York, took a hotel room there, and invited his father to visit him. In the hotel room, he asked his father to stop abusing his mother, to leave them alone. Mansfield promised he would, but Frank did not believe him. He took out a gun, a gift from his grandfather, and shot his father four times. Then he summoned the police and turned himself in.

At trial, Frank Walworth's lawyer made a case for hereditary insanity. He emphasized Frank's honorable though misguided desire to be his mother's protector. What the lawyer could not do, on the other hand, was justify Frank's act as a matter of right. And the judge instructed the jury on the value of human life. Bad as Mansfield Walworth had been, his son had no right to make himself into the "avenger" of the wrongs his father had done to his mother. "[I]n the eye of the law all men, without respect to their condition of character, bad devices, or their moral or physical nature," remained under the law's protection. "The same shield that is over the bad is over you." It was, the judge continued, "a wild and foolish notion that a man may be called to have his grave laid open to shop up his character and his pursuits in life, for the purpose of creating a public sentiment that he was so bad a man that he ought to die."[52]

The jury obediently convicted Frank Walworth of second-degree murder. And he spent many years in an insane asylum.

The moral seems obvious. Whatever exemption husbands had from the ordinary rules of criminal responsibility would not be extended to sons, even to a son who had assumed the responsibilities that his father had abandoned. Husbands' rights were not general male rights; they were rights specific and peculiar to marriage itself.

Yet there is another moral to be drawn from Mansfield Walworth's story, one closer to the ideal of the Christian husband that Reuben Walworth had developed in the Barry case. And it is one, ironically, that Mansfield Walworth himself told in a novel he had just completed at his death.

Beverly, or, the White Mask begins with a New York City journalist, MacGregor, sitting in a lonely room, while a storm beats against the windows. There MacGregor swears vengeance. "Cruelty had maddened him." His wife has abandoned him, taking their child with her. She has adopted "the usual treachery" of women. Now, alone in the "storm-wrapped house," he is busily "plotting the murder of the woman who made his home desolate."[53]

MacGregor is then sued by his wife for a judicial separation. He decides not to resist. "The tie was severed, and MacGregor was alone for life." He realizes that his marriage has been "a delusion and a snare." And he turns back to his profession, and seeks "literary immortality."[54]

The novel becomes a gothic narrative, centering on lost fortunes and old estates in the Hudson Valley. The plot is too complicated to recapitulate. Suffice to say that MacGregor eventually gains a new child and a woman who loves him and whom he loves. The child teaches him sympathy and care. Eventually he forgives his wife in his heart, even though he realizes that her survival means that he cannot ever marry his true love. True Christianity, untouched by the churches, has come to him.[55]

Still, it seems deeply unjust that he can never have someone "to nestle close to his lion-heart, to receive all the weight and richness of the tenderness born in him and quivering in every vein of his body." Because of the happenstance that he had once married "a traitoress, and been deserted in a temporary trouble," should he be condemned to a solitary life? "He was wrestling like a giant with his enemy, Sin, sin by the law of the church, felony by the law of the state." He will win the struggle, given his "high sense of honor and his religious instinct." Nevertheless, the sense of unfairness remains. Remarriage is forbidden him.[56]

Then, in the mansion of a benefactor, he comes across his ex-wife, who has just married the benefactor's neighbor. She is, he realizes, just a common woman. More important, she is a bigamist and, as a result, she is now in his power. "Her inordinate craving for wealth had entrapped her at last. . . . The man she had deserted could place her in a felon's cell."

But the newly reformed MacGregor struggles against his desire for revenge and, of course, masters his struggle. He vows not to harm her, never to recognize her, never to speak to her. He forgives her, and he writes her a note to that effect.

Still, he can't have his true love because he won't be a bigamist. And though his benefactor gives him an estate and a million dollars, still he has sealed his own solitary doom. He is unhappy.

Then the ex-wife conveniently dies. He can remarry. All is resolved. And the novel ends.[57]

In this forgotten novel, Mansfield Walworth, whose own unhappy life was about to end, sketched an answer to the question, what should a husband do when honor is challenged? Men like MacFarland and Cole and Sickles had all acted on their immediate impulses, impulses shaped by an imagined husbandly identity, impulses shaped by a world in which women—wives—could and did leave. The work their lawyers had done in those cases had been, in the first place, to make their reactions understandable in the peculiar context of nineteenth-century America and, in the second place, to give a moral gloss to their actions. Husbands could retain their honorable identities by resisting change. Their murderous behavior became, in the lawyers' presentation, a defense of a marital order imagined as unchanging.

By contrast, MacGregor, an obvious stand-in for Mansfield Walworth himself, traced a trajectory of change over the course of the novel. He restrained his own murderous impulses; he buried himself in his work; he accepted as his fate the misery of a life without a husbandly identity; his former rage was transformed into Christian love; and, eventually, he found a new and true and permanent marital union—a family—in a new relationship.

Whether that narrative course was any truer than the narrative of resistance that the lawyers told is not the point. The narrative of remarriage was, by the last third of the nineteenth century, becoming a dominant story in American culture. Murderous husbands remained a presence, as they do to the present. And in the law, there would still be ways of excusing them from culpability. But, both within the law and outside of it, in the emerging American context, the usual answer to the question, What should a man do?, was simple: get on with life; make a career; forgive, if you can; forget, if you can. And remarry.

9

The Geography of Remarriage

[H]e . . . desired to leave and abandon his own wife and children, and take defendant's wife and go to a new country where they would not be known, and could marry and live together as man and wife.
Rinehart v. Bills, 82 Mo. 534, 536 (1884)

Everywhere, even in antidivorce New York, men and women remarried before their spouses' deaths. Sometimes they divorced, but frequently their divorces were invalid. And sometimes men and women lived as married, even though they knew they were not "really," that is, legally, married.

Abby Sage McFarland Richardson's marital history provides an exemplary scandal. In 1868 she had moved to Indiana "to get free" from Daniel. She stayed for sixteen months. Then, having met Indiana's residence requirements, she filed her petition for a divorce. The complaint charged Daniel with cruelty, drunkenness, and a failure to support. Over the previous two years, he had led "a life of idleness and vice" and had not contributed toward her or their children's support. They had survived only by her "industry." She, on the other hand, had been "ever . . . a faithful and dutiful wife." Notice of the pending divorce was published for four weeks successively in a small Indiana newspaper, but Daniel was never notified directly. The divorce was quickly granted, and she went back to New York, "free" of Daniel and also "free" to remarry Albert Richardson.[1]

In December 1869, after Daniel McFarland had mortally wounded Albert Richardson, public opinion (at least as expressed in the newspapers) was outraged: less by the murder, more by the deathbed marriage of Albert and Abby. One contemporary account began with damning characterizations of everyone involved. Everyone that is but poor and innocent Daniel McFarland. Abby Sage McFarland Richardson had sought "notoriety, money and dress." And for the sake of these she had driven her husband "to a state of frenzy, and ruined the future prospects of her offspring." She was "a fine woman as regards looks," but her morals were "rotten to the core." Worse than Abby, however, worse even than Albert Richardson and the free lovers who had seduced Abby away from duty and marriage, were the "men of standing in Church and State" who had orchestrated and officiated at the bigamous marriage of the dying Albert and the Indiana-divorced Abby. For these men—including Schuyler Colfax, the vice president of the United States, Horace Greeley, the editor of the New York Tribune, and the Reverends Henry Ward Beecher, O. B. Frothingham, and Henry M. Field—the writer felt "unmitigated contempt and disgust."[2]

Beecher, Frothingham, and Greeley all went to some lengths to deny the charge that they had given "benedictions to bigamy."[3] Horace Greeley gave an interview to a reporter from the rival New York Sun. In it, he began by minimizing the marriage ceremony itself. It was "only the matter of a name," whether "Mrs. McFarland should be called Mrs. Richardson." "Only the matter of a name?" asked the reporter. Yes, nothing more. And since Richardson was about to die, "nobody could be hurt by the marriage." "But what had Mr. Richardson's dying got to do with his right to McFarland's wife?" Greeley: "Why, as I understand it, though I have not given the subject much attention, there was a divorce between the original parties which seems to me to have been all right enough in justice, though I don't know about the technicalities of the case; and besides all this, Mr. McFarland had given up all right in his wife long ago."[4]

Later, during the murder trial, Greeley testified for the prosecution about his conversations with Daniel McFarland. John Graham cross-examined him. He read from Greeley's New York Sun interview. Greeley, a nervous and uncomfortable witness, denied that he had been quoted accurately. Graham asked whether he believed "if a man tells you his wife shall never more be his wife, that is a divorce?" Greeley denied it. Did he think that McFarland had "given up absolutely all rights to his wife?" Yes, Greeley had understood him to have renounced her.[5]

One year after his acquittal, in May 1871, Daniel McFarland went to Indiana to challenge Abby's divorce. His lawyers claimed that a variety of reversible errors had been committed by the local county court: the court had no jurisdiction to grant the divorce, Abby had never been a resident in Indiana, Daniel had never received notice so he had no opportunity to defend himself, and the record of the proceedings did not show that the wrongs alleged (Daniel's intemperance and nonsupport) actually existed. The Indiana Supreme Court dismissed the appeal summarily. (Indeed, one suspects that the appeal was published only because of the notoriety of the appellant.) There was nothing before it to decide. There was certainly no need to discuss the policy that lay behind "our" divorce laws. And the court affirmed the judgment of the Morgan County court divorcing Abby from Daniel.[6]

Horace Greeley must have found it galling to have had to take the position he did during the McFarland-Richardson affair. Although he often made the pages of the *New York Tribune* available to radical voices, he had always disagreed with divorce reformers and free lovers. In debates published in 1852–1853 and 1860, Greeley took his stand as the guardian of orthodoxy, opposed to all divorce except where adultery had been proved. New York's rigid divorce law, allowing divorce only for adultery, was his model of a good law.[7]

In 1860 his critique of liberal divorce incorporated a defense of separation. The law in conservative New York did not leave the abused wife without a remedy. In such cases, New York law granted a formal separation, "not a disruption of the marriage, with liberty to marry again." Greeley thought this "just right." A victimized wife should be able to live apart from her husband. But "such a wretch" should not be allowed "to delude and torture another 'pure and virtuous girl.' Let one victim suffice him." No matter how outrageous or brutal the conduct of the husband, an innocent wife, that is, a woman who truly understood "the nature and purposes of marriage," would never remarry during her husband's lifetime. As a mother, she could not look her children in the eye "with all a mother's conscious purity and dignity while realizing that their father and her husband, both living, were different men." Greeley felt sorry for those "unfitly" married. In the end, however, the goal was the "protection" of society, not individual happiness. One was not punished for stealing a horse, but that horses not be stolen.[8]

Greeley's arguments resembled those found in conservative anti-divorce polemics throughout the second half of the nineteenth century. The fundamental wrong of easy divorce was not divorce as such, that is to say, the actual breakup of a marriage and a family. It was remarriage that constituted the greater threat to the moral fabric of the society. Yale President Theodore Woolsey's influential *Essay on Divorce and Divorce Legislation* (1869) exemplified much theologically driven writing. Just as Christ had challenged the Mosaic law of divorce, so a Christian understanding of modern law required a critical perspective on the legal order as it existed in the United States. Woolsey distinguished separations from divorces, regarding the former as often defensible and permitted. Secular authorities, however, had no right to allow divorces, by which he meant the right to remarry, except where wife or husband had been guilty of adultery. States like Indiana gave "a bounty to immorality" by granting easy divorces. Indeed, all of the American states, as parts of the decentralized structure of American federalism, participated in these corrupt practices, and together these states were bringing on a general corruption of the moral order.[9]

In the course of an editorial review of the McFarland case, *The Nation* played out a secular version of the same perspective. The public had no interest in whether Mr. and Mrs. McFarland lived together. On this matter, "husbands and wives" were "the sole and sovereign judges." So long as children were taken care of, "society" had "no right to force a man and woman between whom, for any reason, mutual repugnance has sprung up, to remain under the same roof as members of the same family." Divorce, by contrast, was a question entirely within the jurisdiction of "society." Abby's supporters had knowingly confused her right to separate with her claimed right to be courted by another man, "with a view to marriage," even before divorce or a formal separation. Her friends pretended that her 1867 separation from McFarland effectively ended and dissolved the marriage. The Indiana divorce was then merely a ratification of an existing state of affairs. But their position masked the real consequences. If a wife or husband could be released from a marriage "by a mere verbal announcement," the result was "free love"—where marriages rested solely "on inclination." "The sane and healthy-minded portion of the public," that is to say, all who understood "the influence of sexual passion in clouding the judgment and enfeebling the will," knew what a disaster that would be. "[S]ociety would have even fewer guarantees for the legitimacy of children and the preservation of the family institution than it has for the paternity of calves or the rearing of young birds."[10]

Antidivorce writers had no doubts what marriage meant: "There may be something better than Marriage; but nothing *is Marriage* but a solemn engagement to live together in faith and love *till death*." Everything else, in particular everything begun by the already married before the death of a spouse, was just adultery and/or bigamy.[11] Couples who understood they had to live together softened "by mutual accommodation that yoke" that they knew they could not shake off. They became good husbands and good wives "from the necessity of remaining husbands and wives." According to the "philosophical" David Hume, a favorite source for the defenders of orthodoxy, men and women delighted in liberty and hated to be confined. Thus, they yearned for freedom and for divorce. Yet, at the same time, men and women also submitted to necessity and lost "an inclination" when there was no way to gratify it. "These principles of human nature may appear contradictory. But what is man but a heap of contradictions?" By tightening the marriage knot, friendship and stability were reinforced, more durable values than transitory love. Necessity led wife and husband to "a repose and satisfaction sufficient for their happiness."[12]

Proponents of easier divorce typically portrayed divorce as a cure for ordinary human errors and, in particular, for the wrongs done by husbands to wives. To Henry James Senior, traditional marriage was an "intrinsically good" institution "very *badly administered*." Divorce improved the administration of marriage by doing away with the ineffective and distorting remedy of separation. Separation left a couple locked in legal embrace, even as they lived apart and went their disparate ways, continually tempted to adultery. Divorce, by contrast, emancipated the poor wife from her intemperate or violent or selfish abuser, and it took away "one great, existing stimulant to conjugal inconstancy." For divorce apologists, the psychological vectors went in precisely the opposite direction of those drawn in the orthodox literature. James, like Hume, began with the observation that individuals did not willingly obey compulsion. For James, though, the central insight was the inability of law to compel the good. It was "a matter of daily observation" that "legal bondage" failed to produce "conjugal fidelity" if "mutual love and respect" were "wanting." Americans refused to submit to the duties articulated in the law because the law lacked the coercive power that conservatives imagined it possessed. The only result of a conservative divorce regime was disrespect, both for marriage as an institution and for the law as a normative order.[13]

Some took this psychological framework in more radical directions. According to Elizabeth Cady Stanton, it was "a sin against nature, the family, [and] the state for a man or woman to live together in the marriage relation in continual antagonism, indifference, disgust." Indissoluble marriage was the mark of women's slavery, and there was "no other slavery so disastrous in its consequences on the race, or to individual respect, growth and development." Divorce was emancipatory, precisely because it made marriage into exactly what the conservatives feared: a free, contractual relationship between partners, each of whom remained capable of leaving when the relationship no longer suited. Loving, happy, and harmonious marriages would only be strengthened by easy public divorce, for "the very fact of freedom" would purify relationships. Marriage would become "a life long friendship and not a heavy yoke." On the other hand, the knowledge that wives had a right to leave might force bad husbands to act better if they would remain married. Every public divorce helped "educate other wives similarly situated into higher ideas of purity, virtue, self respect."[14]

In the case law of the second half of the nineteenth century, one can read sentences and paragraphs that resemble those found on both sides of the cultural politics of marriage and divorce.[15] But, with the odd exception, the voices of the wives and husbands in the case records did not evoke either side in the ideological struggle. Litigants often resembled Abby Sage McFarland Richardson: conventional in their marital yearnings, yet aware of the possibilities for marital reinvention across the jurisdictional landscape. When they appeared in court they assumed conventional marital identities. However, they also married and remarried and sometimes remarried several times more—and they rarely waited until the death of a spouse. Many lived with continuing uncertainty about the legality of their remarriages, at risk that divorces and marriages legal in one state had become something less in another. The accusation of bigamy lurked around the edges of their lives. Yet they could also find support for their wants and desires in the extended, multi-jurisdictional environment of the United States.

Both the conservatives and Elizabeth Cady Stanton were surely right. Ease of exit, sometimes through divorce, in combination with remarriage, often without divorce, was changing the expectations and under-standings of the unhappily married. But the trajectory of change played a minimal role in the decisions of late nineteenth- and early twentieth-century American courts. In court the problems raised by the (allegedly) remarried formed two constellations. The first were problems of judicial discretion. Men and women remarried; often enough, the remarried were the still married. Some remarriages were legal; some were not. For any one man or woman, however, no more than one marriage at a time could ever be legal. So how to choose who was the real wife or widow? Who was the real husband? How to distinguish valid from invalid acts in a context (litigation) where at least two contradictory stories would be told, in a time and place often far removed from the determining events? The second set of problems reflected a contradiction at the heart of American federalism. Each state had the right to construct its own mari-tal regime, including the right to define the grounds for divorce, who was eligible to receive a divorce, and who could remarry. And the valid acts of each state (including marriages and divorce decrees) were sup-posed to be recognized as entitled to "full faith and credit" in any other state in the union. Yet each state also, as part of its possession of a mari-tal regime, remained largely free to decide whether to recognize and to enforce the divorces and remarriages made in other states. So what was a judge do when faced with a divorce decree granted in another state, for reasons and using procedures that would not have passed muster in his own state? What did the constitution demand of the conscientious judge?

Judges were trapped by their institutional and managerial responsibil-ities (inheritances had to be distributed, divorces decreed or rejected, al-imony and maintenance awards enforced, juries instructed), as well as by the varying and changing rules passed by state legislatures. They had to decide the almost metaphysical question of who was really married in a constitutional order with multiple marital regimes, in a mobile and in-creasingly industrialized country with a railroad system that allowed individuals to move quickly and temporarily to "divorce havens," in a nation without centralized recordkeeping, in a legal culture that encour-aged and supported contractual entry and exit, in a culture that made marriage an economic and social necessity. There were innumerable in-centives to be or to pretend to be married, and legal doctrine offered ex-cuses and justifications, explanations, and a general policy in favor of marriage. Nothing was exactly as it seemed, and everyone lied when they came to court.

The point is not that laws against remarriage lacked all coercive force. The crime of bigamy existed and played a critical role in the constitutional narrative of nineteenth-century law. But at no time did a moral and theological understanding of marriage as permanent and indissoluble exhaust the legal options available to husbands and wives as they exited and reassembled. Those who became caught up in the law because of multiple marriages, a very few of whom became convicted bigamists, apparently thought of themselves as having exited and recreated a new, permanent, and monogamous relationship. They were rarely free lovers, sexual radicals, or knowing criminals. Indeed, like Abby Sage McFarland Richardson, they typically asserted their conventionality, their conformity with public marital identities and with the cultural expectations to which coverture gave legal expression. If and when they ended up as bigamists, they must have experienced the law as a randomly oppressive structure, doing to them what was not done to others similarly situated, punishing them for having done what they thought they were entitled to do.[16]

WAYS NOT TO TALK ABOUT BIGAMY

Edwin Christy insisted he had invented blackface minstrelsy in the late 1830s or early 1840s. Competitors challenged his claim. But through the 1840s his troupe of Christy's Plantation Minstrels were an enormous and unprecedented success in New York and around the world, in part because of the songs that Stephen Foster wrote for Christy. Another piece in the Christy formula was the presence of George Christy, often described as Edwin's adopted son, who often performed in drag as a black "wench" and who quickly became the most famous of the early minstrels.

In the early 1850s George Christy left Edwin's troupe and set up a rival production company. Christy's Plantation Minstrels collapsed and, over the next decade, Edwin may have lost his mind, though he also made many successful investments. On May 9, 1862, he threw himself out of an upper-story window and, after several weeks of excruciating pain, died, leaving an estate worth $200,000 and two wives.[17]

Edwin Christy began his career in Buffalo. There he had a wife, Harriet, whom he had married sometime before 1835, and with whom he had four children. In the mid-1840s, when Christy's Plantation Minstrels began to perform in New York City, Harriet remained in Buffalo, until 1849 when she moved to the city with two surviving sons. In the city, Edwin lived with Mary Miller (sometimes known as Mary Maples).

For a time Edwin maintained two households. After George Christy left his company, however, Edwin at once refused to support Harriet. He also rejected his own sons after they refused to horsewhip George. George, it turned out, was the son of Harriet, and his real name was George Harrington. At about the same time, Mary Miller began to call herself Mrs. Christy. Before then, Edwin had referred to her in letters to his children as "Aunt Mary." And at some time Edwin and Mary visited Ithaca, where a marriage ceremony may have been performed.

On May 17, 1862, eight days after he had thrown himself out of the window, another marriage ceremony was performed at Christy's house, allegedly between Edwin Christy and Mary Miller Maples. A will was executed and witnessed. A group of doctors was brought in to test Edwin's mental capacity, and they all concluded that his mental condition was "sound." He inspected a bag of diamond jewelry that he had entrusted to a friend. He made a few small gifts. And then a few days later he died. His will gave a small annuity to his mother and a life estate to Mary Miller Maples, under the name "Mary Maples Christy." Neither Harriet nor her children received anything.[18]

Harriet and her son, Edwin junior, sued to void the alleged will and to establish their rights as the legitimate heirs of Edwin senior. In June 1865 they lost before the New York City Surrogate, who admitted the will to probate.[19] But in early 1866 the New York Supreme Court reversed and sent the case back to the surrogate for a jury trial.

Three questions framed the legal struggle before the New York Supreme Court: whether Harriet was the "lawful wife" of Edwin, whether the alleged will was executed while he was of sound mind, and whether that alleged will was procured by fraud. The latter two questions, questions of the testator's capacity and of what happened during Edwin Christy's last days, occupied the New York courts for the next two years. Justice George Barnard's opinion, however, focused on the first question. If Harriet's marriage was valid, then everything that happened in the house on 18th Street around May 17, 1862, came under the cloud of bigamy.[20]

Barnard believed the evidence for a marriage between Harriet and Edwin was very strong. He quoted from letters written by Edwin to Harriet in the late 1840s. In none was there much love or passion, but that counted in Harriet's favor. They were not the sort of letters "a man would address to a mistress of whom he was passionately enamored." Instead, they showed the "deep feeling of mutual interest" only found in "recognized domestic relations." Likewise, there was evidence that they had been known among friends and relatives as husband and wife. In an 1848 letter his mother had addressed her as "your affectionate mother." One of his brothers wrote her as "Sister Harriet." Harriet herself had provided a detailed description of their marriage ceremony—describing who performed the ceremony, where it was performed, and who the witnesses were.[21]

Mary's lawyers raised five challenges to the evidence. The first was "almost too trivial" to be taken seriously. In none of the letters did Edwin ever call Harriet his wife or call himself her husband.[22]

The second challenge was a more serious matter. At the time of her supposed marriage to Edwin, Harriet was already married to George Harrington (the father of George Christy, the minstrel), and George Harrington was still alive at the time of her marriage to Edwin. Thus, her marriage to Edwin was bigamous and void, and Edwin was a single man, fully capable of marrying Mary and of willing her his estate.

The evidence mobilized to prove Harriet's marriage to George Harrington resembled the evidence used to prove her marriage to Edwin. Harrington's brother, for example, testified that there was a "general understanding" in the family that George and Harriet were married. Harriet's sister testified to a similar understanding in her family. Justice Barnard conceded that there was "no dispute" that they had lived together as husband and wife for a time. But he emphasized George Harrington's unhusbandly conduct. Harriet had told one witness that she was a "decent woman" until she married George, but he had put her into a "whore house, and made a whore of her." The same witness had heard Harriet call George her husband, but George had only laughed when asked if she were his wife.

Whatever had actually happened in the early 1830s, Barnard ruled that the evidence was insufficient to prove a marriage to such a man. He found the attitude of Mary's counsel "singular" in insisting that weak evidence established the marriage of George and Harriet, while challenging "far stronger" evidence in support of the marriage of Edwin and Harriet. More, he was convinced by Harriet's own testimony that she had been seduced by George and that she had never been married to him. "This is a fact about which she could not be mistaken, and which she must have remembered." Presumably, a woman's admission to seduction was an admission against interest (even if it laid the foundation for a large inheritance), and thus no woman would swear to such a fact if it were not true.[23]

Barnard then rejected the other challenges that Mary's lawyers raised. The third, that Harriet herself had stated to witnesses that she was never married to Edwin, was disposed of by challenging the reliability and credibility of the witnesses. The fourth challenge, that Harriet had never taken any action against Edwin, even after he had abandoned her for another woman, raised the implication that she must not have believed that she possessed any marital rights. But Barnard emphasized Christy's known disposition as "an irritable and violent man." She might well "have feared personal violence to herself and children." Or she might have worried that any action on her part would make his "return" less likely. Instead, she had waited "with patient resignation" for Edwin to tire of Mary.[24]

The fifth challenge, that Edwin had married another woman, Mary Miller Maples, took a bit more work on Barnard's part. At face value, that challenge should have been easily countered, if one were convinced, as Barnard was, that Harriet was already legally married to Edwin. But Barnard knew that the challenge reflected an evidentiary presumption announced in 1850 by the New York Court of Appeals, the highest court in the state. The evidentiary presumption was a version of the presumption in favor of innocence. Where facts remained contested, not clearly proved, a court should not make factual determinations that could lead to a conviction for crime. Therefore, one had to presume that Edwin was not married to Harriet, so that his later marriage to Mary would not be considered bigamous. To invoke the presumption, however, one first had to demonstrate that a later marriage had occurred between Edwin and Mary. Barnard characterized the evidence for this third marriage as "strong, but not stronger" than the evidence on behalf of Harriet's earlier marriage to Edwin. More important, Mary had revealed a lack of "wifely feelings" when she excluded his sons from Edwin's presence in his last days and when she imposed on him "the excitement" of an apparently unnecessary marriage ceremony. Just as George Harrington was not the sort of person Barnard wanted to recognize as a husband, so Mary Miller Maples was not entitled to be a Mrs. Christy. And Barnard ruled that a jury would likely hold that there had never been a marriage between Mary and Edwin.[25]

Thus, Harriet and her son were reinstated as Edwin Christy's rightful heirs.[26]

Edwin Christy was a man of the theater, part of a relatively Bohemian subculture. We might imagine that subculture as standing apart from the more rigid sexual mores of Victorian America. Yet, as a courtroom saga about marriage and the law, *Christy v. Clarke* was neither unusual nor unrepresentative.[27] Justice Barnard's approach typified how judges dealt with such situations. He worked to make Harriet Harrington Christy into a wifely and motherly heroine and a victim of the seducer George Harrington. She was not the sort of woman who would lie about a seduction. Mary Miller Maples Christy, for reasons that are not entirely clear, though it may simply be that there could not be two heroines in Barnard's story, became a sexual predator, not a wife. Barnard's story showed some strains. Formally perhaps none of the three "marriages" in *Christy* were valid. As social enactments, as expressions of the (perhaps only momentary) commitment of the couple to live together for the rest of their lives, perhaps all were "real," although only one, Mary's, lasted until death.

Clayton v. Wardell, the 1850 decision that had troubled Barnard, was also the case that established the evidentiary approach he mobilized. Catherine Clayton had petitioned the New York City Surrogate for payment of the principal of a trust. Her grandfather had died in 1826 leaving his son (Catherine's father) $10,000 in trust. The son was to have the trust income for the rest of his life, and on his death the principal would go to the son's legitimate children. In 1825 the son had married Sarah Maria Youngs, Catherine's mother, and in 1828 Catherine was born. Catherine's father died in 1835, but the executors of his estate resisted giving Catherine the trust principal. They believed she was a bastard, since her parents' marriage had been void. The New York City Surrogate agreed, ruling that Sarah Maria Youngs was already married when she "married" in 1825.

Thus, Catherine Clayton's inheritance depended on her mother's marital history. That history began when Richard Schenck was arrested in

1822 as the father of Sarah Maria Youngs's unborn child. Sarah was either thirteen or fourteen years old at the time. Either a wedding followed, or it didn't. In any case, Richard was not convicted of bastardy, Sarah gave birth in 1823 to a child who lived for less than one year, and, for a time, Richard and Sarah lived together in her mother's house. Richard's family understood that they were married, and Sarah was received by them as his wife. Richard did not support Sarah, however, who continued to work with her mother as a cigar maker. In 1824, after their child's death, Richard moved out. And in June 1825 Sarah and Richard signed a separation agreement. (Actually, only Richard signed. Sarah could not write, and she only left her mark.) In the agreement, they were described as husband and wife. Richard then disappeared, and one month later, Sarah married Catherine Clayton's father.

In 1849 the New York Supreme Court reversed the New York City Surrogate's decree, a decision affirmed the next year by the New York Court of Appeals. Majorities on both courts held that there had not been a marriage between Richard Schenck and Sarah Maria Youngs, clearing the way for Catherine's inheritance. According to the New York Court of Appeals, the only piece of counterevidence was the separation agreement the two of them had agreed to in 1825. The judges admitted there was "something singular," even "unaccountable," about the agreement. The unmarried, after all, don't need separation agreements to part. But they concluded that "the mere naked fact" of such an agreement did not furnish enough "to justify the inference of a marriage," a conclusion reinforced and expanded by the strong presumption both courts found against recognizing an earlier marriage that would make a later marriage bigamous and void.[28]

Clayton v. Wardell modeled how lawyers and courts in New York and elsewhere dealt with contested marriages. In *Christy v. Clarke,* both sides adopted the *Clayton* framework. For Harriet Christy, her marriage to Edwin was presumptively valid, and her marriage to George Harrington was presumptively invalid, because not to hold in that manner would have made her marriage to Edwin bigamous. But likewise, for Mary Miller Maples Christy, her marriage to Edwin was presumptively valid and his earlier marriage to Harriet was presumptively invalid, because not to hold in that manner would have made her marriage to Edwin bigamous. In order to rule for Harriet, Justice Barnard relied on the *Clayton* analysis in the first part of his opinion and then worked to avoid it in the second.[29]

In the midst of the detritus of multiple and uncertain marriages, mid-nineteenth-century judges turned to the emerging law of evidentiary presumptions. In law, a presumption is a rebuttable inference about an unknown or contested fact, given certain established facts. We have seen the operation of factual presumptions in various aspects of the law of marriage in early and mid-nineteenth-century America. Presumptions cut short potentially interminable inquiries (for example, had a wife really been coerced or who was the better parent), and they may be an inevitable part of any process committed to establishing factual truth in a world where many "facts" will be dependent on uncertain and conflicting memories. So what was novel in *Clayton* was not the mobilization of presumptions. Rather, it was the Court of Appeals' adoption of a ranking of competing presumptions. The presumption against criminality (that bigamy had not been committed) prevailed over the presumption in favor of marriage. The presumption in favor of marriage was itself an important statement, embodying the preference for legitimate children and a belief in the ordinary and proper presence of matrimony in people's lives. But the presumption against criminality weighted the "facts" in favor of later marriages. Allowing that presumption to trump the presumption in favor of marriage gave judges the means to avoid upsetting present settled relations. As in other areas of nineteenth-century American law, particularly those involving property rights, the security of past rights—title, the originally married—would be defeated by later present occupants, by those who had taken over the relevant identities and made them their own. That approach would not solve every problem faced by the judges, as *Christy* demonstrates, but it appeared to offer a method to end inquiries that often threatened to become metaphysical and unresolvable.[30]

In John Lawson's 1886 text, the first illustration of the presumption of innocence in both civil and criminal cases was the now familiar inference that when a man and woman lived and cohabited together, the presumption must be that they were married. "Their conduct being susceptible of two opposite explanations," one was "bound to assume it to be moral rather than immoral." In the context of the 1880s, it was perhaps inevitable that his second illustration imagined that when "a negro and a white woman live together," the presumption was that they were not married, given criminal miscegenation laws. But the third and fourth illustrations returned to the standard image of legitimated (and implicitly white) remarriage: if husband and wife separated, and husband went and lived and cohabited with another woman, it was presumed that he had obtained a divorce and that his former wife was capable of remarrying. If husband married wife while her previous husband was still alive and undivorced, and if the undivorced husband subsequently died, and if the second husband and wife continued to live together, then the presumption was that they had "been" married after the first husband's death.[31]

As always, the law did not speak with one voice. Indeed, there was already a strongly voiced dissent in *Clayton*. The dissenter thought it absurd to analyze the situation through a presumption against criminality. The petitioner, Catherine Clayton, was merely seeking to acquire money; she was not concerned with the "guilt or innocence" of her parents. Furthermore, "between the moral guilt of prostitution, continued under the roof of her mother, . . . and that of bigamy," there was "very little to choose." A woman "with any pretension to character" would have considered "the imputation of the former offence quite as degrading as the latter."[32]

Doctrinal conflict swirled with particular intensity around the question of the legitimacy of remarriages by husbands and wives divorced by their previous spouses. In New York, as in several other jurisdictions, the wife or husband judged guilty in a divorce decree was forbidden from remarrying during the lifetime of the innocent ex-spouse. And the man or woman who did so anyway was, at least in legal theory, a bigamist of a sort.[33]

The 1854 decision in *Cropsey v. Ogden* exemplifies the rigors of this policy. Eliza Ann Ridgway Cropsey sued to recover her dower interest in the estate of James Ridgway. She had married Ridgway in 1825, and they had lived together until his death in 1847. Unfortunately for her, James Ridgway had already been twice married. In 1822 his second wife had divorced him for adultery. Under New York law, that meant that James Ridgway was prohibited from marrying again during his second wife's life. According to the Court of Appeals, there was "no moment" after 1822 when marriage in New York was lawful for him and, as a result, Eliza had never been a wife and possessed no dower rights in his estate.[34]

Eliza, who had given birth to twelve children during her twenty-two years with Ridgway, then went back to court, bringing an action for services rendered as her "husband's" employee. With her aid his estate had grown from less than $1,000 when they married to $150,000 at his death. And she asked, reasonably, for an award of $40,000 out of his estate. The New York Supreme Court, however, rejected her assumption that her wifely labors deserved compensation. The law presumed that all work done as a servant or laborer was done with a view to compensation. But the law did not presume that the work of a wife was performed with an expectation of pay. "Her own (no doubt truthful) story of her long, devoted, faithful love, and services, as a *wife and mother*," prevented her from claiming pay as a servant. Out of what they described as respect for the plaintiff herself, the judges held that her services were performed "from higher and holier motives." Thus, she lost again. In every way but legally, she had always remained a wife and thus was not entitled to compensation.[35]

Eliza Ridgway Cropsey gained nothing from her long marriage with James Ridgway because he had been divorced. On the other hand, Mary Jane Blossom won an award of $9,000 from William Hall. He had been divorced twenty years earlier for adultery, and Mary Jane sued him for fraud in inducing her to marry and cohabit with him when he had no capacity to remarry. She had known that he had been twice divorced when she married him, but the court decided that Mary Jane had a right to rely on his claim that he was lawfully divorced from his former wives. She did not need to confirm his claim by an exhaustive search of the public records. And the court saw her as suing for exactly what she was entitled to, compensation for her mistreatment by William Hall, unlike Eliza Cropsey, who had sued twice for exactly what she was not entitled to: first, dower, a consequence of marriage, and then wages, a consequence of some different relationship.[36]

By the 1880s, New York's rule weakened. The ban on remarriage continued as law, but courts imported a legislatively defined presumption of death that took effect when the previous spouse had been absent or unheard of for five years. Even if the presumed dead spouse reappeared thereafter, the new marriage was regarded as still valid. And in 1889, the legislature allowed a court that had granted a divorce to modify its decree forbidding remarriage. After five years, if the court then determined that the innocent spouse had remarried and that the conduct of the defendant throughout that time had been "uniformly good," the ban could be lifted.[37]

DOMICILES AND DIVORCE

Well before 1889, however, guiltily divorced New Yorkers, at least those who had "lived quietly" and avoided a "disorderly" life, had learned that they could ignore the rule against remarriage. They simply had to go elsewhere to remarry. New Jersey was near at hand, and the New Jersey courts ignored the disability imposed by New York. In 1847 Judge Samuel Betts of the federal district court in New York City had already declared that capacity to marry depended on the law of the place where the marriage was contracted, not the couple's domicile. Each state was sovereign and independent with regard to its marital regime, free to define the rules of entry, including disabilities. And so, if New Jersey, as a legal jurisdiction, wished to regard the guiltily divorced as capable of marriage, that was its right.[38]

At this point, the small story of the remarriage rights of New York's divorced adulterers joins up with the much larger and longer constitutional history of divorce and remarriage across state lines. Adulterers from New York were no different than many other women and men in their desires to do (to escape, to remarry) what they could not in their home states. Indeed, the guiltily divorced had it somewhat easier than others, for they only wanted a marriage elsewhere. They did not need a "foreign" divorce. Marriages made anywhere were, in constitutional theory, valid everywhere, entitled to full faith and credit (always excepting Mormon polygamous marriages). Thus, the New York courts could hardly avoid recognizing a New Jersey remarriage by a New York divorcé, even if that recognition qualified and undercut New York policy. Foreign divorces, on the other hand, were far less certain in their extraterritorial effects, for reasons that make little sense in abstract constitutional theory but have much to do with a general cultural sensibility that marriage was a good thing while divorce a bad one.[39]

So-called foreign divorces divided into two characteristic situations. In the first, a husband (and it was typically a man who instigated this situation) abandoned his wife in one place and then remarried elsewhere, usually in the West or Midwest, sometimes getting a divorce along the way. In the second, wife or husband went to a liberal divorce jurisdiction, met whatever statutory requirements were set to acquire a divorce, and then returned to her or his home, where she or he remarried. The two situations intersected and intertwined. The first situation often evolved into a variant of the second, when the wife who had remained behind remarried relying on her husband's divorce elsewhere, or when the husband moved back. Yet the two affected different state jurisdictions (although both played important roles in the evolution of federal constitutional law). The first became a problem for newer, more liberal states, as judges there confronted the mixed motivations and marital decisions of settlers. The second tested and challenged the marital regimes of older, more conservative, southern and eastern states, like New York.[40]

The first was an old story. Men had always come to America, or had moved across America, leaving wives behind. American men had always disappeared when their failure to support or their behavior in other ways made them subject to public discipline. Sometimes they found a more liberal jurisdiction where they could divorce their wives. More often they had simply remarried elsewhere. Some proportion of those who left surely did so as part of negotiated agreements with the wives they left behind, although neither wife nor husband could rely on the other once out of sight and control. Husbands forgot to transfer property promised or to send support; wives who had promised to remain behind changed their minds.

An old story, yet still a constant presence in the case records of western and midwestern states throughout the second half of the nineteenth century. In the late 1860s, for example, the Wisconsin Supreme Court heard an extended challenge to the will of Ephraim Chafin. The children from his first marriage, who had been excluded from his estate, described his mind as "swarming with delusions. . . . [N]otions the most erratic and chimerical flocked into it as owls and bats infest the upper rooms of an old ruin," though they also conceded that in business matters he remained quite capable. Ephraim had married Charlotte in New York State sometime before 1828. They had lived together until 1843, when he had moved, first to Illinois and then to New Glarus, Wisconsin. When he had left New York, he provided for his wife, leaving her ten acres of land, a cow, and furniture, enough, according to the lawyers, to provide for her and their daughters for two years. (He had taken their son with him.) Then, in January 1849 he had married Nancy Miller. Six months later Charlotte arrived in New Glarus. Nancy left Ephraim and went to live with her brother. Charlotte and Ephraim tried to negotiate. One witness, who evidently served as a kind of arbitrator, reported that they each stated their deep and long-standing hatred of the other. But they reached an apparent settlement: Chafin had forty acres of Wisconsin land conveyed to one daughter and forty more conveyed jointly to his son and to Charlotte. Two years later, however, Charlotte, evidently unsatisfied by the settlement, had Chafin indicted for bigamy, and then she filed for a divorce, which she obtained in 1854. Chafin remarried Nancy Miller, and the two of them lived for the rest of his life in the town of Jefferson.[41]

The only unusual aspect of the Chafin narrative was Charlotte's willingness to mobilize the criminal law. In the typical case, a husband left his wife in the East, telling her that he would bring her out west as soon as he was settled. Then the husband remarried, sometimes writing his wife that he had divorced her in his new state. What happened next depended on the wife. Often she stayed where she was, and then nothing happened legally until the man died and an inheritance was at issue. But much law was made by women who followed their husbands to their new homes and then filed for divorce. There, in California or Wisconsin or wherever, the continuing commitment of the law to marital unity meant that newly arrived wives would be recognized as having an already established residence or domicile in the state. A divorce for adultery and a property settlement quickly followed.[42]

Damon v. Damon, for example, involved a couple married in 1851 in Massachusetts, where they had lived "peaceably and happily together" until 1865, when he left her to take a short trip to Dane County, Wisconsin. In January 1866 the husband wrote his wife that he had divorced her and, at exactly the same time, he married a new wife. In 1870 the first wife discovered that he had lied about the divorce, and it was then that she first came to Wisconsin, where she filed a petition for divorce based on his adultery in living with his new wife. The magic of coverture and domicile allowed her lawyer's brief to describe her as having "removed" to Wisconsin in 1865 and that "her residence" had "been for five years last past and still is in Dane county." In legal theory, she lived wherever her husband lived, and so she had immediate standing to sue him in Wisconsin, even though state law required two years' residence before a newcomer was permitted to sue for divorce.[43]

The paradigm of western remarriage was *Maynard v. Hill* (1888), a case whose phrases still remain a presence in American family law casebooks. David Maynard had moved west, in this case to Oregon Territory, leaving Lydia, his wife of twenty-two years, and his children, promising to bring them out as soon as he was settled. Once in Oregon he made a claim as a married man to a 640-acre tract, received a legislative divorce from the territorial legislature giving no notice to his wife, and then remarried. He and his new wife took joint title to the tract in 1853 under the Oregon Donation Act. That title was soon voided. Lydia, who had only just heard that she had been divorced, appeared through counsel, and the land office decided to give her the east half of the tract, leaving the west half to David. That decision was appealed first to the commissioners of the General Land Office and eventually to the Secretary of the Interior, both of whom decided that David would retain the west half, and the east half belonged to no one. It was to be treated as public land, to be platted and sold. The case that eventually reached the U.S. Supreme Court was brought by Lydia's children (Lydia died in 1870), who were still trying to regain the east half of the 640-acre tract.[44]

Their right to do so turned on their claim that David Maynard's legislative divorce was a nullity. But Stephen Field, writing for the Court, held that the fact that the divorce had resulted from David's "loose morals" and "shameless conduct" was irrelevant. "Marriage, as creating the most important relation in life, as having more to do with the morals and civilization of a people than any other institution," had "always been subject to the control of the legislature." States owned their marital regimes, and their legislatures could do as they pleased with marriage, including granting divorces directly if they chose to do so. Indeed, the fact that many state constitutions prohibited legislative divorces (of the sort granted to David Maynard) demonstrated that the presumption had to be in favor of their legality, where, as had been the case in territorial Oregon, no such prohibition existed. That no apparent cause existed for this divorce and that it was obtained without the knowledge of the wife did not affect its validity, given the power of the territorial assembly to pass such an act. Divorce was an aspect of state sovereignty.[45]

Marriage was "more" than "a mere contract," meaning that married individuals like Lydia Maynard had fewer constitutional protections than ordinary contractors. Unlike other contracts, which could "be modified, restricted, or enlarged, or entirely released upon the consent of the parties," a marriage, once made, became a public relationship, and the law established and enforced its terms. It was "an institution, in the maintenance of which in its purity, the public" was "deeply interested, for it" was "the foundation of the family and of society, without which there would be neither civilization nor progress." All of which meant that Lydia Maynard and her children had no way to challenge her husband's divorce.[46]

Field's opinion articulated what was by the 1880s a reconfigured understanding of the state's role in marriage, one often characterized as a shift from contract to status. But Field's language manifests two other legal changes as well. For him, divorce was no longer a near-criminal process, external to and separated from the ordinary terms and practices of marriage law. Instead, he understood divorce law as an integral part of a state's marital regime. For him too, as for other judges who dealt with divorce in late nineteenth-century America, the received legal identity of husband and wife, the merger symbolized by traditional rules of domicile, had blown apart. Domicile survived as a concept derived from coverture and marital unity, but its survival would take immense intellectual work by conservative judges and lawyers and treatise writers. And it would survive peppered with serious gaps and contradictions and exceptions.[47]

By the 1880s, much of the law of divorce had been reduced to a question of how to determine a wife's domicile. Husbands who abandoned and remarried, as in *Damon* or in *Maynard*, offered relatively easy cases, ones that fit well within traditional understandings. The first principle remained, as coverture and marital unity demanded, that a wife's domicile was her husband's. That meant that wives who followed their husbands to their new homes had the right (standing) to sue for divorces there. Courts regarded the wife who remained where she had been abandoned as a second easy situation. Her husband's wrongful act invested her with a domicile where she remained. Thus, she too could sue in the couple's old domicile, even though her husband no longer lived there.[48]

But other couples played out more complicated scenarios. What if David Maynard had asked Lydia to move west with him, but she had refused? Did she then become the one guilty of desertion? The traditional answer would have been yes. But mid- and late-nineteenth-century judges kept expanding the exceptions. Older English doctrine had held that the "mere circumstance of unhealthy climate, the inconvenience of travelling, the bad health or the weak constitution of the wife" did not free her from an obligation to accompany her husband wherever he chose to go. American judges, however, insisted that a husband could not exercise his right to choose a home in an arbitrary manner. He could not drag his wife across the country against her will. Or, as a widely cited Pennsylvania case put it, a wife "enjoying . . . the comforts of home, friends, and refinement," who refused "to follow the whim or caprice of her husband in the western wilds, or to encounter the perils and hardships of a journey to the mines of California," would not be considered guilty of desertion. More important, courts worked to prevent a husband from using his capacity to choose the marital home as a way to construct or coerce his wife into becoming a deserter.[49]

A divorced wife was restored the power to establish her own domicile; she was "emancipated" from her dependent status. Likewise, a judicial separation based on a husband's fault empowered a wife to choose her own residence.[50] But other wives, even wives who had grounds for a divorce or a judicial separation but who had not yet acted on them, were in a less secure position. *Cheever v. Wilson,* decided by the U.S. Supreme Court in 1869, held that a wife could establish her separate domicile whenever it was necessary and proper that she do so. That equitable language meant, on the one hand, that a trial court ought to hear the wife's story before ruling that she did not have standing to sue and, on the other hand, that a husband should not be able to assert his wife's desertion or abandonment because she did not accompany him when he left her. M. W. Jacobs, the author of the leading treatise on the law of domicile, tried to distinguish a wife's right to a separate domicile in "the place of their common domicile" (after a husband's abandonment) from her right to establish a new domicile in a different place. He acknowledged that there were many decisions that recognized a wife's capacity to leave her home and move to a new jurisdiction where she could receive a divorce, but he worried that it was "dangerous" ground, as it acknowledged the wife's capacity as a strategic legal actor, who might choose her jurisdiction for its legal usefulness.[51]

We return to the situation of Abby Sage McFarland Richardson, who had, so it was claimed, committed bigamy when she married the dying Albert Richardson after her Indiana divorce. How to understand the situation of women (and men) who migrated elsewhere in order to leave a marriage, but who then returned "home" where they then remarried? The foundation of legal analysis was the same positivist constitutional understanding of state sovereignty that Field enunciated in *Maynard v. Hill,* but the constitutional difficulties Abby's situation raised were quite different. Because of state sovereignty there was no way to challenge the decision of states like Indiana to recognize the separate domicile of a separated wife like Abby Sage, entitling her to receive a divorce. But, by the same token, there was no way for Indiana to insist that its divorce made Abby Sage into a free woman once she had returned to New York, once she had (re)subjected herself to the jurisdiction of New York's courts. Abby's situation, endlessly repeated, confronted judges with the paradox that a man or a woman might be married in one state and divorced in another, that one could be a scrupulous paragon of virtue in one part of the United States and a criminal bigamist in another.

The problem had long existed in theory, but the transportation revolution of the middle years of the nineteenth century made it a real constitutional dilemma. The railroad meant that movement across the continent became bidirectional. It was as easy to return as to stay. A state could grant divorces to "residents" or "domiciliaries" (women and men who had established their residence in the state according to the standards set out in the state's legislation), who would quickly and efficiently return to their real homes, to states where their divorces would not have been possible.

The apparently simple legal question who was a resident—who had established domicile—sank into the mud of unascertainable intentions and strategic behavior. In a free society, a society where people's motives were understood as private and irrelevant to their legal rights, a society that identified freedom with mobility, was any reason for moving less legitimate than any other? As Joel Bishop noted, people had a right to change their minds. They could come for one reason and stay for another. Or perhaps they had come with an intention to stay, but then found the weather or the business opportunities or the marriageability of the available men or women not attractive. As a matter of law, it was not necessary when moving "that there should be an absolute, fixed resolution never to come back."[52]

Meanwhile, a few states, Indiana first, capitalized on the mobile and uncertain meaning of residence and domicile. Such states created a competitive niche for themselves as providers of divorce to the women and men who were willing to come. Two legislative innovations identified Indiana as the pioneer. The first, instituted in 1824, gave Indiana judges the right to grant divorces for any reason they regarded as legitimate if the petitioner failed to demonstrate a ground predefined by legislation. The second, passed into law in 1852, allowed a judge to grant a divorce to anyone (wife or husband) who had established "bona fide" residence in his county, without insisting on proof of any prior period of residence. The first innovation placed Indiana on the liberal end of a continuum of state divorce laws and made it one of a number of states hated by antidivorce polemicists. The second innovation pushed Indiana into uncharted territory and tested the limits of jurisdiction and state sovereignty in nineteenth-century America.

In 1852 Indiana thus became the first divorce haven. Indiana's legal preeminence was momentary (although more long-standing in the popular imagination). By the late 1860s, by the time Abby Sage McFarland arrived in the state, Indiana's residency law had already been weakened (or strengthened depending on one's point of view). And in the 1870s and through the rest of the nineteenth century, other jurisdictions—Illinois, Rhode Island, Iowa, the District of Columbia, South Dakota, Utah, Arizona, and others—took over the migratory divorce business. But what mid-century Indiana had modeled for those later competitors was a way of practicing divorce law: local judges treated divorces as routine bureaucratic acts, as facilitative work; assumed that petitioners were entitled to their divorces in the absence of evidence to the contrary; and refused to regard a divorce as a threat to the moral fiber of the community.[53]

So, from the early 1850s on, women and men could establish a residence in a county in Indiana (later on in South Dakota or Arizona) by renting a room in a boardinghouse or hotel, hire a lawyer, get a divorce, and then return to their true, their real, their unchanged homes. Like Abby Sage McFarland, they could leave ex-husband-to-be and fiancé in New York, do their business in Indiana, and return with problem apparently solved. They never really had to move. They always remained New Yorkers.

But if they remained New Yorkers, what was the significance of the Indiana divorce? New York law mandated permanent marriage, except where adultery had been proved. Clearly Indiana as a state had the right to construct its own divorce regime, for Hoosiers and for those who were willing to become permanent Hoosiers. But did Indiana's easy divorce law become a supplement, a qualification, a subversion, of New York's law so that any unhappy spouse with sufficient resources could do legally in Indiana precisely what she or he could not do in New York? Or to ask the question in the terms of American federalism: were New York judges obligated to recognize Indiana divorce decrees as entitled to full faith and credit?[54]

In February 1864, in the midst of the Civil War, Isaac Redfield, a War Democrat and the former chief justice of the Vermont Supreme Court, published an essay in the *American Law Register.* The essay offered judges and other legal actors an array of arguments to reject foreign divorces while still remaining committed to state sovereignty.

The essay began with the English case of *Warrender v. Warrender* (1835), where the House of Lords had ruled that an English marriage could be dissolved by a Scottish court (at a time when English marriages were still understood as absolutely indissoluble except by parliamentary act). The Lords' language Redfield regarded as of "universal application." Marriage was not a contract like other contracts. Were it such, its terms would be fixed by the place where it was entered into. Rather, marriage was a relationship (a status) whose terms were entirely "ambulatory." The law in place where and when a couple married fixed nothing. Wife and husband always remained subject to the marital rules of the place where they happened to live.

In language that prefigured Field's in *Maynard v. Hill,* Redfield wrote of marriage as "one of those things, so essentially affecting society, and the civil and economic relations of social existence, that it must of necessity be under constant and perpetual legislative control." Redfield wrote that he did "not desire to state offensive, and surely not painful, illustrations," but he could see no reason why it would not be within the theoretical power of any state legislature to insist that a man take more than one wife or that a wife have more than one husband. Marriage, unlike other contracts, was so "inherent and interwoven with the very framework of social life" that it needed to possess "the quality of perfect uniformity." The paradoxical result of that need was that all married couples were compelled to accommodate themselves "to the existing law of the moment" and of the place. The individual wills of the parties were irrelevant. All marriages became the same, that is, subject to the same rules, in the moment and in the place (the state) where they found themselves, in spite of the diversity of their origins.[55]

Writing in the midst of the Civil War, Redfield recognized that some aspects of social life would become national, theoretically unified across the nation. But, asserting a Democratic sensibility, he insisted that marriage, like "naturalization" and "citizenship," remained matters exclusively under the control of the states. No state would consent to surrender such matters to any other state. And "control" of marriage, of its "rights, obligations, and duties," he thought involved questions even more vital to the state's "prosperity" than those affecting citizenship.[56]

Redfield knew that American law differed from the law set out in *Warrender.* The English Lords had decided that Scotland had jurisdiction over the Warrenders' marriage because the husband had moved there, even though the wife had remained in England. By the 1860s, few American courts would have agreed. Separated American wives, certainly wives separated because of the desertion of their husbands, could always establish a separate domicile. Thus, marital conflict that implicated the differing marital or divorce regimes of differing states was always a possibility.[57]

Redfield's goal was to destroy the capacity of American divorce havens (Indiana) to tempt the unhappily married from more conservative states. State laws that made migratory divorces possible were the products of inexperienced legislators, too tender in their desire to relieve "misfortune," who had succumbed to the itch to try "a new experiment in the matrimonial scheme." Succumbing to the pressures of apparently victimized women, they had so shortened their residence requirements that their laws had become a public scandal, a matter "of wonder throughout the civilized world."

Unlike antidivorce polemicists, however, Redfield insisted that he was making no claim with regard to "the propriety" of easier divorce, and he would have rejected the nationalizing solutions that late nineteenth-century conservatives often promoted. Different states were free to make differing choices. Decrees were valid where granted. Each state legislature could provide divorces for any cause, or for no cause, in its own discretion. And divorces allowed those divorced to remarry, *"within that particular forum."* That this meant that in Indiana Abby Sage McFarland could marry Albert Richardson, even though she had a husband in New York, he would have accepted as logically entailed by federalism.[58]

In Redfield's version of the American marital dilemma, the problem was fundamentally about federalism and the American constitutional order. The core evil lay in the capacity of an Indiana to destroy the marital regimes of more conservative jurisdictions, the ability of Indiana "to bind the rights of the whole world." "All" he desired was "that the practice of the [more conservative state] courts . . . be preserved from contamination." How could a state restrain its inhabitants, keep them from "throwing off all obedience to its own laws and institutions, and subverting, by the interposition of a foreign tribunal, its own fundamental policy"? How could New York legally sustain its commitment to the inviolability of Abby's marriage to Daniel McFarland?[59]

Redfield's answers rested on his insistence that divorce proceedings were like criminal proceedings. Marriages were transitory and personal; they moved with the couple. At issue in a divorce case, however, was not the marriage but the legislatively prescribed and delimited wrongs—desertion, adultery, cruelty—on which the divorce petition was founded. Unlike the marriage, such wrongs were not transitory and personal. They did not move with the plaintiff. To the contrary, they were local and fixed. A valid "cause" had to be a "breach" of the state law at the time that the cause occurred. Such causes were like criminal charges, and they were "of such a police and disciplinary character" that no state could delegate them to any other sovereignty. Indiana could not "punish" a defendant for a wrong done in New York.[60]

Redfield's analysis drew on an older and embattled understanding of divorce as an extraordinary act of state power comparable to the criminal law, as radically separable from the laws of marriage. Even as he insisted on the constitutional sovereignty of each state as a marriage maker and breaker, his answer challenged exactly the kind of routinized divorce regimes that legislatures in states like Indiana were enacting, and it reified and sanctified a way of divorce that those state legislatures had explicitly rejected.

Redfield's approach also rested on a rights-based conception of state sovereignty redolent of parallels to the national law of slavery. To him, any other way of thinking about divorce law would be destructive of patriarchal civil liberties. There would be "no security," no safety, in one's private life. (And here Redfield's "one" is clearly male.) An isolated act of neglect or cruelty that was a divorceable wrong in some other state, but not in the state one lived in, "might become the instrument of forfeiting the most important and vital interests pertaining to social life." One was always at the mercy of a wife's capacity to move to that other state. The easy solution to the problem would have been a national decision (akin to Taney's bludgeoned solution in the *Dred Scott* case) that denied separated wives the capacity to establish their own separate domiciles. But that easy solution would have been radically inconsistent with Redfield's first principle of state sovereignty. Instead, Redfield posited that a foreign or migratory divorce decree would be entitled to recognition in other states only when both husband and wife were "constructively" within the state where the decree was made. The "constructively" gave away Redfield's patriarchal mindset. It meant that an "innocent" New York husband who had gone to Indiana alone to free himself from his marriage could do so, even within the terms of Redfield's restrictive analysis. The magic of coverture meant that his wife was always "constructively" with him, even when she was actually somewhere else. A similarly situated New York wife, Abby Sage McFarland for example, would possess no comparable right to recognition of her foreign divorce; no nineteenth-century court, not even in Indiana, would have recognized her husband's constructive domicile along with her real presence.[61]

Redfield believed that the full faith and credit clause of the federal Constitution had no relevance when only one party to a judgment was present. The clause applied only to judgments where courts had full jurisdiction over all parties. And his domicile-based understanding of full faith and credit shaped the development of constitutional law through the first half of the twentieth century. But in 1864 his goal was to protect the policies of conservative divorce regimes against the depredations of other states that had made divorce a way to reconstitute new marital relations instead of a punishment for wrongdoing. Comity, the legal understanding that sovereign states ordinarily owed a duty to respect the valid decisions made by other sovereign states, was the unstated but crucial concept at issue. Constitutionally, Redfield could not challenge a state court's decision to grant comity to a foreign divorce. The point of his piece, however, was to lay out the reasons why no state court could be compelled to do so or, to put it more strongly, why a state court ought not to do so.

At exactly the same time that Redfield's essay appeared, Joel Prentiss Bishop published a new edition of his treatise on marriage and divorce. In it he set out what would become the dominant approach to the problem of the foreign divorce. And his approach stood as a point-by-point refutation of the moral and constitutional assumptions of men like Isaac Redfield.

The source of Bishop's immense influence over the next century were six specific propositions about how to determine the extraterritorial legality of a divorce. The first proposition was entirely uncontroversial: no court could have jurisdiction if neither party had a bona fide domicile in the state. The second proposition, on the other hand, changed American constitutional law: only one party to a divorce needed to be domiciled in a jurisdiction. If either wife or husband possessed a domicile in the state that granted the divorce, then the courts of other jurisdictions had to recognize the validity of the foreign divorce.

This second proposition followed logically from the modern American recognition that separated wives often possessed separate domiciles. Once one understood that a wife could be a resident of a state where her husband had no residence, then state sovereignty itself demanded recognition of a foreign divorce. Otherwise, a state, say Indiana, would be "deprived" of the right to determine the status of its own subjects; the state would be forced to "yield to foreign power in the management of its domestic concerns." It could not "redress" its citizens' wrongs. It would be unable to provide "the solace of actual married life" to those subject to its laws, and it would have deprived "itself of any increase of population which might result from the actual marriage of the citizen." Like Redfield, Bishop played with the apparent absurdity of a framework that seemed to make it possible to be married in one state and unmarried or a bigamist in another. The home state of a man divorced in another state by his separated wife could regard him as still married to his absent and divorced wife (much as New York regarded Daniel McFarland as still married to Abby Sage). But for Bishop, unlike Redfield, the conundrum that state sovereignty appeared to create was, in the end, nonsense because no state could "invent a way of causing a husband to exist without a wife." The goal of a just legal order was to encourage marriage. The "permanent" marriage ("a mere theoretical thing") that Redfield defended, however, was nothing but an "impediment" to real matrimony.[62]

The other four propositions stood as corollaries to this second proposition. The place where the "offence"—that is, the wrong that justified the divorce petition—took place was immaterial (Proposition Three). The actual domicile of the couple at the time the offence occurred was irrelevant (Proposition Four). It was immaterial where—in what state or country, or under what divorce laws—the marriage was celebrated (Proposition Five). And finally, a valid divorce, one based on jurisdiction founded on the legal domicile of either a wife or a husband, did not violate the provision in the U.S. Constitution against laws that impaired the obligations of contracts (Proposition Six).[63]

Bishop's third, fourth, and fifth propositions countered Redfield's older understanding of divorce as a near-criminal process. The effect was to lower the apparent legal stakes. To Redfield, the divorce process mobilized the power of the state against an accused defendant; it was a punitive process that ought to be limited and circumscribed in a free society. Bishop, by contrast, saw divorce as a facilitative process shaped by a reality principle—by the desire of liberal states to provide mechanisms to undo relationships that had become merely theoretical, merely legal— and by a policy in favor of remarriage. Bishop himself was not entirely comfortable with a vision of divorce as merely bureaucratic and routine, with the practices that were emerging in the divorce havens. Yet, in opposition to the patriarchal and civil libertarian vision of Redfield, he placed the rights of the (apparently female) complainant ahead of those of the (apparently male) absent defendant.[64]

Bishop shared with divorce reformers like Robert Dale Owen a visceral hatred of separation as a legal status. To him, a judicial separation was a "corrupting device," a "monster," an institution that would never have been tolerated but for the religious fantasy that a legal dissolution of marriage was an offence against God ("from which point, the slope was easy toward any compromise with good sense"). Separation existed as the dark underbelly of the received law of marriage. Against the values of unity and continuity and support and care that permanent marriage ought to nurture, it counterposed an incentive structure that produced abandonment and neglect and illicit relationships. Once separated, only divorce, by which Bishop meant the possibility of remarriage, could save women and men from lives of sin and disorder. The liberal divorce regimes of the western states constituted, as such, both reasonable responses to human frailty and humane recognitions of human potential.[65]

Bishop's treatise can therefore be read as a defense of liberal divorce regimes, as a liberal Protestant response to those like Redfield who thought "happiness . . . too plentiful and woe too scarce." He meant to provide a method that legitimated extraterritorial divorces. The method was startlingly simple. Where an extraterritorial divorce was asserted, all a judge had to do was to determine if a bona fide domicile had been established by the complainant in the divorcing state. If so, then the divorce was entitled to recognition wherever the divorced ex-spouse moved or lived. In other words, so long as someone had the resources and the will to go where divorce was possible, divorce should be an available option.[66]

Both the treatise and the method were huge successes. Well into the twentieth century, Bishop on domicile remained an obligatory citation for judges and for lawyers who dealt with out-of-state divorces. Yet the application of Bishop to actual situations transformed the startlingly simple into the inexplicably complex. The domicile-based standard grew Ptolemaic epicycles and qualifications and elaborations. A whole discipline of academic legal study—conflicts of law—emerged out of the struggle to rationalize and to explain, a discipline that transformed divorce cases into problems in logic shorn of the human relations that had produced them.

Bishop's standard had the apparent virtue of allowing judges to avoid inquiries into the motives of the parties standing before them. Yet judges found themselves unable to accept Bishop's gift, unable to step away from moralism and the human situations of the litigants. Their paternalistic and moralistic reactions led the judges toward complexity, away from simplicity. Where, for example, a court determined that a husband had abandoned his wife to go to a divorce mill, it would often recognize his divorce for purposes of protecting the husband from bigamy charges, if he had remarried in his home state. And Bishop would be cited in support of that holding. Yet the court would also insist on granting support or alimony to the abandoned wife, on the basis of her later petition to a local court for a divorce on grounds of abandonment or adultery. Her right to a divorce—her right both to support and to the moral status of being the victimized party—could not be precluded by his preexisting divorce.[67]

New York's decisions were both crucial and especially problematic. The state's continuing refusal to liberalize its divorce law produced many cases. For New Yorkers a legal divorce usually required a foreign divorce. Meanwhile, New York's place at the center of a national communication and news network and also as the center of the professionalized legal culture meant continuing publicity for its decisions. When Indiana politicians criticized Indiana divorce law, they cited New York cases and the critical language of New York judges. The scandalous character of divorce havens like Indiana was epitomized by the willingness of Indiana lawyers to advertise in the commercial and legal pages of New York journals.[68] And when, after the turn of the twentieth century, the U.S. Supreme Court tried to reconcile the conflicts among the states and to solve the problem of the extraterritorial divorce, it did so using appeals from New York cases and elaborating on categories and concepts drawn from New York law.

During the 1850s, 1860s, and 1870s, at least two different analytic approaches vied for ascendancy in New York jurisprudence. Trial judges, like Recorder Hackett in the McFarland case, sometimes instructed juries to regard the foreign divorce as void and illegal. When trial judges did so, they used language like Redfield's, and they relied on a line of New York appellate decisions that had protected the support claims of separated New York wives after their husbands had exited west.[69] But another line of New York decisions, typically involving marital stories less reducible to stereotypes of victim and victimizer, recognized that both women and men had the right to go west "to procure" divorces and that right meant inevitably that those foreign divorces would shape the marital rights of women and men still living in New York. In *Kinnier v. Kinnier* (1871), for example, the New York Court of Appeals rejected a husband's claim that his wife's prior Illinois divorce was not entitled to any recognition in New York. The judges had no doubt that in the best of all legal worlds, all states would conform their laws with those of New York. They also knew, however, that they could not escape a constitutional obligation to recognize at least some foreign divorces.[70]

According to Bishop, the courts of New York appeared to have been moving "step by step" toward his vision of the validity of foreign divorces. The false "dicta" that he identified with the first line of decisions were gradually being replaced by the true understanding represented in cases like *Kinnier*. But then, in a decision Bishop found both inexplicable and horrifying, "a mere jump in the dark . . . without looking, thinking, or reasoning," the New York Court of Appeals reversed course in *People v. Baker* (1879).[71]

Frank M. Baker was a bigamist who had married four different women between 1871 and 1876, and he had been sentenced to three consecutive five-year terms, one for each bigamous marriage. At issue in his appeal was the first five-year sentence. The New York Supreme Court had reversed his conviction on the theory that he could not have been guilty of that particular bigamy because his first wife, Sallie West, had divorced him in Ohio six months before he had married his second wife. Sallie had moved back to Ohio in 1872 to be with her parents at the time of childbirth. Frank had promised to follow her there, but he never did. Nor did he ever ask her to return to him. Nor did he tell her where he was living. Nor did he ever contribute to her support. So, not surprisingly, when Sallie petitioned for divorce, she asserted that Frank had been guilty of "gross neglect of duty," and that she had established a bona fide domicile in Ohio, based on his abandonment.[72]

But then, in the decision that horrified Bishop, the New York Court of Appeals reinstated Baker's full conviction because his wife's Ohio divorce had no validity in New York. To Judge Charles Folger, who wrote for the court and who mobilized the same language that Redfield had in 1864, the case raised only one question: could a court in another state end a New York marriage. And to Folger the answer was plainly no. There was, he conceded, much variety in the divorce rules of the states, and he recognized that the U.S. Supreme Court might one day have to arbitrate or choose between the competing divorce regimes of the states. Until it did, however, "diversity in policy" did not mean that the state whose courts acted first should control beyond its borders. There was no conception of comity that demanded that New York had to allow Ohio law to change the status of its citizens, against public policy or public morality.[73]

In New York, *People v. Baker* remained an obligatory citation, good law, for the next sixty-four years. It helped to define the distinctive jurisprudential path of New York. And to Bishop and others concerned with articulating a coherent understanding of divorce and federalism it remained emblematic of bad law, inconsistent with good policy. It was one of a number of influential late nineteenth-century appellate decisions that reproduced Redfield's strong state sovereignty understanding of federalism. Nationally that understanding became the minority understanding, as more and more jurisdictions moved toward Bishop's approach. Yet toting up what was the majority rule, what was the minority rule, doesn't get us far toward a historical understanding of the legal structures and practices that women and men faced as they struggled with one another and for recognition of their remarriages.[74]

For divorcing and remarrying New Yorkers, on the other hand, *People v. Baker* was nothing but a legal problem. And evidently it was a problem easily solved. New York's lawyers developed predictable techniques to ensure that their clients' migratory divorces would be recognized in New York. New York grew full of men who had remarried in reliance on their ex-wives' foreign divorce decrees. Unlike Frank Baker, none of them appeared at risk of being charged as bigamists.[75]

In three decisions between 1901 and 1906, all involving the marital struggles of New Yorkers, the U.S. Supreme Court did interject itself onto the terrain of the foreign divorce. In the first case, *Atherton v. Atherton*, Justice Horace Gray invoked the concept of a matrimonial domicile to justify his decision that a Kentucky divorce trumped a New York separation order. The Kentucky divorce was entitled to full faith and credit because Kentucky was the state where the couple had lived as a couple (their matrimonial domicile), and Kentucky was also where the wrong had occurred (the wife's abandonment and departure for New York) on which the divorce was founded.[76] The second case, *Bell v. Bell*, sketched the converse situation, using the same conceptual structure. A husband, who had married in Illinois and then lived with his wife in New York, could not rely on a Pennsylvania divorce (where neither husband nor wife had ever lived) as a defense to his wife's New York divorce petition on grounds of his adultery. Again, the matrimonial domicile allowed the court to dismiss the Pennsylvania divorce, even though the husband had met the state's residency requirements.[77]

The third case, *Haddock v. Haddock,* also relied on the concept of a matrimonial domicile. As in *Atherton* and so many other decisions, *Haddock* tested the legitimacy of a husband's claimed divorce as a defense against his wife's suit for a separation and for support. In this case the couple had married in New York in 1868, the husband had divorced his wife in Connecticut in 1881 on the ground of her desertion, though he had apparently abandoned her immediately after their marriage, and the wife brought an action for a legal separation in 1899, more than thirty years after their actual separation. The majority voted to affirm the decision of the New York courts in favor of the wife. In support of that decision, Justice Edward White constructed a complex method that he fantasized would solve the constitutional problem of the extraterritorial divorce. White's holding could be reduced to two complementary propositions: if a husband had wrongfully left his wife and sought a new domicile, he could not get a divorce entitled to full faith and credit; if, on the other hand, he had acquired a new domicile after her wrongful conduct, his divorce was entitled to full faith and credit.[78]

For forty years *Haddock* remained both the leading case on the problem of the foreign divorce and a focus of continuing criticism. Figuring out what *Haddock* meant became the work of both divorce lawyers and legal academics. And their work shaped constitutional law, the conflicts of law, and divorce law. Much of this moves far afield from the concerns of this book, but two particular implications drawn out of *Haddock* are important for the narrative of federalism that we have been tracing: only when wives or husbands left the "matrimonial domicile" because of their spouses' misconduct (misconduct as defined by the law of the state that was the matrimonial domicile) were their divorces entitled to full faith and credit. State courts were free to recognize any and all other extraterritorial divorces, and most state courts would do so, increasingly so throughout the first forty years of the twentieth century. But nothing in the U.S. Constitution required them to do so. That meant that state courts that refused to recognize such foreign divorces, like those of New York, were constitutionally empowered to continue to maintain their separate path. Second, the effect of *Haddock* was to undercut the premise on which a case like *People v. Baker* had been decided. Each state no longer had the right to be as strict or as loose as it chose with regard to the recognition of foreign divorces. The federal Constitution now served to discipline apparent state sovereignty. As Joseph Beale wrote in 1926 on the twentieth anniversary of the decision, *Haddock* forced conservative states like New York to recognize some foreign divorces based on the domicile of a wife alone. That paved the way for a general recognition of foreign divorces obtained by New York wives, as women entitled to establish separate domiciles and assert their husbands' fault under other states' laws.[79]

For Joseph Beale, who by 1926 had come to epitomize legal formalism and orthodoxy, *Haddock* was a conundrum. On the one hand, the decision made no sense. On the other hand, he had reluctantly come to the conclusion that the holding might have been the best that American law could do under the circumstances. The whole confusing story of divorce jurisdiction had been set on course back in the middle years of the nineteenth century: by the odd American insistence that marital unity could be divided, that separated wives could live apart from their husbands, that wives and their husbands could be legal residents of different states, subject to differing rules. This was "an undesirable condition of affairs," inconsistent with a rational legal order and with the rules that prevailed in the rest of the civilized world outside of the United States. But in the United States, on the terrain of American federalism, separation allowed wives and husbands to establish separate domiciles, to divorce under competing legal regimes, and to know themselves as married in one state and divorced or remarried in another.[80]

Let us skip ahead to the early 1940s. In the intervening years, men and women still abandoned marriages and remarried and remarried, sometimes stopping for a legal ending. But the continuously rising rate of divorce suggests that more and more separating spouses were choosing to formalize endings through divorces. It was the era of "the road to Reno," an era when the "migratory divorce" was both a sociological fact of life and a problem for legal and public policy. In 1882 W. D. Howells had imagined himself as opening up a new, previously unexplored subject when he published *A Modern Instance,* a novel that dealt seriously with an Indiana divorce. By the 1920s and 1930s, divorce stories (including the obligatory "foreign" divorce) were clichés, the stuff of slapstick comedy, routine enough to serve as an almost unspoken backdrop to the real narrative of the film, the play, the novel.[81]

By the 1940s Nevada was long established as the epitome of a divorce haven, replacing all competitors. In Nevada lawyers and the hotel industry worked to create a divorce regime that was "speedy, painless, and profitable." When in 1931 Arkansas and Idaho tried to compete by enacting comparable ninety-day residence requirements, Nevada countered by reducing its requirement to six weeks. Nevada's commercial success (and hotel industry) was driven, as Indiana's before it, by the unwillingness of New York and a few other jurisdictions to liberalize their divorce laws. Around 60 percent of all divorces granted in the state were to women and men who had come from New York and New Jersey. And realistic voices understood Nevada as a kind of safety valve that allowed more conservative jurisdictions to sustain apparently rigid rules that conformed to Catholic and conservative Protestant theology without actually preventing divorce and remarriage.[82]

By the 1940s sociologists and legal realists also understood "the institution of divorce," including foreign divorces, as an ordinary, though not everyday, event. "[L]ike sickness," divorce could be understood as the "means of livelihood for a profession." They emphasized the disjuncture between the apparent and the real, between the formal structure symbolized by *Haddock v. Haddock* and *People v. Baker* and a workaday world where divorce never evoked risk of bigamy. And that disjuncture became one way to characterize life in twentieth-century America. A 1935 article by the young Fowler Harper explored "the myth" of the void divorce. Void divorces were foreign divorces received by women and men, who then lived remarried lives in states that refused to recognize such divorces as legal. To him the gap between doctrinal law and social practice in divorce law was of a piece with the recently concluded experiment in Prohibition. Citizens had come to realize that legal doctrine was one thing, the law to which they were "actually subject" was "something very different." When nearly everyone acted "as if" a rule were not law, "the 'as if'" became "the actuality."[83]

The last act in the long nineteenth-century constitutional drama of domiciles and divorces began one day in early May 1940 in little Granite Falls, North Carolina, deep in the Blue Ridge mountains. On that day, O. B. Williams, the local grocer, ran off to Las Vegas with Lilly Shaver Hendrix. Both were married at the time. Not to each other.

In Las Vegas they lived together in the Alamo trailer court for the six weeks needed to establish Nevada residence. They used the same lawyers. They testified for each other, each of them repeating the prescribed formula to establish that their respective spouses had committed "extreme cruelty." Their lawyers dutifully mailed notices of the pending divorces back to the appropriate addresses in North Carolina and published a notice in a Las Vegas newspaper. And then, as soon as the divorce was "final," O. B. and Lilly married.

So the story would have ended had they stayed in Nevada, or if they had moved practically anywhere other than back to where they had come from. Instead, they moved to Pineola, North Carolina, one county over and a few miles away from Granite Falls. In Pineola, they invited old friends to visit them, and they joined the local Baptist Church. And apparently their presence nearby, flaunting their remarried identities, outraged old neighbors and spouses. Late in the year the Caldwell County grand jury indicted both O. B. Williams and Lilly Shaver Hendrix for bigamy, for pretending to be married while each had a living spouse.

At the trial, which began and ended on February 24, 1941, the state proved their first marriages and then had four witnesses describe Lilly and O. B.'s life together in Pineola. The defendants then introduced the divorce proceedings in Nevada. And the judge then charged the jury to disregard the Nevada divorces as entirely void, unworthy and unentitled to any respect or recognition. Even though both of the spouses who had remained in North Carolina had apparently received actual notice of the divorces, the judge charged that service by publication in Nevada did not give Nevada jurisdiction to grant a divorce to North Carolinians. The judge did not charge the jury that the Nevada divorce was a sham or a fraud. Instead, he asserted the strong theory of state sovereignty that Redfield had developed in 1864: that the apparent legality of the Nevada divorce constituted no constraint on the power of North Carolina courts to enforce North Carolina's criminal law of bigamy. The jury obediently convicted O. B. and Lilly. He was sentenced to three to ten years' imprisonment at hard labor; she was sentenced to three to five years' imprisonment.[84]

After their convictions were upheld by the North Carolina Supreme Court, the case went to the U.S. Supreme Court, which reversed.[85] *Haddock* was no longer good law, according to Justice William O. Douglas. Divorces, even Nevada divorces, were entitled to full faith and credit under the U.S. Constitution. Douglas's holding was of a piece with the Court's general withdrawal from substantive due process. And it was also, he stressed, a limited decision. He assumed that O. B. Williams and Lilly Shaver Hendrix Williams had each established a bona fide domicile in Nevada. He reserved the question whether North Carolina could refuse to recognize a Nevada divorce after a North Carolina court had made an independent determination that a Nevada divorce was fraudulent. The Constitution he was "expounding" drew much of its significance from its capacity to bring "separate sovereign states into an integrated whole through the medium of the full faith and credit clause." North Carolina had a right to its policy, but when a Nevada court, "acting in accord with the requirements of procedural due process," issued a divorce decree to a Nevada resident, that decree was entitled to full faith and credit, even though the recognition of that decree violated North Carolina's marital policy.[86]

In North Carolina, the prosecutors in Caldwell County went back to work. O. B. Williams and Lilly Shaver Hendrix were indicted again, and in late November 1943 the two were brought to trial. A new judge, Sam Ervin, who many years later would become famous as the senator who led the Watergate inquiry, was brought in to hear the case. The defendants moved to dismiss the charges on the grounds of double jeopardy, a motion Ervin rejected. Then much the same evidence used in the first trial was reintroduced.[87] Judge Ervin prepared a complex set of jury instructions that challenged the Nevada divorces while still recognizing the obligation to grant full faith and credit to valid Nevada decrees. Ervin asserted that Nevada decrees were not valid, that is, not entitled to any recognition in North Carolina, when the only reason for "moving" to Nevada had been to avoid North Carolina law. The defendants had the burden of satisfying the jury that they had been legally domiciled in Nevada at the time they obtained their divorces. Otherwise, they had never lost their North Carolina domiciles, and their Nevada divorces were both fraudulent and collusive. Nevada could do whatever it wanted, could recognize them as divorced if it so chose, but a court in North Carolina remained free to determine whether the Nevada proceedings were valid under Nevada law. The result, as before, was that both defendants were convicted: he this time to one to three years' imprisonment, she to eight to twenty-four months.[88]

On appeal to the North Carolina Supreme Court, the couple's attorney tried to focus the court's attention on the wartime context. National existence depended on "a free and easy flow" of citizens from one state to another. Yet the effect of upholding these bigamy convictions was to "freeze" citizenship within each of the forty-eight states. "[S]ociety could not exist as an organized branch of human endeavor if . . . each time a divorced man or woman" crossed "the boundary of a state line" he or she were "subject to indictment for this or some similar offense." "Obviously," the founders of the country had not intended to permit legislation that "would confine the citizenship of the respective states within their respective boundaries" or to make them vulnerable to "some snoopy or envious neighbor." And times "of great national emergency," as World War II surely was, made even greater the need for "the free and easy transmigration" of citizens across the United States. There were many divorced individuals among the soldiers and defense workers temporarily living in North Carolina. A "strict application" of the law put them all at risk.[89]

But again the North Carolina Supreme Court affirmed the convictions.[90] And this time, in *Williams II,* the U.S. Supreme Court agreed. The right of a state to grant a divorce was founded on domicile. North Carolina, however, was not required, according to Justice Felix Frankfurter, to "yield" her state policy once a Nevada court had decided that O. B. and Lilly were domiciled in the state. North Carolina's courts had the right to determine that the couple was not ever domiciled in Nevada, and once they had made that determination, they were clearly free to decide that a Nevada divorce had no capacity to "liberate" O. B. and Lilly from a bigamy conviction.[91]

Like so many doctrinal narratives, the story of the recognition of the foreign divorce does not end with a bang. What did *Williams II* mean? Apparently, neither O. B. nor Lilly ever saw the insides of a prison, and it appears that the two of them spent the rest of their lives together in total obscurity. On August 18, 1945, shortly after the Supreme Court affirmed their bigamy convictions, the two of them married each other again, this time in Caldwell County.[92] One commentator imagined the holding as standing for the continuing authority of conservative divorce jurisdictions to hold at bay the transgressive power of the Nevadas of the world. But Max Rheinstein, who would emerge as the leading scholar of family law in the postwar world, thought otherwise. His careful narrative of the constitutional history of the foreign divorce after *Williams II* started with the premise that a Nevada divorce would carry a presumption of "nationwide effectiveness," so long as the divorcing party carefully followed "the advice of experienced counsel" in her or his home state. He was surely right, though it soon became clear that even without experienced counsel, the risk of becoming the next Williams had practically disappeared. In case after case, the Supreme Court eroded the apparent moral of *Williams II*. And in the face of clear signals of disinterest from the U.S. Supreme Court, conservative states soon ceased to police their marital boundaries, letting remarriages occur without comment. The competition between differing marital and divorce regimes within American federalism would no longer be understood as raising central constitutional issues (at least not until the potential recognition of gay marriages came into consciousness).[93] Long before the official starting date of the "no-fault revolution," long before conservative divorce jurisdictions like New York formally changed their divorce law, divorce had become, in New York and North Carolina and elsewhere, an expectation, even a right, for those who would remarry.[94]

BEHIND THE LAW OF DIVORCE

In 1867, after Abby Sage McFarland had left her husband but before her Indiana divorce, she lived for a time in the house of Samuel Sinclair, the publisher of Horace Greeley's *New York Tribune*. Sinclair, who was a bit straitlaced, had heard that Abby intended to marry Albert Richardson. One day he spoke to her about the rumor. He said: "her friends thought it strange she should engage herself so soon after their separation." As he remembered it, she replied: "that having separated, she thought she had a right to."[95]

Abby's statement can be read as a declaration of independence, telling Sinclair that she had broken with her marital identity, her covered self, and that she had begun a process that would inevitably lead to divorce and legal emancipation. That reading may define a modern understanding of the meaning of divorce. Divorce is about an ending to a relationship. It opens up a world of new possibilities. It liberates from the past.

Fragments of that modern understanding float through the rhetoric of nineteenth-century debates and the case law. Men reclaimed their independence from the ties and the financial obligations of married life, sometimes divorcing, often just walking, occasionally talking openly about their desires and their "right" to be free. Woman's rights activists across the feminist spectrum talked of women's need to emancipate themselves or to be emancipated from abusive men. Lawyers sometimes tried to convince juries and judges that their female clients were entitled to the freedom that divorce offered. Of one such wife, the New York lawyer Henry Lauren Clinton explained, "The hope of emancipation . . . ever [hung] . . . upon her life as lightning in a cloud."[96] And surely emancipation was also implicit in Abby's answer to Samuel Sinclair. Divorce, in the sense of an ending to her marriage to Daniel McFarland, must have been somewhere on her mental horizon.

But that was not what Sinclair had asked about. His question was about Abby's "engagement" to another man, about the fact that she was already moving toward a new relationship. Her imagined emancipation was not an emancipation from marriage but an emancipation to remarry. That was what bothered Sinclair.

Today, remarriage is simply one of a number of possibilities presented to the newly unencumbered formerly married self. Adultery is a symptom, not a cause. If people divorce when they fall in love with someone new, that is because something had already gone wrong with the marriage. If people remarry soon after their divorces, that "fact" will be explained in terms of habits or social practices, of an order of experience beneath or to the side of the law and legal practice.

But in late nineteenth- and early twentieth-century America, remarriage was the goal and the problem that legal policy confronted, divorce only one of several means to that end. To achieve lives as (re)married, men and women consulted lawyers, conspired, colluded, traveled to distant states, obtained "fraudulent" divorces, remade their memories, signed "separation agreements," and risked bigamy convictions. They exploited ambiguities in the law, even as they also sometimes became the victims of bad advice and unwarranted expectations. They rarely talked or wrote publicly about their "rights" against conventional morality and law. They acted and lived lives as married, and when caught they looked for help from lawyers.

Often, they found in legal doctrine and in judicial interpretations of doctrine odd reflections of their own complicated understandings of marriage. What was bigamy, after all? If a second marriage was a void act, then how could anyone be a bigamist? The very fraudulence of the second ceremony meant that the apparent bigamist was merely an adulterer. Statutes typically dealt with that difficulty by defining the crime as committed by one who "cohabited as" or pretended to be husband or wife, when already in possession of a spouse. But what did it mean to cohabit as if, or to pretend to be, married? A wife may have known that her husband had a wife already; presumably she knew that she was not (really) married to him. Perhaps "she would not have married him, if she had known he had another wife." At the same time, however, so long as she lived with him she might as well say they were married. With time, the law might conclude that they were, or had become, married because they resided together and said that they were married. In the end, the legal question, the question that required a yes or no answer (married/not married) had been one such couples bracketed off over years together. They had lived as husband and wife; that was enough.[97]

Behind the law of bigamy and of divorce, behind the law that shaped the cases strewn across this chapter, behind the complexities generated by wives who established separate domiciles from their husbands, behind the sense of crisis and of moral challenge that motivated the anti-divorce polemicists, lay the perceived right to (re)marry. Abby Sage McFarland and Albert Richardson, like any number of couples across nineteenth-century America, assumed that they had a right to marry. In spite of whatever legal disabilities they faced. In spite of "existing" legal marriages. And that common sense of right, that demand, remade the law.

To most nineteenth-century Americans, marriage was a concrete necessity. Women needed husbands in order to survive. Men too needed wives; certainly, they needed wives if they were going to flourish, to live productive lives, to be recognized as adults. In part, the need for marriage was a story about labor, about the impossibility of doing what was needed without at least two sets of adult hands. In part, this was a story about vast American distances and about the long breakdown of traditional community networks, and about the absence of imagined alternatives to marriage. Coupledom was, within the nineteenth-century mindset, usually the only alternative to isolation. And isolation was not a possibility that many nineteenth-century women or men wished to contemplate. Nor was going back home to family. Even for young or middle-aged women abandoned by husbands, going home to parents or family was no longer the usual or expected outcome.[98]

The marriages women and men needed were real ones, real relationships, not imaginary legal ones. Formal relationships, the abstract ties of past commitments, were worthless. The illusions of permanent marriage, the religious images that had shaped Abigail Bailey's memoirs, images still of enormous power in the culture and in the formal law, were of no use to them. They were unwilling to accept lives as the sinfully married, as adulterers, unwilling to be anything other than really married.

Economics obviously provides much of the explanation for the practices we have been exploring. But, as obviously, it is not enough. What drove many women and men toward divorce and remarriage was not simply the need for labor, for collectivization and economies of scale.

(Otherwise, one can imagine that the communitarian experiments that littered the nineteenth-century landscape would have had more success.) It was, rather, the desire for a particular person, call it love, for happiness, for this marriage, not the old marriage, for a life as a wife or a husband with this one other person. The women and men in these cases drew from the culture and from their experiences a sense of a right to marital happiness, a right to undo decisions once made, a right to second and third and fourth chances.

In the world of the very long nineteenth century, a world that continued into the 1950s, it was hard to escape marriage. Marriage, or at least the promise of marriage, was the usual precondition for sexual relations. Often, sex required "marriage" or at least the promise of marriage. Sex without marriage was overlaid by the dangers—physical, cultural, spiritual, emotional—that bastardy rules and restricted access to birth control produced. Many women apparently decided that even knowing bigamy was better than unmarried sex. At the level of legal theory, their choice was no choice at all, for a bigamous marriage was a void marriage and so whatever went on within it was unmarried sex: fornication or adultery. But with time and distance, with a public life as wife and husband, the void bigamous marriage often became the true, the real, the unquestionable. The law reflected in legal presumptions, as well as in the risk assessments of women and men who took their chances on a life together, was a very complex thing indeed. And in its complexity it served the needs of those who calculated (or speculated) that they could become happily "married."[99]

In December 1909 the novelist Margaret Deland spoke at a New York meeting of the National League for the Civic Education of Women, an antisuffrage organization. The *New York Times* reported the speech under the headline "Girls today are learning to say I want instead of I ought." Mrs. Deland's speech blamed modern individualist women for the rise of divorce. (And she thought her speech as a whole would reduce the average suffragette to tears.) Like other antidivorce polemicists, she recognized that it was "frequently better" that a couple should live apart from one another. But a separation was all that was ever necessary. The bad news for her listeners: "I am afraid that we cannot close our eyes to the unwelcome truth that the majority of divorces are obtained with the prospect in view of a subsequent union with another person who it is presumed will be more congenial." Those who sought and received such divorces did not understand that no one had a right to be happy at the expense of society. Duty trumped happiness.[100]

I can't help imagining Margaret Deland as Margaret Dumont, with Groucho Marx lurking in the wings of the auditorium. And like Margaret Dumont, her call to arms in defense of duty would be ignored as the forces of chaos and disorder, the Marx Brothers, took center stage. Even so, Deland knew what was going on in the society, and her voice serves as a useful close to this chapter. There was a real phenomenon of people searching for congenial spouses, insisting on their right to marital happiness. They were not seeking emancipation from marriage. Rather, they insisted on happiness in their marital identities. They moved across America, women as well as men. The women claimed and eventually won the right to separate domiciles, violating a fundamental tenet of the traditional law of husband and wife. Yet they did so in order to make new marriages, marriages that were by and large conventional, that conformed to the norms of the traditional law of husband and wife, that would be, they hoped, "real" and permanent. Together and separately, the men and women who lived behind the developing law of divorce pushed and pulled at a received structure, wrestled with it, sometimes suffered because of it, but in the end made it, for the most part, serve their limited and concrete goals: to live as husband and wife, to be married.

10

Coverture in a New Age

[T]he law of servitude in marriage is repealed in this State.
Bryant v. Smith, *187 S.C. 453, 198 S.E. 20 (1938)*

In 1871, more than a quarter century after state legislatures had begun to reform the inherited law of marital property, Joel Prentiss Bishop published the first volume of a new treatise on the law of married women. In his hugely successful treatises on marriage and divorce, Bishop had assumed a confident and authoritative voice. By contrast, the law of husband and wife, the law that regulated the space between marriage and divorce, seemed to defeat him. Repeatedly he conceded he had no idea "whether any doctrine . . . set down in the text" would "be held by any court hereafter." "Nothing" was "now fixed and certain"; "all" was "in . . . a state of ferment." The law was, and was likely to remain, in a "very unsatisfactory state," "a jumble of chaotic things."[1]

What was the law of husband and wife after the passage of married women's property acts and earnings acts? Observers of the legal scene knew that the new legislation had not effected a revolution. Coverture survived, and the states remained the only arenas for continuing reform.[2] Still, something had happened and was happening to legal understandings of marital identities, to the law of husband and wife. In 1856 a law dictionary definition of "wife" had taken six paragraphs to set out her limited rights and duties under the traditional law; "husband" had an equally long definition focusing on his rights. In the 1877 edition of the same dictionary, nothing had changed in the definition of "husband." "Wife," however, now included a survey of statutory changes, for a "great change in favor of the wife has been produced by recent statutes in a majority of the United States." In the 1892 edition, the 1856 definition of "husband's" obligations and rights was again reprinted, with all verbs changed from present to past tense. By contrast, "wife" included a survey of recently enacted laws. And in the new Black's *Law Dictionary* (1891), "husband" had become simply "the correlative" of "wife," both definitions lacking any further content.[3]

For lawyers, the changing nature of the law of husband and wife would have been a matter of little interest if posed as a historical problem or as a question of legal theory. What they needed were ways to answer the particular and concrete questions that clients brought them. The complexities of married life in modern America—full of wages earned but uncollected, leases broken, properties bought and sold, separations, contracts, creditors, accident victims, strangers, seductions, abuse, and neglect—led wives and husbands to lawyers. What those clients wanted were answers and ways to assess the risks and opportunities raised by particular situations. To provide that, lawyers needed both a knowledge of the law and how to situate a legal problem within a family of categories, how to give useful advice: how to justify, how to critique, how to explain. Their advice necessarily incorporated a perspective on the changes enacted by several generations of state legislatures. To what extent had transitory legislative enactments been grafted on to the ostensibly permanent categories of coverture? Lawyers could not pretend that the world was still as it no longer was. They needed analytic tools that worked for clients who moved across and through many American jurisdictions.

Prior to the Civil War, the knowledge and the methods lawyers needed would have been learned in apprenticeships, by watching experienced lawyers at work. By the end of the nineteenth century, however, young men usually learned law in law schools. And in the law schools, casebooks became the primary pedagogical tool through which legal subjects, like the law of husband and wife, were taught. Casebooks reproduced and disseminated crucial features of the common sense of legal practice: the ordinary phrases and categories that allowed a lawyer to conceptualize a problem and to make plausible predictions, the conventional reasons and explanations for maintaining particular rules, as well as those forms of criticism that might effectively destabilize or challenge an existing practice. The editors' arrangements of limited numbers of cases made a subject appear knowable, in spite of the unmasterable quantities of competing and conflicting decisions that actually made up "the law" on any legal subject. The editors also socialized law students and lawyers into a particular historical consciousness about change and permanence: about what was settled and what was contested within a professional domain.[4]

Most of all, the editor's selection and ordering of materials defined a student's understanding. This is "family law," a law student would think, a subject contained within familiar red or blue covers. The subject appeared transparently, naturally, through the cases, with only an occasional note to mark an authorial intent. The fact that parts of the edited subject bore an almost accidental connection to the world of legal practice or to what most cases were really about barely entered the law student's consciousness, only entered if an instructor mentioned it. And, though generations of young lawyers later complained that they were unprepared for the legal world they encountered outside of the law school casebooks, still the categories those young lawyers mobilized to solve legal problems and to manage that legal world were decisively shaped by the casebooks.

STATUTES IN DEROGATION

The first casebooks dealing with domestic relations date from the 1890s, a good twenty years after similar works appeared for the "core" courses in the new law school curriculum pioneered at Christopher Columbus Langdell's Harvard. The late arrival of these casebooks reflects both the low status of the field within elite legal practice and its conceptual untidiness, its unscientific nature. Its gendered character, the inescapable presence of women as wives, as sexual beings, of dishonored husbands suing for compensation, and of dependent children, also played some part in shaping the inattention of legal academics concerned to create a curriculum that evoked manliness and the strenuous life. The makers of the classic law school curriculum could not ignore the subject entirely. Yet in no law school was the subject anything more than a relatively minor elective, typically assigned as an ancillary task to junior faculty, to practitioners, and to other marginal faculty members.[5]

Still, four law school casebooks on domestic relations were published between 1891 and 1899.[6] Like other casebooks, the editors worked to reveal the internal structure of the subject. They did not collect all the cases, as treatise writers had; their goals were pedagogical, and so they were unconcerned with helping attorneys with practical chores, such as hunting up cases from a particular jurisdiction to make a winning point. Moreover, the cases they emphasized were heavily edited to hide the social and cultural contexts that full reports might have revealed. But, unlike contract law and other subjects imagined as purely private, state legislative incursions into married women's traditional disabilities were an inescapable part of domestic relations law. Thus, all the casebooks included cases in which appellate courts interpreted the reach and limitations of a variety of statutory modifications. These cases posed a variety of questions that presumably framed class discussions: To what extent had two generations of statutes (which by the 1890s were being consolidated into general married women's acts) changed the inherited understandings of coverture and of the distinctive personalities that husbands and wives possessed? Had the legislatures "annihilated" coverture, or had they merely made limited adjustments? And how to draw right answers out of the language of the statutes?

In Jeremiah Smith's 1899 casebook, the law of husband and wife was divided into three chapters: at common law, in equity, and under modern legislation. He began the first of these with an editor's note: "The common-law doctrines as to the civil rights and liabilities of married persons no longer exist in full force in any jurisdiction. Those doctrines have been materially modified, and in many instances reversed, by modern legislation." But, he continued, "[s]ome knowledge of the old law" was "still desirable": first, because few "if any" states had completely abolished the old law, and second, because one could not understand the statutes without such knowledge.[7] His chapter on husband and wife "under modern legislation" began with another note. The "greatest difficulty" for courts arose when they had to rule on matters implicitly but not expressly covered by legislative language. How ought a court (or a law school class studying the opinion of a court) to regard a statute that abolished particular features of the inherited law, using broad and expansive justifications, when that statute did not speak directly to the legal problem that the court had been asked to decide? "The trouble is largely as to matters upon which the statutes are silent."[8]

From the 1840s on, reformers and legislators had trumpeted married women's property acts and earnings acts as abolitions of the law of coverture, analogizing the statutes to the end of slavery. As many proponents were forced to concede, however, courts resisted and undercut expansive or transformative interpretations of the new laws. They chained up legislation "by means of the most rigid construction."[9] While judges did not often declare the new statutes unconstitutional, they mobilized language and interpretive tools that permitted them to continue to apply received common law orthodoxy and to ignore transformative visions apparent in the new legislation, without directly challenging legislative authority.

The most important such judicial tool was the interpretive standard that "statutes in derogation of the common law," which is what all those statutes were, ought to be interpreted strictly and narrowly, against any expansive meaning. The "statutes in derogation" standard operated at the ambiguous boundaries of legislative intent: when litigants attempted to apply statutory language to situations that a legislature had not directly covered in the statute or when legislative language appeared imprecise or overinclusive. Confronted by poorly drafted statutes that seemed to transform and to assume legislative control over huge areas of legal practice that had once belonged to the courts alone, judges reasserted authority. Courts used the standard to tell legislatures to be explicit if they meant to change common law rules and practices. The standard disciplined legislatures, forced them to draft laws more clearly and with a greater awareness of judicial sensibilities and of the situations—the cases—that new laws inevitably produced.[10] In the context of marriage law, the standard also reflected a pessimism about change and a sentimental attachment to traditional rules. When statutes challenged the received structure of marital rights and duties, courts used the "statutes in derogation of the common law" standard to reimpose, at least for a moment, a threatened orthodoxy. The judges who mobilized the standard worried about disturbances to "family solidarity"; they remained committed to the subordination of wives; and they often understood the statutes as unjustified redistributions of rights and powers from husbands to wives.[11]

Sometimes the standard gave courts words to reject the explicit language of a statute. Thus in *Cole v. Van Riper,* an 1867 case that found its way into Smith's casebook, the Illinois Supreme Court answered the question, could a wife convey her separate real estate without the acknowledgment of her husband, with a resounding negative. The statute clearly said that she could. But the court thought the legislators must not have intended what they had written or, better, must not have understood the implications. According to the court, if a wife owned as her separate property the house or farm on which the family lived, and if she did not need to secure her husband's permission before acting, she could kick her husband out of the house, make him into a trespasser. "It is simply impossible that a woman married should be able to control and enjoy her property as if she were sole, without leaving her at liberty, practically, to annul the marriage tie at pleasure."[12]

Other opinions reproduced in the casebooks mobilized the standard to test whether wives who had contracted for wages with their husbands could enforce their contracts. Judges regularly declared such contracts unenforceable, even though many legislatures had passed statutes allowing wives to keep earnings and to sue to secure wages. It could not, wrote the judges, have been the intent of the legislatures to empower wives to sue their husbands, even though many of the statutes did not explicitly exclude contracts with husbands. Wives owed labor to their husbands, and earnings acts did not change those duties. Any other conclusion would lead to disregard of the mutual obligations of marriage.[13]

The casebooks of the 1890s were not all alike. Smith's was generally more "liberal" than others; that is to say, he included more cases that affirmed a wife's new rights and that recognized an expansive legislative intent, and he presented as contested questions that other editors regarded as closed. For example, he used Justice John Brady's 1882 opinion for the New York Supreme Court in *Schultz v. Schultz* as the "leading" opinion on whether a wife could sue her husband for damages for his violence. Brady had ruled that New York's famous 1860 married women's statute (a statute that among other new rights recognized a wife's capacity to keep her earnings and her equal custodial rights) necessarily implied a wife's right to sue when beaten. The old rule, Brady wrote, had "succumbed to more liberal and more just views" under "the scrutiny and analysis of modern civilization." Smith followed Brady's opinion with a note revealing that the Court of Appeals had reversed him. It was, concluded the judges of New York's highest court, "settled" that a wife could not maintain such an action against her husband. But, in reproducing Brady's opinion (and in only noting the reversal), Smith made it clear that he disagreed with the Court of Appeals.[14]

By contrast, Marshall Ewell's 1891 casebook took a more conservative line.[15] Often he counterposed an eighteenth- or early nineteenth-century English case with a recent case that affirmed or reestablished the "old" law. And his arrangement of cases tended to emphasize inegalitarian implications. So, after reproducing a leading New York case on a wife's inability to sue her husband for wages, Ewell followed with one where the same New York court allowed a husband to sue successfully to be compensated for his management of his wife's separate business. The first case rested on the fundamental principle "that the marital duty of the wife required her to perform . . . duties when necessary in the household of her husband." As a result, her husband's explicit contract to pay her (for taking care of his mother) was unenforceable. That principle was irrelevant to the second case, however. There was no equality of duty between husband and wife. And no one could claim that a husband owed "any legal duty to his wife to render services for her, in her separate business, without compensation."[16] On the question whether a wife could sue her husband for abuse, Ewell ignored *Schultz* and reproduced the older 1863 New York case of *Longendyke v. Longendyke,* which had held that such an imagined cause of action was "destructive of that conjugal union and tranquillity, which it has always been the object of the law to guard and protect."[17]

In spite of differences, all four books shared a common orientation toward their subject: that contemporary domestic relations law was in complicated continuity with its past. Coverture and marital unity were to be "modernized," made suitable to a modern nation, not abolished. Being a wife still meant having an identity shaped by duties owed to your husband; being a husband still meant both that you had a right to demand duties and that you owed your wife support. These remained baseline assumptions, for the most part inescapable, of what it meant to be married, at least within the imagined world of the casebooks.[18]

From all these casebooks, students would have learned how to situate a legal problem involving a married couple and how to portray a client. Marital identities remained primary, contractual and autonomous selves secondary. If a client had acted, or wanted to act, in ways that violated traditional expectations, the law student learned to look to explicit statutory language authorizing behavior (or to make statutory language appear explicit). On the other hand, if a client needed or wanted to challenge behavior (such as a contract with a spouse), the law student learned to demonstrate that behavior as standing outside the received understanding of a marital identity and that nothing explicit in the reform statutes legitimated what had occurred.

The absences the casebooks shared were equally striking. Divorce, first of all. Though many of the reproduced cases dealt with separated litigants, the general and growing availability of legal exits was barely acknowledged. Only one casebook devoted a section to the law of divorce, and it gave less than fifty pages to the subject.[19] Divorce appeared primarily as a situation that created difficult issues with regard to whether marital obligations and duties continued after "the end" of the marriage. For example: Could a court order alimony for a deserted wife if she did not choose to seek a divorce? (Yes.) Would a court force a husband to continue to make payments after a divorce, under a separation agreement negotiated before the divorce? (Yes.) After divorce, could a wife maintain an action against her husband for an assault he had committed during their marriage? (No.)[20] For the rest, the word "divorce" sat in judicial opinions in the early casebooks only as a "horror" avoided.[21]

A second absence, unlike divorce a near-total absence, was of the discourse of nonjudicial public intervention and public regulation. At a time when treatise writers and polemicists defined marriage as a public status subject to the police power of the state, at a time when moralists and temperance workers and early social workers were all formulating ways to mobilize state intervention, particularly into the family lives of the urban poor, the early casebooks presented the law of husband and wife without public actors or nosy neighbors or friendly visitors. To the casebook editors of the 1890s, the only question wife beating (or other forms of abuse) raised was if a wife had a private cause of action against her husband. Whether answered positively or negatively, the question as framed narrowed the range of options that had once seemed to be part of the relevant law.

Even as they linked present law to a long and continuous past of marital identities, the early casebook editors also made the older law of husband and wife a harsher, more limited, less complicated place than it had appeared in the works of eighteenth- and early nineteenth-century law writers. Wives, in particular, were imagined as (re)subjected to their husbands through the law, only occasionally as the beneficiaries of coverture's protections.[22] The judicial opinions the editors emphasized, opinions that rejected and constrained the expansive egalitarian and contractual language of the statutes, also incorporated a new historical understanding present in the statutes: that the old law subjugated women as wives to their husbands. The overarching lesson of the 1890s casebooks was that wives lost, only rarely gained, from their marital identities. And, of equal importance, that husbands possessed important and valuable rights as husbands.

COVERTURE IN 1950

Over the next half century, domestic relations law remained both a minor feature of legal education and a staple of legal practice. When four new domestic relations casebooks appeared in 1951 and 1952, the first since the beginning of World War II, three of the four looked much like their predecessors of the 1890s.[23] And all of them presented the twentieth-century law of husband and wife in complicated continuity with a nineteenth-century past.

What was new in these works reflected changes overtaking postwar American society. The work lives of wives—their participation in the economy, their relative economic independence from husbands—had become an inescapable and continuing presence in the cases. New technologies produced new facts—for example, auto accidents—that produced much new law. Divorce and separation percolated through every legal topic, and all the casebooks provided separate sections on "the law of divorce." Two of the four also gave substantial space to *Williams v. North Carolina* (both I and II) and the transformed understanding of "full faith and credit" *Williams I* had signaled.[24]

A close reader of the casebooks could have found glimmers of new constitutional rights and of egalitarian understandings. The Columbia casebook of the legal realist Albert Jacobs and the legal historian Julius Goebel introduced "husband and wife" with a historical note: the judicial construction of married women's statutes had once been conservative, "and to this day" there remained "many places where the old law" cast "its shadow upon the new." But against continuing conservatism, Jacobs and Goebel noted contrary impulses: "a respect for the individual regardless of sex, a self-conscious and determined liberalism and even a certain sensitivity to the things implicit in the changed status of women."[25] "In our society," went one reproduced opinion, "where almost no bride promises to obey her husband, and where it is not accepted as the usual that a wife does what her husband wishes by way of yielding obedience to a dominant will," the basis for the presumption of coercion had disappeared. When the common law was in force, according to a second judge, a husband had been able "to collect his wife's pay check, he could direct its use, he could appropriate her separate property and direct the course of her career or business." Thankfully, those rules had "not only been abrogated by law," they had "been abrogated by custom, the very thing out of which the common law was derived."[26]

Change was everywhere, but the new casebooks emphasized the continuities. Indeed, all presented a continuing marital legal order, surviving in the face of a changing culture and society. Public actors—social workers and others—still played no roles in the construction or the enforcement of the law.[27] Cases that had appeared in the 1890s casebooks still took up space in the 1950s editions. Novelties of twentieth-century legal practice recreated nineteenth-century legal questions and perspectives. Though divorce had become a background circumstance, unproblematic in itself but constitutive of the stories through which legal issues of support rights and contractual capacity would be discussed, and though that sense of divorce as routine would have been incomprehensible to nineteenth-century editors, still the law of support rights retained much from the nineteenth-century past. It remained unquestioned that a wife—even an ex-wife—was entitled to be supported by her husband, at least so long as she had not violated her obligations of duty and obedience. The nineteenth century remained the home of most of the relevant categories used to organize the materials, though the twentieth century provided complexity, new wrinkles on older problems, and occasional challenges to the received structure.

In William McCurdy's Harvard casebook, for example, his section on a wife's earnings began with an 1895 case where the court had actually enforced a wife's contract to be paid as an employee in her husband's restaurant. But McCurdy followed that case with a series of excerpted early cases, in none of which the wife recovered. And then he turned to three twentieth-century cases.

In the first, decided in New Jersey in 1923, the court held that a husband still had the sole right to collect from an estate for the services his wife had provided to an elderly neighbor. (She had cleaned house, carried coal, tended fire, carried out ashes, mowed grass, mended clothes and bed linen, sewed new sheets, given alcohol rubs, dressed injuries when the old man fell, did errands such as placing flowers on his wife's grave, collected rents from tenants, shopped, cooked meals, and washed clothes.) The statute that entitled a wife to collect her own wages was irrelevant here because the services she had performed were so "interwoven" with her ordinary household duties as to be inseparable from what she still owed her husband as a wife. The value of her work belonged entirely to her husband.

The second was a 1942 appeal from a decision awarding an Alabama woman unemployment compensation after she had left Alabama and her job in a textile factory to join her husband in New York. Her award had been justified on the theory that her departure was not a voluntary decision, for wives were obligated to move with their husbands. But the Alabama Supreme Court reversed. When a wife worked, her labors were her contribution to family support, and were at her husband's direction. Under Alabama law, her status as an employee depended on her husband's consent. She was "not wholly a free person to determine whether she shall thus be employed." And when she quit a job because of her husband's voluntary decision to move, his voluntary act became her voluntary act, became "attributable" to her. "His will" had "to a limited extent and in a legal sense become hers." Marital unity still lived.

In the third case (1913), an Ohio wife had taken care of her husband's mother in the mother's home. The Ohio Supreme Court noted that there was a statute that would have required the husband to care for his mother if she had been unable to pay for her own support. But though he might have become obligated to care for his mother, that duty would never have devolved onto his wife as part of her domestic duties. The wife had made her own separate contract to care for her mother-in-law, and she had a right to recover on it. Her work was her own voluntary act, and she did not need her husband's consent to enter into such a contract.[28]

How McCurdy or some other family law teacher would have presented these cases is a mystery. Given the ordinary premises of twentieth-century law teaching, the right answer would not have been that different states had different laws and practices. Nor would it have been enough to insist that Alabama and New Jersey were right, while Ohio was wrong. Nor that Ohio was right and Alabama and New Jersey wrong. Nor does an evolutionary or chronological narrative seem available, given McCurdy's arrangement of the cases. Still, somehow, a principle was supposed to work its way out, a principle that would reconcile the irreconcilable. And though that principle escapes me (and, I dare say, any reader of this work), what law students of the early 1950s surely learned was something of the continuing power of an analytic dilemma that late nineteenth-century courts had first confronted and that had, by 1950, become a pervasive feature of marriage law. Was it possible to understand a married woman as both a free contractual actor and as a wife? Which characterization—contractor? wife?—should take precedence when conflict occurred? And what became of a husband's identity whenever a court chose between those identities?

The problem of the wife as economic actor had been conceptually central to the law for nearly a century. At a time, however, when more and more married women entered and remained in the paid labor force, even as many other women were being forced to leave war jobs, the conflict resonated throughout the contemporary culture. Law students (still nearly all young men in the early 1950s) would have found themselves whipsawed by the instructor as they bounced from one side to the other. No answer that obliterated either contractual freedom or wifedom would have satisfied. But the received categories provided no principle to hold the two together.

All the casebooks organized units around the tort action for loss of consortium, again a topic that focused the student's attention both on the problem of what a wife owed her husband and what had changed in the law. Could a husband recover for injuries to his wife resulting from an auto accident or a street car accident or any of the other "accidents" typical of modern life? What rights did a husband retain in the body and capacities of his wife, at a time when a wife possessed the right to sue in her own name for harms that had been done to her? What loss did a husband suffer when his wife was harmed? And was his loss one that entitled him to separate damages?[29]

Twentieth-century law writers always identified loss of consortium as part of received common law doctrine. But actually, before the late nineteenth century, there had been no cases framed as actions for loss of consortium; loss of consortium was an invented tradition, one that softened and blunted inherited legal categories. The only early source was an enigmatic passage where Blackstone had noted that occasionally a husband could use the pleading form per quod to recover for the battery of his wife by a third party, but only when the abuse was "very enormous" so that a husband lost his wife's "company and assistance" (per quod consortium amisit).[30]

Blackstone's language had to be wrested out of its historical context.

For eighteenth-century lawyers, per quod was identified with hierarchical relationships. Wives, children, servants, and others similarly situated were defined by what they owed their superiors. And when inferiors were harmed, husbands, parents, and masters recovered from wrongdoers for costs incurred in substituting for what was lost (such as having to hire a maid when a wife could not clean because of injuries).[31] But twentieth-century judges found the direct language of service, a language that made monetary compensation possible, discomforting. "Service" was not how modern men—including judges—wanted to think about marriage. And so "consortium" was remade as a protean term that suggested the complex yet irreducible qualities of a loving marriage, its romantic and sentimental and erotic features, while minimizing the embarrassing yet inescapable language of services and obligations. As Judge Charles Clark put it in 1950: "although it embraces within its ambit of meaning the wife's material services, [consortium] also includes love, affection, companionship, sexual relations, etc., all welded into a conceptualistic unity."[32]

Still, service remained the mark of a husband's recovery, and in the leading case of *Guevin v. Manchester Street Railway* (1916) (found in three casebooks), the New Hampshire Supreme Court danced warily around the word. A husband sued for loss of consortium resulting from his wife's injuries. In 1911 the Connecticut Supreme Court had rejected a similar claim, insisting that a husbandly right to consortium violated the marital equality to which the Connecticut legislature had committed the state. Loss of consortium made no sense without a concept of service, and service had been torn out of the concept of marriage.[33] But the New Hampshire court rejected Connecticut's approach, even though New Hampshire's statutes were similar to Connecticut's. In New Hampshire, the cause of action survived, "since some right to services still remains in the husband."

But what was the nature of that right to services? The New Hampshire court knew it was on dangerous terrain. The opinion began with the claim that services had always been voluntarily rendered. While traditional authorities insisted that a wife's services belonged to her husband and that it was "her duty to render them to him," still a husband "had no legal remedy if she chose to refuse performance of that duty." And he had no right to enforce obedience. In the court's retelling, her services became a lovingly offered gift. Why then allow a husband to recover from third parties for loss of services that he had no right to expect or to impose? One answer: if the action for alienation of affections survived, if a husband had a remedy for total loss of consortium (because his wife had deserted him under the influence of another), then "logic" led to the conclusion that he should be able to recover for a partial loss. More important, and even less logically, the husband was "entitled to the whole of his wife's marital affection, and to the whole of such society and comfort" as she was willing to give him. A third party that stole "any substantial part of that affection," or that disabled her from "rendering such aid and comfort," was guilty and could be required to make compensation.[34]

Though the "statutes in derogation of the common law" standard still appeared in the 1950s casebooks, it mostly appeared as raised and rejected. Courts had come to recognize and to accept the expansive and transformative implications of state legislation. The law they enforced and interpreted was no longer rooted in common law coverture. Although the old law still provided many of the operative phrases and categories, legislation had become the foundation of the law of husband and wife.

Thus, in a 1938 case that three of the books reproduced, the South Carolina Supreme Court held that the elderly wife of a Confederate veteran would be solely liable, after she had knocked down an eighty-nine-year-old veteran who had voted the wrong way at a meeting of the United Confederate Veterans. The injured veteran's lawyer insisted that "as a matter of [common] law," her husband had to be liable as well. South Carolina held "tenaciously" to the rule that statutes in derogation of the common law were to be strictly construed, so the only question was whether the common law rule was still in force. But when the court surveyed the South Carolina Code, it found that various statutes that had gradually and piecemeal enlarged the legal capacity of a wife had collectively destroyed the common law rule. The legislature had made "successive" steps toward a larger liberty and a corresponding responsibility; "the law of servitude in marriage" had been repealed; the work of "emancipation" had been completed. And that meant that married women—even Confederate veterans' wives—were subject alone to all the laws, and their husbands were free of derivative liability.[35]

In place of the "statutes in derogation of the common law" standard, casebook editors emphasized the language of "public policy." In the older casebooks, the derogation standard had given drama and weight to apparently mundane stories. Now, in the early 1950s, invocations of "public policy" played something of a similar role. Once editors had scoured the reports for cases that had played out an institutional struggle between judiciary (or common law order) and legislature. Now editors peppered their works with cases that countered assertions of individual rights with the constraints of the public marriage relationship.

Remember the pivotal sentence in *McGuire v. McGuire* (1953): "Public policy requires such a holding." Lydia McGuire could not expect a court to intervene in her marriage, could not expect a court to force Charles, her husband, to provide her with the material goods that she thought she was entitled to. A court would not, absent allegations of abuse or absent a justified separation, attempt to determine her entitlements. Her entitlements were those of a wife: to live within her husband's household, to be supported by him in a manner that he was entitled to determine. Public policy meant that Charles's private freedom would not be violated.

Jacobs and Goebel were particularly assiduous in using such cases to highlight various doctrinal topics. Three examples: Could a wife sue her husband for injuries she had received in an auto accident he had caused before their marriage? No, she couldn't. Husband and wife could not sue each other in such situations, "during coverture at least," because "so to do would disturb and tend to disrupt the marriage and family relations, which it is the public policy of the state to protect and maintain inviolable." Could a widow sue her husband's estate to enforce an oral antenuptial contract whereby he had promised to give her all his property if she took care of him? No, she couldn't. A contract to do what was already "a part of her duties as a wife" was "without consideration, against public policy, and void." What of the agreement between a separated couple that the husband would pay the wife $100 a week, but her right to support would be suspended if she went into business in competition with him? Could he stop payments when she did open a competing store? No, he could not. His support obligation could not be conditioned, and his attempt to do so offended public policy. His obligation sprang from "the marital relationship itself," and from the state's "uncompromising determination to preserve the important incidents of the marriage relationship during its continuance whatever the contrary sentiments of the parties themselves may be." Neither of them was capable "of bargaining away the woman's right to the man's support."[36]

"Public policy" served several purposes in such cases. It allowed courts to define the space between marital entry and exit as distinctive legal space, subject to its own "fundamental" rules. The conceptual boundaries of that space were necessarily porous in mid-twentieth-century America. Private contracting, choice, variation, none could be excluded from marital behavior within a capitalist culture that made freedom of choice appear normative and of right, in a marital regime that recognized the separate identities of wives as contractors and property owners. But "public policy" allowed courts to constrain choice within this space, within this legal relation. Public policy also appeared as a way to mediate among past, present, and future, between inherited legal understandings and the tendency of litigants to press the boundaries of statutory reforms. It served as a legal discipline on wealthier and more powerful husbands. It substituted an analysis of duties and obligations for litigants' insistence on rights. Most of all, courts and editors used it to reimpose marital identities, wifedom and husbandom, on those who had exceeded the limits of normal variation.

Two prominent cases exemplify the reimposition of marital identities. *Kelley v. Kelley* was a 1931 Rhode Island decision that found its way into two of the casebooks. Mrs. Kelley sued to have her separated husband evicted out of her separately owned house, in which he lived and worked. She had bought the place in 1910, and at one time it had been the family home. Her husband had joined with her in execution of a mortgage, and he had always paid the interest on the mortgage and part of the repair costs, insurance, taxes, and water bills. In 1923 Mrs. Kelley had wanted to move to another part of the city. When Mr. Kelley refused, she moved anyway with their children. After she left, she rented out a separate apartment in the house, and until 1928 or 1929 she did not charge her husband rent. But then she demanded that he pay rent in addition to the monthly allowance that he regularly paid her. When he refused, she went to court.

The Rhode Island Supreme Court's opinion denied her the right to evict her husband and, along the way, the court danced between older and newer understandings of marriage, holding the two together through the mantra of public policy. While a wife's legal identity was no longer merged with her husband's, still she was not and never had been "held to be in the same legal position as an unmarried woman." Nothing in the statutes giving her the right to hold separate property showed any intention "to so modify the marriage relation as to authorize an action of this character against her husband." Marriage contemplated that a couple lived together, and the law favored "the marital relation and the permanence of the family." Her "voluntary" separation constituted desertion, which would have provided a ground for a divorce if the husband chose to seek one. Meanwhile, her house was still "the lawful home of both husband and wife." His occupancy never became "adverse" to her title, and therefore he never became a trespasser, subject to eviction. And where he lived remained her proper home.[37]

Or consider the 1940 case of *Graham v. Graham*. She was an older wealthy woman, he a hotel employee. After marrying in 1932, they made an agreement: she promised to pay him $300 per month indefinitely; he promised to quit his job and accompany her in her travels. They divorced a year later, but he claimed the agreement survived and that she owed him more than $25,000.

Federal District Judge Arthur J. Tuttle doubted whether such an agreement was even within the capacity of a married woman. In Michigan, where the contract had been made, wives possessed no general power to contract (unlike the case in many other states). But Tuttle did not rest on this ground. Instead, he ruled that the contract was void because it contravened public policy. Individual men and women were not permitted to change "essential" features of the marriage contract, including a wife's obligation to follow her husband's choice of domicile and a husband's "right to engage in such work as he sees fit to do, unrestrained by contract with his wife." A wife was free to pay her husband a monthly sum; a husband was free to quit his job. These freedoms, however, could only be understood as gratuitous and voluntary, without enforceable consequences.[38]

The phrase "public policy" had long existed in the law of husband and wife as a shorthand for the state's interest in restricting individual freedom. Judges had always tried (usually unsuccessfully) to rein in the strategic and contractual behavior of wives and husbands. Indeed, in some ways, the twentieth-century invocations of the phrase represented a return to an older, pre–Civil War, judicial rhetoric, one that assumed that judges and legislators shared a common commitment to "a well ordered society." Unlike late nineteenth-century judges, who often insisted that their grasp of marriage was superior to, but in inevitable conflict with, that of legislators, the twentieth-century judges understood themselves as articulating a common sense shared with legislators and the educated public. All knew what was and what was not "fundamental" to marriage.

Still, there was something novel in these invocations of "public policy." Why, for example, make *Kelley* and *Graham* turn on the "essential" nature of marriage? Both *Kelley* and *Graham* portray private individuals who should have lost on any number of grounds. On what possible basis should Graham have been entitled to insist on a continuing debt, years after the foundation of that debt, the marriage, had ended? Mrs. Kelley, likewise, seems a bit mean-spirited in trying to evict a husband who was apparently paying support as well as his share of the maintenance costs on the house. Yet in both cases the courts worked to root their holdings in fixed marital identities rather than in contractual fairness. A wife must accept her husband's right to choose the marital domicile. Where he lives is where she lives, at least in legal theory. And a husband must support his wife. Wives obey; husbands support.

Where did the courts get these fundamental terms? Not as such from the legislation on which their authority depended. Nor from older treatises or cases, the sources of the old common law of coverture. Rather, they found those terms as implied premises on which modern legislation rested. Public policy was what remained, after common law, equity, the old law, tradition had all faded away. Unlike the "statutes in derogation of the common law" standard, "public policy" was less an assertion of historical continuity, more a claimed metahistorical understanding about the role played by courts in maintaining marital identities.

The practices of modern marriage law—what lawyers and their clients actually did—undermined the judges' faith in public policy as a constraint. Public policy may have demanded that the marriage relationship be kept "sacred and inviolate" and that all incentives to exit be countered. Yet this was, by the middle of the twentieth century, empty language. Mrs. Kelley may have been stopped momentarily from evicting her husband, but nothing presumably could prevent her from selling her house to someone else, who would have been free to evict Mr. Kelley. Graham may have failed to secure his $25,000 (as if he ever had a chance), but the twentieth-century casebooks were full of cases that revealed how husbands could negotiate control over a wife's property and earnings. Judges tried to resist the escape plans of wealthier husbands who refused to share resources with their separated or divorcing wives; judges insisted on support—and alimony—as fundamental rights that wives possessed, so long as the wives or ex-wives portrayed themselves as proper wives. The reality that anyone with experience with the legal system knew, however, was that support and alimony were rare and intermittent. Distance and/or moderately clever lawyering would leave many, perhaps most, ex-wives unsupported.[39]

Judges (and casebook editors) could not prevent strategic behavior by individuals in struggle with spouses. All they could do was offer guides to the wary, to lawyers and compliant clients, about how to strategize, about how to be (at least transitionally) a wife or a husband in order to achieve the individual advantages that one sought. Lawyers would learn from these cases how to use, how to fit a client's interests in with, predictable and expected invocations of public policy. Public policy became a tool of the litigating Mrs. Grahams, the Mr. Kelleys, and the Mr. McGuires of the mid-twentieth century.

We might speculate that these cases taught lawyers and clients (and law students) to think more cynically about the law itself. Cynicism about the law of marriage was nothing new. The law of the "intact" marriage and of marital unity had always been played out on the terrain of separation and of separated identities. There had always been a disjuncture between the normative language of the legal order and the strategic behavior and the calculated self-presentations of litigants. And judicial language may have long had the paradoxical result of encouraging litigants—wives and husbands—to produce false selves (for example, the "ever-obedient" wife) that conformed to judicial expectations. Still, the cynicism of the twentieth-century language seems stronger, less buried, less repressed, than its nineteenth-century predecessors. The claim that "public policy" demanded a particular result had a different quality than earlier language: thinner and more authoritarian. The twentieth-century judges, unlike their predecessors, made little effort to connect justifications to the actual situations of the litigants before them. The reasons why wealthy men should be kept from impoverishing their separated or divorcing wives were inadequately captured by invocations of an increasingly illusory public policy against divorce. Much of the time, "public policy" seemed almost empty: without a vision of right conduct, reduced to the bare and unenforceable assertion "this far and no farther."

What "public policy" lacked that earlier judicial approaches to marriage possessed was a sense of reciprocity: of identities defined and constituted in a chosen relationship. Reciprocity and the explicit assumption of a relational identity (by marriage) had provided the underlying justification for the duties courts had imposed on wives and husbands. In that sense, a husband restrained or a wife disciplined was always understood as restrained or disciplined by his or her own commitments and moral undertakings, by the values and aspirations that had made him or her take on an identity as husband or wife. By contrast, the modern language of public policy implied a loss of confidence that individuals shared any committed understanding. Duties and disabilities would be maintained only because, to use Holmes's famous phrase, "of that which is so much more powerful than we are," because of the assertion of external public power.[40]

In 1950 (and still in 1960 and even in 1970), much of the nineteenth-century law of husband and wife remained. A husband was still entitled to manage resources and to decide where the family lived. Wives had a right to be supported, though not to decide how resources would be spent. Domestic violence remained within the private sphere. Spouses still could not testify for or against one another.

Marital identities survived. What had changed was little, except the forms of justification and argument. Explanations had eroded. And the law of husband and wife (re)produced in mid-twentieth-century casebooks often seemed little more than an unexplained, perhaps inexplicable, authority.

Consider, as a coda, marital rape. Or, rather, consider a mid-twentieth-century effort to explain why marital rape was not rape. Today marital rape is a term that describes a known and recognized occurrence, a fact in the world, a crime. Until recently, by contrast, marital rape was an oxymoron. "Rape . . . consisted of having illicit sexual intercourse with a woman not his wife without her consent."[41] No domestic relations casebook gave space to marital rape. Not in the 1890s, nor in the early 1950s.[42]

Criminal law was a different matter. In the 1950s the leading casebook and the leading short treatise placed the "problem" of why a wife could not be raped by her husband at the heart of the general definition of rape. "A man does not commit rape by having sexual intercourse with his lawful wife, even if he does so by force and against her will." Why not? Some older writers had answered that a wife had given an irrevocable consent to sexual intercourse at the time of marriage. But Rollin Perkins, the author of the one and the editor of the other, thought this "rationalization" mere "double talk" and "out of date." A better explanation lay inherent in the nature of marriage. Sexual intercourse between husband and wife was authorized by law; thus, "the element of *unlawfulness*" was lacking when a husband coerced his wife. By contrast, all other sexual intercourse was unlawful. And thus, unmarried sexual intercourse, when coerced, became rape.[43]

Perkins's formulation can be understood as one late attempt to retain a male marital sex right. Many other husbandly privileges and exemptions had died; sexual access remained.[44]

What is striking, though, is the absence of elaboration, the absence of the explanatory work that assertions of husbands' rights once provoked. Perkins's husbandly sex right appeared without context or justification. If earlier law writers would have wanted to justify a wife's incapacity to claim rape, they might have rooted it in the complex ways a wife was constructed to submit to her husband. Or her incapacity would have been understood as of a piece with a husband's right to recover in criminal conversation, when his wife was seduced by another. Or we could imagine it emerging out of reciprocity, in which the sex right was exchanged for guarantees of support and care. Or marital privacy—both as a moral barrier and as a functional description of the evidentiary difficulties that proving marital rape raised—might have carried weight as a justification for the exemption. None of these justifications seems particularly compelling in the face of the arguments of several law writers, Tapping Reeve and James Kent, for example, that the law of husband and wife existed as a protection against coercive male power. Indeed, all the nineteenth-century authorities insisted that the state retained a residual right to intervene when it became aware of serious violence and abuse within the household. Still, we can imagine arguments of the sort that nineteenth-century lawyers might have made for a husband's exemption and for a wife's disability.

But such imagined justifications would have depended on a thick context of rights and duties, on culturally resonant relational marital identities, on an understanding of what it was to be a wife or a husband. In Perkins's formulation, on the other hand, all reciprocity had disappeared. He rested, instead, on a bare—and barren—contrast. Intercourse was legal in marriage; not outside of marriage. And then, the final move, only illegal violent intercourse became rape.

Perkins's assumption that sex outside of marriage was definitionally illegal was not true in the 1950s, except in an abstract and formalistic sense. He grudgingly conceded as much when he admitted that sometimes "the secret act of fornication" was not punished. By the late 1950s there was already a serious decriminalization movement that would gain strength in the 1960s, as birth control became publicly and easily available. Nonmarital heterosexual sex was decriminalized, effectively and constitutionally, over the postwar era. And Perkins's bright-line distinction between marriage and nonmarriage would be lost. Within a decade after Perkins's treatise appeared, the thin assumption that legal sex provided a basis for distinguishing marital coerced sex from nonmarital rape had become ridiculously wrong.[45]

The disappearance of a justification for the exemption did not mean that the exemption itself disappeared. Real change awaited an aroused feminism that in the 1970s made marital rape a symbol of male wrongdoing. And real change is today still uncertain and incomplete. But by 1980 rape had become a violent crime that husbands, like all other men, could commit on wives, who were entitled as women to be free from sexual assault.

Epilogue

In casebooks of the 1990s, the law of husband and wife is an odd presence. The subject today survives to teach family law students about the intrusions of norms identified with the Fourteenth Amendment into the "state action" that was once the law. Chapters on "the law of the intact marriage" or "the meaning of marriage" or "towards equality in marriage" summarize the older structure. The books still reproduce a few older cases, like *McGuire v. McGuire* and *Graham v. Graham,* to explain the need for contemporary constitutional norms and to reflect on complexities in evolving understandings of "privacy." Archaic rules, for example, the inability of one spouse to testify for or against the other or a husband's singular duty to support his wife, are set out only to show how recent constitutional decisions have destroyed them. Editors include expanded sections on domestic violence. They also remind students that marriage survives as an institution and that being married remains a privileged status. But as a pedagogical subject, as an area to explore systematically and in extensive detail, the law of husband and wife has been replaced by other subjects: child custody law, which had only a small presence in earlier generations of domestic relations casebooks, and the law of "nontraditional families," which had no existence at all in 1950, let alone in 1895.[1]

By the mid-1970s, perhaps earlier, the very long nineteenth century had become the foreshortened twentieth century. Marital identities no longer appeared inscribed in the law. Wives not only worked, but courts recognized that wives worked for wages. Identities as workers and mothers had become for many women more important, more salient, than their identities as wives. A few men still killed when patriarchal identities were threatened. And lawyers struggled, as in the past, to explain and to excuse them. But no one rooted those fragile but violent selves in the fact of being a husband. In the 1970s and 1980s, legislative drafting offices worked to remove gendered language from the statutory law of marriage. Domiciles belonged to individuals. Wives could support husbands. Husbands did not represent their families; they did not presumptively manage family resources. The law of necessaries, where it survived, became an economic calculus of neutered expectations made between degendered spouses. The moral and legal language of duty disappeared. No lawyer in recent years ever drafted a plea for her client framing the legal self as one who had been "always obedient," as Lydia McGuire's lawyer still had. No husband's lawyer asserted that her client's wife had been disobedient.

Across America jurisdictional diversity lessened. Anywhere a couple resided, they got roughly the same divorce. Men and women still disappeared to escape unhappy marriages. But disappearing had become unnecessary legally if all one wanted was an end to a marriage (although child support obligations were a continuing incentive for many men). And disappearing had become more difficult, given the income tax and the social security card, given the reach of a pervasive and powerful federal government.

More, the bright line between marriage and nonmarriage weakened. Unmarried couples, heterosexual and homosexual alike, gained property rights that imitated marriage. The language of "public policy" no longer restricted most of the contractual choices married couples made. "Marriage" may still have been "dangerous for women," or so went the feminist line of the 1970s, but it was no more so than any number of other relational situations where the relatively vulnerable, the weaker, still found themselves under the control of the strong and the violent.

Increasingly marriage was imagined, both in its inception and in its concrete shape, as a private choice and as a collection of private practices. The question "What does it mean to be married?" was answered through multiple social descriptions, laying out and classifying the varieties of marital and nonmarital arrangements assumed by couples. It was not answered by invoking a normative legal description, certainly not one that endowed marriage with necessary characteristics, as implicating obligatory or inescapable reciprocal duties, as shaped by the rights— to sex, to support, to care, to respect—held by one spouse against the other.

Change produced new forms of unjust domination. The law was formally out of the gender business. Contractual equality was the rule. As a result, courts did even less than they once had to protect weaker parties from coercion. Women often found themselves defined, in the law, by identities as mothers. And many women remained impoverished, as mothers, in and out of marriage. But their impoverishment could not be understood as caused by coverture, by legal rules that imposed marital identities.

And yet men and women still marry. And when they marry, their marriages often look much like their parents' and grandparents' marriages. They love; they hate; they scheme; they negotiate; they run; they return; they fight, occasionally they kill; they go on to new relationships.

Many of us still fixate on marriage, making our marriages (or our several marriages) integral to our histories as individuals. We, like men and women of the nineteenth century, construct them to fit our own individual identities; we negotiate, strategize, commit ourselves to preset forms, play with and distort those same forms.

Nineteenth-century marriages were not the same as ours, in part because nearly everyone began their marriages committed to an understanding that their marriages were, definitionally and factually, for life. Their marriages were not the same as ours because their marriages were constructed in part out of a received legal orthodoxy, call it coverture, that gave a husband power and a wife protection, that united them in theory, and insisted that they adopt distinctive identities in legal practice. Their marriages were not the same as ours, as well, because they lived their marriages in a decentralized federal polity with many jurisdictions, in which there were many small variations in the marital regimes and large differences in the rules of exit.

But their marriages were like ours because we, like they, remain gripped by a sense of the centrality of marriage for an adult life.

Today marriage is still an immensely conventional institution, constructed out of a common sense about how lives and relationships ought to be conducted, about the ordering of time and change and generations and genders, about what it means to be an adult, about the duties differently situated persons owe to each other. Why did I marry? Hell, I married. Reasons fail. I am happy I did, but why I did will always remain just beyond my horizon of self-knowledge. I thought I was acting as a free agent, but I was also working off of scripts and patterns that I barely recognized. And then what happened? What did we do, the new couple?

What did we become, once married? We assumed our freedom to create a union—a private sphere—that would express creatively our individuality, our shared identity, and our changing commitments, our love. And we worked to make that a reality. Once married we did not settle down to preset roles. Yet again, through struggle, improvisation, and innovation, we produced what? A marriage, one recognizably akin to those that our parents and grandparents had created for themselves, linked to a past. Yet also our marriage, one that belonged only to the two of us.

Like us, the women and men of the nineteenth century believed their marriages were their own individual possessions. Others might have an interest as well—children, parents, other family members, God, perhaps the state. But first of all, their marriages belonged to them.

They would rarely have thought of themselves as makers of law. Even less often would they have accepted a sense of themselves as products of law, as made by law. When they went to court, voluntarily or involuntarily, because of conflicts with spouses, with creditors, or with governments, because they hoped to save or to destroy their marriages, it was not to defend or to challenge the political institution of marriage, still less the legal forms and practices that sustained that institution. Sometimes marriage itself was beside the point, an instrument, a means to an end. Sometimes marriage, or, as often, the apparent honor that came with marriage, was so important that life itself seemed trivial by comparison. Some litigants infused their marriages with reformist zeal or religious conviction. A few might have thought deeply, even passionately, about the place of marriage within the political order. But even they, once in a lawyer's office, found themselves playing in the law of marriage, bound by its ground rules.

In the course of living (or of escaping from) lives as married, they came to court, to the law. In the law, they discovered a strategic field full of dangers and opportunities, legacies and desertions, children and abandonments, unearned rewards and undeserved punishments. They became users of the law as they pursued dreams and ambitions: of love, of wealth, of security, of an end to misery, of happiness.

And along the way, as they worked in and with the law to make it serve their individual ends, their uses of law reproduced, recreated, and changed a familiar legal order, the nineteenth-century law of marriage.

A Note on Method

The law of marriage is too huge to be encompassed. All anyone can do is identify particular points of entry that "worked," that rewarded exploration. For this project there were three such points of entry:

1. With the help of Andrea Friedman, I constructed a database of published (mostly appellate) cases dealing with the legal consequences of marriage, divorce, and separation. This database included all published New York cases up to 1870, with samplings thereafter, all published California cases to 1870, with samplings thereafter, and samplings of the published case law of Wisconsin and Delaware.
2. I read virtually all of the nineteenth-century commentary on the law of husband and wife (sometimes called "baron and femme") and on the law of marriage, divorce, and separation. (In the nineteenth century these were separate subjects.) I reviewed treatises, law review articles, casebooks, and more overtly polemical works. I read these both to identify persistent positions and perspectives and also to identify particular cases that appeared to raise core problems and issues.
3. I surveyed law libraries and other research libraries to identify published trial transcripts and trial narratives that dealt with contested issues in the law of marriage. Many of the trials I found were scandalous divorces; others were adultery trials or murder trials or property disputes.

Beyond these points of entry, all pretense of system disappeared. I found myself reading and rereading, pursuing leads, tracking changes, and looking where I could for information about particular litigants or lawyers. I relied on a growing intuitive grasp of the subject that came after much time spent with my sources.

As should be obvious, I made an initial decision not to emphasize local county court records or manuscript sources. And as a result, the claims made throughout this book need to be tested with work in other American jurisdictions and using different sources.

Notes

Introduction

1. Alexander M. Burrill, *A New Law Dictionary and Glossary* (New York: John S. Voorhies, 1850), 707. By way of contrast, both the 1979 edition of *Black's Law Dictionary* and the 1992 edition of the *American Heritage Dictionary* remove the phrase "for life" from their definitions.
2. We can distinguish three legal meanings of separation in marriage. The first of these restates the idea of marital unity. By marriage, a man and a woman separated from their families of origin; through a legal act, they became something new, a couple. The second meaning of separation is founded on marital conflict. Marriages aspire to unity, but the law of marriage also created wife and husband as distinct and relationally opposed identities, with rights and duties peculiar to their distinctive identities. The theological and legal mystery of marriage was that it created separate marital identities, even as it also created unity, "one flesh." Third, there is the physical separation of husband from wife (our particular concern), including exit and divorce. What happened when couples lived apart? Were they still a unity, a marriage? Were they still bound by their marital duties and their marital identities?
3. See Sally Falk Moore, "Introduction: Moralizing States and the Ethnography of the Present," in *Moralizing States and the Ethnography of the Present,* ed. Sally Falk Moore, American Ethnological Society Monograph Series, no. 5 (Arlington, Va: American Anthropological Association, 1993), 1–16; Pierre Bourdieu, *The Logic of Practice* (Cambridge: Cambridge University Press, 1990); Barbara Yngvesson, *Virtuous Citizens, Disruptive Subjects: Order and Complaint in a New England Court* (New York: Routledge, 1993); Karl Llewellyn, "Behind the Law of Divorce," *Columbia Law Review* 32 (1932): 1281–1308; ibid., 33 (1933): 249–294.
4. Some historians and critics deny that historical study of legal documents can illuminate the lives and self-understandings of ordinary women and men. They insist that for most couples, and particularly for wives, the law is nothing but an alien and imposed structure; as a result, the apparent

317

presence of wives in legal texts is an illusion. Wives' selves are so distorted, so strategically shaped, so mediated by legal constructs that the historian can learn nothing that is truly "about" them. Ordinary wives—those who are not exceptionally powerful or wealthy—cannot "speak" in or through legal texts. Indeed, a historian who manages to make a wife speak through the text of the law has both asserted an illegitimate intellectual power and masked the pervasive and shaping power of law. Gayatri Spivak, "Can the Subaltern Speak?" in *Marxism and the Interpretation of Culture,* ed. Cary Nelson and Lawrence Grossberg (Urbana: University of Illinois Press, 1988), 271–313; Carroll Smith-Rosenberg, "The Female World of Love and Ritual: Relations between Women in Nineteenth-Century America," *Signs* 1, no. 1 (Summer 1975): 1–29.

How to respond to such a critique? As the chapters that follow make clear, I reject the premise of law as a monotonal imposition of domination, at least in the case of American law in the nineteenth century. There was domination aplenty, but also opportunity, critique, renewal through law, and contradiction and indeterminacy. I also reject, at least provisionally, a conception of a "realer" self, unrevealed in legal texts. Wives came to law, sometimes voluntarily, sometimes not. When they came "voluntarily," there are many questions we should always raise about the meaning of their acts. It is important to note that some of those questions were ones already raised in the law of the nineteenth century. But to question the relative degrees of coercion or freedom that brought wives (and husbands) to court, or that made them assume particular stances or positions in court, is not to assume that the self presented in the texts was a "false" self. This is who they were, in their legal dealings and identities. Other selves, other presentations and performances, occurred elsewhere. But those too were constructed performances, of uncertain voluntariness and freedom.

5. See Daniel Scott Smith, "The Curious History of Theorizing about the History of the Western Nuclear Family," *Social Science History* 17 (Fall 1993): 325–353; Daniel Scott Smith, "The Meanings of Family and Household: Change and Continuity in the Mirror of the American Census," *Population and Development Review* 18 (November 1992): 421–456.

6. The nostalgia that animates this side is wonderfully captured by a recent *New Yorker* cartoon of a modern mother reading to her young daughter: "And, because a princess can't be forced to testify against her prince, they lived happily ever after." *New Yorker,* June 23–30, 1997, 137.

7. The concept of patriarchy plays a continuing role in this work. I use it to describe "a set of practices and assumptions . . . that position women and children in the context of their relation to men and that deny them legiti-

macy (in both private and public life) unless they are officially connected to a man as wife or child. . . . It is expressed not as absolute right but as 'custom and bargaining.' As this implies, patriarchy is not ubiquitous and should not be reified as an unchangeable moral/legal code. Its hegemony is always incomplete." Barbara Yngvesson, "Negotiating Motherhood: Identity and Difference in 'Open' Adoptions," *Law and Society Review* 31, no. 1 (1997): 37 (quoting Linda Gordon, *Heroes of Their Own Lives* (New York: Vintage, 1988), 256).

1. The Scene of a Marriage

1. See *Lydia McGuire vs. Charles W. McGuire,* Transcript of Case No. 5437 (District Court of Wayne County, Nebraska, 1952); *McGuire v. McGuire,* 157 Neb. 226, 59 N.W.2d 336 (1953). At some point prior to 1952 Lydia transferred her interest in her first husband's farm to her daughters.
2. On the expectations of Nebraska farmwives, see Margaret Cannell, "The Kitchen Frontier," in *Roundup: A Nebraska Reader,* ed. and comp. Virginia Faulkner (Lincoln: University of Nebraska Press, 1957), 444–449. Farm women were eager to get telephones; men, on the other hand, were likely to disdain the telephone and labeled it "a woman's instrument." Deborah Fink, *Agrarian Women: Wives and Mothers in Rural Nebraska* (Chapel Hill: University of North Carolina Press, 1992), 50–51. Charles McGuire's land would have put him in the top quarter of farm holdings, perhaps in the top tenth. Ibid., 54.
3. *McGuire,* Transcript, 30–32. See letter (April 18, 1977) from Charles McDermott, attorney for Charles McGuire, in Judith C. Areen, *Cases and Materials on Family Law* (Mineola, N.Y.: Foundation Press, 1985), 68.
4. *McGuire,* 157 Neb. at 230–231, 59 N.W.2d at 388. The defense also argued that it was wrong to force Charles to pay Lydia's attorney fees.
5. Ibid., 157 Neb. at 238, 59 N.W.2d at 342.
6. If they had separated because of his "wrongdoing," Lydia could have purchased the goods and services she needed on Charles's credit, and merchants could have sued him for payment for "necessaries." Under Nebraska law, a wife's separate estate could become liable for necessaries only if "execution against the husband" had "been returned unsatisfied." *Dreamer v. Oberlander,* 122 Neb. 335, 240 N.W. 435 (1932) (quoting Neb. Comp. St. 1929, §42-201).
7. Ellen Wright Clayton and Jay Clayton, "Afterword: Voices and Violence—A Dialogue," *Vanderbilt Law Review* 43 (November 1990): 1807, 1815; Barbara Allen Babcock, Ann E. Freedman, Eleanor Holmes Norton, and Susan C. Ross, *Sex Discrimination and the Law: Causes and Remedies*

(Boston: Little, Brown, 1975), 619–626; Lee Teitelbaum, "Family History and Family Law," *Wisconsin Law Review*, 1985: 1335. Modern casebook editors leave unclear whether *McGuire* is still "good law," that is, whether it stands as an accurate expression of contemporary doctrine. Many casebooks give it an identity as an atavism: certainly for the lifestyle of its litigants, but also for the doctrine expounded. One places it under the heading of "the heritage of coverture." J. Ralph Lindgren and Nadine Taub, *The Law of Sex Discrimination* (St. Paul: West Publishing Co., 1988), 308; Leslie J. Harris, Lee E. Teitelbaum, and Carol Weisbrod, *Family Law* (Boston: Little, Brown, 1996), 34–42; Areen, *Cases and Materials on Family Law*, 62–68; Carl E. Schneider and Margaret F. Brinig, *An Introduction to Family Law* (St. Paul, Minn.: West Publishing Co., 1996), 235–243; Ira Mark Ellman, Paul M. Kurtz, and Katherine T. Bartlett, *Family Law: Cases, Text, Problems*, 2d ed. (Charlottesville, Va.: Michie, 1991), 84–87. A July 1998 search of the Lexis law review database, which does not include all law reviews, revealed thirty-nine citations between 1983 and 1998. On *McGuire* as the paradigmatic horror story, see Martha Fineman, "Implementing Equality: Ideology, Contradiction and Social Change: A Study of Rhetoric and Results in the Regulation of the Consequences of Divorce," *Wisconsin Law Review*, 1983: 855. For the suggestion that Lydia was abused, see Mary Becker, Cynthia Grant Bowman, and Morrison Torrey, *Cases and Materials on Feminist Jurisprudence: Taking Women Seriously* (St. Paul, Minn.: West Publishing Co., 1994), 503. In her original petition, Lydia had described Charles as "a very headstrong man" and that she was "afraid of what might happen to her personally when legal service of summons has been served upon the defendant," and she asked and received a temporary restraining order while the suit was pending. *McGuire*, Transcript, 2–3. But both the district court and the Nebraska Supreme Court dismissed her worries.

8. The casebook editors all edit out two-thirds of the opinion, where the court laboriously worked its way through the Nebraska case law on the support rights of wives. 157 Neb. at 231–237, 59 N.W.2d at 338–342.

9. *Earle v. Earle*, 27 Neb. 277, 43 N.W. 118 (1889); *Cochran v. Cochran*, 42 Neb. 612, 60 N.W. 942 (1894).

10. *Polster v. Polster*, 145 Mo. App. 606, 123 S.W. 81 (1909); *Bucknam v. Bucknam*, 176 Mass. 229, 57 N.E. 343 (1900); *Randall v. Randall*, 158 Fla. 502, 29 So. 2d 238 (1947).

11. The dissenting opinion in *McGuire* argued that the majority had drawn that boundary too restrictively. 157 Neb. at 239–247, 59 N.W.2d at 342–346.

12. To the district court judge there was something lacking in both litigants: "The objective of the defendant in life seems to be the accumulation of

money. The plaintiff has also adopted the habit of attempting to accumulate, in her own name. . . . It is commendable that neither is concerned with separation in any form. However, there is a conspicuous absence of companionship or affection. Each performs some marital obligations." *McGuire,* Transcript, 24.

13. See Sophinisba P. Breckinridge, *The Family and the State: Select Documents* (Chicago: University of Chicago Press, 1934; New York: Arno Press and The New York Times, 1972); Grace Abbott, *Legal Status in the Family, Apprenticeship, and Child Labor,* vol. 1 of *The Child and the State* (Chicago: University of Chicago Press, 1938; New York: Greenwood Press, 1968).

14. On early Nebraska law, see Othman A. Abbott, *Recollections of a Pioneer Lawyer,* ed. Addison E. Sheldon (Lincoln: Nebraska State Historical Society, 1929). The provision in the 1850 California constitution mandating community property and married women's property rights was taken verbatim from the Texas constitution of 1846. Those delegates who debated its passage were all easterners and all lawyers. Bonnie L. Ford, "Women, Marriage, and Divorce in California, 1849–1872" (Ph.D. diss., University of California, Davis, UMI no. 8521204, 1985), 20–23. On Texas, see Kathleen Elizabeth Lazarou, *Concealed under Petticoats: Married Women's Property and the Law of Texas, 1840–1913* (New York: Garland, 1986).

15. *Report of the Debates in the Convention of California on the Formation of the State Constitution in September and October 1849,* comp. J. Ross Browne (Washington, D.C.: J. T. Towers, 1850).

16. Nelson Manfred Blake, *The Road to Reno: A History of Divorce in the United States* (New York: Macmillan, 1962).

17. I am analogizing state marital regimes to the suburban local governments famously and controversially analyzed in Charles M. Tiebout, "A Pure Theory of Local Expenditures," *Journal of Political Economy* 64 (1956): 416–424.

18. In South Carolina, for example, not only were no divorces ever granted (except for a short moment during Reconstruction), but no divorce granted elsewhere to a South Carolinian would be recognized by a South Carolina court. See Janet Hudson, "From Constitution to Constitution, 1868–1895: South Carolina's Unique Stance on Divorce," *South Carolina Historical Magazine* 98, no. 1 (January 1997): 75–96.

19. Common law marriages entered into in New York before 1933 continued to be recognized as valid. William E. Nelson, "Patriarchy or Equality: Family Values or Individuality," *St. John's Law Review* 70, no. 3 (Summer 1996): 444. On the history of common law marriage, see Michael Grossberg, *Governing the Hearth: Law and the Family in Nineteenth-Century America* (Chapel Hill: University of North Carolina, 1985), 64–102.

20. *The People, ex rel. Brooks v. Brooks,* 35 Barb. 85 (N.Y. Sup. Ct. 1861). For

a typical European response, see Auguste Carlier, *Marriage in the United States*, trans. B. Joy Jeffries (New York: Leypoldt and Holt, 1867), 59.

21. *Anderson v. Dunn*, 19 U.S. 204, 226 (1821).

22. See generally Grossberg, *Governing the Hearth*.

23. James Willard Hurst, *The Growth of American Law: The Law Makers*, (Boston: Little, Brown and Co., 1950), 249–378.

24. See the decision of the Wisconsin Supreme Court in *Todd v. Lee*, reprinted in *American Law Register* 1 (September 1862), 657–669. A systematic reading of all published cases in California and Wisconsin between 1850 and 1870 dealing with the law of husband and wife (combined with a more selective reading of cases elsewhere) reveals the constant reliance on New York decisions.

25. Compare Joel Prentiss Bishop, *Commentaries on the Law of Marriage and Divorce, of Separations without Divorce, and of the Evidence of Marriage in All Issues; Embracing Also Pleading, Practice, and Evidence in Divorce Causes, with Forms* (Boston: Little, Brown and Co., 1864) with Joel Prentiss Bishop, *New Commentaries on Marriage, Divorce, and Separation as to the Law, Evidence, Pleading, Practice, Forms and the Evidence of Marriage in All Issues on a New System of Legal Exposition* (Chicago: T. H. Flood and Co., 1891); James Schouler, *A Treatise on the Law of the Domestic Relations: Embracing Husband and Wife, Parent and Child, Guardian and Ward, Infancy, and Master and Servant*, 2d ed. (Boston: Little, Brown and Co., 1874). The treatise writers' optimistic belief that they could produce a true (scientific) law of marriage warred against their empiricist sense of obligation to present the law accurately. Sometimes they conceded that their enterprise was rooted in the irreducibility of the law to first principles: since a lawyer could not apprehend the true rule simply through the exercise of deductive reason, he needed treatises. See Tapping Reeve, *The Law of Baron and Femme, of Parent and Child, Guardian and Ward, Master and Servant, and of the Powers of the Courts of Chancery; with an Essay on the Terms Heir, Heirs, Heirs of the Body*, ed. Amasa J. Parker and Charles Baldwin (Albany: William Gould, 1862), 297–300.

26. Earl M. Maltz, *Civil Rights, the Constitution, and Congress, 1863–1869* (Lawrence, Kans.: University Press of Kansas, 1990), 56–58; William E. Nelson, *The Fourteenth Amendment: From Political Principle to Judicial Doctrine* (Cambridge, Mass.: Harvard University Press, 1988), 136–138.

27. Only in the case of Mormon polygamy did Congress interfere with the instituted marital rules of the territorial legislatures. On the Mormon antipolygamy campaign, see Sarah Barringer Gordon, "'The Liberty of Self-Degradation': Polygamy, Woman Suffrage, and Consent in Nine-

teenth-Century America," *Journal of American History* 83, no. 3 (December 1996): 815–847. Another moment of federal activity over marriage occurred as a result of the Civil War. The Freedmen's Bureau devoted much energy to establishing and regulating the marriages of ex-slaves. The Pension Bureau also often had to determine who had been a "real" wife in order to award a widow's pension. See Beverly Schwartzberg, "Grass Widows, Barbarians, and Bigamists: Documenting and Describing Marital Irregularity in Nineteenth Century America" (unpublished manuscript, University of California, Santa Barbara, 1998). For the argument that images of marriage were crucial in national policy formation, see Nancy F. Cott, "Marriage and Women's Citizenship in the United States, 1830–1934," *American Historical Review* 103, no. 5 (December 1998): 1440–1474.

28. Peggy Pascoe, "Miscegenation Law, Court Cases, and Ideologies of 'Race' in Twentieth-Century America," *Journal of American History* 83, no. 1 (June 1996): 44–69; Peter Wallenstein, "Race, Marriage, and the Law of Freedom: Alabama and Virginia, 1860s–1960s," *Chicago-Kent Law Review* 70, no. 2 (1994): 371–438.

29. Conversation with Marygold Melli, 1991.

30. Until the late nineteenth century, the takings clause was understood as not applicable to the states. Thereafter, there were occasional invocations of the clause in litigation challenging particular state laws. Late nineteenth- and early twentieth-century courts, however, rarely held that the property rights of a spouse were so "vested" that a state could not reframe the terms of marriage for its citizens. As for the contract clause, Joseph Story had ruminated on its potential significance for marriage and divorce in his famous concurrence in the *Dartmouth College* case. *Trustees of Dartmouth College v. Woodward,* 17 U.S. 518, 695 (1819). A few mid-nineteenth-century courts similarly applied the contract clause to married women's property acts, holding that legislation changing the inherited law violated the obligation of contracts. See *Holmes v. Holmes,* 4 Barb. 295 (N.Y. Sup. Ct. 1848). Yet even when legislation changed existing marriages and existing marital rights, that is, applied changes retrospectively, courts rarely invoked the contract clause. See *Maynard v. Hill,* 125 U.S. 190 (1887), discussed in Chapter 9, for the end of the story. State constitutional provisions were occasionally significant. See, e.g., *Clark v. Clark,* 10 N.H. 380 (1839), where the court took it as beyond argument that there were "vested rights" in the existence of a marriage.

31. See Michael M. O'Hear, "'Some of the Most Embarrassing Questions': Extraterritorial Divorces and the Problem of Jurisdiction before *Pennoyer*," *Yale Law Journal* 104 (1995): 1507–1537; Neal R. Feigenson, "Extraterri-

torial Recognition of Divorce Decrees in the Nineteenth Century," *The American Journal of Legal History* 34, no. 2 (April 1990): 119–167; Larry Kramer, "Same-Sex Marriage, Conflict of Laws, and the Unconstitutional Public Policy Exception," *Yale Law Journal* 106, no. 7 (May 1997): 1965–2008.

32. Ellen DuBois, "Outgrowing the Compact of the Fathers: Equal Rights, Woman Suffrage, and the United States Constitution, 1820–1878," *Journal of American History* 74 (December 1987): 836–862.

33. See generally Blake, *Road to Reno;* William L. O'Neill, *Divorce in the Progressive Era* (New Haven: Yale University Press, 1967).

34. See Benedict Anderson, *Imagined Communities: Reflections on the Origins and Spread of Nationalism* (New York: Verso, 1985).

35. *Hall v. Hall,* 1870, briefs, University of Wisconsin Law Library; *Hall v. Hall,* 25 Wis. 600, 605–606 (1870). On wives who remained behind when husbands moved west, see Linda Peavy and Ursula Smith, *Women in Waiting in the Westward Movement* (Norman: University of Oklahoma Press, 1994).

36. Robert V. Remini, *Andrew Jackson and the Course of American Empire, 1767–1821* (New York: Harper and Row, 1977), 37–69. On the political uses made of Rachel's marriage, see Norma Basch, "Marriage, Morals, and Politics in the Election of 1828," *Journal of American History* 80, no. 3 (December 1993): 890–918.

37. *Cochran v. Cochran,* 42 Neb. 612, 60 N.W. 942 (1894). She was designated in the suit as L. Letitia Cochran, even though, according to her, she had always gone publicly by her husband's name as Mrs. Warren Cochran.

38. James G. Snell, "The International Border as a Factor in Marital Behavior: A Historical Case Study," *Ontario History* 81 (December 1989): 289–302; Eli Lilly, ed., *Schliemann in Indianapolis* (Indianapolis: Indiana Historical Society, 1961).

39. Mary Astell, *The First English Feminist: Reflections upon Marriage and Other Writings by Mary Astell,* ed. Bridget Hill (New York: St. Martin's Press, 1986); Carole Pateman, *The Sexual Contract* (Stanford: Stanford University Press, 1988); Harriet Beecher Stowe, *Uncle Tom's Cabin* (1852; New York: Washington Square Press, 1962), 9.

40. *McGuire,* Transcript, 33–34.

41. On "mandarin legal texts," see Robert W. Gordon, "Critical Legal Histories," *Stanford Law Review* 36 (1984): 57–125. Prior to the middle years of the nineteenth century, the subject was often called the law of "baron and femme." By the end of the century, it was usually called the law of "domestic relations."

42. On the Forrest case, see the transcript, *Report of the Forrest Divorce Case, Containing the Full and Unabridged Testimony of All the Witnesses, the Affidavits and Depositions, Together with the Consuelo and Forney Letters* (New York: Robert M. De Witt, 1852). There is a huge literature on the Beecher-Tilton controversy. A good starting point is Laura Hanft Korobkin, *Criminal Conversations: Sentimentality and Nineteenth-Century Legal Stories of Adultery* (New York: Columbia University Press, 1998), 55–118.

43. Oliver Wendell Holmes, "The Path of the Law," *Harvard Law Review* 10 (1897): 457.

44. *McGuire,* Transcript; *Cochran,* 42 Neb. at 616.

45. My father solved the problem by sending his brother's wife on a train to Nevada.

46. Katherine L. Caldwell, "Not Ozzie and Harriet: Postwar Divorce and the American Liberal Welfare State," *Law and Social Inquiry* 23, no. 1 (Winter 1998): 1–54.

47. *Forrest v. Forrest,* 25 N.Y. 501, 503 (1862); 16 N.Y. Super. Ct. 650, 661, 668, 671–673, 699 (1859).

48. *McGuire,* Transcript, 23.

49. *Eisenstadt v. Baird,* 405 U.S. 438, 453 (1972).

50. McGuire, 157 Neb. at 236–238, 59 N.W.2d at 341–342.

51. See Roderick Phillips, *Putting Asunder: A History of Divorce in Western Society* (Cambridge: Cambridge University Press, 1988); William J. Goode, *World Changes in Divorce Patterns* (New Haven: Yale University Press, 1993).

52. James Schouler, *A Treatise on the Law of the Domestic Relations: Embracing Husband and Wife, Parent and Child, Guardian and Ward, Infancy, and Master and Servant,* 1st ed. (Boston: Little, Brown, and Co., 1870), 290; *Marshall v. Rutton,* 8 T.R. 545 (K.B. 1800).

53. Even when separations were undisguised, they often became statistically unknowable because of inherited legal categories. A separated wife might retain her husband's domicile, wherever he was. Moreover, those exited wives and husbands who remarried, whether or not they had a theoretical legal right to do so, would have been counted as married in the census returns. Past separations would have been masked by present marriages. No census taker would have checked back through the records to find evidence of bigamy. Moreover, demographers have long known that there were always more women who identified themselves as widows than could possibly be true. Paul H. Jacobson, *American Marriage and Divorce,* in collaboration with Pauline F. Jacobson (New York: Rinehart & Co., 1959), 5; Caldwell, "Not Ozzie and Harriet: Postwar Divorce and the

326 Notes to Pages 33–38

American Liberal Welfare State"; Paul Bohannon, "Divorce Chains, Household of Remarriage, and Multiple Divorcers," in *Divorce and After,* ed. Bohannon (Garden City, N.Y.: Doubleday & Co., 1970), 113–123. On the other hand, there were separations that can be counted. See Jacobson, *American Marriage and Divorce,* 3; Richard Sennett, *Families against the City: Middle Class Homes of Industrial Chicago, 1872–1890* (Cambridge, Mass.: Harvard University Press, 1970), 113–116; Phillips, *Putting Asunder,* 273–313.

54. *Barber v. Barber,* 2 Pinney (Wis.) 297 (1849).
55. *Barber v. Barber,* 62 U.S. 582 (1858).
56. Ibid. at 595, 598 (1858). In the nineteenth century, most law writers used the "law French" "domicil" instead of "domicile."
57. See M. W. Jacobs, *A Treatise on the Law of Domicil* (Boston: Little, Brown, and Co., 1887); Isaac F. Redfield, "Conflict of Laws Affecting Marriage and Divorce. The Distinction between the English and Scotch Law. The Validity and Effect of Foreign Divorces," *American Law Register* 3 (new series) (February 1864): 193–222. It is possible to read Justice Stephen Field's opinion in *Maynard v. Hill,* 125 U.S. 190 (1888), as a partial vindication of Daniels's perspective.
58. 62 U.S. at 601–602.
59. Ibid. at 602.
60. Ibid. at 603.
61. See *Cruger v. Cruger,* trial papers and pleadings (1844), New York University Law Library, 31, 590–592; Henry Lauren Clinton, *Extraordinary Cases* (New York: Harper, 1899), 316–318.
62. See Chapter 7.
63. In the 1920s, the first act of a notorious New York case, *Mirizio v. Mirizio,* concluded with a Court of Appeals decision that a separated husband had no obligation to support his young wife when she refused to consummate the marriage. Her rights as a (separated) wife were contingent on her willingness to meet her duties as a wife. In the second act, she, having learned the law's lesson, told her husband that she had changed her mind, that she was now willing to consummate the union. He still refused to support her, insisting that her offer came too late. But now the Court of Appeals disagreed with him. In making her offer, she established her rights as a wife, including her right to be supported by her absent husband. *Mirizio v. Mirizio,* 242 N.Y. 74, 150 N.E. 605 (1926); *Mirizio v. Mirizio,* 248 N.Y. 175, 161 N.E. 461 (1928). Refusal of sexual intercourse was not understood as the same as refusal to cohabit, and it did not usually constitute desertion. See *Southwick v. Southwick,* 97 Mass. 327, 93 Am. Dec. 95 (1867); David Stewart, *The Law of Marriage and Divorce,*

as *Established in England and the United States* (San Francisco: Sumner Whitney & Co., 1884), 142–143.

2. Abigail Bailey's Divorce

1. Abigail Abbot Bailey, *Religion and Domestic Violence in Early New England: The Memoirs of Abigail Abbot Bailey*, ed. Ann Taves (Bloomington: Indiana University Press, 1989). All citations in this chapter are to this edition. Earlier references to Bailey's memoirs can be found in Mary Beth Norton, *Liberty's Daughters* (Boston: Little, Brown and Co., 1980), 49–50; Nancy Cott, "Divorce and the Changing Status of Women in Eighteenth-Century Massachusetts," *William and Mary Quarterly* 33 (1976): 586–614.
2. See Jane Fishburne Collier, *Marriage and Inequality in Classless Societies* (Stanford: Stanford University Press, 1988), 231–232.
3. On eighteenth-century evangelical Protestantism, see Philip Greven, *The Protestant Temperament* (New York: Alfred A. Knopf, 1980); Susan Juster, *Disorderly Women* (Ithaca: Cornell University Press, 1996).
4. Taves asserts that position in her introduction, as did Bailey's early nineteenth-century clerical editor. Bailey, *Memoirs*, 24–35, 72.
5. Ibid., 58; Ellen K. Rothman, *Hands and Hearts, a History of Courtship in America* (Cambridge, Mass.: Harvard University Press, 1987).
6. With "prudent management," she could sometimes keep him in "a pleasant mode" for weeks. Bailey, *Memoirs*, 57–58, 65–66.
7. Ibid., 77–78.
8. Ibid., 68.
9. Ibid., 78, 69, 56–57.
10. Ibid., 112–113.
11. Ibid., 135.
12. Ibid., 56–58.
13. Ibid., 58–76.
14. Ibid., 76–94.
15. Ibid., 94–111. Assuming that the land was in fact land owned by Asa, its sale would still require the consent of Abigail to release her dower rights in the property.
16. Ibid., 112–150.
17. Ibid., 150–178.
18. In 1791 the New Hampshire legislature granted both husbands and wives the right to seek judicial divorces for incest, bigamy, adultery, abandonment for three years, and/or extreme cruelty. *Laws of New Hampshire*, c.94, 732–733. Abigail's petition, recorded in May 1793, alleged that Asa had repeatedly committed adultery, had abused her, and had abandoned

her for more than two years. It is unclear why she raised the issue of abandonment. Only a three-year abandonment would do under the statute. Furthermore, it made little sense to claim that he had utterly forsaken her even for two years, given that he had left her only in June of 1792. Before he left, Asa had made a property settlement with Abigail, hardly leaving her in the position of a neglected or forsaken woman. Perhaps the allegation was meant simply to indicate the aggravated quality of the adultery and the abuse. More likely, the language was formulaic. Bailey, *Memoirs*, 197.

19. Ibid., 90–91.
20. Ibid., 77–79.
21. Ibid., 79.
22. Ibid., 82, 176.
23. In the treatise literature, an abandoning husband was sometimes analogized to a man who had "abjured" the realm and who had thereby suffered "civil death." In that case, his feme covert became a feme sole, capable of acting independently. See Zephaniah Swift, *A System of the Laws of the State of Connecticut* (Windham: John Byrne, 1795), 198; James Kent, *Commentaries on American Law*, vol. 2 (New York: O. Halsted, 1827), 127–130.
24. Bailey, *Memoirs*, 177–178.
25. William Blackstone, *Commentaries on the Laws of England*, ed. William Carey Jones (Baton Rouge: Claitor's Publishing Division, 1976), 1:*453.
26. Bailey, *Memoirs*, 76.

3. Early Exits

1. See Nancy Cott, "Divorce and the Changing Status of Women in Eighteenth-Century Massachusetts," *William and Mary Quarterly* 33 (1976): 586–614; Sheldon S. Cohen, "'To Parts of the World Unknown': The Circumstances of Divorce in Connecticut, 1750–1797," *Canadian Review of American Studies* 11, no. 3 (Winter 1980): 275–293; Sheldon S. Cohen, "The Broken Bond: Divorce in Providence County, 1749–1809," *Rhode Island History* 44 (August 1985): 67–79; Kathleen M. Brown, *Good Wives, Nasty Wenches, and Anxious Patriarchs: Gender, Race, and Power in Colonial Virginia*, Institute for Early American History and Culture (Chapel Hill: University of North Carolina Press, 1996); Richard H. Chused, *Private Acts in Public Places: A Social History of Divorce in the Formative Era of American Family Law* (Philadelphia: University of Pennsylvania Press, 1994); Merril D. Smith, *Breaking the Bonds: Marital Discord in Pennsylvania, 1730–1830* (New York: New York University Press, 1991).
2. The degendered "spouse" hides differences. In England, an explicit dou-

ble standard shaped the law of divorce. See "An Act to amend the Law re-lating to Divorce and Matrimonial Causes," 20 and 21 Victoria, c.85 (1857, 1858); Keith V. Thomas, "The Double Standard," *Journal of the History of Ideas* 20 (1959): 195–216. Throughout the United States, there was no explicit double standard distinguishing husbands from wives. Anonymous, "The Law of Divorce," *North American Review* 90 (April 1860): 427. Implicitly, however, distinctions were drawn both by judges and juries. See *Matchin v. Matchin,* 6 Pa. St. (Barr) 332 (Pa. Sup. Ct. 1847). On South Carolina, see George Elliott Howard, *A History of Matri-monial Institutions* (Chicago: University of Chicago Press, 1904), 3:76–78; Jane Turner Censer, "'Smiling through Her Tears': Antebellum South-ern Women and Divorce," *American Journal of Legal History* 25 (January 1981): 24–47.

3. By the 1830s there were also vice-chancellors who heard specific divorce pleadings, including Aaron Burr's, subject to review by the chancellor. On Burr and Eliza Jumel, see Milton Lomask, *Aaron Burr: The Conspiracy and Years of Exile, 1805–1836* (New York: Farrar, Straus, Giroux, 1982), 395–403.

4. Aaron Burr, *The Papers of Aaron Burr, 1756–1836,* ed. Mary-Jo Kline (Glen Rock, N.J.: Microfilming Corporation of America, 1977).

5. In New York prior to 1846, a contested trial meant that a jury had to be impaneled by a district court judge to hear a "feigned issue" sent over by the chancellor.

6. *Williamson v. Williamson,* 1 Johns. Ch. 488 (N.Y. Ch. 1815), *Williamson v. Parisien,* 1 Johns. Ch. 388 (N.Y. Ch. 1815), and Burr, *Papers,* 77–5187, reel 20.

7. In other states that might have been true, but not in New York. See the 1791 *Laws of New Hampshire,* c.94, 732–733. Later in the nineteenth cen-tury, marriages like Jane's second marriage came to be known as "Enoch Arden" marriages, after a poem of Tennyson's. See William Lamartine Snyder, *The Geography of Marriage or Legal Perplexities of Wedlock in the United States* (New York: G. P. Putnam's Sons, 1889), 78.

8. 1 Johns. Ch. 388, 393.

9. What she could not have done legally was to remarry Philip Parisien.

10. 1 Johns. Ch. 488, 490–491, 493.

11. Twenty years after the *Williamson* case, Chancellor Walworth echoed his predecessor Kent, holding against another man suing to divorce his aban-doned and long remarried (indeed, widowed) wife. *Valleau v. Valleau,* 6 Paige's Ch. 207, 209–210, 212 (N.Y. Ch. 1836). See "Can a Person Have Two Wives or Two Husbands in New York?" *The University Law Review* 1 (March 1894): 183–186.

12. James Kent, *Commentaries on American Law,* vol. 2 (New York: O.

Halsted, 1827), 88–89; *Betts v. Betts,* 1 Johns. Ch. 197 (N.Y. Ch. 1814); *Palmer v. Palmer,* 1 Paige's Ch. 276 (N.Y. Ch. 1828).

13. See generally Marylynn Salmon, *Women and the Law of Property in Early America* (Chapel Hill: University of North Carolina Press, 1986); Marylynn Salmon, "Republican Sentiment, Economic Change, and the Property Rights of Women in American Law," in *Women in the Age of the American Revolution,* ed. Ronald Hoffman and Peter J. Albert (Charlottesville: University Press of Virginia, 1989), 447–475.

14. *Laws of New Hampshire,* c.94, 732–733.

15. *Mary F— v. Samuel F—,* 1 N.H. 198 (1818). See *Washburn v. Washburn,* 9 Cal. 475 (1858), where *Mary F—* was interpreted to mean that a husband could not be held guilty of neglect if he lacked the means to provide for his wife.

16. *Wait v. Wait,* 4 N.Y. 95 (1850). In Rhode Island, the state supreme court ruled that even a wife who had eloped and lived in adultery did not lose her claim to dower. Only an actual divorce barred her claim. A husband who knew of the adultery and had not divorced his wife had effectively condoned it (or reconciled with her). *Bryan v. Batcheller,* 6 R.I. 543, 78 Am. Dec. 454 (1860).

17. *Trustees of Dartmouth College v. Woodward,* 17 U.S. (4 Wheat.) 518 (1819). On the concept of the "well ordered society," see William Novak, *The People's Welfare* (Chapel Hill: University of North Carolina Press, 1996); Thomas R. Meehan, "'Not Made out of Levity': Evolution of Divorce in Early Pennsylvania," *Pennsylvania Magazine of History and Biography* 92 (October 1968): 441.

18. Story's concurrence in *Dartmouth College* suggested that legislative divorces might not pass constitutional muster because vested marital rights were "impaired." 4 Wheat. at 695. The leading case declaring legislative divorces constitutional was *Starr v. Pease,* 8 Conn. 541 (1831). See Samuel Harrington's survey of the question, without a final ruling, in *Townsend v. Griffin,* 4 Harrington 440 (Del. 1846). Two state supreme courts held that such legislation impaired "the obligations" of contracts. *Ponder v. Graham,* 4 Fla. 23 (1851); *State v. Fry,* 4 Mo. 120 (1835). Joel Prentiss Bishop, *Commentaries on the Law of Marriage and Divorce, of Separations without Divorce, and of the Evidence of Marriage in All Issues; Embracing Also Pleading, Practice, and Evidence in Divorce Causes, with Forms* (Boston: Little, Brown and Co., 1864), 1:545–575. In Maryland the legislative committees to which divorce petitions were referred acted much as courts did. Chused, *Private Acts.*

19. See Meehan, "'Not Made out of Levity': Evolution of Divorce in Early Pennsylvania"; Chused, *Private Acts;* Lawrence B. Goodheart, Neil

Hanks, and Elizabeth Johnson, "'An Act for the Relief of Females . . .': Divorce and the Changing Legal Status of Women in Tennessee, 1796–1860, Part I," *Tennessee Historical Quarterly* 44 (Winter 1985): 318–339; Lawrence B. Goodheart, Neil Hanks, and Elizabeth Johnson, "'An Act for the Relief of Females . . .': Divorce and the Changing Legal Status of Women in Tennessee, 1796–1860, Part II," *Tennessee Historical Quarterly* 44 (Winter 1985): 402–416; Donna Elizabeth Sedevie, "The Prospect of Happiness: Women, Divorce and Property," *Journal of Mississippi History* 57 (Fall 1995): 189–206.

20. *Laws of New York*, 1787, c.69; *Laws*, 1813, c.102, 197; *Revised Statutes*, vol. 2, pt. II, c.8, art. 2, 76–78 (1836). In the late 1820s, husbands gained the same theoretical right as their wives to go to a court of equity and ask for a divorce à mensa et thoro, although very few ever did.

21. Lawyers for female defendants often emphasized the presumption of innocence and that a jury ought to treat an accusation of adultery as equivalent to a criminal charge. See, e.g., *Richard Cox against Ellen C. Cox: Argument of J. W. Gerard, Esq. for the Defendant, on Summing Up to the Jury* (New York: Bryant and Co., 1856). Proof of adultery by a man was not held to the same standard, although there was much controversy over how precisely the date and place of the acts alleged had to be specified. See *Van Epps v. Van Epps*, 6 Barb. 320 (N.Y. Sup. Ct. 1848). Under California's early (1851) divorce law, it was entirely within the discretion of the judge whether to call a jury. In Sacramento during the next twenty years, the district court called a jury only when a wife was accused of adultery. Bonnie L. Ford, "Women, Marriage, and Divorce in California, 1849–1872" (Ph.D. diss., University of California, Davis, UMI no. 8521204, 1985), 143–144. Ford interprets California practice as a mobilization of public shame against adulterous wives. It is much more likely that the practice reflected the perception of adultery as crime and the "accused" wife as entitled to all the protections of a criminal process, including a right to potential jury nullification. In that sense the process served to moderate legally a cultural double standard.

22. In New York, although legislative divorces were theoretically available until 1846, only one petition for a legislative divorce was ever granted. See Carol Weisbrod, *The Boundaries of Utopia* (New York: Pantheon, 1980), 46–47. On the other hand, legislative petitioners kept asking for special divorce relief. To these petitions, as for others, the "Committee on Grievances," speaking for the legislature, gave a consistent set of denials. See, e.g., "Report on the petition of Nathaniel Winslow," 1833 Assembly Document 97 (v.2), January 23, 1833; "Report . . . on the petition of Louisa Crandall," 1836 Assembly Document 328, May 26, 1838; Petition

of David Frost, Report of the Committee on Grievances, Assembly Document 78, January 17, 1839; Document 21, 1839; Document 324, April 18, 1840; Document 189, March 12, 1841.

23. Isaac Ray, *A Treatise on the Medical Jurisprudence of Insanity*, 5th ed. (Boston: Little, Brown, and Co., 1871), 30–31; *Pomeroy v. Wells*, 8 Paige's Ch. 406 (N.Y. Ch. 1840); *Appleton v. Warner*, 51 Barb. 270 (N.Y. Sup. Ct. 1868); *Cook v. Cook*, 53 Barb. 180 (N.Y. Sup. Ct. 1869); *Hamaker v. Hamaker*, 18 Ill. 137, 65 Am. Dec. 705 (1856). But see John Bannister Gibson's opinion in *Matchin v. Matchin*, 6 Pa. St. (Barr) 332 (Pa. Sup. Ct. 1847).

24. *R.F.H. v. S.H.*, 40 Barb. 9, 12 (N.Y. Sup. Ct. 1862); *Leseuer v. Leseuer*, 31 Barb. 330 (N.Y. Sup. Ct. 1860); *Wood v. Wood*, 2 Paige's Ch. 108 (N.Y. Ch. 1830).

25. Kent, *Commentaries*, 2:102.

26. Kent, *Commentaries*, 2:88–89.

27. The "feigned issue" appears to have been Kent's innovation, shaped by the novelty of the jurisdiction of a court of equity in divorce as well as by the general understanding that a judgment of "guilt" in divorce was equivalent to a criminal judgment and required the protections incorporated in a jury trial. *Betts v. Betts*, 1 Johns. Ch. 197 (N.Y. Ch. 1814); Kent, *Commentaries*, 2:83. For the later development of practice with a feigned issue, see *Morrell v. Morrell*, 1 Barb. 318 (N.Y. Sup. Ct. 1847); *Morrell v. Morrell*, 3 Barb. 236 (N.Y. Sup. Ct. 1848).

28. *Hanks v. Hanks*, 3 Edw. Ch. 469 (N.Y. Ch. 1841); *Banta v. Banta*, 3 Edw. Ch. 295 (N.Y. Ch. 1839). See *Bokel v. Bokel*, 3 Edw. Ch. 376 (N.Y. Ch. 1840); *Hanford v. Hanford*, 3 Edw. Ch. 468 (N.Y. Ch. 1841); *Graves v. Graves*, 2 Paige's Ch. 62 (N.Y. Ch. 1830). For the efforts of the Mississippi legislature to prevent collusion, see Sedevie, "The Prospect of Happiness: Women, Divorce and Property."

29. See the comments of Vice-Chancellor Edwards in *Dobbs v. Dobbs*, 3 Edw. Ch. 377 (N.Y. Ch. 1840), and *Hanks*, 3 Edw. Ch. 469 (N.Y. Ch. 1841). See also Note, "Collusive and Consensual Divorce and the New York Anomaly," *California Law Review* 36 (1936): 1121–1133; Lawrence M. Friedman, "Rights of Passage: Divorce Law in Historical Perspective," *Oregon Law Review* 63 (1984): 649–669.

30. James Schouler, *A Treatise on the Law of the Domestic Relations: Embracing Husband and Wife, Parent and Child, Guardian and Ward, Infancy, and Master and Servant*, 2d ed. (Boston: Little, Brown, 1874), 314–315.

31. *Ringsted v. Lady Lanesborough*, Scone Place MSS, Box 68, No. 29, quoted in James Oldham, *The Mansfield Manuscripts and the Growth of English Law in the Eighteenth Century* (Chapel Hill: University of North Carolina

Press, 1992), 1245–1251; *Ringsted v. Lanesborough,* 3 Doug. 197 (K.B. 1783); *Barwell v. Brooks,* 3 Doug. 371 (K.B. 1784); *Corbett v. Poelnitz,* 1 T.R. 5 (K.B. 1785). See R. J. Peaslee, "Separation Agreements under the English Law," *Harvard Law Review* 15 (1905): 638–656; Susan Staves, *Married Women's Separate Property in England, 1660–1833* (Cambridge, Mass.: Harvard University Press, 1990), 162–195. In theory, the separation occurred "through the intervention of trustees," who became responsible for the wife. The role of trustees in managing a separated wife's estate was, however, understood as essentially formal. R. S. Donnison Roper, *A Treatise on the Law of Property Arising from the Relation between Husband and Wife,* vol. 2 (New York: Stephen Gould and Son, 1824), 272–273.

32. See *Rex v. Mary Mead,* 1 Burr. 542 (K.B. 1758), where Mansfield denied the writ of habeas corpus taken out by John Wilkes for the return of his wife because he had "used her very ill," and they had negotiated articles of separation.

33. *Marshall v. Rutton,* 8 T.R. 545 (K.B. 1800). The other great source of phrases hostile to voluntary separations was William Scott's opinion in *Evans v. Evans,* 1 Hagg. Con. 35, 161 Eng. Rep. 466 (1790). Lord Eldon relied on *Marshall* in *St. John (Lord) v. St. John (Lady),* 11 Ves. Jun. *526 (Ch. 1805). See Lawrence Stone, *Road to Divorce: England 1530–1987* (Oxford: Oxford University Press, 1990), 154–156; Staves, *Married Women's Separate Property,* 162–195.

34. *Simpson v. Simpson,* 4 Ky. (Dana) 140, 141–142 (1836).

35. *Beach and Wife v. Ranney and Wife,* 2 Hill 309 (N.Y. Sup. Ct. 1842); *Beach v. Beach and Wife,* 2 Hill 260, 38 Am. Dec. 584 (N.Y. Sup. Ct. 1842).

36. A husband possessed the right to recover for many legal wrongs done to his wife. He owned the causes of action. Slander was different. As a wrong done to a wife's personal reputation, a husband had to join his wife's name to the complaint. If he won, he would own the money recovered in the suit after it had been "reduced to possession." But he did not own the cause of action or the judgment itself. And if he died before the property had been reduced to possession, the judgment would not become part of his estate but would, rather, go to the wife as part of her newly uncovered identity as a widow. Nothing in the existing law, however, required him to sue to protect her reputation. In that respect, slander was indistinguishable from other legal wrongs—torts—done to a wife. Only a husband possessed the right to decide whether to initiate suit on behalf of his wife. Therefore, Mrs. Beach needed her husband to acknowledge that she had the right to use his name along with hers in a slander case. Otherwise, she might be remediless. See Tapping Reeve, *The Law of Baron and*

Femme, of Parent and Child, Guardian and Ward, Master and Servant, and of the Powers of the Courts of Chancery; with an Essay on the Terms Heir, Heirs, Heirs of the Body, ed. Amasa J. Parker and Charles Baldwin (Albany: William Gould, 1862), 212–221.

37. 2 Hill at 261–264.

38. Ibid. at 264–265. See *Robinson v. Reynolds,* 1 Aiken's Vt. Rep. 174 (1826); *Ballard v. Russell,* 33 Me. 196 (1851); *Baker v. Barney,* 8 Johns. 72, 5 Am. Dec. 326 (N.Y. Sup. Ct. 1811). Sometimes the language of *Marshall v. Rutton* was mobilized in cases of divorce à mensa et thoro. See *Barber v. Barber,* 2 Pinney 297 (Wis. 1849).

39. See *Fenner v. Lewis,* 10 Johns. 38 (N.Y. Sup. Ct. 1813); *Kelly v. Harrison,* 2 Johns. 29, 32 (N.Y. Sup. Ct. 1800) (Kent, concurring). Compare Chief Justice John Lansing's dissent in ibid., 33. There were also a number of English treatises, available in the United States, that provided arguments justifying separate maintenance agreements. See James Clancy, *A Treatise of the Rights, Duties and Liabilities of Husband and Wife, at Law and in Equity,* 2d ed. (American), from the last London ed. (New York: Law Press, 1837); John Joseph Powell, *Essay upon the Law of Contracts and Agreements* (Dublin: Chamberlaine and Rice, 1790).

40. Reeve, *Baron and Femme,* 178–179.

41. Ibid., 191. The editors of the 1862 edition thought *Marshall v. Rutton,* and the cases that followed it, established the disability of a separated wife to sue or be sued alone "too positively to be controverted." Ibid.

42. *Rogers v. Rogers,* 4 Paige's Ch. 516 (N.Y. Ch. 1834); *Carson v. Murray,* 3 Paige's Ch. 483 (N.Y. Ch. 1832); *People v. Mercein,* 8 Paige's Ch. 47 (N.Y. Ch. 1839); *Emery v. Neighbour,* 2 Halsted 142, 145 (N.J. 1824); *Helms v. Franciscus,* 2 Bland Ch. 544, 554–556, 20 Am. Dec. 402 (Md. Ch. 1830); *Champlin v. Champlin,* Hoffman's Ch. 55 (N.Y. Ch. 1839); *Heyer v. Burger,* 1 Hoffman's Ch. 1 (N.Y. Ch. 1839). Often agreements were enforced when they were understood as providing a "separate maintenance" for a wife in the context of an existing separation rather than an agreement to separate. See, e.g., *Rolette v. Rolette,* 1 Pinney 370 (Wis. 1843), which surveyed the New York cases.

43. *Rogers v. Rogers,* 4 Paige's Ch. 516 (N.Y. Ch. 1834).

44. Thus, the editors of the 1862 edition of Reeve's treatise criticized *Simpson v. Simpson* not because the court refused to enforce the contract between separated husband and wife, but because the court misunderstood the traditional responsibility of a court of equity to offer a remedy to a wife under coverture, who would otherwise be totally remediless. Reeve, *Baron and Femme,* 258.

45. *Emery v. Neighbour,* 2 Halsted 142, 146 (N.J. 1824); Joseph Story, *Commentaries on Equity Jurisprudence as Administered in England and America,* vol. 2, 7th ed. (Boston: Little, Brown and Co., 1857), 652.

46. *Florentine v. Wilson,* Hill and Denio 303, 305 (N.Y. Sup. Ct. 1844); *Rogers,* 4 Paige's Ch. at 517.

47. Lawrence Stone notices the same phenomenon in England. Stone, *Road to Divorce,* 163. Separate maintenance agreements typically asserted that they were confirming and regularizing the terms of an existing separation.

48. Abigail Abbot Bailey, *Religion and Domestic Violence in Early New England: The Memoirs of Abigail Abbot Bailey,* ed. Ann Taves (Bloomington: Indiana University Press, 1989), 176.

49. See J. Willard Hurst, *Law and the Conditions of Freedom in the Nineteenth-Century United States* (Madison: University of Wisconsin Press, 1956); Amy Dru Stanley, *From Bondage to Contract: Wage Labor, Marriage and the Market in the Age of Slave Emancipation* (New York: Cambridge University Press, 1998).

50. Patricia Williams makes a similar argument—on the connections between possession of a bounded self and African-American emancipation—in "Alchemical Notes: Reconstructing Ideals from Deconstructed Rights," *Harvard Civil Rights–Civil Liberties Law Review* 22 (1987): 401–433.

51. Rufus W. Griswold, *Statement of the Relations of Rufus W. Griswold with Charlotte Myers (Called Charlotte Griswold)* (Philadelpia: H. B. Ashmead, 1856).

52. See *Fry v. Drestler,* 2 Yeates 278 (Pa. 1798); Mary Ann Salter, "Quarreling in the English Settlement: The Flowers in Court," *Journal of the Illinois State Historical Society* 75 (1982): 101–114; Elizabeth Crook, "Sam Houston and Eliza Allen: The Marriage and the Mystery," *Southwestern Historical Quarterly* 94, no. 1 (1991): 1–37.

53. For England, see Stone, *Road to Divorce,* 142; Stephen Parker, *Informal Marriage, Cohabitation and the Law, 1750–1989* (New York: St. Martin's Press, 1990). Kathleen Brown describes bigamy as "the quintessential colonial crime." Brown, *Good Wives,* 94.

54. *People v. Humphrey,* 7 Johns. 314 (N.Y. Sup. Ct. 1810).

55. *Fenner v. Lewis,* 10 Johns. 38 (N.Y. Sup. Ct. 1813). See Michael Grossberg, *Governing the Hearth: Law and the Family in Nineteenth-Century America* (Chapel Hill: University of North Carolina, 1985), 64–101.

56. *Valleau v. Valleau,* 6 Paige's Ch. 207, 208–209 (N.Y. Ch. 1836). For an example of the use of a second marriage to prove adultery justifying di-

vorce, see *Hoffman v. Hoffman*, in Burr, *Papers*, reel 22. See also *McNeil v. McNeil*, 3 Edw. Ch. 550 (N.Y. Ch. 1842); *Lewis v. Lewis*, 3 Johns. Ch. 519 (N.Y. Ch. 1818), and in Burr, *Papers*, reel 22.

57. *Valleau*, 6 Paige's Ch. 207.

58. The emergence of an American law of common law marriage was therefore the necessary complement of the general unwillingness of the courts to punish bigamy. Grossberg, *Governing the Hearth*, 64–101.

59. *Rose v. Clark*, 8 Paige's Ch. 574 (N.Y. Ch. 1841). See likewise *Jackson, ex dem. Van Buskirk v. Claw*, 18 Johns. 346 (N.Y. Sup. Ct. 1820); *Baker v. Metzler*, Anthon's Nisi Prius 193 (N.Y. Sup. Ct. 1807).

60. Doyce B. Nunis, Jr., *The Trials of Isaac Graham* (Los Angeles: Dawson's Book Shop, 1967), 67. Later, Catherine claimed that Isaac had represented that they were married according to the "laws of the land" (Mexico), a representation she had accepted out of ignorance. *Graham v. Bennett*, 2 Cal. 503 (1852).

61. Meanwhile, Isaac's son by the earlier marriage had managed to kill Catherine's brother and to wound her mother.

62. *Graham*, 2 Cal. 503. See David J. Langum, *Law and Community on the Mexican California Frontier: Anglo-American Expatriates and the Clash of Legal Traditions, 1821–1846* (Norman: University of Oklahoma Press, 1987), 226–267. Common law marriage resembled the "marriage by bond" relied on by the English settlers of Spanish North America as a way to avoid Catholic conversion. But the decision of the California Supreme Court was not an application of preannexation Mexican California law. Hans W. Baade, "The Form of Marriage in Spanish North America," *Cornell Law Review* 61 (November 1975): 1–89.

63. Hurst, *Law and the Conditions of Freedom*, 1–31.

4. Being a Wife

1. Margaret A. Burnham, "An Impossible Marriage: Slave Law and Family Law," *Law and Inequality* 5 (July 1987): 187–225; George L. Christian and Frank W. Christian, "Slave-Marriages," *Virginia Law Journal* 1, no. 11 (November 1877): 641–652. Well after Emancipation and the passage of the Thirteenth Amendment, treatise writers continued to use slavery as a heuristic category to delimit capacity for marriage. David Stewart, *The Law of Marriage and Divorce, as Established in England and the United States* (San Francisco: Sumner Whitney & Co., 1884), 62–64; Joel Prentiss Bishop, *New Commentaries on Marriage, Divorce, and Separation as to the Law, Evidence, Pleading, Practice, Forms and the Evidence of Mar-*

riage in All Issues on a New System of Legal Exposition (Chicago: T. H. Flood and Co., 1891), 281–296.

2. *Cruger v. Cruger*, trial papers and pleadings (1844), New York University Law Library, 365–367.

3. Noah Webster, *An American Dictionary of the English Language*, revised by Chauncey Goodrich (Springfield, Mass.: George and Charles Merriam, 1856), 365–366.

4. *Barnes v. Allen*, 30 Barb. 663 (N.Y. Sup. Ct. 1860); James Schouler, *A Treatise on the Law of the Domestic Relations: Embracing Husband and Wife, Parent and Child, Guardian and Ward, Infancy, and Master and Servant*, 2d ed. (Boston: Little, Brown and Co., 1874), 57–58.

5. *Hutcheson v. Peck*, 5 Johns. 196 (N.Y. Sup. Ct. 1809); *Bennett v. Smith*, 21 Barb. 439 (N.Y. Sup. Ct. 1856).

6. *Barnes*, 30 Barb. 663 (N.Y. Sup. Ct. 1860); *Schuneman v. Palmer*, 4 Barb. 225 (N.Y. Sup. Ct. 1848); *Bennett*, 21 Barb. 439 (N.Y. Sup. Ct. 1856).

7. *Barnes v. Allen*, 1 Keyes 390, 1 Abbott 111 (N.Y. 1864). The holding placed the burden of proof on the husband to demonstrate that the defendant acted with knowing ill will and with knowledge that the wife's fears or assertions were false. In most contexts, that destroyed the cause of action. On the other hand, in *Heermance v. James*, 47 Barb. 120 (N.Y. Sup. Ct. 1866), the New York Supreme Court ruled on a demurrer that a defendant who had prejudiced and poisoned the mind of a wife could be held liable. Justice Platt Potter's decision referred approvingly to the New York Supreme Court's decision in *Barnes*, without mentioning the Court of Appeals' reversal. In *Hoard v. Peck*, 56 Barb. 202 (N.Y. Sup. Ct. 1867), a druggist was held liable for enticing a wife to use laudanum as a beverage "so that she was unable to perform her duties as a wife." A dissent emphasized that modern law regarded the wife "as a responsible being, capable of determining for herself what is for her own good." Ibid., 216–217.

8. Only violence justified an annulment for fraud. *Ferlat v. Gojon*, Hopk. Ch. 478 (N.Y. Ch. 1825). In *Wightman v. Wightman*, 4 Johns. Ch. 343 (N.Y. Ch. 1820), Kent granted an annulment at the request of a young woman who had been insane when she married. But both *Ferlat* and *Wightman* were criticized and probably overruled in *Burtis v. Burtis*, Hopk. Ch. 557 (N.Y. Ch. 1825). See also *Fry v. Fry*, 7 Paige Ch. 461 (N.Y. Ch. 1839); Isaac Ray, *A Treatise on the Medical Jurisprudence of Insanity*, 5th ed. (Boston: Little, Brown, and Co., 1871), 300–301. For other unsuccessful efforts to escape from a wife discovered to be flawed, see *Crehore v. Crehore*, 97 Mass. 330, 93 Am. Dec. 98 (1867) (chastity of wife); *Hamaker v. Hamaker*, 18 Ill. 137, 65 Am. Dec. 705 (1856) (insanity of wife); Peti-

tion of David Frost, Committee on Grievances, N.Y. Assembly, Document 21, 1839; Document 78, January 17, 1839; Document 324, April 18, 1840; and Document 189, March 12, 1841. But see *Baker v. Baker,* 13 Cal. 87 (1856), where Stephen Field ruled that a husband was entitled to a remedy when his wife gave birth to another man's child five months after the marriage.

9. *Scroggins v. Scroggins,* 14 N.C. 535 (1832). Ruffin's opinion in *Scroggins* was reversed shortly thereafter because of a public outcry that made it impossible "to follow those rules which . . . dispassionate judgment sanctions."

10. Rufus W. Griswold, *Statement of the Relations of Rufus W. Griswold with Charlotte Myers (Called Charlotte Griswold)* (Philadelpia: H. B. Ashmead, 1856).

11. Amy Dru Stanley, *From Bondage to Contract: Wage Labor, Marriage and the Market in the Age of Slave Emancipation* (New York: Cambridge University Press, 1998); Reva B. Siegel, "The Modernization of Marital Status Law: Adjudicating Wives' Rights to Earnings, 1860–1930," *Georgetown Law Journal* 82, no. 7 (September 1994): 2127–2211.

12. Tapping Reeve, *The Law of Baron and Femme, of Parent and Child, Guardian and Ward, Master and Servant, and of the Powers of the Courts of Chancery; with an Essay on the Terms Heir, Heirs, Heirs of the Body,* ed. Amasa J. Parker and Charles Baldwin (Albany: William Gould, 1862), 53–55, 143–147, 152. For cases that realized Reeve's fears, see *Cotton and Uxor v. Moon,* N.Y. Jud. Ops. 11 (1802), and *Hawk v. Harman,* 5 Binney 43 (Pa. 1812).

13. Married women were regularly excused from criminal liability after they invoked the coercive presence of their husbands. *Martha Boyd's Cases* (People v. Boyd), 3 New York City-Hall Recorder 134 (1818); *People v. William Brown and Elizabeth, his wife,* 3 New York City-Hall Recorder 56 (1818). By contrast, an unmarried woman, arrested for theft or any other crime, could not excuse herself with the claim that she had acted under the control of the man she was with, that she had been coerced into theft. *People v. Brandon and Griffiths,* 4 New York City-Hall Recorder 140 (1819).

14. Until the middle of the nineteenth century, however, political identity was distinguished from marital identity. A foreign wife did not become a citizen because of her marriage to an American. See *Kelly v. Harrison,* 2 Johns. Cases 29 (N.Y. Sup. Ct. 1800), and *Sutliff v. Forgey,* 1 Cowen 89 (N.Y. Sup. Ct. 1823).

15. Caleb Cushing, "Legal Conditions of Woman," *North American Review* 26 (April 1828): 318; E. P. W. Packard, *Modern Persecution, or Married*

Woman's Liabilities, as Demonstrated by the Action of the Illinois Legislature, vol. 2 (Hartford: Case, Lockwood & Brainard, 1875), 67.

16. See Ruth Bloch, "The Gendered Meanings of Virtue in Revolutionary America," *Signs: Journal of Women in Culture and Society* 13 (1987): 37–58; Linda Kerber, et al., "Forum: Beyond Roles, Beyond Spheres: Thinking about Gender in the Early Republic," *William and Mary Quarterly,* Third Series 46 (July 1989): 565–585.

17. *Trial of James Berrian, for Criminal Conversation with Catherine Blakney, Wife of Jacob Blakney, Had in the Mayor's Court of the City of New-York, in the Term of July, 1807* (New York, 1807), 1–15.

18. Abigail Abbot Bailey, *Religion and Domestic Violence in Early New England: The Memoirs of Abigail Abbot Bailey,* ed. Ann Taves (Bloomington: Indiana University Press, 1989), 87, 97, 101, 102.

19. Alexis de Tocqueville, *Democracy in America,* ed. J. P. Mayer; trans. George Lawrence (13th ed., 1850; Garden City, N.Y.: Doubleday & Company, 1969), 592–594, 602.

20. Elisha P. Hurlbut, *Essays on Human Rights and Their Political Guaranties,* ed. George Coombe (Edinburgh: Maclachlan, Stewart, & Co., 1847), 53–55.

21. *Report of the Debates and Proceedings of the Convention for the Revision of the Constitution of the State of Indiana* (Indianapolis: A. H. Brown, 1850), 503.

22. Edward Deering Mansfield, *The Legal Rights, Liabilities and Duties of Women* (Salem, Mass.: J. P. Jewett & Co., 1845), 270.

23. Proponents of marital reform were more likely to claim that husbands and wives naturally assumed marital identities. See, e.g., Milo M. Quaife, ed., *The Struggle over Ratification* (Madison, Wis.: State Historical Society, 1920), 567–575; Hurlbut, *Human Rights,* 55.

24. *Indiana Convention,* 470–471; *Debates and Proceedings in the New-York State Convention, for the Revision of the Constitution,* ed. S. Croswell and R. Sutton (Albany: The Albany Argus, 1846). See Anonymous, "Rights and Wrongs of Woman in the United States," *Themis* 1 (1844): 89–90.

25. Anonymous, "The State v. Henry Day," *American Jurist* 20 (October 1838): 237–242.

26. This was, we should remember, lawyer's verse, and so the poem's final image of connubial bliss and gluttony bore a footnote. Literally. The footnote quoted Chancellor Kent on his skepticism about "legislation in regard to sexual matters." Anonymous, "The State v. Henry Day," 242.

27. See *A Faithful Report of the Trial of Doctor William Little, on an Indictment for an Assault and Battery, Committed upon the Body of His Lawful Wife, Mrs. Jane Little, a Black Lady* (New York, 1808), 5.

28. See Christine Stansell, *City of Women* (New York: Alfred A. Knopf, 1986), 29; Elizabeth Pleck, *Domestic Tyranny* (New York: Oxford University Press, 1987).

29. *State v. Rhodes,* 61 N.C. 453 (1868); Irving Browne, "Wife-Beating and Imprisonment," *American Law Review* 25 (1891): 551–568.

30. See, e.g., *Govane's Case,* 2 Bland Ch. 570 (Md. 1750–1752), a case reported in footnote to *Helms v. Franciscus,* 2 Bland Ch. 544 (Md. Ch. 1830); *People v. Winters,* 2 Park. Cr. Rep. 10 (N.Y. 1823); and *Morris v. Morris,* 14 Cal. 76 (1859).

31. Zephaniah Swift, *A System of the Laws of the State of Connecticut* (Windham: John Byrne, 1795), 203; Rollin C. Hurd, *A Treatise on the Right of Personal Liberty, and on the Writ of Habeas Corpus and the Practice Connected with It: A View of the Law of Extradition of Fugitives,* 2d ed. (Albany: W. C. Little & Co., 1876), 25. The best-known case on the other side was *State v. Rhodes,* 61 N.C. 453 (1868). Yet Justice Edwin Reade's opinion conceded that his opinion was not "in unison" with that in other states "or with the philosophy of some very respectable law writers." The ruling in *Rhodes* was soon reversed. *State v. Oliver,* 70 N.C. 60 (1874). On family law in North Carolina, see Laura F. Edwards, *"Gendered Strife and Confusion": The Politics of Reconstruction* (Urbana-Champaign: University of Illinois Press, 1997).

32. *William Brook's Case,* 6 New York City-Hall Recorder 66 (1821). The judge decided that a man had a right to govern his family but no right to beat his wife. See likewise *State v. Buckley,* 3 Harr. 552 (Del. Super. Ct. 1838).

33. Reeve, *Baron and Femme,* 141. Oregon wife beaters in the 1890s did not justify their acts by referring to a right to do so. See David Peterson, "Wife Beating: An American Tradition," *Journal of Interdisciplinary History* 23, no. 1 (Summer 1992): 106.

34. Blackstone, *Commentaries,* 1:*442–443.

35. James Kent, *Commentaries on American Law,* vol. 2 (New York: O. Halsted, 1827), 109. See likewise St. George Tucker, *Blackstone's Commentaries: With Notes of Reference, to the Constitution and Laws, of the Federal Government of the United States; and of the Commonwealth of Virginia* (Philadelphia: Birch and Small, 1803), 108; Swift, *System,* 193–194.

36. James Wilson, *Works,* ed. Robert Green McCloskey (Cambridge, Mass.: Harvard University Press, 1967), 601.

37. Blackstone, *Commentaries,* 1:*442–443.

38. Reeve, *Baron and Femme,* 182–184.

39. *Fenner v. Lewis,* 10 Johns. 38, 42 (N.Y. Sup. Ct. 1813)(argument of Slosson and Ogden); Richard Newcombe Gresley, *A Treatise on the Law of*

Evidence in the Courts of Equity, 2d ed., ed. Christopher Alderson Calvert (Harrisburg, Pa.: I. G. M'Kinley & J. M. G. Lescure, 1848), 344.

40. *Fenner,* 10 Johns. at 42. Kent's position was controversial. Yet other judges also allowed such testimony where they regarded it as necessary for the resolution of a case. *People ex rel. Ordrenaux v. Chegary and Condert,* 18 Wend. 637 (N.Y. Sup. Ct. 1836); *People v. Mercein,* 8 Paige Ch. 47 (N.Y. Ch. 1839).

41. Swift, *System,* 203; *People v. Goodman and Goodman,* 6 New York City-Hall Recorder 21 (1821); Henry St. George Tucker, *Commentaries on the Laws of Virginia, Comprising the Substance of a Course of Lectures Delivered to the Winchester Law School* (Winchester, Va.: Printed at the office of the Winchester Virginian, 1820), 116–117. Tapping Reeve agreed that wives were theoretically subject to punishment under the criminal law, but he regarded husbands' coercion as a compelling excuse. Reeve, *Baron and Femme,* 150–156, 220, 230. In John D. Lawson's 1886 treatise, the presumption that wives had been coerced by husbands when they committed criminal or tortious acts came "from the course of nature." Lawson, *The Law of Presumptive Evidence, Including Presumptions Both of Law and of Fact, and the Burden of Proof Both in Civil and Criminal Cases, Reduced to Rules* (Littleton, Colo.: Fred B. Rothman & Co., 1982), 279–307.

42. Mansfield, *Legal Rights,* 273–274; Wilson, *Works,* 599; *Mason v. Mason,* 1 Edw. Ch. 278 (N.Y. Ch. 1831).

43. *Helms v. Franciscus,* 2 Bland Ch. at 561–562; Wilson, *Works,* 602.

44. James Willard Hurst, *The Growth of American Law: The Law Makers* (1950), 199–246; Jacob Katz Cogan, "The Look Within: Property, Capacity, and Suffrage in Nineteenth Century America," *Yale Law Journal* 107 (1997): 473–498. From the time of the Revolution, state legislatures had asserted a constitutional capacity to make new law, to change inherited bodies of law and practice. Gordon Wood, *The Radicalism of the American Revolution* (New York: Vintage, 1991), 169–189. Until the 1840s, though, the characteristic legislative product was modest.

45. Richard H. Chused, "Married Women's Property Acts," *Georgetown Law Journal* 71 (1983): 1359–1425; Elizabeth Warbasse, *The Changing Legal Rights of Married Women, 1800–1861* (New York: Garland, 1987).

46. In New York, the constitutional measure was defeated, although the married women's property act the New York legislature passed in 1848 became a model statute throughout the nation. Norma Basch, *In the Eyes of the Law: Women, Marriage, and Property in Nineteenth-Century New York* (Ithaca: Cornell University Press, 1982); Peggy A. Rabkin, *Fathers to Daughters: The Legal Foundations of Female Emancipation* (Westport, Conn.: Greenwood Press, 1980). In Wisconsin, the measure was included

in the 1846 draft constitution, which then went on to defeat by the voters. The 1848 constitution included no such measure, but the new state legislature passed a married women's property act as one of its first acts. Catherine B. Cleary, "Married Women's Property Rights in Wisconsin, 1846–1872," *Wisconsin Magazine of History* 78, no. 2 (Winter 1994–1995): 110–137. In California and Indiana, measures won.

47. *Indiana Convention*, 474.

48. Ibid., 462–469.

49. Ibid., 1189.

50. *New York Debates and Proceedings*, 907–908. This speech was much reproduced. See, e.g. Quaife, *The Struggle over Ratification*, 404–409, 421.

51. Lucy Stone and Henry B. Blackwell, *Loving Warriors: Selected Letters of Lucy Stone and Henry B. Blackwell, 1853 to 1893*, ed. Leslie Wheeler (New York: Dial Press, 1981), 135–136; J. Ross Browne, *Report of the Debates in the Convention of California on the Formation of the State Constitution, in September and October 1849* (Washington: J. T. Towers, 1850), 265.

52. *Indiana Convention*, 498–499.

53. *New York Debates and Proceedings*, 907. See Browne, *California Convention*, 267–269; Milo M. Quaife, ed., *The Convention of 1846* (Madison, Wis.: State Historical Society, 1919), 631. O'Conor was the lawyer for Mrs. Forrest in the Forrest divorce case and represented several other wives in prominent New York divorce cases.

54. Quaife, *The Struggle over Ratification*, 593. The image of breeches or pantaloons was also used to represent male identities that might be put on by a wife. See ibid., 564–574, 602–604; *Indiana Convention*, 1161–1166. On spritual and sexual union, see Karen Lystra, *Searching the Heart: Women, Men, and Romantic Love in Nineteenth-Century America* (New York: Oxford University Press, 1989).

55. Mansfield, *Legal Rights*, 270, 306–310.

56. Blackstone, *Commentaries*, 1*443–445. What is missing are passages describing the property rights a husband acquired by marriage, his remedies against those who interfered or trespassed on his marital rights, and an expanded consideration of a wife's criminal responsibility. Ibid., 2:*433–436; 3:*139–140; 4: 28–30.

57. At the same time, Blackstone conceded she could be indicted and punished for criminal offenses, for her marriage was only "a civil union" that did not absolve her of responsibility to obey the law. For reformers this concession was crucial. It signaled Blackstone's own awareness that marriage in the law was a merely human institution, subject to reform and reconceptualization. See Hurlbut, *Human Rights*, 2.

58. Kent, *Commentaries*, 109. See Joseph Story, *Commentaries on Equity Juris-*

prudence as Administered in England and America, 2d ed. (London: A. Maxwell, 1839), 2: 622–659; John Joseph Powell, *Essay upon the Law of Contracts and Agreements* (Dublin: Chamberlaine and Rice, 1790), 59. Even in 1870, James Schouler began his discussion of coverture and marriage with an extended paraphrase of Blackstone. Schouler, *Domestic Relations*, 51.

59. Sarah Grimké, *Letters on the Equality of the Sexes and Other Essays*, ed. Elizabeth Ann Bartlett (New Haven: Yale, 1988), 71–77; Stone and Blackwell, *Loving Warriors*, 136. The Seneca Falls Convention included a reading of the relevant passages of Blackstone on coverture. See Nancy Gale Isenberg, "'Co-Equality of the Sexes': The Feminist Discourse of the Antebellum Women's Rights Movement in America" (Ph.D. diss., University of Wisconsin—Madison, 1990), 53.

60. See Peregrine Bingham, *The Law of Infancy and Coverture* (Burlington, Vt.: Chauncey Goodrich, 1849); Reeve, *Baron and Femme*; James Clancy, *A Treatise of the Rights, Duties and Liabilities of Husband and Wife, at Law and in Equity*, 2d ed. (American), from the last London ed. (New York: Law Press, 1837); R. S. Donnison Roper, *A Treatise on the Law of Property Arising from the Relation between Husband and Wife*, vol. 2 (New York: Stephen Gould and Son, 1824).

61. Blackstone, *Commentaries*, 1:*443–445; E. P. W. Packard, *Modern Persecution, or Insane Asylums Unveiled, as Demonstrated by the Report of the Investigating Committee of the Legislature of Illinois*, vol. 1 (Hartford: Case, Lockwood & Brainard, 1875), 70–71. A legitimate child who had lost her or his father might be called an "orphan," even if the child's mother still lived. See *Report of the Second Trial of Silas E. Burrows, for the Alleged Seduction of Mary Crew: In the Superior Court of the City of New York, before Chief Justice Jones* (New York: Bell, 1834), 43–44.

62. Blackstone, *Commentaries*, 1:*54–55. Elisha P. Hurlbut quoted this passage as his starting point for his libertarian critique of all legal rules—in particular those affecting marriage—that were not declaratory of natural rights. Hurlbut, *Human Rights*, 2. Early treatises described the wife's incapacities "in consideration of law" or "by policy of law." Roper, *Treatise*, 2:97–98; Powell, *Essay*, 59.

63. See Danaya C. Wright, "From Feudalism to Family Law: Inter-Spousal Custody Disputes and Repudiation of Mother's Rights" (Ph.D. diss., Johns Hopkins University, 1998).

64. Lawrence Stone, *Road to Divorce: England 1530–1987* (Oxford: Oxford University Press, 1990), 27; Martin Ingram, *Church Courts, Sex and Marriage in England, 1570–1640* (Cambridge: Cambridge University Press, 1987). A very high percentage of nonelite English couples, even after

Lord Hardwicke's Act of 1753, were "married" in ways that would not be recognized by the royal courts. See Stephen Parker, *Informal Marriage, Cohabitation and the Law 1750–1989* (New York: St. Martin's Press, 1990).

65. See Amy Louise Erickson, *Women and Property in Early Modern England* (London: Routledge, 1993).

66. Alan Macfarlane, *The Origins of English Individualism: The Family, Property and Social Transition* (New York: Cambridge University Press, 1978); Frederic William Maitland and Frederick Pollock, *The History of English Law before the Time of Edward I* (Cambridge, England: Cambridge University Press, 1968), 2:364–447.

67. Mary Beard, *Woman as Force in History* (New York: Persea, 1987), 77–105.

68. In New York, Chancellor Kent argued that his court of equity had assumed some of the "power over matrimonial causes" of the English ecclesiastical courts when the legislature granted it jurisdiction over divorces and judicial separations. *Wightman v. Wightman,* 4 Johns. Ch. 343 (N.Y. Ch. 1820). His successors as chancellor, however, rejected this interpretation and insisted that the chancellor's jurisdiction was not founded on a reception of English law but on specific legislative mandates. *Burtis v. Burtis,* Hopk. Ch. 628 (N.Y. Ch. 1828).

69. William E. Nelson, *The Americanization of the Common Law* (Cambridge, Mass.: Harvard University Press, 1995), 65–175; Lawrence M. Friedman, *A History of American Law,* 2d ed. (New York: Simon and Schuster, 1985), 107–156; Hendrik Hartog, "The Public Law of a County Court: Judicial Government in Eighteenth Century Massachusetts," *American Journal of Legal History* 20 (May 1976): 282–329.

70. Marylynn Salmon, *Women and the Law of Property in Early America* (Chapel Hill: University of North Carolina Press, 1986); Stanley N. Katz, "The Politics of Law in Colonial America: Controversies over Chancery Courts and Equity Law in the Eighteenth-Century," *Perspectives in American History* 5 (1971): 257.

71. Michael Grossberg, *Governing the Hearth: Law and the Family in Nineteenth-Century America* (Chapel Hill: University of North Carolina, 1985).

72. Indeed, as Beard herself revealed, their reliance on Blackstone was consistent with the beliefs and practices of most contemporary lawyers. Beard, *Woman as Force in History,* 108–113.

73. See Anonymous, "Facetiousness of the Law. Husband and Wife," *The New York Legal Observer* 3 (March 1845): 155–156.

74. Lucy Stone and Antoinette Brown Blackwell, *Friends and Sisters: Letters between Lucy Stone and Antoinette Brown Blackwell, 1846–93,* ed. Carol

Lasser and Marlene Deahl Merrill (Urbana-Champaign: University of Illinois Press, 1987), 56.

75. See Hurlbut, *Human Rights*, 57. See likewise Elizabeth Cady Stanton's 1854 speech to the joint judiciary committee of the New York legislature, in Beth Waggenspack, ed., *The Search for Self-Sovereignty: The Oratory of Elizabeth Cady Stanton* (New York: Greenwood Press, 1989), 101–102.

76. Anonymous, *The Laws Respecting Women, As They Regard Their Natural Rights, Or Their Connections and Conduct* (London: J. Johnson, 1777), 55.

77. Packard, *Modern Persecution*, vol. 1, at 39–41.

78. When, for example, could a wife sue in her own name? A separating or separated wife had no such right, needed a *prochein ami*, a next friend, a legal representative answerable for her costs if she could not sustain her allegations of ill treatment by her husband. *Wood v. Wood*, 2 Wend. 357 (N.Y. 1831), affirming *Wood v. Wood*, 2 Paige Ch. 454 (N.Y. Ch. 1831); *Garlick v. Strong and Garlick*, 3 Paige Ch. 440 (N.Y. Ch. 1832). In *Hay v. Warren*, 8 Paige Ch. 609 (N.Y. Ch. 1841), Walworth held that Mrs. Hay, the wife of a lunatic and drunkard who had recently abandoned her, had no right to bring suit against the committee appointed under the lunacy law to care for her husband's person and estate.

79. *Fenner v. Lewis*, 10 Johns. 38 (N.Y. Sup. Ct. 1813); *M'Cutchen v. M'Gahey*, 11 Johns. 281 (N.Y. Sup. Ct. 1814); *M'Gahey v. Williams*, 12 Johns. 293 (N.Y. Sup. Ct. 1815); *Sykes v. Halstead*, 3 N.Y. Super. (1 Sand.) 483 (N.Y. Super. Ct. 1848); *Pomeroy v. Wells*, 8 Paige Ch. 406 (N.Y. Ch. 1840); *Hay v. Warren*, 8 Paige Ch. 609 (N.Y. Ch. 1841).

80. *Ross v. Singleton*, 1 Bates 149 (Del. Ch. 1821). See John C. Miller, *The Federalist Era, 1789–1801* (New York: Harper and Row, 1960), 147.

81. See *Dutton v. Jackson*, 2 Bates 86 (Del. Ch. 1840).

82. *Ross*, 1 Bates 149. The chancellor was obviously uncomfortable with his decision and noted that he would be "extremely willing" to change his mind if new facts were forthcoming. Evidently Ross got the message, and in 1823 the chancellor granted the request for an injunction because a case of "intentional fraud" had been made out. One presumes that Ross was able to demonstrate that Sarah knew all along that Joseph was alive. Ibid., 156.

83. *Ratcliff v. Wales*, 1 Hill 63 (N.Y. Sup. Ct. 1841). My reading of divorce trial transcripts reveals no challenges to a wife's testimony, even though many a wife would eventually lose her suit for divorce and "return" to the status of a feme covert.

84. Hartog, "Public Law of a County Court."

85. *Overseers of the Poor of the Town of Sherburne v. Overseers of the Poor of the Town of Norwich*, 16 Johns. 186 (N.Y. Sup. Ct. 1819). Conversely, by mar-

riage, a man might gain a settlement in the town of his wife's birth if at the time of marriage she owned property in the town. What was hers became his. *Overseers of the Poor of the Town of Whitestown v. Overseers of the Poor of the Town of Constable,* 14 Johns. 469 (N.Y. Sup. Ct. 1817).

86. *Overseers of the Poor of the Town of Otsego v. Overseers of the Poor of the Town of Smithfield,* 5 Cow. 760 (N.Y. Sup. Ct. 1827).

87. See Robert William Fogel and Stanley L. Engerman, "Philanthropy at Bargain Prices: Notes on the Economics of Gradual Emancipation," *Journal of Legal Studies* 3, no. 2 (June 1974): 377–401.

88. Why didn't the child's own place of birth become her settlement? The court ignored the question. According to Reeve, the child's place of birth would become his or her place of settlement if neither father nor mother had any settlement. If, on the other hand, his or her father had one, it would become the child's as well. But if the father had none but the mother did, the mother's settlement became the child's. Reeve, *Baron and Femme,* 434.

89. *Overseers of the Poor of the Town of Marbletown v. Overseers of the Poor of the Town of Kingston,* 20 Johns. 1 (N.Y. Sup. Ct. 1822).

90. *People ex rel. Ordronaux v. Chegaray and Condert,* 18 Wend. 637, 642 (N.Y. Sup. Ct. 1836); *People v. Mercein,* 3 Hill 63, 74 (N.Y. Sup. Ct. 1840). The chancellor also allowed the wife's testimony in *People v. Mercein,* 8 Paige Ch. 47, 50–52 (N.Y. Ch. 1839). See Reeve, *Baron and Femme,* 298–299; *People v. Carpenter,* 9 Barb. 580 (N.Y. Sup. Ct. 1850); *Forrest v. Forrest,* 10 Barb. 46 (N.Y. Sup. Ct. 1850), 25 N.Y.R. 501 (1862).

91. *Clagett v. Gibson,* 5 Fed. Cases 808 (D.C. Cir. 1828), offers a poignant example. Phillis Clagett, a slave, petitioned for her freedom and the freedom of her children. Their master, Gerard Gibson, was being sued for alimony by his separated wife Ann when he recorded a deed of manumission to take effect on his death. He died a year later while his wife's suit was still pending. His slaves demanded their freedom. But his wife argued that she had become Gerard's creditor the minute she went to court to demand maintenance or alimony, and the deed of manumission had been an attempt to defraud her. The court agreed and so instructed the jury. Phillis Clagett and her children remained enslaved.

92. Stone and Blackwell, *Loving Warriors,* 108–111.

93. H. N. Hudson, *Lectures on Shakspeare* [sic] (New York: Charles Scribner, 1848), 302–303, 333–345.

5. Acting Like a Husband

1. The right to recapture and restrain and confine a wife was understood as a logical corollary of the law of coverture, but treatise writers could point

to only one modern English case where the right was sustained. *In re Cochrane*, 8 Dowl., P.C. 630 (Q.B. 1840). Writs of habeas corpus and actions for enticement and alienation of affections, all of which had more tangible presence in the law, might be brought against a woman as well as against a man if the woman were a fully competent legal actor (that is, not a wife or an infant).

2. On the explosive growth in recorded crim. con. cases in England, see Lawrence Stone, *Road to Divorce: England 1530–1987* (Oxford: Oxford University Press, 1990), 231–300; Susan Staves, "Money for Honor: Damages for Criminal Conversation," *Studies in Eighteenth-Century Culture* 11 (1982): 279–297; Peter Wagner, "Trial Reports as a Genre of Eighteenth-Century Erotica," *British Journal for Eighteenth-Century Studies* 5, no. 1 (Spring 1982): 117–121. American publishers often reprinted the English trials.

3. Tapping Reeve, *The Law of Baron and Femme, of Parent and Child, Guardian and Ward, Master and Servant, and of the Powers of the Courts of Chancery; with an Essay on the Terms Heir, Heirs, Heirs of the Body*, ed. Amasa J. Parker and Charles Baldwin (Albany: William Gould, 1862), 139.

4. *Trial of James Berrian, for Criminal Conversation with Catherine Blakney, Wife of Jacob Blakney, Had in the Mayor's Court of the City of New-York, in the Term of July, 1807* (New York, 1807); John Andrew Graham, *Speeches, Delivered at the City-Hall of the City of New York, in the Courts of Oyer and Terminer, Common Pleas and General Sessions of the Peace* (New York: M'Gillda and Co., 1812), 9–11. The verdict may have been set aside. See *George Parker vs. Alexander M'Dougall, Being an Action for Crim. Con. Tried at the Present Sitting of the Mayor's Court, before the Recorder of the City of New-York, on Wednesday, the 19th of October, 1808* (New York: H. C. Southwick, 1808).

5. *Parker v. M'Dougall*, 22.

6. *William Jeffers vs. John Tyson, Being an Action for Crim. Con. (Common Pleas, October 28, 1808)* (New York, 1808), 20–22.

7. Lawyers' arguments to juries often played on husbands' uncertain control of wives. "You," declaimed John Graham in one closing statement, "dare not, by your verdict, . . . set at nought the marriage covenant, and make your wives commoners of lust and intemperate passion." Graham, *Speeches*, 24.

8. Stone, *Road to Divorce*, 231–300; Staves, "Money for Honor." On early modern statecraft, see Albert O. Hirschman, *The Passions and the Interests: Political Arguments for Capitalism before Its Triumph* (Princeton: Princeton University Press, 1977).

9. Only crim. con. and bigamy prosecutions required actual proof of a marriage ceremony. Reeve, *Baron and Femme*, 140–141. See *People v.*

Humphrey, 7 Johns. 314 (N.Y. Sup. Ct. 1810) (bigamy); Joel Prentiss Bishop, *Commentaries on the Law of Marriage and Divorce, of Separations without Divorce, and of the Evidence of Marriage in All Issues; Embracing Also Pleading, Practice, and Evidence in Divorce Causes, with Forms,* vol. 1 (Boston: Little, Brown and Co., 1864), 425.

10. *Torre v. Summers,* 2 Nott and McCord 267, 271–272 (S.C. 1820). The theory that justified introducing such evidence was that a wife's bad reputation depreciated her husband's loss. Courts allowed juries to consider such evidence only in mitigation of damages, not in determining guilt. Still, if a husband had "connived" in his wife's sexual conduct, if he had pimped for her, there would be no guilt at all. On the other hand, if the wife did so against his wishes, her reputation would be relevant to the size of the damages but not to liability itself. Reeve, *Baron and Femme,* 140–141; *Sanborn v. Neilson,* 4 N.H. 501, 510–511 (1828); *Cook v. Wood,* 30 Ga. 891 (1860).

11. *Norton v. Warner,* 9 Conn. 172, 174 (1832); *Van Vacter v. McKillip,* 7 Blackf. 578, 581 (Ind. 1845); *Smith v. Masten,* 15 Wend. 270, 273 (N.Y. Sup. Ct. 1836).

12. Stone, *Road to Divorce,* 266–267; John Joseph Powell, *Essay upon the Law of Contracts and Agreements* (Dublin: Chamberlaine and Rice, 1790), 318–319.

13. *Fry v. Drestler,* 2 Yeates 278 (Pa. 1798); Reeve, *Baron and Femme,* 174–175 (but see note of 1862 editors); James Kent, *Commentaries on American Law,* vol. 2 (New York: O. Halsted, 1827), 178. See the defense arguments of Henry Lauren Clinton in *Brown v. Davidson* (1860) and *Millspaugh v. Adams* (1865); also, his argument for the plaintiff in *Favre v. Monvoisin* (1873). Clinton, *Extraordinary Cases* (New York: Harper, 1899), 223–251, 281–341, 573–599.

14. *Torre,* 2 Nott and McCord at 269, 270; *Smith v. Masten,* 15 Wend. at 272.

15. *Sanborn v. Neilson,* 4 N.H. at 508 (Bell, for the defendant). See *Cook v. Wood,* 30 Ga. 891 (1860); also the argument of William Sampson in *Jeffers v. Tyson,* 20–22. In the South, the shameful intimation was posed more strongly. See, e.g., *An Authenticated Report of the Trial of Myers and Others, for the Murder of Dudley Marvin Hoyt* (New York: Richards and Co., 1846); Bertram Wyatt-Brown, *Southern Honor* (New York: Oxford University Press, 1982).

16. H. D., "The Domestic Constitution—Criminal Constitution," *The New York Legal Observer* 8, no. 1 (January 1850): 1–6. Oddly, Elisha P. Hurlbut, the woman's rights advocate, made an even stronger case against criminal conversation, one that combined the discourse of honor with the requirements of a public code of justice. Hurlbut, *Essays on Human*

Rights and Their Political Guaranties, ed. George Coombe (Edinburgh: Maclachlan, Stewart, & Co., 1847), 44–49.

17. This possessory right would soon become a reactive foundation for the enormous body of feminist writing that took sexual possession (and the inability to refuse sex or to refuse childbearing) as definitive of domestic servitude and of the absence of self-ownership. See Sarah Grimké, *Letters on the Equality of the Sexes and Other Essays,* ed. Elizabeth Ann Bartlett (New Haven: Yale, 1988), 138–153. See generally Linda Gordon, *Woman's Body, Woman's Right,* rev. ed. (New York: Penguin, 1990).

18. Dower was the model, and the most common problem, but there were any number of other situations where a husband, in managing property or resources, required the formal acknowledgment or release or participation of his wife. For example: if he sold the property he managed for her by right of curtesy, or if they lived in a community property state like California, where all property of the marriage was presumptively held in common, although under the husband's managerial control, or if property was held as tenancy by the entireties.

19. Two things had to occur (at least after 1285) to bar a wife's right to dower: her voluntary abandonment of her husband and the fact of adultery. Neither alone was enough. Richard R. Powell, *The Law of Real Property* (Matthew Bender & Co., 1950), *216.

20. Her personal property, that is, her clothing, her furniture, her things, as well as her stock certificates, all became his automatically and absolutely as soon as they wed, unless she (or her family) had used a separate use agreement and the resulting trust to cut short a husband's curtesy rights.

21. Morton Horwitz, *The Transformation of American Law* (Cambridge, Mass.: Harvard University Press, 1977), 56–58; Joan Hoff, *Law, Gender, and Injustice: A Legal History of U.S. Women* (New York: New York University Press, 1991), 106–115; Marylynn Salmon, *Women and the Law of Property in Early America* (Chapel Hill: University of North Carolina Press, 1986), 163–168.

22. See *Carson v. Murray,* 3 Paige Ch. 483 (N.Y. Ch. 1832); *Garlick v. Strong and Garlick,* 3 Paige Ch. 440 (N.Y. Ch. 1832). It also became the subject of judically ordered separations or divorces à mensa et thoro. See *Miller v. Miller,* 6 Johns. Ch. 91 (N.Y. Ch. 1822). As late as 1850, dower remained a vested right that survived divorce if the husband were held to be the one at fault. *Wait v. Wait,* 4 N.Y. 95 (1850).

23. For two early American examples, see *Govane's Case,* 2 Bland Ch. 570 (Md. Ch. 1750–1752)(case reported in footnote to *Helms v. Franciscus,* 2 Bland Ch. 544), and Laurel Ulrich, *Good Wives* (New York: Oxford University Press, 1982), 23–24.

24. Elisha Hurlbut used the ineffectuality of the separate examination as an argument for separate property rights for women. Hurlbut, *Human Rights,* 59–60. Reeve, on the other hand, offered a limited defense of separate examinations as ratifying the law's concern with a husband's potential coercion. Reeve, *Baron and Femme,* 196–199.

25. See, e.g., *Boykin v. Rain,* 28 Ala. 332, 65 Am. Dec. 349 (1856).

26. See *Dacy v. New York Chemical Manufacturing Company,* 2 Hall's 550 (N.Y. Super. Ct. 1829); *Ogden v. Prentice,* 33 Barb. 160 (N.Y. Sup. Ct. 1860). How far would the presumption of trust go? At what point would a husband's liability for his wife's acts cease? The traditional answer: at the point when she was no longer acting "as wives, according to the usage of the country," ought to act. A wife who bought food fell on the right side of the line. But if she tried to buy a ship or a yoke of oxen, no presumption. Of course, if the husband were in "foreign parts" or separated, then, "necessarily," she would acquire a "more than ordinary power" to bind him. Reeve, *Baron and Femme,* 157–158.

27. *Robinson v. Reynolds,* 1 Aikens 174 (Vt. 1826). See *Gregory v. Pierce,* 4 Met. 478 (Mass. 1842).

28. *Woodward v. Murray,* 18 Johns. 400 (N.Y. Sup. Ct. 1820).

29. On custody, see Chapter 7. *Kettletas v. Gardner,* 1 Paige Ch. 488 (N.Y. Ch. 1829). A second reason to remove Mrs. Gardner as guardian was that her niece had just married. According to the chancellor, the authority of a guardian over a female ward ended with her marriage; control of her person now belonged to her husband. See *Badgley v. Decker,* 44 Barb. 577 (N.Y. Sup. Ct. 1865); Reeve, *Baron and Femme,* 471. See Silas Burrows's defense in *Report of the Second Trial of Silas E. Burrows, for the Alleged Seduction of Mary Crew: In the Superior Court of the City of New York, before Chief Justice Jones* (New York: Bell, 1834), 19–20.

30. Further, it required that the treasurer be an unmarried woman who could give bond for herself. Lori D. Ginzberg, *Women and the Work of Benevolence: Morality, Politics, and Class in the Nineteenth-Century United States* (New Haven: Yale University Press, 1990), 48–54.

31. William Warren Sweet, ed., *Religion on the American Frontier: The Baptists, 1783–1830* (New York: Henry Holt and Company, 1936), 370–371. There was no quicker way to identify one's radicalism than to reject the traditional rules of representation. See Fanny Wright's 1826 "Deed of Trust," which included the following instructions concerning the admission of new members to her utopian community at Nashoba: "[T]he admission of a husband will not carry along with it the admission of a wife. . . . [E]ach admission shall . . . be strictly individual." Julia C. Ott, "Slavery, Sex, and Sorority: Frances Wright's Nashoba Experiment in Ten-

nessee" (senior thesis, Princeton University, 1997), 49 (quoting Shelby County Register, Book B, Deed of Trust, 82, 86).

32. *The New Whole Duty of Man*, 227, quoted in Alan Macfarlane, *Marriage and Love in England* (Oxford, U.K.: Basil Blackwell, 1986), 176.

33. Even slaveholders recognized that a slave wife owed obedience to her slave husband. See J. W. Page, *Uncle Robin in His Cabin in Virginia and Tom without One in Boston* (Richmond, Va.: J. W. Randolph, 1853), 152–153.

34. A father's right to recover against his daughter's seducer was variously and controversially understood as a father's right to his daughter's labor and/or his right to profit from her marriage. Lea VanderVelde, "The Legal Ways of Seduction," *Stanford Law Review* 48, no. 4 (April 1996): 817–901. The responsibility of stepfathers for their wives' children from earlier marriages was an unsettled question throughout the nineteenth century. See *Whispell v. Whispell*, 4 Barb. 217 (N.Y. Sup. Ct. 1848). According to Kent, from the moment a husband took a wife's child into his own house, he was understood as standing in loco parentis and was responsible for the maintenance and education of the child. Kent, *Commentaries*, 161–162.

35. *Maguinay v. Saudek*, 5 Sneed 146 (Tenn. 1857).

36. Edward Deering Mansfield, *The Legal Rights, Liabilities and Duties of Women* (Salem, Mass.: J. P. Jewett & Co., 1845), 271.

37. Rollin C. Hurd, *A Treatise on the Right of Personal Liberty, and on the Writ of Habeas Corpus and the Practice Connected with It: A View of the Law of Extradition of Fugitives*, 2d ed. (1858; Albany: W. C. Little & Co., 1876), 25.

38. Hurd, *Personal Liberty*, 28–40. *In re Cochrane*, 8 Dowl., P.C. 630 (Q.B. 1840), was the English case. For the story of one husband's unsuccessful effort to confine his wife, see Hendrik Hartog, "Mrs. Packard on Dependency," *Yale Journal of Law and the Humanities* 1, no. 1 (December 1988): 79–104.

39. *People v. Mercein*, 8 Paige Ch. 47, 65–68 (N.Y. Ch. 1839).

40. Zephaniah Swift, *A System of the Laws of the State of Connecticut* (Windham: John Byrne, 1795), 201–202; Reeve, *Baron and Femme*, 141–143.

41. Hurd, *Personal Liberty*, 34.

42. Mansfield, *Legal Rights*, 271, 273–274.

43. Nancy Gale Isenberg, "'Co-Equality of the Sexes': The Feminist Discourse of the Antebellum Women's Rights Movement in America" (Ph.D. diss., University of Wisconsin—Madison, 1990), 145–150; Elizabeth Clark, "Religion, Rights, and Difference in the Early Woman's Rights Move-

ment," *Wisconsin Women's Law Journal* 3 (1987): 29–58; Hoff, *Law, Gender, and Injustice,* 138–140; Grimke, *Letters,* 71, 77, 78.

44. She thought about the conflict between the passage (Ephesians, 22) and obedience to Christ and decided, predictably, that all churches must have abandoned the passage since "all encouraged wives to join their communion with or without the consent of their husbands." Jane Grey Swisshelm, *Half a Century,* 2d ed. (Chicago: Jansen, 1880), 66–68. On Packard, see Hartog, "Mrs. Packard on Dependency."

45. Swisshelm, *Half a Century,* 72–73.

46. Warren Chase, well on his way in the 1830s toward a lifelong commitment to socialism and woman's rights, still assumed that his new bride would naturally give up her Baptist beliefs and instead adopt "the more rational religion of her husband." Warren Chase, *The Life-Line of the Lone One; or, Autobiography of the World's Child* (Boston: William White & Co., 1868), 71.

47. *Lawrence v. Lawrence,* 3 Paige Ch. 267, 272 (N.Y. Ch. 1832).

48. Clark, "Religion, Rights, and Difference"; Hartog, "Mrs. Packard on Dependency."

49. Swisshelm, *Half a Century,* 42–53.

50. *Mason v. Mason,* 1 Edw. Ch. 278 (N.Y. Ch. 1831). Jane Swisshelm acknowledged her disobedience and "cheerfully" accepted being divorced by her husband and her "legal guilt." Swisshelm, *Half a Century,* 168.

51. This is an explicit theme in Michael Grossberg, *A Judgment for Solomon* (Cambridge, U.K.: Cambridge University Press, 1996). Jane Swisshelm, who described herself as having cheerfully accepted her husband's right to divorce her because of her disobedience and desertion, also insisted on her right to the custody of her children, a right she declared willing to "defend to the death." Swisshelm, *Half a Century,* 165.

52. In 1879 the editor of the *Albany Law Review* (20:262) commented on the use of this passage in a Pennsylvania custody case, *Snyder v. Snyder:* "This, which Shakespeare puts into the mouth of a woman, is poetry, but at the same time law." See H. N. Hudson, *Lectures on Shakspeare* vol. 1 (New York: Charles Scribner, 1848), 231–233. On the other hand, an 1888 burlesque, in which Kate turns the tables on Petruchio and gains a life that is free, signals the standard modern understanding: "I thought the libretto called for submission. There's been a conspiracy in the intermission." John Kendrick Bangs, "Katherine: A Travesty," in *Nineteenth-Century Shakespeare Burlesques,* American Shakespeare Travesties (1852–1888), vol. 5, ed. Stanley Wells (London: Diploma Press Limited, 1978), 299.

53. See *Burr v. Burr,* 10 Paige Ch. 20 (N.Y. Ch. 1842), affirmed, 7 Hill 207

(N.Y. Ct. of Errors, 1843), for a full-scale debate on the boundaries of this principle. See also *Barlow v. Heine* (New York City Ct. of Common Pleas), reported in *Law Reporter* 3 (1843): 453, and in *New York Herald,* February 4, 1842.

54. See *Burr,* 10 Paige Ch. 20, affirmed, 7 Hill 207; *Denton v. Denton,* 1 Johns. Ch. 364 (N.Y. Ch. 1815); and *Fabre v. Colden,* 1 Paige Ch. 166 (N.Y. Ch. 1828).

55. *Maguinay v. Saudek,* 5 Sneed 146 (Tenn. 1857).

56. When a wife applied for poor relief, the question became more complicated. In 1854 the New York Supreme Court held, in a case that presaged *McGuire,* that overseers of the poor had no business ordering a husband to support his wife, so long as they were not separated formally. Doing so constituted an intervention into the private sphere of marriage. *Norton v. Rhodes,* 18 Barb. 100 (N.Y. Sup. Ct. 1854). That case was criticized and eventually overruled. *Goodale v. Lawrence,* 88 N.Y. 516 (1882).

57. Anonymous, *A Treatise of Feme Coverts: Or, the Lady's Law* (1732; South Hackensack, N.J.: Rothman, 1974), 91. The English law is summarized in James Clancy, *A Treatise of the Rights, Duties and Liabilities of Husband and Wife, at Law and in Equity,* 2d ed. (American), from the last London ed. (New York: Law Press, 1837), 24–47. See Reeve, *Baron and Femme,* 164. A husband's continuing duty to provide necessaries was sharply distinguished from his wife's implied or express agency to purchase goods on his account, which could be cut off. See *Cromwell v. Benjamin,* 41 Barb. 558 (N.Y. Sup. Ct. 1863).

58. 1 Sid. 109, 1 Mod. Rep. 124 (Ex. Ch. 1659), reprinted in Anonymous, *Lady's Law,* 177–200. The clearest picture of the English law in the early nineteenth century, including its continued reliance on *Manby,* can be found in Clancy, *Treatise,* 23–47. See argument of George Wood, *Henry D. Cruger vs. George Douglas & William Douglas, Trustees of Mrs. Harriet D. Cruger* (New York: Herald Book and Job Printing Office, 1844), 22–23.

59. Anonymous, *Lady's Law,* 183–186.

60. Reeve, *Baron and Femme,* 161. Kent, on the other hand, thought Hide's opinion no longer stated the prevailing rule. Kent, *Commentaries,* 123–127.

61. *M'Cutchen v. M'Gahey,* 11 Johns. 281 (N.Y. Sup. Ct. 1814); *M'Gahey v. Williams,* 12 Johns. 293 (N.Y. Sup. Ct. 1815). See *Hanberry v. Hanberry,* 29 Ala. 719 (1857).

62. Reeve, *Baron and Femme,* 162. See *Pomeroy v. Wells,* 8 Paige 609 (N.Y. Ch. 1840); Ariela R. Dubler, "Governing through Contract: Common Law Marriage in the Nineteenth Century," *Yale Law Journal* 107, no. 6 (April 1998): 1885–1920.

63. Reeve, *Baron and Femme,* 164; Lyman Beecher, *Autobiography,* ed. Barbara M. Cross (Cambridge, Mass: Harvard University Press, 1961), 1:162–163. Both Clancy's and Roper's treatises made the question whether a husband could be held responsible for his adulterous wife's necessaries depend on the circumstances. See Clancy, *Treatise,* 34; R. S. Donnison Roper, *A Treatise on the Law of Property Arising from the Relation between Husband and Wife,* vol. 2 (New York: Stephen Gould and Son, 1824), 117–118; *Howard v. Whetstone Township,* 10 Ohio 365 (1841).

64. See *Mott v. Comstock,* 8 Wend. 544 (N.Y. Sup. Ct. 1832); *Kimball v. Keyes,* 11 Wend. 33 (N.Y. Sup. Ct. 1833).

65. *Sykes v. Halstead,* 3 N.Y. Super. (1 Sandf.) 483, 484 (1848).

66. *Baker v. Barney,* 8 Johns. 72, 5 Am. Dec. 326 (N.Y. Sup. Ct. 1811). Such agreements usually included a release by the husband of the "fortune" the wife had brought to or inherited during the marriage.

67. *Helms v. Franciscus,* 2 Bland Ch. 544, 554–556, 558 (Md. Ch. 1830).

68. Ibid. at 557–558.

69. Ibid. at 562.

70. Ibid. at 578, 579.

71. Kent carried the principle farther than other chancellors. In *Kenny v. Udall,* 5 Johns. Ch. 464 (N.Y. Ch. 1821), he held that a wife's equity attached to her property whenever it became subject to the chancellor's jurisdiction, even if the property had been previously sold to a third party. Those who purchased from a husband, those who dealt in such property, had first to satisfy themselves that the husband was dealing fairly and justly with his wife. *Dumond v. Magee,* 4 Johns. Ch. 318 (N.Y. Ch. 1820), held that a man who had abandoned his wife, and married another, had abandoned all claims on his wife's personal property. Her equity became the whole of the property, all of which was put to her separate use. Kent suggested that equity courts ought to prevent husbands from using any legal means, either at law or in equity, to gain possession of their wives' property until husbands demonstrated that they had adequately provided for their wives. But he admitted that no court had ever gone so far as to interfere with a husband's legal rights outside of a court of equity. Kent, *Commentaries,* 117–118. For South Carolina, see Marylynn Salmon, "Woman and Property in South Carolina: The Evidence from Marriage Settlements, 1730 to 1830," *William and Mary Quarterly* 39 (October 1982): 655–686. A court of equity could also intervene to protect a husband's interest in his wife's property, forcing her to do equity. The circumstances rarely arose. But see *Martin v. Martin,* 1 N.Y. 473 (1848).

72. Anna had asked the court to give her full control over the property she had inherited. Bland, however, ruled that she could only receive income

from the property, and he denied her the right to convey the property during coverture (that is, for the rest of her husband's life). Anna and Lewis later joined together to petition the court to give her greater control over her property. The court refused. *Helms*, 2 Bland Ch. at 574–576, 580, 583–585.

73. Reeve, *Baron and Femme*, 70.

74. *Van Duzer v. Van Duzer*, 6 Paige Ch. 366 (N.Y. Ch. 1837). See also *Van Epps v. Van Deusen*, 4 Paige Ch. 64 (N.Y. Ch. 1833). Other New York decisions that appeared to limit the principle included *Dewall v. Covenhoven*, 5 Paige Ch. 581 (N.Y. Ch. 1836); *Holmes v. Holmes*, 3 Paige Ch. 363 (N.Y. Ch. 1832); *Fry v. Fry*, 7 Paige Ch. 461 (N.Y. Ch. 1839); and *Shirley v. Lambert*, 3 Edw. Ch. 336 (N.Y. Ch. 1839).

75. See *Carter v. Carter*, 1 Paige Ch. 463 (N.Y. Ch. 1829); *Van Duzer*, 6 Paige Ch. 366 (N.Y. Ch. 1837); *Smith v. Kane*, 2 Paige Ch. 303 (N.Y. Ch. 1830).

76. Jane Maria McManus Cazneau, pseudonym: Cora Montgomery, *Eagle Pass, or Life on the Border*, ed. Robert Crawford Cotner (1852; Austin: Pemberton Press, 1966), 153, 165–167.

77. Carole Pateman, *The Sexual Contract* (Stanford: Stanford University Press, 1988).

78. *Report of the Debates in the Convention of California on the Formation of the State Constitution in September and October 1849*, comp. J. Ross Browne (Washington, D.C.: J. T. Towers, 1850), 259–260. See Joel Prentiss Bishop, *Commentaries on the Law of Married Women Under the Statutes of the Several States, and at Common Law and in Equity* (Boston: Little, Brown, and Co., 1871–1875), 26–28. But see Nicholas St. John Green, "Married Women," *American Law Review* 6 (October 1871): 57–73.

6. Coercion and Harriet Douglas Cruger

1. See Duncan Kennedy, *Sexy Dressing Etc.* (Cambridge, Mass.: Harvard University Press, 1993), 63–125.

2. Alan S. Rosenbaum, *Coercion and Autonomy*, Contributions in Philosophy, no. 31 (New York: Greenwood Press, 1986); Alan Wertheimer, *Coercion* (Princeton, N.J.: Princeton University Press, 1987); Anne M. Coughlan, "Excusing Women," *California Law Review* 82, no. 1 (January 1994): 1–94.

3. William Blackstone, *Commentaries on the Laws of England*, ed. William Carey Jones (Baton Rouge: Claitor's Publishing Division, 1976), 1:*445. A much-reprinted note by Edward Christian concluded: "From this impartial statement . . . , I fear there is little reason to pay a compliment to our laws for their respect and favour to the female sex." See St. George

Tucker, *Blackstone's Commentaries: With Notes of Reference, to the Constitution and Laws, of the Federal Government of the United States; and of the Commonwealth of Virginia* (Philadelphia: Birch and Small, 1803), 2:445. James Kent ended his discussion of the law of marriage with a paragraph that reversed Blackstone, praising the civil law recognition of a wife's separate identity. Kent, *Commentaries on American Law,* vol. 2 (New York: O. Halsted, 1827), 157.

4. *Methodist Episcopal Church v. Jaques,* 3 Johns. Ch. 77 (N.Y. Ch. 1817); *Jaques v. Methodist Episcopal Church,* 17 Johns. 548 (N.Y. Ct. Err. 1817); John D. Jaques, appellant, *In the Court for the Trial of Impeachments and the Correction of Errors, John D. Jaques and Robert Jaques: Who Are Impleaded with Henry Cruger, Appellants, and the Trustees of the Methodist Episcopal Church in the City of New-York, & Others, Respondents, Case on the Part of the Appellants* (New York: W. H. Creagh, printer, 1818), 10, 86. The church also attacked Robert Jaques, John's brother, who had served as his adviser, as a "young man without visible property or responsibility," who had been "made" Mary's "trustee by the artful persuasion and influence of John D. Jaques." Ibid., 11. The case is discussed, from a somewhat different perspective, in Gregory S. Alexander, *Commodity and Propriety: Competing Visions of Property in American Legal Thought, 1776–1970* (Chicago: University of Chicago Press, 1997), 165–168.

5. See Jaques, *In the Court,* 76.

6. William Kent, ed., *Memoirs and Letters of James Kent, LL.D. Late Chancellor of the State of New York, Author of "Commentaries on American Law," Etc.* (Boston: Little, Brown, and Co. 1898), 159.

7. *Methodist Episcopal Church,* 3 Johns. Ch. 77, 86, 87.

8. Ibid., 3 Johns. Ch. at 88–90. Since the purposes were valid, such agreements were valid, even though they constituted restraints on alienation. The rule against such restraints was in this case merely a "technical" rule. Ibid. at 89.

9. This is the language of the church's lawyers. *Jaques,* 17 Johns. 548, 575 (argument of Harison and Jones).

10. *Methodist Episcopal Church,* 3 Johns. Ch. 77, 90, 92, 96, 105, 100–101. Kent argued that Lord Eldon, the English chancellor, agreed with him but felt bound by precedents. Ibid. at 110.

11. On Kent's politics, see John T. Horton, *James Kent: A Study in Conservatism, 1763–1847* (New York: D. Appleton-Century, 1939); John H. Langbein, "Chancellor Kent and the History of Legal Literature," *Columbia Law Review* 93, no. 3 (April 1993): 547–594.

12. Jaques, 17 Johns. 548, 582–585, 577–578.

13. Ibid., 17 Johns. at 583–584.

14. Ibid., 17 Johns. at 583–585, 577–578.

15. The Court of Errors' reversal of Kent's decision meant that a new master had to be assigned by a new chancellor. (In 1821 Kent was forced into retirement.) *Methodist Episcopal Church v. Jaques,* Hopk. Ch. 453, 459–460 (N.Y. Ch. 1824).

16. Kent, *Memoirs and Letters,* 185–186.

17. Kent, *Commentaries,* 139.

18. Peregrine Bingham, *The Law of Infancy and Coverture* (Burlington, Vt.: Chauncey Goodrich, 1849), 277–278; Joel Prentiss Bishop, *Commentaries on the Law of Married Women under the Statutes of the Several States, and at Common Law and in Equity* (Boston: Little, Brown and Co., 1871–1875), 1:663–666; Tapping Reeve, *The Law of Baron and Femme, of Parent and Child, Guardian and Ward, Master and Servant, and of the Powers of the Courts of Chancery; with an Essay on the Terms Heir, Heirs, Heirs of the Body,* ed. Amasa J. Parker and Charles Baldwin (Albany: William Gould, 1862), 266; James Schouler, *A Treatise on the Law of the Domestic Relations: Embracing Husband and Wife, Parent and Child, Guardian and Ward, Infancy, and Master and Servant,* 2d ed. (Boston: Little, Brown and Co., 1874), 241. Elisha P. Hurlbut critiqued Platt's reactionary sentiments. Hurlbut, *Essays on Human Rights and Their Political Guaranties,* ed. George Coombe (Edinburgh: Maclachlan, Stewart, & Co., 1847), 57–58.

19. Daniel D. Barnard, "A Discourse on the Life, Character and Public Services of Ambrose Spencer, late Chief Justice of the Supreme Court of New York: Delivered by Request before the Bar of the City of Albany, January 5, 1849," in *Memorial of Ambrose Spencer* (Albany: Joel Munsell, 1849), 74–76; Speech of Charles O'Conor in *Debates and Proceedings in the New-York State Convention, for the Revision of the Constitution,* ed. S. Croswell and R. Sutton (Albany: The Albany Argus, 1846), 907–908; "Marriage Settlements," *American Law Magazine* 3 (April and July 1844): 16–22; "Cruger v. Douglas," *New York Legal Observer* 4 (February 1846): 55–69.

20. See the remarks of "Agricola," in Milo M. Quaife, ed., *The Convention of 1846* (Madison, Wis.: State Historical Society, 1919); *Report of the Debates and Proceedings of the Convention for the Revision of the Constitution of the State of Indiana* (Indianapolis: A. H. Brown, 1850), 519–521. *See New York Times,* February 10, 1860, at 4 (on the 1860 earnings act).

21. See *North American Coal v. Dyett,* 7 Paige Ch. 9 (N.Y. Ch. 1837), affirmed, 20 Wend. 570 (N.Y. Ct. of Errors 1838); *Albany Fire Insurance v. Bay,* 4 Barb. 407, 413–414 (N.Y. Sup. Ct. 1848), affirmed, 4 Comst. 9 (N.Y. 1850); *Miller v. Newton,* 23 Cal. 554, 566–567 (1863); *Cheever v. Wilson,* 76 U.S. 108, 119 (1869); *Walker v. Beal,* 76 U.S. 743 (1870).

22. *Albany Fire Insurance v. Bay,* 4 Barb. 407, 413–415 (N.Y. Sup. Ct. 1848),

affirmed, 4 N.Y. 9 (1850); *Colvin v. Currier,* 22 Barb. 371, 380 (N.Y. Sup. Ct. 1856). But for some qualms, see *Noyes v. Blakeman,* 6 N.Y. 567, 581–582 (1852) (Watson, concurring).

23. *Cruger v. Cruger,* trial papers and pleadings (1844), New York University Law Library, 43–44; Angus Davidson, *Miss Douglas of New York* (London: Sidgwick and Jackson Limited, 1952), 100.

24. *Cruger Papers,* 44.

25. Ibid., 448–455.

26. This portion of her life is detailed in Davidson, *Miss Douglas,* 66–216.

27. *Cruger Papers,* 455–460.

28. Ibid., 45–46.

29. Ibid., 460–464.

30. Ibid., 46–47, 137, 467–468. See Davidson, *Miss Douglas,* 166–169.

31. *Cruger Papers,* 1–7. At least in one letter, Henry conceded that this gift was coupled with a stipulation that he should account to her for his expenditures. Ibid., 545–546.

32. Ibid., 47–48.

33. Ibid., 499–500.

34. Ibid., 520—521.

35. Ibid., 52–55, 496–501.

36. Ibid., 68–69.

37. Ibid., 541.

38. Ibid., 373–374, 407–408. See the sarcastic letter from Stephen Munn, ibid., 371–372.

39. *Ibid.,* 8–9.

40. *Ibid.,* 235, 549.

41. *Ibid.,* 547–548. Meanwhile, though, Henry was keeping a journal of "chance readings" emphasizing patriarchal readings of husbandly authority. Ibid., 549–550. At various times he exchanged similar texts with James Monroe. In July 1839, for example, Monroe sent Cruger a magazine that reprinted a letter from Patrick Henry to his daughter on her marriage, advising her to be perpetually submissive to her new husband. Ibid., 370–371.

42. Ibid., 564–566.

43. Ibid., 576–578, 386.

44. Harriet also let Monroe know that she did not regard him as a neutral arbiter (which he wasn't). Ibid., 74–75, 169. Monroe himself had had to sign a premarital agreement keeping all his wife's property outside of his control. See Davidson, *Miss Douglas,* 45–46.

45. On November 7, Monroe wrote Cruger, prematurely, that he was happy that a settlement had been agreed to. All that remained was the reconcili-

ation: "Write a kind letter to your Wife and say all that a generous man can afford to say to his Wife or to the sex even." *Cruger Papers*, 336.

46. Ibid., 583.

47. Ibid., 582–587, 590–592.

48. Ibid., 18.

49. Ibid., 409–414, 601–605. Harriet had recently learned that her husband had had an affair with a married woman in the 1820s, long before their marriage. In September, Bard wrote that he remained anxious that she insisted on Henry's religious conversion as a condition to the end of the separation. She answered that she didn't care about communion as such. But until he saw his "desperate errors," she would not put herself "in his power." Ibid., 434–435.

50. Bard congratulated Harriet for "coming up to all we expect of her." She had shown that she was "governed by higher motives than a love of money, or a love of oppression." Ibid., 430–434.

51. See Chapter 4 for William Whetten's response to his return.

52. *Cruger Papers*, 146–148.

53. Ibid., 31. Henry also wanted her trustees discharged for incompetence.

54. Ibid., 34–42. In *Hackney v. Hackney*, 8 Humph. 452 (Tenn. 1847), a husband succeeded in defeating his wife's suit for specific performance of his promise to let her keep her property (slaves) to her separate use. Joseph Hackney, like Henry Cruger, had convinced his wife not to make a prenuptial agreement because such a settlement violated "all his preconceived opinions concerning the anticipated relation of husband and wife; that it was calculated to impair the independence of the husband, and to subject them both to the strictures and animadversions of others."

55. *Cruger v. Douglas*, 4 Edw. Ch. 446, 552–553 (N.Y. Ch. 1844); argument of George Wood, *Henry D. Cruger vs. George Douglas & William Douglas, Trustees of Mrs. Harriet D. Cruger* (New York: Herald Book and Job Printing Office, 1844), 3032. In *Shepard v. Shepard*, 7 Johns. Ch. 57 (N.Y. Ch. 1823), Chancellor Kent had held that equity would, under particular circumstances, enforce a postnuptial settlement.

56. *Cruger v. Cruger*, 5 Barb. 225, 268, 269–271 (N.Y. Sup. Ct. 1849). The vice-chancellor's decision had been appealed to the new New York Supreme Court because the old chancellor's court of equity had been abolished by the state constitution of 1846. The new court was created as a court of law and equity. In his argument on behalf of Henry Cruger, George Wood interpreted *Jaques* to mean that courts of equity should only protect a wife's separate property "in harmony with that other great Common Law principle, that the Husband is to be the head of his own household." Wood, *Cruger v. Douglas*, 24.

57. "Cruger v. Douglas," *New York Legal Observer*. The New York Supreme Court made the division by giving Henry most of the income of Harriet's personal estate, leaving her with full control over her real estate. *Cruger v. Cruger*, 5 Barb. 225 (N.Y. Sup. Ct. 1849).

58. George Templeton Strong, *Diary*, ed. Allan Nevins and Milton Halsey Thomas (New York: Octogon Books, 1974), 4:131–132.

59. Davidson, *Miss Douglas*, 255.

60. 18 N.Y. 265 (1858). James Schouler described *Yale* as an "important" case that established new doctrine "under cover of legislative policy." The doctrine, Schouler recognized, contradicted New York's own precedents, by which he meant the Court of Errors' holding in *Jaques*. Schouler, *Domestic Relations*, 243.

61. 18 N.Y. 265, 269, 271, 272, 277, 284. Two years later, when the case came back for review on factual findings that Eliza Ann Dederer had "intended" to charge her separate estate, Judge Samuel Selden reaffirmed the court's earlier decision. Whatever her intentions, those intentions were not expressed in the writing, and therefore her separate estate could not be bound. Selden used his opinion as an opportunity to mimic Kent in providing a critical survey of the English precedents. He also analyzed the new 1860 statute that authorized wives to carry on trade or business on their own account. That statute, he concluded, had not removed a wife's common law disability to bind herself by her contracts. *Yale v. Dederer*, 22 N.Y. 450, 460 (1860). Seventeen years later, the case appeared again before the Court of Appeals. Chief Judge Sanford Church wrote for a unanimous court that, while he wished the rule in the case had been decided differently in favor of the wife's enlarged capacity under the statutes, the rule was "too long established" to be overturned judicially now. The problem should be referred to the legislature. *Yale v. Eliza Ann Dederer*, 68 N.Y. 329 (1877). The legislature did change the law in 1884 (c.384). See *Bank v. Sniffen*, 54 Hun 394 (N.Y. Sup. Ct. 1889).

For an indication of the centrality of *Yale v. Dederer*, see the opinion for the Wisconsin Supreme Court in *Todd v. Lee*, reprinted in *American Law Register* 1 (September 1862), 657–669, with a comment by Isaac F. Redfield. The opinion opens: "Before the case of *Yale v. Dederer* . . . , it was well settled in New York, if, in fact, anything can ever be said to be settled in that state . . ." In California, a state that formally had abandoned the whole structure of common law marital property rules and had committed itself constitutionally to a community property regime, *Jaques* and *Yale* were mobilized repeatedly by the state supreme court in cases that allowed wives to escape from contracted obligations. See *Selover v. American Russian Commercial Company*, 7 Cal. 266, 273 (1857), and *Miller v.*

Newton, 23 Cal. 554, 568 (1863). In *McLay v. Love,* the court's opinion quoted at length from *Yale.* In mid-opinion, however, the judge stopped himself, suddenly remembering that in California the "rights of the parties" had never been determined by common law or equity, had always been "fixed" by statute. He apologized to his readers for having been "educated under the double system of common and equity law." Yet, as if unable to break the hold of past legal socialization, he then immediately quoted again from *Yale.* 25 Cal. 367, 378–382 (1864).

62. *Gage v. Daughy,* 28 Barb. 622, 625–627, 629–630 (N.Y. Sup. Ct. 1859).

63. *Gage v. Daughy,* 34 N.Y. 293 (1866); *Knapp v. Smith,* 27 N.Y. 277 (1863). The issue was bound up with the merger of legal and equitable title achieved by the new statutes. Under the old rules, or at least the rules as defined in *Jaques,* a wife had equitable ownership as a feme sole while legally she remained a feme covert. Thus, a court could imagine that she owned land equitably yet remained her husband's dependent on the farm.

64. *Winans v. Peebles,* 31 Barb. 371, 374–378 (N.Y. Sup. Ct. 1860). See *White v. Wager,* 32 Barb. 250, 257–262 (N.Y. Sup. Ct. 1860) (Campbell, dissenting).

65. *White,* 32 Barb. at 253, 254–255, 257. See also *Graham v. Van Wyck,* 14 Barb. 531 (N.Y. Sup. Ct. 1851).

66. *White v. Wager,* 25 N.Y. 328, 329, 331, 332–333 (1862).

67. She was dead by the time of the suit, which was brought by her executor. *Boyd v. De La Montagnie,* 73 N.Y. 498, 500–501 (1878), affirming 1 Hun 696 (N.Y. Sup. Ct. 1874).

68. *Stickney v. Stickney,* 131 U.S. 227, 238–240 (1889).

69. *Garner v. Second National Bank,* 151 U.S. 420 (1894); *Allen v. LaVaud,* 213 N.Y. 322, 107 N.E. 570 (1915); *Estate of Brundage,* 185 Wis. 558 (1925). But see *Smith v. Hughes,* 292 Ky. 723, 167 S.W.2d 847 (1942), where the court held that the rule prohibiting a wife from conveying property directly to her husband had no place in modern jurisprudence. On continuing limits at mid-century, see Albert C. Jacobs and Julius Goebel, Jr., *Cases and Other Materials on Domestic Relations,* 3d ed. (Brooklyn: The Foundation Press, 1952), 680.

7. John Barry and American Fatherhood

1. Laura Edwards tells a more complicated story about what marriage meant to African-American women after the Civil War; they sometimes resisted marriage precisely because of its custodial implications. Laura F. Edwards, *"Gendered Strife and Confusion": The Politics of Reconstruction* (Urbana-Champaign: University of Illinois Press, 1997). See generally Eric

Foner, *Reconstruction, 1863–1877* (New York: Harper and Row, 1988), 85–98.

2. William Blackstone, *Commentaries on the Laws of England,* ed. William Carey Jones (Baton Rouge: Claitor's Publishing Division, 1976), 1:*453. By contrast, an unmarried father had no custodial rights; his bastards were legally fatherless. And to be a married mother was to be "entitled to no power, but only to reverence and respect."

3. Michael Grossberg, *Governing the Hearth: Law and the Family in Nineteenth-Century America* (Chapel Hill: University of North Carolina, 1985), 237–240.

4. *In the Matter of Deming,* 10 Johns. 232, 483 (N.Y. Sup. Ct. 1813); Danaya C. Wright, "From Feudalism to Family Law: Inter-Spousal Custody Disputes and Repudiation of Mother's Rights" (Ph.D. diss., Johns Hopkins University, 1998).

5. *Codd v. Codd,* 2 Johns. Ch. 141 (N.Y. Ch. 1816). See also Charles Edwards, *Pleasantries about Courts and Lawyers of the State of New York* (New York: Richardson & Co., 1867), 108–109. See *Barrere v. Barrere,* 4 Johns. Ch. 187, 188, 191, 197 (N.Y. Ch. 1819). See Kent's decisions in *In the Matter of Wollstonecraft,* 4 Johns. Ch. 79 (N.Y. Ch. 1819); *Haviland v. Myers,* 6 Johns. Ch. 25, 178 (N.Y. Ch. 1822); and *Bedell v. Bedell,* 1 Johns. Ch. 604 (N.Y. Ch. 1815). For similar decisions by other judges, see *Pawling v. Bird's Executors,* 13 Johns. 192 (N.Y. Sup. Ct. 1816); *Graves v. Graves,* 2 Paige Ch. 62 (N.Y. Ch. 1830); *In the Matter of Rachel Hansen,* 1 Edmunds' Select Cases 9 (N.Y. Ch. 1834).

6. James Kent, *Commentaries on American Law,* vol. 2 (New York: O. Halsted, 1827), 164–165.

7. Joseph Story, *Commentaries on Equity Jurisprudence as Administered in England and America,* 2d ed. (London: A. Maxwell, 1839), 529–533.

8. John A. Barry, *The Barry Case. A Review of, and Strictures on the Opinion of His Honor the Chancellor of the State of New York, Delivered 26th August, 1839, in the Late Case of the People, Ex Relatione John A. Barry, versus Thomas R. Mercein. Affording Also, a Correct View of the Circumstances of the Case, and the Persecutions of the Reviewer by His Wife's Father and Family, and Others Their Partisans, up to the Present Time* (New York: D. Appleton, 1839), 16–20. Many nineteenth-century women feared leaving their parental home, as Eliza Barry did. Michael Grossberg, *A Judgment for Solomon* (Cambridge, U.K.: Cambridge University Press, 1996), 21; Ellen K. Rothman, *Hands and Hearts, a History of Courtship in American* (Cambridge, Mass.: Harvard University Press, 1987), 67–75; Mary Ryan, *Cradle of the Middle Class: The Family in Oneida County, New York, 1790–1865* (Cambridge, U.K.: Cambridge University Press, 1981), 194–195; Carroll

Smith-Rosenberg, "The Female World of Love and Ritual: Relations between Women in Nineteenth-Century America," *Signs* 1, no. 1 (Summer 1975): 1–29. Smith-Rosenberg describes such feelings as defined by the mother-daughter bond. In legal cases, however, the daughter's lost home was always described as the parental or paternal home.

9. *People v. Mercein,* 8 Paige Ch. 47, 59 (N.Y. Ch. 1839).
10. Barry, *The Barry Case,* 50.
11. A summary procedural history of the litigation can be found in Hendrik Hartog, "John Barry's Custodial Rights: Of Power, Justice, and Coverture," in *Justice and Power in Sociolegal Studies,* ed. Bryant G. Garth and Austin Sarat (Chicago: Northwestern University Press, 1997), 186.
12. 46 U.S. 103, 120 (1847).
13. See, e.g., *In re Baby M,* 217 N.J. Super. 313, 525 A.2d 1128 (1987). See Jamil Zainaldin, "The Emergence of a Modern American Family Law: Child Custody, Adoption, and the Courts, 1796–1851," *Northwestern Law Review* 73 (1979): 1038–1089; Mary Ann Mason, *From Father's Property to Children's Rights: The History of Child Custody in the United States* (New York: Columbia University Press, 1994), 21.
14. This statement ignores the federal judges who saw the case solely as a problem of federal jurisdiction.
15. It was also about the right of an "alien" husband to compel his wife to follow him to foreign lands. Justices Cowen and Bronson emphasized the equal rights of foreign fathers. It is important to remember, further, that the notion of a foreign father was itself a contested and fuzzy concept in an America with many jurisdictions. For a New York judge, a man from Nova Scotia was not much more of an alien than someone from Oregon or Texas. On the attempt (perhaps motivated by the Barry case) to pass a statute in New York that would have deprived alien fathers of custody rights whenever the father attempted or threatened "to carry the child into a foreign country" without the mother's consent, see Grossberg, *Judgment for Solomon,* 63–65.
16. In 1844 Eliza Barry unsuccessfully petitioned the vice-chancellor for an injunction to keep her husband from bringing more writs of habeas corpus. 3 Saratoga Chancery Sentinel 13 (1844).
17. Barry, *The Barry Case,* 7.
18. *People v. Mercein,* 3 Hill 399, 407 (N.Y. Sup. Ct. 1842).
19. *In re Waldron,* 13 Johns. 418 (N.Y. Sup. Ct. 1816).
20. *Mercein,* 8 Paige Ch. 47, 53–54. In *Coverdill v. Coverdill,* 3 Harr. 13 (Del. 1839), a judge complained about the absence of legislation giving courts power to order restitution of conjugal rights. But no legislature ever responded.

21. *People v. Mercein,* 25 Wend. 64, 80 (N.Y. Sup. Ct. 1840); *People v. Mercein,* 3 Hill 399, 406–407 (1842). See Barry, *The Barry Case,* 8.

22. 25 Wend. at 72–73. Bronson had admitted that fathers' rights were not absolute in *People ex rel. Ordronaux v. Chegaray,* 18 Wend. 637, 642–643 (N.Y. Sup. Ct. 1836).

23. 8 Paige Ch. at 57–58.

24. 8 Paige Ch. at 60, 58.

25. 8 Paige Ch. at 61–64.

26. While sitting as a member of the Court for the Correction of Errors in 1840, Walworth changed his mind on this question and decided that this was an agreement founded upon a present separation, and therefore valid. *Mercein v. People,* 25 Wend. 83, 98 (N.Y. 1840).

27. 8 Paige Ch. at 68.

28. 8 Paige Ch. at 61, 65–69.

29. 8 Paige Ch. at 69–70. See M. W. Jacobs, *A Treatise on the Law of Domicil* (Boston: Little, Brown and Co., 1887), 292–297.

30. Part of the conflict rested on a dispute about whether a chancellor hearing a writ of habeas corpus was sitting as a judge at law or as a chancellor in equity. See Barry, *The Barry Case,* 47, 9.

31. 25 Wend. at 72–73.

32. 25 Wend. at 75.

33. 25 Wend. 83, 92, 98 (N.Y. 1840). Apparently, one of the dissenters in the Court of Errors was Lieutenant Governor Luther Bradish. John Barry wrote him repeatedly in January and February 1841 vainly trying to get Bradish to publish an opinion. See letters from John A. Barry to Luther Bradish, January 11, 1841, January 15, 1841, and February 26, 1841, and letter from Luther Bradish to John A. Barry, February 3, 1841. Luther Bradish Papers, uncarded correspondence, New-York Historical Society.

34. John Barry to Luther Bradish, February 26, 1841. Oakley's opinion can be found in the uncarded correspondence of the Luther Bradish Papers, New-York Historical Society.

35. This time Chief Justice Samuel Nelson dissented, on the ground that the earlier reversal by the New York Court of Errors had settled the law for this case. The conflict was now res judicata. 3 Hill 399, 423.

36. The decision of the Court of Errors in 1842 was unreported (although it is noted in the summary of the case history made to the U.S. Supreme Court; see also 42 F. 113 (1844)). As a result, the opinions of the New York Supreme Court in 1842 were often considered as the final word on New York law and continued to be cited everywhere as significant authority.

37. 3 Hill at 408–411.

38. 3 Hill at 412–415.
39. Barry, *The Barry Case*, 27, 44.
40. Ibid., 13–14, 33. On the invocation of "Wrightism" as epithet, see Lori D. Ginzberg, "'The Hearts of Your Readers Will Shudder': Fanny Wright, Infidelity, and American Freethought," *American Quarterly* 46, no. 2 (June 1994): 195–225.
41. Barry, *The Barry Case*, 31.
42. Ibid., 47, 9.
43. Ibid., 47–48.
44. Grossberg, *Governing the Hearth*; Jay Fliegelman, *Prodigals and Pilgrims* (Cambridge, Mass.: Harvard University Press, 1984); *In re O'Neil*, in 3 *American Law Review* 578 (Mass. 1869); *Chapsky v. Wood*, 26 Kan. 650 (1881).
45. 25 Wend. at 101–106.
46. 25 Wend. at 103. The future Supreme Court Justice Joseph Bradley, a close observer of the *Mercein* case, described the "spirit" of the holdings in terms very like Paige. Joseph P. Bradley Papers, New Jersey Historical Society, Law Notes, Folder 9. Dan Ernst was kind enough to share this with me.
47. Unpublished manuscript, Luther Bradish papers, uncarded correspondence, New-York Historical Society. For a description of the uses Barry's case played in the D'Hautville litigation in Philadelphia, see Grossberg, *Judgment for Solomon*.
48. Edward Deering Mansfield, *The Legal Rights, Liabilities and Duties of Women* (Salem, Mass.: J. P. Jewett & Co., 1845), 336–344.
49. Between 1840 and 1950, citations in all state jurisdictions to the opinions in *Mercein*, excluding the federal court opinions, numbered approximately 145. Of those, the opinions were referenced 33 times for the position that the best interests of the child (or parens patriae) stood superior to inherited notions of the father's right (8 times in New York, 25 times in other states). The opinions were also mobilized 13 other times (3 times in New York, 10 times in other states) for a general invocation of the best interests of the child. By contrast, the opinions of the New York Supreme Court that confirmed a father's right were invoked 17 times over the same period (10 times in New York, 7 times in other states). The single most frequent citation to the Barry case, again for both sides of the question, was on issues of res judicata, both involving child custody and not. Here the opinions were mobilized 55 times between 1840 and 1950 in New York and elsewhere. Other uses of the opinions include: as authority on the validity of separation agreements (13), as authority on issues of jurisdiction and habeas corpus (12), and, oddly, since the case

involved an infant, on giving a child the discretion to choose her or his custodian if of sufficient age and judgment (2).

50. Thomas M. Cooley, *A Treatise on the Constitutional Limitations Which Rest upon the Legislative Power of the States of the American Union* (Boston: Little, Brown and Co., 1868), 348. See R. F. G., "The Rights and Liabilities of Parents in Respect of Their Minor Children," *American Law Register* 1 (old series) (September and October 1853): 641–654, 705–716.

51. Rollin C. Hurd, *A Treatise on the Right of Personal Liberty, and on the Writ of Habeas Corpus and the Practice Connected with It: A View of the Law of Extradition of Fugitives*, 2d ed. (Albany: W. C. Little & Co., 1876), 511–517.

52. Joseph Story, *Commentaries on Equity Jurisprudence as Administered in England and America*, 7th ed. (Boston: Little Brown and Co., 1857), 703.

53. *In the Matter of William Gregg, an Infant*, 5 New York Legal Observer 265, 267 (N.Y. Super. 1847).

54. *Marshall v. Reams*, 32 Fla. 499, 502, 14 S. 95 (1893), cites *Mercein* for the term, although it doesn't appear as best I can tell.

55. *Wand v. Wand*, 14 Cal. 512, 515 (1860). In the appeal, both sides relied on the Barry precedents. See Bonnie L. Ford, "Women, Marriage, and Divorce in California, 1849–1872" (Ph.D. diss., University of California, Davis, 1985), 218–232. See *Bennett v. Bennett*, 3 Fed. Cas. 212, 214 (Dist. Ct., Or., 1867).

56. See *People ex rel. Olmstead v. Olmstead and Randell*, 27 Barb. 9 (N.Y. Sup. Ct. 1857); *Latham v. Latham*, 71 Va. 307 (1878); *People ex rel. Sinclair v. Sinclair*, 47 Misc. 230, 95 N.Y. Supp. 861 (1905).

57. Judges often used failed divorce suits by mothers to develop their commitment to paternal custody rights. See *Latham*, 71 Va. 307 (1878), and *Bryan v. Bryan*, 34 Ala. 516 (1859).

58. See Art. 15, sec. 6 of the 1859 Kansas constitution; *Bennet v. Bennet*, 13 N.J. Eq. 114, 116 (1860). For a campaign to pass such a law in Iowa, see E. P. W. Packard, *Modern Persecution, or Married Woman's Liabilities, as Demonstrated by the Action of the Illinois Legislature*, vol. 2 (Hartford: Case, Lockwood & Brainard, 1875), 364.

59. Laws of 1860, c.90, sec. 4; "Address to the New York State Legislature, 1860," in Beth Waggenspack, ed., *The Search for Self-Sovereignty: The Oratory of Elizabeth Cady Stanton* (New York: Greenwood Press, 1989), 111–118; Elisabeth Griffith, *In Her Own Right: The Life of Elizabeth Cady Stanton* (New York: Oxford University Press, 1984), 101.

60. *The People, ex rel. Clark B. Brooks v. Lydia H. Brooks*, 35 Barb. 85, 90–95 (N.Y. Sup. Ct. 1861). Allen continued: if he were wrong in his interpretation of the meaning of the statute, then the "most" that could be claimed

on the wife's side was that she and her husband were equal, and the court ought to look to their respective equities. In that case, a mother who lived in "open violation of her conjugal duties," defying the claims of her husband to her company and assistance, showed herself "unfit" to be entrusted with custody. "Her sins" worked "a forfeiture." And the father's right regained its customary sway.

61. Laws of 1862, c.172, sec. 2. See *People ex rel. Boice v Boice,* 39 Barb. 307 (N.Y. Sup. Ct. 1862).

62. *Allen v. Affleck,* 64 Howard's Pr. 380, 10 Daly 509 (N.Y. Common Pleas 1882); *Lee v. Lee,* 157 N.Y. Supp. 821 (N.Y. Sup. Ct. 1916). See *People v. Mt. St. Joseph's Academy,* 189 N.Y. Supp. 775, 198 App. Div. 75 (N.Y. Sup. Ct. 1921).

63. *People v. Sinclair,* 95 N.Y. Supp. 861, 47 Misc. 230, affirmed, 94 N.Y. Supp. 1159 (N.Y. Sup. Ct. 1905). The earlier award to the mother can be found at 86 N.Y. Supp. 539. See Mason, *Father's Property,* 61.

64. *Stafford v. Stafford,* 299 Ill. 438, 132 N.E. 452 (1921). See *In re Reynolds,* 8 N.Y. Supp. 172 (N.Y. Sup. Ct. 1889); *Markwell v. Pereles,* 69 N.W. 798 (Wis. 1897); *In re Jacquet,* 82 N.Y. Supp. 986, 40 Misc. 575 (N.Y. Surrogate Ct. 1903); *Ullman v. Ullman,* 135 N.Y. Supp. 1080, 151 App. Div. 419 (N.Y. Sup. Ct. 1912); *State v. Bollinger,* 101 So. 282 (Fla. 1924); *Finlay v. Finlay,* 208 N.Y. Supp. 585, 212 App. Div. 786 (N.Y. Sup. Ct. 1925).

65. *Allen,* 64 Howard's Pr. at 384, 10 Daly at 516. See *Rising v. Dodge,* 2 Duer 42 (N.Y. Super. 1853).

66. Peter Hitchcock Family Papers, 1788–1898, MSS 3325, Western Reserve Historical Society, Cleveland, Ohio (thanks to Ann Fidler).

67. *Burritt v. Burritt,* 29 Barb. 124, 129–130 (N.Y. Sup. Ct. 1859). See *Finch v. Finch,* 22 Conn. 411 (1853).

68. See Elizabeth Clark, "Religion, Rights, and Difference in the Early Woman's Rights Movement," *Wisconsin Women's Law Journal* 3 (1987): 29–58; Ellen DuBois, "Outgrowing the Compact of the Fathers: Equal Rights, Woman Suffrage, and the United States Constitution, 1820–1878," *Journal of American History* 74 (December 1987): 836–862.

8. The Right to Kill

1. It became a written "unwritten law" in Texas, Utah, and New Mexico: Tex. Penal Code Ann. art. 1220 (Vernon 1961); N.M. Stat. Ann. secs. 780, 401 (1948); Utah Code Ann. sec. 76-30-10(5) (1953). See generally Leo Kanowitz, *Women and the Law: The Unfinished Revolution* (Albuquerque: University of New Mexico Press, 1969), 92–93.

2. William Blackstone, *Commentaries on the Laws of England,* ed. William

Carey Jones (Baton Rouge: Claitor's Publishing Division, 1976), 4:*191 (quoting Hale). Both acknowledged that Roman law recognized such a right. Tapping Reeve, *The Law of Baron and Femme, of Parent and Child, Guardian and Ward, Master and Servant, and of the Powers of the Courts of Chancery; with an Essay on the Terms Heir, Heirs, Heirs of the Body,* ed. Amasa J. Parker and Charles Baldwin (Albany: William Gould, 1862), 300. See Henry Campbell Black, *A Law Dictionary,* 2d ed. (St. Paul, Minn.: West, 1910), 1188.

3. "Lessons of the McFarland Case," *Albany Law Journal* 1 (May 21, 1870): 385–387. Joel Prentiss Bishop concluded that a husband who immediately killed either wife or lover (like a father who killed a man sodomizing his son) would be guilty of manslaughter, not murder. But Bishop insisted that delay, or a killing founded on hearing rather than seeing, made the act murder. Bishop, *Commentaries on the Criminal Law* (Boston: Little, Brown and Co., 1882), 400–401.

4. Felix G. Fontain, reporter, *Trial of the Hon. Daniel E. Sickles: For Shooting Philip Barton Key, Esq. U.S. District Attorney, Washington, D.C., February 27, 1859* (New York: R. M. De Witt, 1859); Thomas Dunphy, ed., "George W. Cole (Trial Transcripts, for the Murder of L. Harris Hiscock)," in *Remarkable Trials of All Countries; with the Evidence and Speeches of Counsel, Court Scenes, Incidents, &c. Compiled from Official Sources,* vol. 2 (New York: S. S. Peloubet & Co., 1882), 194–421; *The Richardson-McFarland Tragedy. Containing All the Letters and Other Interesting Facts and Documents Not Before Published* (Philadelphia: Barclay and Co., 1870); A Practical Law Reporter, *The Trial of Daniel McFarland for the Shooting of Albert D. Richardson, the Alleged Seducer of His Wife* (New York: W. E. Hilton, 1870).

5. See, e.g., John Graham, lawyer, *Opening Speech to the Jury, on the Part of the Defence, on the Trial of Daniel E. Sickles, in the Criminal Court of the District of Columbia, April 9th and 11th, 1859* (New York: T. R. Dawley, 1859); John Graham, *Summing Up of John Graham, Esq., to the Jury, on the Part of the Defense, on the Trial of Daniel MacFarland, in the Court of General Sessions, at the City of New York, Recorder John K. Hackett, Presiding May 6th and 9th, 1870* (New York: W. A. Townsend & Adams, 1870).

6. In the Cole case it took two trials before he was acquitted. See *People v. Cole,* 6 Parker's Crim. R. 695 (Albany Oyer and Terminer 1868), for his unsuccessful petition for habeas corpus between the first and second trials.

7. "This I have written with my bed-room open [to prove that no violence was used], and my maid and child in the adjoining room, at half past eight o'clock in the evening." Fontain, *Sickles,* 42.

8. Dunphy, "Cole," 194–210, 219–222; *Cole's Trial*, 7 Abb. Pr. (new series) 321, 327–334 (Albany Oyer and Terminer 1868).

9. During the Civil War, McFarland profited from his unusual character as an Irishman who was also an active committed member of the Republican Party, and he obtained a small political position in New York City. Earlier, in Wisconsin, he had been a founding member of the party. Daniel McFarland to Lysander Spooner, September 12, 1854, Papers of Lysander Spooner, New-York Historical Society.

10. See Lucy Calhoun to Abby Sage McFarland, February 22, 1867, in A Practical Law Reporter, *McFarland*, 61–63. Albert Richardson became famous for reports in the *New York Tribune* on his travels through the West. During the Civil War he wrote a thrilling description of his capture as a spy in the South and his later escape. In 1868 he wrote Grant's official campaign biography. Many of his writings were collected by Abby in a volume that included her reverential biographical introduction. Albert D. Richardson, *Garnered Sheaves from the Writings of Albert D. Richardson, Collected and Arranged by His Wife [Mrs. Abby (Sage) Richardson]; to Which Is Added a Biographical Sketch of the Author.* (Toledo, Ohio: W. E. Bliss, 1871).

11. A Practical Law Reporter, *McFarland*, 226–240; *Richardson-McFarland Tragedy*, 97–109. There was, however, very little disinterested testimony in the trial to prove that McFarland was an alcoholic. And in nineteenth-century America it was always convenient to accuse an Irishman of intemperance.

12. *Richardson-McFarland Tragedy*, 58.

13. George Templeton Strong, *Diary*, ed. Allan Nevins and Milton Halsey Thomas (New York: Octagon Books, 1974), 2:447–449.

14. Dunphy, "Cole," 294–295. They also played up what was constructed as mental illness caused by serious chronic injuries to their client's bowels suffered during the Civil War. See L. B. Proctor, *The Bench and Bar of New-York* (New York: Diossy & Co., 1870), 264–265.

15. A Practical Law Reporter, *McFarland*, 28.

16. On James T. Brady (1815–1869), see *Dictionary of American Biography*, vol. 2, 583; Proctor, *The Bench and Bar of New-York*, 238–276; *In Memoriam: James T. Brady: Report of Proceedings at a Meeting of the New York Bar Held in the Supreme Court Room on Saturday, February 13, 1869* (New York: Baker, Voorhis, 1869); Henry Lauren Clinton, *Extraordinary Cases* (New York: Harper, 1899), 84–86. Other than the Sickles and Cole cases, Brady's greatest reknown came from his losing representation of Edwin Forrest in the actor's endless divorce suit against his wife. John Graham (1821–1894), the son and brother of prominent New York law-

yers, was a more controversial figure within the bar. His most famous case was as the lead counsel in the trial of William Marcy Tweed. See David McAdam, et al., *History of the Bench and Bar of New York* (2 vols., New York: New York History Company, 1897), 1:337–338; Clinton, *Extraordinary Cases,* 440–468.

17. Parker and Charles Baldwin appended a note to follow Reeve's 1816 discussion of a husband's right to kill. It concluded that a man who killed his wife's seducer "deliberately, and upon revenge, and after sufficient cooling time," was a murderer. Reeve, *Baron and Femme,* 300–301. See Charles S. Spencer, *Eulogy on Charles Sumner: Delivered in the Assembly Chamber of the State of New York, March 18, 1874* (Albany, 1874); Henry Ward Beecher and James Topham Brady, *Addresses on Mental Culture for Women* (New York, 1858). For cases in which Brady opposed fathers' or husbands' rights, see *People ex rel. Fowler v. Pillow,* 6 New York Legal Observer 106 (N.Y. Super. Ct. 1848), and *People ex rel. Tappan v. Porter, alias Cooper,* 1 Duer 709, 11 New York Legal Observer 228 (N.Y. Super. Ct. 1853). See John Graham, *Peter R. Strong against Mary E. Strong: Closing Address of John Graham, Esq. to the Jury for the Defence, December 26th and 27th, 1865* (New York City: The Superior Court, 1865). (Peter Strong happened to be George Templeton Strong's cousin.) It may be coincidence, although I don't think so, but "Brady" and "Graham" together make Braham, which is the name of the famous lawyer who dominates the trial scene at the end of Mark Twain and Charles Dudley Warner, *The Gilded Age* (Hartford, 1873).

18. Brady, in particular, was eulogized as the greatest oral advocate of his generation. Graham was detested by more conventional lawyers like George Templeton Strong, but he too was universally recognized as a superb advocate and legal strategist. Strong, *Diary,* 4:54.

19. Who were the jurors? In *McFarland,* the jury included three merchants, one broker, an insurance man, a "rectifier," five in sales, and an actor. See A Practical Law Reporter, *McFarland,* 9. The jury in *Sickles* included two farmers and ten men from the city, including one merchant, four grocers, a man in "gent's furnishing," a shoemaker, a tinner, a coach maker, and a cabinet maker. See Fontain, *Sickles,* 6–15.

20. John Graham himself never married, a fact he noted at the beginning of his closing speech in the McFarland case. A Practical Law Reporter, *McFarland,* 173.

21. Dunphy, "Cole," 212. For McFarland, see A Practical Law Reporter, *McFarland,* 25. Hadley emphasized Cole's terror that men were looking at him, his sense of visible dishonor. Dunphy, "Cole," 225–227.

22. *Richardson-McFarland Tragedy,* 55 (comment by editor). See Dunphy, "Cole," 219–220, 226.

23. Fontain, *Sickles,* 27.

24. A Practical Law Reporter, *McFarland,* 178–179, 197–198.

25. Ibid., 28–29, 30, 51, 61–68, 189. The transcript has Graham describing Abby as "vibrating between her affection for her husband and the desire to keep disgrace away from them." Either this is a mistake by the reporter who covered the trial, or it is an even more interesting "mistake" by Graham. Perhaps Graham realized in mid-speech that the contrast he was drawing between her love for Richardson and her love for her children conceded too much autonomy and free will to her, and so he "accidently" changed the referent to "her husband."

26. Fontain, *Sickles,* 44. Interestingly, John Graham made exactly the same argument in the Strong divorce case of 1865. Graham, *Closing,* 93.

27. *State v. John (a slave),* 8 Ired. 330 (N.C. 1848); Fontain, *Sickles,* 50–51, 62. In identifying Key with both the alleged seducer of John's wife and the slaves' master, defense lawyers were making a rhetorical point that had no connection to the facts in *State v. John.* The murdered man in that case was another slave.

28. See Robert M. Ireland, "Insanity and the Unwritten Law," *American Journal of Legal History* 32, no. 2 (April 1988): 157–172. In each of the cases, witnesses for the defense testified as to the obsessed or distracted manner with which the defendant had behaved. And in both the Cole and the McFarland cases, William Hammond, a controversial medical expert on insanity, testified on behalf of the defense. Dunphy, "Cole," 262; William A. Hammond, *A Medico-Legal Study of the Case of Daniel McFarland* (New York: D. Appleton & Co., 1870); William A. Hammond, *A Synopsis of the General Subject of Insanity, and Especially Of Temporary Insanity of Morbid Impulse, as Applicable to the McFarland Case* (New York: W. E. Hilton, 1870). Brady was already identified with the emerging insanity defense because of his famous argument in 1857 on behalf of the accused forger Charles Huntington. See Proctor, *The Bench and Bar of New-York,* 256–263. On the development of the insanity defense, see Norman Dain, *Concepts of Insanity in the United States, 1789–1865* (New Brunswick: Rutgers University Press, 1964); John P. Reid, *Chief Justice: The Judicial World of Charles Doe* (Cambridge, Mass.: Harvard University Press, 1967); John S. Hughes, *In the Law's Darkness: Isaac Ray and the Medical Jurisprudence of Insanity in Nineteenth-Century America* (New York: Oceana, 1986).

29. A Practical Law Reporter, *McFarland,* 183. The lawyers' argument bears comparison to recent "diminished capacity" cases, for example, where the "battered wife syndrome" has been invoked. The husbands in the nineteenth-century cases, like wives who murder abusive husbands, were portrayed as having done what anyone who had experienced something like that might have done. On the battered wife syndrome defense, see

State v. Baker, 424 A.2d 171 (N.H. 1980); *Smith v. State,* 277 S.E.2d 678 (Ga. 1981); David L. Faigman, "The Battered Wife Syndrome and Self-Defense: A Legal and Empirical Dissent," *Virginia Law Review* 72 (April 1986), 619–647; Elizabeth M. Schneider, "The Dialectic of Rights and Politics: Perspectives from the Women's Movement," *New York University Law Review* 61 (October 1986), 589–652; Martha Mahoney, "Legal Images of Battered Women: Redefining the Issue of Separation," *Michigan Law Review* 90, no. 1 (October 1991): 1–94.

30. A Practical Law Reporter, *McFarland,* 180, 213, 109–110, 185; Dunphy, "Cole," 233.
31. Dunphy, "Cole," 237.
32. A Practical Law Reporter, *McFarland,* 25.
33. Ibid., 149–152, 208–209.
34. Dunphy, "Cole," 334–338; A Practical Law Reporter, *McFarland,* 220.
35. "The Crime of Adultery," *American Law Register* 7 (new series) (November 1868): 769–777; Theodore Tilton, "Sober Second Thought," editorial, *The Independent,* May 10, 1870, 311–312; H. B. B., "Woman Suffrage and the McFarland Case," *The Revolution,* December 16, 1869; Isabella Beecher Hooker, "The M'Farland-Richardson Tragedy," *The Revolution,* December 16, 1869.
36. Dunphy, "Cole," 237.
37. *In Memoriam: James T. Brady.*
38. *Richardson-McFarland Tragedy,* 90; A Practical Law Reporter, *McFarland,* 194.
39. On the need to make adultery a crime, see Theodore D. Woolsey, *Essay on Divorce and Divorce Legislation, with Special Reference to the United States* (New York: Scribner, 1869), 260. See also Henry Lauren Clinton's argument in *Favre v. Monvoisin* (1873), in Clinton, *Extraordinary Cases,* 592–594. For judicial interpretations of the statutory crime of adultery, where it existed, see *Wright v. State,* 5 Blackf. 358 (Ind. 1840); *State v. Jolly,* 20 N.C. 110 (1838); and *Collins v. State,* 14 Ala. 608 (1848).
40. Dunphy, "Cole," 229; A Practical Law Reporter, *McFarland,* 31.
41. Dunphy, "Cole," 323–335.
42. Ibid., 235–236; Fontain, *Sickles,* 27. There is less of this language in McFarland-Richardson because McFarland had in fact sued Richardson for alienation of affections. *Richardson-McFarland Tragedy,* 41–42. Still, see A Practical Law Reporter, *McFarland,* 32. Lawyers representing plaintiffs in crim. con. cases sometimes emphasized a client's restraint in asking for money damages, when a jury would have acquitted him if he had murdered the seducer. See Clinton, *Extraordinary Cases,* 592–594.
43. Fontain, *Sickles,* 92–93.

44. Dunphy, "Cole," 345.

45. A Practical Law Reporter, *McFarland*, 46–47.

46. Ibid., 197–198.

47. Ibid., 208–209.

48. On Walworth's life after being forced from his position as chancellor with the passage of the 1846 state constitution, see Irving Browne, "Reuben Hyde Walworth," *The Green Bag* 7, no. 6 (June 1895): 257–267. Ellen Hardin Walworth became a well-known local historian of Saratoga Springs and one of the founders of the Daughters of the American Revolution.

49. Thomas Dunphy, ed., "The Walworth Parricide (Trial Transcript)," in *Remarkable Trials of All Countries; with the Evidence and Speeches of Counsel, Court Scenes, Incidents, &c. Compiled from Official Sources*, vol. 2 (New York: S. S. Peloubet & Co., 1882), 148–152.

50. His insanity was understood as long-standing. In 1861 or 1862, he claimed to have had a commission in the Confederate army. In a letter to his sister Ellen Backus, he insisted that he was the true Messiah. Dunphy, "Walworth Parricide," 154–165, 175.

51. Ibid., 152–153.

52. Ibid., 187, 193.

53. Mansfield Tracy Walworth, *Beverly, or, The White Mask: A Novel*, Wright American Fiction, vol. 2 (New York: G. W. Carleton, 1872), 13–14.

54. Ibid., 19–20.

55. Ibid., 300–301, 341.

56. Ibid., 359.

57. Ibid., 384–389.

9. The Geography of Remarriage

1. A Practical Law Reporter, *The Trial of Daniel McFarland for the Shooting of Albert D. Richardson, the Alleged Seducer of His Wife* (New York: W. E. Hilton, 1870), 238–239; *New York Times*, December 4, 1869, 4:6; ibid., December 12, 1869, 5:2; *McFarland v. McFarland*, 40 Ind. 458 (1872).

2. *The Richardson-McFarland Tragedy. Containing All the Letters and Other Interesting Facts and Documents Not Before Published* (Philadelphia: Barclay and Co., 1870), 19–21.

3. For Beecher, see *Richardson-McFarland Tragedy*, 48–50, 53–55. For Frothingham, see ibid., 50, and also *New York Times*, December 6, 1869, 8:1. For Greeley, see *Richardson-McFarland Tragedy*, 46–48. "Benedictions to bigamy" comes from Recorder Hackett's charge to the grand jury. See *New York Times*, December 9, 1869, 2:7.

4. *Richardson-McFarland Tragedy,* 51–53.

5. A Practical Law Reporter, *McFarland,* 107.

6. *McFarland,* 40 Ind. 458 (1872).

7. Henry James, Horace Greeley, and Stephen Pearl Andrews, *Love, Marriage, and Divorce and the Sovereignty of the Individual* (1852–1853; New York: Source Book Press, 1972). On Greeley's debates, see Elizabeth B. Clark, "Matrimonial Bonds: Slavery and Divorce in Nineteenth-Century America," *Law and History Review* 8, no. 1 (Spring 1990): 25–54; Nelson Manfred Blake, *The Road to Reno: A History of Divorce in the United States* (New York: Macmillan, 1962), 82–86, 89.

8. Horace Greeley and Robert Dale Owen, *Divorce, Being a Correspondence . . . Originally Published in the New York Daily Tribune* (1860; New York: Source Book Press, 1972), 154, 162, 180. Had Greeley changed his mind about divorce by the time of the McFarland trial? I think it unlikely. See his autobiography, *Recollections of a Busy Life* (New York: J. B. Ford & Co., 1868), to which he appended his 1860 debate. For an echo of Greeley's words, see William D. Howells, *A Modern Instance,* Selected Edition of W. D. Howells, vol. 10 (1882; Bloomington: Indiana University Press, 1977), 430.

9. Theodore D. Woolsey, *Essay on Divorce and Divorce Legislation, with Special Reference to the United States* (New York: Scribner, 1869), 54–57, 69–84, 239–240. See likewise Charles Caverno, *Treatise on Divorce* (Madison, Wis.: Midland Publishing Co., 1889).

10. "The McFarland Case," *The Nation,* May 12, 1870, pp. 301–303.

11. Greeley and Owen, *Divorce,* 155 (emphasis in original).

12. *People v. Mercein,* 8 Paige Ch. 47, 57 (N.Y. Ch. 1839). Hume's views are set out in Henry Folsom Page, *A View of the Law Relative to the Subject of Divorce in Ohio, Indiana, and Michigan* (Columbus, Ohio: 1850), 1–17, 35–43. The same perspective appears in Howells, *A Modern Instance,* 397–398.

13. James, Greeley, and Andrews, *Love, Marriage, and Divorce,* 39, 78 (emphasis in original).

14. Elizabeth Cady Stanton and Susan B. Anthony, *Correspondence, Writings, Speeches,* ed. Ellen Carol DuBois (New York: Schocken Books, 1981), 133–135, 129. A critic described Stanton's vision as a "partnership" in which "contingencies of discord and separation and termination" were never "left out of sight." Carl Benson, "Casual Cogitations," *Galaxy* 16 (August 1873): 197. Stanton did not represent the woman's rights movement when she argued for free divorce. See Clark, "Matrimonial Bonds." The mainstream woman's rights understanding is described in Lewis Perry, *Childhood, Marriage and Reform: Henry Clarke Wright, 1797–1870*

(Chicago: University of Chicago Press, 1980), 251–253. A few "free lovers" or philosophical anarchists imagined a state that had gone entirely out of the business of regulating or licensing marriages. John C. Spurlock, *Free Love: Marriage and Middle-Class Radicalism in America, 1825–1860* (New York: New York University Press, 1988).

15. Occasionally, a litigant like Daniel McFarland challenged divorce law as practiced in a jurisdiction, apparently mad at the law itself as well as at a former spouse. See, e.g., *Kinnier v. Kinnier*, 53 Barb. 454 (N.Y. Sup. Ct. 1868), 58 Barb. 424 (N.Y. Sup. Ct. 1869), 45 N.Y. 535 (1871). There were also wives who challenged their husbands' out-of-state divorces as attempts to escape from mandated support obligations. See *Barber v. Barber*, 62 U.S. (21 How.) 582 (1858), and *Vischer v. Vischer*, 12 Barb. 640 (N.Y. Sup. Ct. 1851). On the other side, husbands sometimes portrayed divorcing wives as captured by a woman's rights ideology inconsistent with a harmonious marriage. See Defendant's brief, Martha E. Williams v. Thompson E. Williams, April 1869, Cases and Briefs, Wisconsin Supreme Court (University of Wisconsin Law School Library). Thompson responded to Martha's charges of abuse, violence, and incest by characterizing her as "a strong minded woman . . . possessed of the idea that she had as much right to dictate in respect to all matters connected with the family and business of the defendant as the defendant himself." See *Williams v. Williams*, 29 Wis. 517 (1872).

16. There were occasional knowing "criminal" bigamists, men who preyed on vulnerable women, marrying them, gaining control of their property, then abandoning them for new prey. There may even have been bigamists of the sort celebrated in novels, who managed by dint of hard work to maintain two or more households at the same time with none of the wives the wiser. And there were, of course, Mormon polygamists, openly defiant flouters, the evil "other" of the late nineteenth-century American legal imagination. There were also a few knowing female bigamists. See Beverly Schwartzberg, "Grass Widows, Barbarians, and Bigamists: Documenting and Describing Marital Irregularity in Nineteenth Century America" (unpublished manuscript, University of California, Santa Barbara, 1998); *Report of the Beardsley Divorce Case, Containing the Full and Unabridged Testimony of All the Witnesses, Together with All the Evidence Suppressed by the Daily Papers*, transcript of trial (Brooklyn: Robert M. De Witt, 1860).

17. On Edwin Christy's mental difficulties, see "Four Undated and Unattributed Newspaper Articles Regarding the Death of Edwin P. Christy" (Houghton Library, Harvard University, 1862). On Christy, see Ken Emerson, *Doo-Dah! Stephen Foster and the Rise of American Popular*

Culture (New York: Simon & Schuster, 1997); Alexander Saxton, "Black-face Minstrelsy," in *Inside the Minstrel Mask: Readings in Nineteenth-Century Blackface Minstrelsy*, ed. Annemarie Bean, James V. Hatch, and Brooks McNamara (Hanover: Wesleyan University Press, 1996), 67–85; *Christy's Plantation Melodies, Published under the Authority of E. P. Christy* (Philadelphia: Fisher & Brother, 1854), v–vii. Much has been written about George Christy (Harrington). See Edward LeRoy Rice, *Monarchs of Minstrelsy from "Daddy" Rice to Date* (New York: Kenny, 1911), 20.

18. The clergyman who officiated remembered the groom as "a small man with dark hair and whiskers moderately long." Christy, however, was "a tall man without either whiskers or hair on his head." *Christy v. Clarke*, 45 Barb. 529, 530–533 (N.Y. Sup. Ct. 1866); "Four Newspaper Articles."

19. *New York Times*, May 5, 1865, 8:4 (William, her other son by Christy, had died in the interim).

20. *Christy*, 45 Barb. at 534. As Barnard realized, this was a question of fact, not one ordinarily answered by an appellate court. Ibid., 534–535. But Barnard persisted, on the theory that answering this question would reveal "the probability" that Harriet and her son would win on a retrial. George G. Barnard is infamous as a wealthy and Yale-educated judge impeached and removed as part of the Tweed Ring. See Leo Hershkowitz, *Tweed's New York: Another Look* (Garden City, New York: Anchor Press/Doubleday, 1978), 225–233.

21. Harriet's testimony had been challenged by Mary's lawyers as incompetent. But the surrogate had received her testimony, and Barnard ruled that once received it would be considered. Mary's lawyers must have faced a classic lawyer's dilemma—were they to challenge the testimony on grounds of coverture, in doing so they would acknowledge Harriet as a wife. 45 Barb. at 536–538.

22. 45 Barb. at 538–39.

23. 45 Barb. at 539–541. Barnard did not mention it in his opinion, for it was inconsistent with his conclusions, but in 1855 Harriet and one of her sons had sued Edwin twice for necessaries. Both suits had been rejected because her "husband" Harrington was still alive, and thus Edwin could not have been her legal husband. "Four Newspaper Articles," 4–5.

24. 45 Barb. at 541–542. Even his defenders conceded that Christy was not an easy man. "Four Newspaper Articles," 1.

25. 45 Barb. at 542–544. The case that worried Barnard was *Clayton v. Wardell*, 4 N.Y. 230 (1850).

26. In late 1867 Harriet was in court again to compel an accounting from the "collector" of the estate. *New York Times*, October 31, 1867, 3: 3; ibid., November 26, 1867.

27. See Schwartzberg, "Grass Widows, Barbarians, and Bigamists"; Ariela R.

Dubler, "Governing through Contract: Common Law Marriage in the Nineteenth Century," *Yale Law Journal* 107, no. 6 (April 1998): 1885–1920.

28. *Clayton v. Wardell,* 5 Barb. 214, 216–217 (N.Y. Sup. Ct. 1849), affirmed, 4 N.Y. 230, 234–238 (1850).

29. See Joel Prentiss Bishop, *Commentaries on the Law of Marriage and Divorce, of Separations without Divorce, and of the Evidence of Marriage in All Issues; Embracing Also Pleading, Practice, and Evidence in Divorce Causes, with Forms* (Boston: Little, Brown and Co., 1864), 2:226–227 (section 272). In California, *Clayton* became a convincing precedent in *Case v. Case,* 17 Cal. 598 (1861), brought by a New York wife, who sued her husband for divorce on grounds of adultery after he had married another woman. The New York wife lost because there was no direct evidence of her marriage. The presumption against criminality overrode the presumption in favor of marriage. When the existence of a marriage was challenged, an actual marriage had to be proved if one were to be entitled to a divorce. The California court's decision might seem logically unassailable. How could a divorce be granted if there were not a marriage? But courts sometimes came to varying conclusions. A marriage in the East, even a recorded marriage with a public ceremony, was hard to prove or disprove when divorcing in California. And some nonmarriages were actually marriages, or would become marriages, because couples acted married long enough and publicly enough to be recognized as married. See *Hamblin v. Hamblin,* 2 Lab. 31 (Cal. Dist. Ct. 1857); *Fuller v. Fuller,* 17 Cal. 605 (1861); *Fox v. Fox,* 25 Cal. 587 (1864). In Kentucky, a "blameless wife" was allowed alimony when she sued for divorce if she had no knowledge that her husband's first marriage was still in effect. *Strode v. Strode,* 3 Bush 227, 96 Am. Dec. 211 (Ky. 1867). In New York, unlike California, courts contemplated granting a divorce where there had been no valid marriage. See *Lincoln v. Lincoln,* 29 N.Y. Superior 525 (1866); *Gall v. Gall,* 114 N.Y. 109 (1889). In the song, "Sweet Betsey from Pike," written by the Gold Rush prospector John Stone and first published in 1858, a young woman travels to California with "her lover, Ike," where he divorces her. John Hollander, ed., *American Poetry: The Nineteenth Century,* The Library of America (New York: Literary Classics of the United States, Inc., 1993), 2:817–818.

30. On the law of presumptions, a cottage industry of nineteenth-century treatise writers, see John D. Lawson, *The Law of Presumptive Evidence, Including Presumptions Both of Law and of Fact, and the Burden of Proof Both in Civil and Criminal Cases, Reduced to Rules* (1886; Littleton, Colo.: Fred B. Rothman & Co., 1982).

31. Ibid., 93–94, 433; David Stewart, *The Law of Marriage and Divorce, as Es-*

tablished in England and the United States (San Francisco: Sumner Whitney & Co., 1884), 103–106. Prosecutions of miscegenous marriages were usually posed as prosecutions for fornication or for "illicit intercourse." Since the marriage was void, the crime was in having nonmarital sexual relations. Peter Wallenstein, "Race, Marriage, and the Law of Freedom: Alabama and Virginia, 1860s–1960s," *Chicago-Kent Law Review* 70, no. 2 (1994): 371–438; Emily Field Van Tassel, "'Only the Law Would Rule between Us': Antimiscegenation, the Moral Economy of Dependency, and the Debate over Rights after the Civil War," *Chicago-Kent Law Review* 70, no. 3 (1995): 873–927.

32. According to the dissenting judge, the only presumption that would have exonerated Catherine's mother from "gross moral delinquency" was that she and her first husband believed that they could divorce themselves with a separation agreement. But their legal ignorance did not make the earlier marriage a nullity. 4 N.Y. at 244. In *O'Gara v. Eisenlohr,* 38 N.Y. 296, 300, 303 (1868), the New York Court of Appeals limited *Clayton v. Wardell: Clayton* settled "no law beyond the fact that the evidence in the case was insufficient to establish the first marriage." The court also challenged broader readings of *Clayton* as exemplifying the judicial sin of "presumptions run mad," of "professing to believe as true, what we are actually convinced is not so." Still, Bishop and the many judges who relied on Bishop regarded the majority's opinion in *Clayton* as stating the correct rule. Joel Prentiss Bishop, *New Commentaries on Marriage, Divorce, and Separation as to the Law, Evidence, Pleading, Practice, Forms and the Evidence of Marriage in All Issues on a New System of Legal Exposition* (Chicago: T.H. Flood and Co., 1891), chs.27, 31–34. See *Blackburn v. Crawford,* 70 U.S. 175 (1865).

33. Although children were sometimes made illegitimate and wives left without inheritance rights, the New York courts avoided criminalizing the act of remarriage by the guiltily divorced. *People v. Hovey,* 5 Barb. 117 (N.Y. Sup. Ct. 1849). Likewise, the courts did not punish the remarried for contempt of court in ignoring an unambiguous judicial decree. Charles Putzel and H. A. Bähr, *Commercial Precedents Selected from the Column of Replies and Decisions of the New York Journal of Commerce, an Essential Work of Reference for Every Business Man* (Hartford, Conn.: American Publishing Co., 1887), 182–184. For other jurisdictions, see the discussion in William Lamartine Snyder, *The Geography of Marriage or Legal Perplexities of Wedlock in the United States* (New York: G. P. Putnam's Sons, 1889), 73–78. In the 1850s and 1860s, New York judges were still resisting collusive divorces. *E.B. v. E.C.B.* 28 Barb. 299 (N.Y. Sup. Ct. 1858); *Lyon v. Lyon,* 62 Barb. 138 (N.Y. Sup. Ct. 1861). And preventing

collusion remained central to divorce policy in California. *Baker v. Baker,* 10 Cal. 527 (1858); ibid., 13 Cal. 87 (1859). But the New York courts refused to set aside collusive divorces after the fact. *Singer v. Singer,* 41 Barb. 139 (N.Y. Sup. Ct. 1863); *Kinnier v. Kinnier,* 45 N.Y. 535 (1871).

34. *Cropsey v. Ogden,* 11 N.Y. 228 (1854). See likewise *Smith v. Woodworth,* 44 Barb. 198 (N.Y. Sup. Ct. 1865).

35. *Cropsey v. Sweeney,* 27 Barb. 310 (N.Y. Sup. Ct. 1858) (emphasis in original).

36. *Blossom v. Barrett,* 37 N.Y. 434 (1868).

37. On the presumption of death, see *Gall,* 114 N.Y. 109 (1889); *Cropsey v. McKinney,* 30 Barb. 47 (N.Y. Sup. Ct. 1859), reversed on other grounds in *Griffin v. Banks,* 37 N.Y. 621 (1868); "Can a Person Have Two Wives or Two Husbands in New York?" *The University Law Review* 1 (March 1894): 183–186; Bishop, *Marriage, Divorce, and Separation* (1891), 119. Bishop thought the New York rule against remarriage so totally wrongheaded that it did not deserve to be labeled a law. The rule had the effect of leaving the wrongdoer "at large under disabilities" that only goaded "his evil nature." The best public defense against such a monster was to tie him up with "the cords of a domestic affection." Ibid., 301–304.

38. *Ponsford v. Johnson,* 19 F. Cas. 983, 2 Blatchf. 51 (S.D.N.Y. 1847); *Van Voorhis v. Brintnail,* 86 N.Y. 18 (1881); *Commonwealth v. Lane,* 113 Mass. 458 (1872). In *Cropsey v. Ogden,* 11 N.Y. 228, 233–234 (1854), dictum claimed that the foreign remarriages of guilty adulterers were void. See *Smith v. Woodworth,* 44 Barb. 198 (N.Y. Sup. Ct. 1865). But by the 1880s, the New York *Journal of Commerce* advised a reader that a remarriage in another state would be valid in New York. Putzel and Bähr, *Commercial Precedents,* 183. For other states, see Snyder, *The Geography of Marriage or Legal Perplexities of Wedlock in the United States,* 98–101; Frank Keezer, *The Law of Marriage and Divorce, Giving the Law in All the States and Territories with Approved Forms* (Boston: William J. Nagel, 1906; Littleton, Colo.: Fred B. Rothman & Co., 1991), 192; Stewart, *Marriage and Divorce,* 97–98. For the later history of the New York rule, see Albert Charles Jacobs and Julius Goebel, Jr., *Cases and Other Materials on Domestic Relations,* 3d ed. (Brooklyn: Foundation Press, 1952), 253–256.

39. Bishop, who almost always defended divorce followed by remarriage, still reproduced the conventional constitutional distinction between marriage and divorce. Bishop, *Marriage and Divorce* (1864), 2:115. See likewise Isaac F. Redfield, "Conflict of Laws Affecting Marriage and Divorce. The Distinction between the English and Scotch Law. The Validity and Effect of Foreign Divorces," *American Law Register* 3 (new series) (February 1864): 209–210; David Rorer, *American Inter-State Law* (Chicago:

Callaghan and Company, 1879; Littleton, Colo.: Fred B. Rothman & Co., 1983), 177–178. Stewart, however, thought the claim that a marriage was valid everywhere was so riddled with exceptions that it was "practically useless." Stewart, *Marriage and Divorce,* 90. Until 1968, the great exception to the rule that a marriage made anywhere was valid everywhere was miscegenation. See generally Peggy Pascoe, "Miscegenation Law, Court Cases, and Ideologies of 'Race' in Twentieth-Century America," *Journal of American History* 83, no. 1 (June 1996): 44–69; Wallenstein, "Race, Marriage, and the Law of Freedom," 403–404.

40. See *Haddock v. Haddock,* 201 U.S. 562 (1906), for a famous example of the intersection of the two situations. *Maynard v. Hill,* 125 U.S. 190 (1888), which exemplifies the first, was often relied on in cases dealing with the second.

41. *In the Matter of the Probate of the Last Will and Testament of Ephraim Bradley Chafin,* circa 1868, Cases and Briefs, Wisconsin Supreme Court (University of Wisconsin Law School Library). Their difficulties began when Ephraim disowned their youngest daughter, claiming that she was not his child. His executors conceded that all the Chafins had "quick and ugly tempers."

42. *Kashaw v. Kashaw,* 3 Cal. 312 (1853); *Cochran v. Cochran,* 42 Neb. 612 (1894); M. W. Jacobs, *A Treatise on the Law of Domicil* (Boston: Little, Brown and Co., 1887), 299; Bishop, *Marriage and Divorce* (1864), 2:104.

43. *Damon v. Damon,* June 1871, Cases and Briefs, Wisconsin Supreme Court (University of Wisconsin Law School Library); *Damon v. Damon,* 28 Wis. 510 (1871).

44. On the history of the Oregon Donation Act, see Richard H. Chused, "Late Nineteenth Century Married Women's Property Law: Reception of the Early Married Women's Property Acts by Courts and Legislatures," *American Journal of Legal History* 29 (January 1985): 3–35.

45. *Maynard v. Hill,* 125 U.S. 190, 205, 209–210 (1888). By the 1880s, legislative divorces had almost disappeared. States passed bans on "special legislation," including legislative divorces, as part of the burst of state constitution-making in the late 1840s and 1850s. See James Willard Hurst, *The Growth of American Law: The Law Makers* (Boston: Little, Brown and Co., 1950), 199–246. See also Thomas M. Cooley, *A Treatise on the Constitutional Limitations Which Rest upon the Legislative Power of the States of the American Union* (Boston: Little, Brown and Co., 1868), 110–111. The practice of legislative divorce continued in Delaware until the beginning of the twentieth century. See Paul H. Jacobson, *American Marriage and Divorce,* in collaboration with Pauline F. Jacobson (New York: Rinehart & Co., 1959), 89; Carroll D. Wright, *A Report on Marriage and Divorce in the*

United States, 1867 to 1886 (Washington, D.C.: U.S. Government Printing Office, 1889), 244–245, 386–387.

46. 125 U.S. at 210–214. Field ruled that the contract clause of the federal Constitution was of no relevance. In so doing, he settled a question that had worried law writers and judges for the previous seventy years. See Cooley, *Constitutional Limitations,* 109–114; Report of the judiciary committee on the petition of George Powlesland for divorce, New York Assembly document #83, February 9, 1855; *Holmes v. Holmes,* 4 Barb. 295 (N.Y. Sup. Ct. 1848); *Todd v. Kerr,* 42 Barb. 317 (N.Y. Sup. Ct. 1864); *Tolen v. Tolen,* 2 Blackf. 407 (Ind. 1831); *Noel v. Ewing,* 9 Ind. 37 (1857). Did Lydia retain any rights to the property, given the validity of the divorce? Field's answer turned on the language of the Oregon Donation Act. The act required four years' cultivation by a white male settler. If the settler were married, the grant of land, "when perfected," belonged equally to the settler and his wife. A wife, however, could not be a settler. "She got nothing except through her husband." Thus, Lydia held nothing at all, for at the time she had been divorced, David held no vested interest in the land. 125 U.S. at 215–216.

47. On the shift from contract to status, see Michael Grossberg, *Governing the Hearth: Law and the Family in Nineteenth-Century America* (Chapel Hill: University of North Carolina, 1985).

48. See *Barber v. Barber,* 62 U.S. 582 (1858). Mid-century courts and treatises sometimes played on older language that "uncovered" a wife whose husband had "abjured" the realm. Peregrine Bingham, *The Law of Infancy and Coverture* (Burlington, Vt.: Chauncey Goodrich, 1849), 262–264; *Wright v. Hays,* 10 Tex. 130, 60 Am. Dec. 200 (1853); *Mead v. Hughes Administrator,* 15 Ala. 141, 50 Am. Dec. 123 (1849); *Osborn v. Nelson,* 59 Barb. 375 (N.Y. Sup. Ct. 1871). In 1860 a deserted Wisconsin wife's lawyer asserted his client's right to sue in her own name because her drunken husband had "abjured" Wisconsin. Brief of Abigail Green, by her next friend, Nicholas Hintgen, Cases and Briefs, Wisconsin Supreme Court (University of Wisconsin Law School Library). But the Wisconsin Supreme Court rejected the claim. *Green v. Lyndes,* 12 Wis. 404 (1860).

49. Jacobs, *A Treatise on the Law of Domicil,* 291–298. The case was *Colvin v. Reed,* 55 Pa. St. 375 (1867). See *Turner v. Turner,* 44 Ala. 437 (1870); *Starkey v. Starkey,* 21 N.J. Eq. 135 (1870). For an example of a husband who did exactly that, see Eli Lilly, ed., *Schliemann in Indianapolis* (Indianapolis: Indiana Historical Society, 1961), 47, 65–68. On the endless negotiations between wives and husbands on whether and when to move west, see Linda Peavy and Ursula Smith, *Women in Waiting in the Westward Movement* (Norman: University of Oklahoma Press, 1994).

50. See *Barber v. Barber,* 62 U.S. 582 (1858); Jacobs, *A Treatise on the Law of Domicil,* 308–309; Bingham, *Infancy and Coverture,* 262–264. On the other hand, where there was a separation by mutual consent or by contractual agreement, Bishop thought that the wife's domicile remained that of her husband; otherwise a voluntary separation "would amount to a *quasi* divorce,—contrary to . . . established doctrine." Bishop, *Marriage and Divorce* (1864), 2:106.

51. *Cheever v. Wilson,* 76 U.S. 108 (1869); Jacobs, *A Treatise on the Law of Domicil,* 310–317. Bishop, by contrast, believed that if a wife had interests "adverse" to her husband, and the law gave her the right to sue, "it must give her, by implication, a domicile in which to bring the suit." Bishop, *Marriage and Divorce* (1864), 2:104–105. In the nineteenth century "domicile" was usually spelled "domicil," following archaic law-French.

52. Bishop, *Marriage and Divorce* (1864), 2:98–99.

53. Abby had to stay in Indiana one year before petitioning for a divorce. After 1873 a two-year residence became the rule, and the "omnibus" clause allowing judges to order divorces for undefined reasons was removed. Why Indiana innovated remains unclear. Robert Dale Owen insisted on a feminist goal: to free abused women from corrupted men. Others assumed the law was the creation of designing men seeking to escape marital responsibilities. Nolan suggests the centrality of lawyers who saw a new source of business, one constructed and developed both through direct advertising and through strategic alliances with lawyers in New York. Val Nolan, "Document: Indiana: Birthplace of Migratory Divorce," *Indiana Law Journal* 26, no. 4 (Summer 1951): 515–527; Norma Basch, "Relief in the Premises: Divorce as a Woman's Remedy in New York and Indiana, 1815–1870," *Law and History Review* 8 (Spring 1990): 1–24. General surveys of early divorce havens include Glenda Riley, *Divorce—An American Tradition* (New York: Oxford University Press, 1991), 62–107; Blake, *Road to Reno,* 116–129. Contemporary accounts of Indiana divorce practice include Lilly, *Schliemann in Indianapolis;* B. V. A., "Indiana Divorces," *American Law Register* 9 (new series) (December 1870): 721–728. *Jenness v. Jenness,* 24 Ind. 355, 87 Am. Dec. 335 (1865), and *Muckenburg v. Holler,* 29 Ind. 139, 92 Am. Dec. 345 (1867), show appellate judges wrestling with divorce law and practice. In California and in Wisconsin, both relatively liberal divorce states, the courts worked to make sure that their states would not become divorce mills like Indiana. *Bennett v. Bennett,* 28 Cal. 599 (1865); *Hall v. Hall,* 25 Wis. 600 (1870). On the other hand, Warren Chase always regretted that he had been unable to convince the Wisconsin legislature to follow Indiana's lead. See Warren Chase, *The Fugitive Wife: A Criticism on Marriage, Adultery and Divorce* (Boston: Bela

Marsh, 1861), 66. Still, Wisconsin also was one of a number of states that those looking for "foreign" divorces went to. See *People v. McCraney*, 6 Parker's Crim. R. 49, 110 (N.Y. 1860); Lilly, *Schliemann in Indianapolis*, 30.

54. See Report of the select committee on the subject "Of divorces dissolving the marriage contract," New York Assembly document #72, February 13, 1850. The corruptions of the "foreign" divorce were compounded by the fact that most decrees were ex parte. The defendant in the typical "foreign" divorce (the accused "guilty" party) had remained in New York, had not been present to defend himself. Sometimes a spouse went to Indiana with the consent and the active connivance of the other party. Notice was then beside the point, publication a genuine formality, at least with regard to the interests of the absent defendant. (There is always the separate problem of the rights of third parties to the marriage.) For those who operated within an orthodox understanding of divorce, however, knowing that the foreign divorce had been collusive did nothing for its legality.

55. Redfield, "Conflict of Laws," 196–197.

56. Ibid., 198–200.

57. Ibid., 222. Redfield was uncomfortable with that liberalizing trend, and his essay reads as a masked critique of the U.S. Supreme Court's 1858 holding in *Barber v. Barber*. But Redfield conceded that in America a guilty husband could not "drag the wife's domicil after him, whither he chooses to go," as the English husband in *Warrender* had.

58. Ibid., 203 (emphasis in original).

59. Ibid., 204.

60. Ibid., 207.

61. Ibid., 209–210.

62. Bishop, *Marriage and Divorce* (1864), 2:136–137. Bishop's assumption that a wife was a citizen was controversial in 1864.

63. Ibid., 2:149–174.

64. Ibid., 2:196–197.

65. Ibid., 1:24–26; Bishop, *Marriage, Divorce, and Separation* (1891), 1:26–28.

66. In the 1881 revision of his treatise, Bishop offered a direct response to Redfield. Joel Prentiss Bishop, *Commentaries on the Law of Marriage and Divorce, with the Evidence, Practice, Pleading, and Forms; Also of Separations without Divorce, and of the Evidence of Marriage in All Issues* (Boston: Little, Brown and Co., 1881), 2:156–159. He drew his domicile-based method from *Ditson v. Ditson*, 4 R.I. 87 (1856), a case Redfield hated. Redfield, "Conflict of Laws," 216.

67. Michael Grossberg has traced the same insistence on moralistic judgment

in other areas of family law. See Grossberg, *Governing the Hearth*. See *Turner v. Turner*, 44 Ala. 437 (1870), for a paradigmatic version of the story told in the text.

68. Nolan, "Document: Indiana: Birthplace of Migratory Divorce."

69. See Recorder Hackett's charge to the grand jury, described in the *New York Times*, December 9, 1869, 2:7. See likewise the judge's instructions in *Millspaugh v. Adams*, in Henry Lauren Clinton, *Extraordinary Cases* (New York: Harper, 1899), 281–341. See also *New York Times*, January 26, 1865, 2:3; *Vischer v. Vischer*, 12 Barb. 640 (N.Y. Sup. Ct. 1851); *McGiffert v. McGiffert*, 31 Barb. 69 (N.Y. Sup. Ct. 1859); *Hoffman v. Hoffman*, 55 Barb. 269 (N.Y. Sup. Ct. 1869); *Kerr v. Kerr*, 41 N.Y. 272 (1869).

70. *Kinnier v. Kinnier*, 45 N.Y. 535, 544 (1871), affirming *Kinnier v. Kinnier*, 53 Barb. 454 (N.Y. Sup. Ct. 1868); *Kinnier v. Kinnier*, 58 Barb. 424 (N.Y. Sup. Ct. 1869); *Hunt v. Hunt*, 72 N.Y. 217 (1878).

71. Bishop, *Marriage and Divorce* (1881), 2:154–155.

72. Justice John Talcott, who wrote the majority opinion, was uncertain whether Bishop's domicile standard was good law in New York, especially when the spouse asserting domicile in the foreign jurisdiction was the wife. And to get around that problem, Talcott presumed that Frank Baker was domiciled in Ohio at the time that the divorce petition was pending. *Baker v. People*, 15 Hun 256, 264 (N.Y. Sup. Ct. 1878).

73. *People v. Baker*, 76 N.Y. 78, 88 (1879). See likewise *State v. Armington*, 25 Minn. 29 (1878); *State v. Westmoreland*, 76 S.C. 145 (1906).

74. See *Dean v. Dean*, 241 N.Y. 240 (1925) (Lehman, J., dissenting); see also *Hubbard v. Hubbard*, 228 N.Y. 81 (1920). *Baker's* reign ended with *Estate of Holmes*, 291 N.Y. 261 (1943), where the New York Court of Appeals followed the U.S. Supreme Court in *Williams v. North Carolina* (see infra) in granting full faith and credit to the foreign divorce. But see Conway's dissent, ibid., at 278. By the early twentieth century, treatises identified only four or five states as hewing to Redfield's line: New York, Pennsylvania, and North and South Carolina (and sometimes New Jersey). Keezer, *The Law of Marriage and Divorce*, 532. On *Baker*, see Joseph Walter Bingham, "Song of Sixpence: Some Comments on *Williams v. North Carolina*," *Cornell Law Quarterly* 29, no. 1 (September 1943): 23–24.

75. Fowler Vincent Harper, "The Validity of Void Divorces," *University of Pennsylvania Law Review* (December 1930): 158–184; Fowler V. Harper, "The Myth of the Void Divorce," *Law and Contemporary Problems* 2, no. 3 (June 1935): 335–347. On some of the remedies that might be available for those left behind when spouses divorced them, see *Baumann v. Baumann*, 250 N.Y. 382, 165 N.E. 819 (1929).

76. *Atherton v. Atherton*, 181 U.S. 155 (1901). On the concept of a matrimo-

nial domicile, see Jacobs and Goebel, *Cases and Other Materials on Domestic Relations,* 403–404.

77. *Bell v. Bell,* 181 U.S. 175 (1901).

78. *Haddock v. Haddock,* 201 U.S. 562 (1906). White rejected Bishop's rule that all one needed for a divorce entitled to full faith and credit was bona fide residence by one spouse in the divorcing state. At the same time, he agreed with Bishop that wives had the same power as husbands to obtain binding divorces. See Jacobs and Goebel, *Domestic Relations,* 399–406.

79. *Haddock,* 201 U.S. at 630–631; Joseph H. Beale, "Haddock Revisited," *Harvard Law Review* 39, no. 4 (February 1926): 417–430. In *Williamson v. Osenton,* 232 U.S. 619 (1914), the court reaffirmed that a wronged wife could establish a separate domicile.

80. Beale, "Haddock Revisited," 428. On Beale, see Laura Kalman, *Legal Realism at Yale, 1927–1960,* Studies in Legal History (Chapel Hill: University of North Carolina Press, 1986), 47–48. On the history of "domicile" as a technical problem, see Mark De Wolfe Howe, "The Recognition of Foreign Divorce Decrees in New York State," *Columbia Law Review* 40, no. 3 (March 1940): 373–403.

81. Standard historical sources on early twentieth-century divorce include Riley, *Divorce;* Blake, *Road to Reno;* William L. O'Neill, *Divorce in the Progressive Era* (New Haven: Yale University Press, 1967); Elaine Tyler May, *Great Expectations* (Chicago: University of Chicago Press, 1980); J. Herbie DiFonzo, *Beneath the Fault Line: The Popular and Legal Culture of Divorce in Twentieth-Century America* (Charlottesville: University Press of Virginia, 1997). Two essays by Karl Llewellyn remain the most perceptive examinations of the place of divorce in the changing culture. Karl Llewellyn, "Behind the Law of Divorce: I," *Columbia Law Review* 32 (1932): 1281–1308; Karl Llewellyn, "Behind the Law of Divorce: II," *Columbia Law Review* 33 (1933): 249–294.

82. Frank W. Ingram and G. A. Ballard, "The Business of Migratory Divorce in Nevada," *Law and Contemporary Problems* 2, no. 3 (June 1935): 302–309.

83. Robert S. Lynd and Helen Merrell Lynd, *Middletown in Transition* (New York: Harcourt, Brace & World, Inc., 1937), 161; Harper, "The Myth of the Void Divorce."

84. *State v. O. B. Williams and Lilly Shaver Hendrix,* February 24, 1941, trial record, Records and Briefs, North Carolina Supreme Court (University of North Carolina Law Library). See *State v. Herron,* 175 N.C. 754 (1918). Prosecutors had also charged Williams with abduction and embezzlement but dropped those charges prior to trial. *Lenoir News-Topic,* February 26, 1941.

85. The couple's brief to the North Carolina Supreme Court asked the court to recognize as a matter of common knowledge that hundreds of North Carolinians had gone to states like Nevada to be divorced. To affirm the convictions would "destroy and disrupt thousands of good, substantial and peaceable homes in North Carolina and bastardize . . . children." The brief for the state insisted that Nevada divorces were not entitled to full faith and credit. *Haddock* had settled it all, where there was only constructive service. Defendant appellants' brief, 24; brief for the state, in *State v. O. B. Williams and Lilly Shaver Hendrix,* February 24, 1941; *People v. Williams,* 220 N.C. 445, 17 S.E.2d 769 (1941).

86. *Williams v. North Carolina,* 317 U.S. 287, 302–303 (1942).

87. There were differences: the first Mrs. Williams had died before the second trial. Thomas Hendrix, Lilly's sometime husband, made himself scarce, as he had remarried in the interim, perhaps relying on Lilly's Nevada divorce. Lilly Shaver Hendrix's lawyer also contended that there was no proof beyond a reasonable doubt that she had ever been legally married to Thomas Hendrix, and an actual marriage had to be proved before one could be convicted of bigamy. *State v. O. B. Williams and Lilly Shaver Hendrix,* November 29, 1943, trial record, Records and Briefs, North Carolina Supreme Court (University of North Carolina Law Library).

88. *State v. O. B. Williams and Lilly Shaver Hendrix,* November 29, 1943, ibid.; *Lenoir News-Topic,* December 1, 1943.

89. Defendants' brief, 23–25, *State v. O. B. Williams and Lilly Shaver Hendrix,* November 29, 1943.

90. 224 N.C. 183, 29 S.E.2d 744 (1943).

91. 325 U.S. 226 (1945).

92. *Caldwell County Marriage Index, S–Z* (at Caldwell County Public Library).

93. Thomas Reed Powell, "And Repent at Leisure: An Inquiry into the Unhappy Lot of Those Whom Nevada Hath Joined Together and North Carolina Hath Put Asunder," *Harvard Law Review* 58 (1945): 930–1017; Max Rheinstein, *Marriage Stability, Divorce, and the Law* (Chicago: University of Chicago Press, 1972), 70–91.

94. Katherine L. Caldwell, "Not Ozzie and Harriet: Postwar Divorce and the American Liberal Welfare State," *Law and Social Inquiry* 23, no. 1 (Winter 1998): 1–54; Grace Ganz Blumberg, "Reworking the Past, Imagining the Future: On Jacob's *Silent Revolution,*" *Law and Social Inquiry* 16, no. 1 (Winter 1991): 115–154. Ten days after the second Williams bigamy jury trial, the Caldwell County court adjourned. The local headline read, "Many Divorces Given." *Lenoir News-Topic,* December 10, 1943.

95. A Practical Law Reporter, *McFarland,* 118.

96. Clinton, *Extraordinary Cases,* 310.

97. *State v. Johnson*, 12 Minn. 476, 483, 486–487, 93 Am. Dec. 241, 246, 249 (1867). See H. M. Hanson, "Jurisdiction of the Courts of One State Over an Act of Bigamy Committed in Another State—the Collins Case," *Central Law Journal* 62, no. 12 (1906): 216–218; Stewart, *Marriage and Divorce*, 133–137.

98. On the consequences of an absence of alternatives, see Charlotte Perkins Gilman, *Women and Economics: A Study of the Economic Relation between Men and Women as a Factor in Social Evolution*, ed. Carl N. Degler (Boston: Small, Maynard & Co., 1898; New York: Harper & Row, 1966), 300. See generally Delores Hayden, *The Grand Domestic Revolution: A History of Feminist Designs for American Homes, Neighborhoods and Cities* (Cambridge, Mass.: MIT Press, 1981).

99. See *Beardsley Divorce*. Occasionally, marriage reappeared at the most inopportune moments. As the headnote to a leading bigamy case put it, "A married man, . . . imagining himself to effect mere seduction, may blunder into bigamy." *Hayes v. The People*, 25 N.Y. 390 (1862).

100. *New York Times*, December 11, 1909, 2:6; ibid., December 12, 1909, 4.

10. Coverture in a New Age

1. Joel Prentiss Bishop, *Commentaries on the Law of Married Women under the Statutes of the Several States, and at Common Law and in Equity* (Boston: Little, Brown and Co., 1871–1875), 1:663–666, 675–677, 696, 2:v. Other late nineteenth-century commentators wrote in similar terms. See James Schouler, *A Treatise on the Law of the Domestic Relations: Embracing Husband and Wife, Parent and Child, Guardian and Ward, Infancy, and Master and Servant*, 2d ed. (Boston: Little, Brown and Co., 1874), 9, 16–18; Henry Hitchcock, "Modern Legislation Touching Marital Property Rights," *Southern Law Review* 6 (new series), no. 5 (December 1880): 633–662; Anonymous, "The Legal Rights of Married Women," *New Englander* 22 (January 1863): 22–35; Francis King Carey, "The Rights of Married Women," *Appleton's Journal* 24 (new series no. 9), no. 53 (1880): 385–395. James Wells was more optimistic. J. C. Wells, *A Treatise on the Separate Property of Married Women, under the Recent Enabling Statutes*, 2d ed. (Cincinnati: Robert Clarke and Co., 1879), iii.

2. Congressmen, who fought with each other over the implications in every phrase of the Fourteenth Amendment, joined together in agreement that the federal government should have no role over the rights and duties of married women. Earl M. Maltz, *Civil Rights, the Constitution, and Congress, 1863–1869* (Lawrence, Kans.: University Press of Kansas, 1990), 56–58; William E. Nelson, *The Fourteenth Amendment: From Political*

Principle to Judicial Doctrine (Cambridge, Mass.: Harvard University Press, 1988), 120, 136–138. Until after World War I, a wife's national citizenship was a very thin and fragile thing. In immigration law, Congress and the federal courts increasingly tied a wife's citizenship to her husband's. See Nancy F. Cott, "Marriage and Women's Citizenship in the United States, 1830–1934," *American Historical Review* 103, no. 5 (December 1998): 1440–1474.

3. John Bouvier, *A Law Dictionary,* 1st ed. (Philadelphia: J. B. Lippincott, 1856); John Bouvier, *A Law Dictionary,* 14th ed. (Philadelphia: J. B. Lippincott, 1877); John Bouvier, *A Law Dictionary,* 15th ed. (Philadelphia: J. B. Lippincott, 1892); Henry Campbell Black, *A Dictionary of Law* (St. Paul, Minn.: West Publishing Co., 1891; New York: The Law Book Exchange, Ltd., 1991). A much-enlarged edition of Bouvier substituted a thirteen-page, double-columned mini-treatise on "husband and wife" for the definition of "husband." "Wife" became "A woman united to a man by marriage." *Bouvier's Law Dictionary and Concise Encyclopedia,* 8th ed. (3d revision), ed. Francis Rawle (Kansas City, Mo.: Vernon Book Co., 1914; Buffalo: William S. Hein Co., 1984).

4. Thomas C. Grey, "Langdell's Orthodoxy," *University of Pittsburgh Law Review* 45, no. 1 (Fall 1983): 1–54; William P. LaPiana, *Logic and Experience: The Origin of Modern American Legal Education* (New York: Oxford University Press, 1994); John Henry Schlegel, *American Legal Realism and Empirical Social Science,* Studies in Legal History (Chapel Hill: University of North Carolina Press, 1995); Robert W. Gordon, "Legal Thought and Legal Practice in the Age of American Enterprise, 1870–1920," in *Professions and Professional Ideologies in America,* ed. Gerald L. Geison (Chapel Hill: University of North Carolina Press, 1984); G. Edward White, *Tort Law in America: An Intellectual History* (New York: Oxford University Press, 1980).

5. LaPiana, *Logic and Experience,* 27–28. When Willard Hurst first started teaching, he took it as the norm that he would be assigned to teach domestic relations law, though as an ambitious young legal academic he got out as quickly as he could. (Conversation with Willard Hurst, June 1993.) None of the legal academics whose casebooks are examined in this chapter were primarily identified with domestic relations law. Jeremiah Smith was known for his torts course; Julius Goebel was a legal historian; Fowler Harper was a torts scholar and a reproductive rights reformer.

6. Marshall D. Ewell, *Cases on Domestic Relations; Leading and Select Cases on the Disabilities Incident to Infancy and Coverture,* student's ed. (Boston: Little, Brown and Co., 1891); James Paige, *Illustrative Cases in Domestic Relations, with Analysis and Citations* (Philadelphia: T. & J. W. Johnson & Co., 1893); Edwin H. Woodruff, *A Selection of Cases on Domestic Relations*

and the Law of Persons (New York: Baker, Voorhis & Co., 1897); Jeremiah Smith, *Cases on Selected Topics in the Law of Persons* (Cambridge: The Harvard Law Review Publishing Association, 1899).

7. Smith, *Law of Persons*, 338. On Smith, see LaPiana, *Logic and Experience*, 21–22, 102–103.

8. Smith, *Law of Persons*, 512. Two-hundred closely printed pages later, Smith finished the chapter with two cases that gave apparently opposing answers to the questions he had posed at the beginning: *Kroessin v. Keller*, 60 Minn. 372 (1895), denying a wife the right to sue her husband's seducer for criminal conversation, and *Haynes v. Nowlin*, 129 Ind. 581 (1891), affirming a similarly situated wife's right to sue for alienation of affections. Ibid., 707–713. Both decisions interpreted statutes that granted wives a general right to sue to redress wrongs done to them as individuals. According to the Minnesota court, that did not mean that a wife had the right to sue in crim. con. Crim. con. was not a right that could be equalized between wife and husband by implication. On the other hand, the Indiana Supreme Court insisted that the wife's right to sue was imminent in the common law itself; the statute merely "uncovered" a right that coverture had prevented her from exercising. "Incidental changes," like a right to sue one's husband's seducer, were inseparable from the essential changes expressed in the legislation.

9. Wells, *Treatise*, iii, 73.

10. The standard was one of a number of tools of statutory interpretation state courts developed during the 1840s and 1850s that allowed judges to limit the invasive powers of democratic legislatures, without challenging legislative supremacy itself. See James Willard Hurst, *The Growth of American Law: The Law Makers* (Boston: Little, Brown and Co., 1950), 46–81. The standard was a characteristic feature of late nineteenth-century public law. Theodore Sedgwick, *A Treatise on the Rules Which Govern the Interpretation and Application of Statutory and Constitutional Law* (New York: J. S. Voorhies, 1857), 313; Thomas M. Cooley, *A Treatise on the Constitutional Limitations Which Rest upon the Legislative Power of the States of the American Union* (Boston: Little, Brown and Co., 1868), 61.

11. Albert Charles Jacobs and Julius Goebel, *Cases and Other Materials on Domestic Relations*, 3d ed. (Brooklyn: Foundation Press, 1952), 542–543.

12. 44 Ill. 58 (1867), in Smith, *Law of Persons*, 550.

13. *Lee v. Savannah Guano Co.*, 99 Ga. 572 (1896), in Smith, *Law of Persons*, 524–537; Ewell, *Domestic Relations*, 500–510. See *Blaechinska v. Howard Mission and Home for Little Wanderers*, 130 N.Y. 497 (1892).

14. Smith, *Law of Persons*, 648–654; *Schultz v. Schultz*, 27 Hun 26 (N.Y. Sup. Ct. 1882), reversed, 89 N.Y. 644 (1882).

15. Marshall Ewell was the dean of the Kent Law School, a Chicago night law

school, and a prolific law writer who had previously published works on medical jurisprudence and a "student" edition of Blackstone's *Commentaries*. His 1891 casebook began by laying out the law of coverture in a 180-page section sandwiched between shorter sections on "infancy" and "idiocy." (The section on idiocy was followed by sections on "deaf and dumb persons" and "drunkenness.") In the section on coverture, all the cases dated from before the middle of the nineteenth century. But then, at the end of the main body of the text, he added a 150-page "supplement," including recent cases dealing with the effects of statutory changes. Ewell, *Domestic Relations*.

16. *Coleman v. Burr*, 93 N.Y. 17, 45 Am. Rep. 160 (1883), and *Bank v. Guenther*, 123 N.Y. 568 (1890), in Ewell, *Domestic Relations*, 500–514.

17. *Longendyke v. Longendyke*, 44 Barb. 366 (N.Y. Sup. Ct. 1863), in Ewell, *Domestic Relations*, 574–577.

18. On "modernization," see Reva B. Siegel, "The Modernization of Marital Status Law: Adjudicating Wives' Rights to Earnings, 1860–1930," *Georgetown Law Journal*, 82, no. 7 (September 1994): 2127–2211.

19. Woodruff, *Domestic Relations*, 208–254.

20. On the right to alimony, see *Galland v. Galland*, 38 Cal. 265 (1869), in Smith, *Law of Persons*, 431–437. On a husband's continuing obligations under a separation agreement, see *Carey v. Mackey*, 82 Me. 516 (1890), in Woodruff, *Domestic Relations*, 88–90. On the wife's right to sue after divorce, see *Abbott v. Abbott*, 67 Me. 307–308 (1877), in Smith, *Law of Persons*, 388–390.

21. For examples, see *Southard v. Plummer*, 36 Me. 64 (1853), in Smith, *Law of Persons*, 517; *Perkins v. Perkins*, 62 Barb. 531 (N.Y. Sup. Ct. 1872), in Ewell, *Domestic Relations*, 577–588.

22. The language of coercion—of disability as protection—was present in all the casebooks, particularly in opinions that characterized the new statutes as limited efforts to increase a wife's protection from her husband, rather than as destructive of the traditional structure of coverture. See for examples Smith, *Law of Persons*, 501, 580, and Ewell, *Domestic Relations*, 577–588.

23. William Edward McCurdy, *Cases on the Law of Persons and Domestic Relations*, 4th ed. (Chicago: Callaghan, 1952); William Randall Compton, *Cases on Domestic Relations* (St. Paul: West Publishing Co., 1951); Jacobs and Goebel, *Domestic Relations*; Fowler V. Harper, *Problems of the Family* (Indianapolis: Bobbs-Merrill, 1952). Three of the four were substantial revisions of earlier casebooks. Harper's *Problems of the Family* was conceived as "an experiment in integration of the various disciplines" that dealt "with problems of the family." Instead of separate chapters on the

law of husband and wife and parent and child, Harper offered two linked chapters—one on "intra-family relations," the other on "relations of family members with others." These merged together confusingly the relative rights and duties of wives and husbands with those of parents and children and other family members. Throughout, Harper used fewer cases; in their place he substituted excerpts from the contemporary social science literature, especially from social work journals. The result replaced the gendered assumptions of traditional marriage law with the mother-blaming and neurosis-labeling misogyny of the Freudianism regnant in postwar social work practice. For an admiring description of Fowler Harper, see David J. Garrow, *Liberty and Sexuality: The Right to Privacy and the Making of* Roe v. Wade (New York: MacMillan, 1994), 147–152.

24. See Jacobs and Goebel, *Domestic Relations*, 386–456; Harper, *Problems*, 660–667.

25. Jacobs and Goebel, *Domestic Relations*, 542–543.

26. *People v. Statley*, 91 Cal. App. 2d Supp. 943, 206 P.2d 76 (1949)(quoting *Smith v. Meyers*, 54 Neb. 1, 74 N.W. 277 (1898)), and *State v. Herndon*, 158 Fla. 515, 27 So. 833 (1946), in Jacobs and Goebel, *Domestic Relations*, 635–637.

27. This absence is particularly striking in Harper's casebook, intended as an experiment to integrate legal opinions with social work writing.

28. *Nuding v. Urich*, 169 Pa. 289, 32 A. 409 (1895) (which had appeared in Smith's casebook); *Kleinert v. Hutchinson*, 98 N.J.L. 831, 121 A. 743 (1923); *Ex parte Alabama Textile Products Corp.*, 242 Ala. 609, 7 So. 2d 303 (1942); *Bechtol v. Ewing, Adm'r*, 89 Ohio 53, 105 N.E. 72 (1913), all in McCurdy, *Law of Persons*, 612–621.

29. Loss of consortium was a cause of action theoretically available to wives as well. But the casebooks focused more on the husband's "right," less on the extension of that right to a wife. But see Jacobs and Goebel, *Domestic Relations*, 579–589; Harper, *Problems*, 604–612.

30. William Blackstone, *Commentaries on the Laws of England*, ed. William Carey Jones (Baton Rouge: Claitor's Publishing Division, 1976), 3:*139–140. Early examples of the modern cause include *Bennett v. Bennett*, 116 N.Y. 584, 23 N.E. 17 (1889); *Skoglund v. Minneapolis Street Railway Co.*, 45 Minn. 330 (1891); *Hoard v. Peck*, 56 Barb. 202 (N.Y. Sup. Ct. 1867); and *Holleman v. Harvard*, 25 S.E. 972 (N.C. 1896). The first time "consortium" appears in law dictionaries was in 1891. Black, *A Dictionary of Law*.

31. In *Skoglund v. Minneapolis Street Railway Co.*, 45 Minn. 330 (1891), in Woodruff, *Domestic Relations*, 184, the court distinguished a husband's right to recover on his wife's behalf, as her representative, for her injuries, and his right to recover for her services. For the use of per quod in labor

law, see Christopher L. Tomlins, *Law, Labor, and Ideology in the Early American Republic* (New York: Cambridge University Press, 1993), 236.

32. *Hitaffer v. Argonne Co.*, 183 F.2d 811 (D.C. Cir. 1950). The shift in language also blurred the boundaries between the traditional remedies for a husband's loss—criminal conversation and alienation of affections—and those few situations in which a husband might have asserted a remedy per quod consortium amisit. Courts and commentators made "loss of consortium" a general term that covered a whole range of marital losses. See *Bigaouette v. Paulet*, 134 Mass. 123 (1883), for an early example of that blurring. See generally Jacob Lippman, "The Breakdown of Consortium," *Columbia Law Review* 30 (1930): 672.

33. *Marri v. The Stamford Street R. Co.*, 84 Conn. 9, 78 A. 582 (1911), in Jacobs and Goebel, *Domestic Relations*, 565–571.

34. *Guevin v. Manchester Street Ry.*, 78 N.H. 289, 99 A. 298 (1916), in Jacobs and Goebel, *Domestic Relations*, 573–577; McCurdy, *Law of Persons*, 706–709; Compton, *Domestic Relations*, 367–373.

35. *Bryant v. Smith*, 187 S.C. 453, 198 S.E. 20 (1938), in Jacobs and Goebel, *Domestic Relations*, 601–604; McCurdy, *Law of Persons*, 753–756; Compton, *Domestic Relations*, 403–408.

36. *Patenaude v. Patenaude*, 195 Minn. 523, 263 N.W. 546 (1935), *Tellez v. Tellez*, 51 N.M. 416, 186 P.2d 390 (1947), and *Haas v. Haas*, 298 N.Y. 69, 80 N.E.2d 337 (1948), in Jacobs and Goebel, *Domestic Relations*, 788–790. See *Fricke v. Fricke*, 257 Wis. 124, 42 N.W.2d 500 (1950), *Hempel v. Hempel*, 225 Minn. 287, 30 N.W.2d 594 (1948), *Goldman v. Goldman*, 282 N.Y. 296, 26 N.E.2d 265 (1940), and *Kull v. Losch*, 328 Mich. 519, 44 N.W.2d 169 (1950), in ibid., 661–663, 810–815, 868–870, 780–785.

37. *Kelley v. Kelley*, 51 R.I. 173, 153 A. 314 (1931) in Jacobs and Goebel, *Domestic Relations*, 680–682; McCurdy, *Law of Persons*, 549–551.

38. *Graham v. Graham*, 33 F. Supp. 936 (E.D. Mich. 1940), in McCurdy, *Law of Persons*, 606–608.

39. Marygold S. Melli, "Constructing a Social Problem: The Post-Divorce Plight of Women and Children," *American Bar Foundation Research Journal* 1986, no. 4 (Fall 1987): 759–772.

40. Oliver Wendell Holmes, "The Path of the Law," *Harvard Law Review* 10 (1897): 457.

41. George L. Clark, *Criminal Law* (Indianapolis: Bobb-Merrill Co., 1954), 43.

42. Two casebooks gave short notes that recited the "uniform understanding" that a husband could not commit rape upon his wife. Harper, *Problems*, 584; Compton, *Domestic Relations*, 428–429.

43. Rollin M. Perkins, *Criminal Law* (Brooklyn: Foundation Press, 1957),

115. The word "unlawful," he conceded, meant different things at different times. But he knew what he meant by the word: "not authorized by
law." Perkins noted that "while a husband cannot rape his wife[,] he can
be guilty of the crime of rape committed upon her." Rollin M. Perkins,
Cases and Materials on Criminal Law (Brooklyn: Foundation Press, 1952),
77. See *State v. Digman,* 121 W. Va. 499 (1939), *Kitchen v. State,* 276 S.W.
252 (Tex. Ct. Crim. App. 1925), and *State v. Dowell,* 106 N.C. 722 (1890),
cases in which a white husband was convicted of having forced a black
man to have sex with his white wife.

44. Rebecca Ryan, "The Sex Right: A Legal History of the Marital Rape Exemption," *Law and Social Inquiry* 20, no. 4 (Fall 1995): 941–1004. See
Susan Estrich, *Real Rape* (Cambridge, Mass.: Harvard University Press,
1987), 72–79; Diana E. H. Russell, *Rape in Marriage* (Bloomington: Indiana University Press, 1990); Mary Irene Coombs, "Crime in the Stacks, or
a Tale of a Text: A Feminist Response to a Criminal Law Textbook," *Journal of Legal Education* 38 (1988): 117.

45. See Ryan's discussion of the gyrations that the drafters of the Model Penal
Code went through to deal realistically with a decriminalized sexual
world while still maintaining the marital rape exemption. Ryan, "The Sex
Right," 959–965. On the constitutional history, see Garrow, *Liberty and
Sexuality.*

Epilogue

1. See David Westfall, *Family Law* (St. Paul, Minn.: West Publishing Co.,
1994), 225–270; Walter O. Weyrauch, *Cases and Materials on Family
Law: Legal Concepts and Changing Human Relationships* (St. Paul, Minn.:
West Publishing Co., 1994), 1–92, 309–482; Carl E. Schneider and Margaret F. Brinig, *An Introduction to Family Law* (St. Paul, Minn.: West Publishing Co., 1996), 2–460; Homer Harrison Clark, *Cases and Problems on
Domestic Relations,* 5th ed. (St. Paul, Minn.: West Publishing Co., 1995),
671–699; Ira Mark Ellman, Paul M. Kurtz, and Katherine T. Bartlett, *Family Law: Cases, Text, Problems,* 2d ed. (Charlottesville, Va.: Michie, 1991),
81–144.

Index

Abandonment (desertion): as form of separation, 9–10, 21–22, 33–36, 47–48, 64, 84, 263, 269; ease of, in early United States, 11, 20, 23, 32, 87; as grounds for separation, 53; of Jane Williamson, 67–70; as grounds for divorce, 71, 268, 274, 303; as contributor to bigamy, 90–91; of Elizabeth Packard, 101; of Sally Emmerson, 147–148; of husbands by wives, 157–159, 221, 236; and remarriage across state lines, 258, 259; and wife's domicile, 262; no longer necessary legally, 310; as "civil death," 328n23. *See also* Domiciles; Mobility (marital)

Abuse: as reason for intervening in marriages, 25, 97, 98, 164, 307, 309; as grounds for separation, 30, 54, 207, 238, 244; by Asa Bailey, 44–46, 58, 59; as grounds for abandonment, 89; of wives, 103–105, 109–110, 119, 146, 152, 190, 320n7; as private matter, 109, 306; remedies for, 152, 162; lack of punishment for husbands', 164–166; damages for, 292, 293; and "battered wife syndrome" defense, 371n29. *See also* Coercion; Cruelty; Incest; Marital rape

Adultery: strategic use of, to obtain divorce, 27, 74; witnesses to, 27, 66, 75; as grounds for separation, 30, 53, 160, 207; by Asa Bailey, 45, 59, 61; as grounds for divorce, 64–73, 244, 245, 256, 257, 265, 268; remarriage as, 67–70, 88, 246, 283; as crime, 72–73, 76, 307, 331n21; money damages for wife's, 123, 127–128, 137–142, 233–234; not a bar to husband's suits against his wife, 140; not a crime, 142, 226, 232–233; by wife as grounds for non-support, 160; husbands' killing of wives'

partners in, 218–241; portrayals of participants in, 225–226; calls for reform of law of, 231–232; perceptions of women's admissions to, 252; remarriage as way of avoiding, 271; as symptom of marital problem, 283; unmarried sex as, 285. *See also* Alienation of affections; Criminal conversation; Enticement; Incest

Alabama Supreme Court, 297

Albert (Prince Consort), 166

Alexander, Mary, 170–172, 174–175, 178, 187

Alexander, William, 170–172, 176

Alienation of affections, 123, 137, 221, 300, 389n8, 392n32

Alimony: during separation, 9–10, 21–22, 28, 34, 72; for divorced wife, 71, 305. *See also* Separate maintenance agreements

Allen, Mr., 96–97

Allen, William, 213–214

American Jurist, 103

American Law Register, 266

Annulments, 99

Arizona, 265

Arkansas, 277

Astell, Mary, 23–24

Atherton v. Atherton, 275

Bailey, Abigail, 40–62, 64, 76–77, 84, 101, 152, 284

Bailey, Asa, 40–62, 76–77, 84, 101, 133

Bailey, Phoebe, 46, 47–48, 55, 60, 61

Baker, Frank N., 273–275

Baldwin, Charles, 163

Baptized Church of Christ Friend to Humanity, 149

Barber v. Barber, 33–35, 383n57

Bard, William, 181, 183, 359n49